Fundamental Considerations in Language Testing

Lyle F. Bachman

Oxford University Press

Oxford University Press
Great Clarendon Street, Oxford OX2 6DP

Oxford New York
Athens Auckland Bangkok Bogotá Buenos Aires Cape Town
Chennai Dar es Salaam Delhi Florence Hong Kong Istanbul Karachi
Kolkata Kuala Lumpur Madrid Melbourne Mexico City Mumbai Nairobi
Paris São Paulo Shanghai Singapore Taipei Tokyo Toronto Warsaw

with associated companies in Berlin Ibadan

Oxford and *Oxford English* are trade marks of Oxford University Press
ISBN 0 19 437003 8

First published 1990
Fifth impression 2001

Typeset in 11 on 12pt Sabon by Pentacor Ltd, High Wycombe, Bucks
Printed in China

For my closest friends and loved ones: Nida, Tina, and Melissa

Acknowledgments

The author and publishers would like to thank the following for permission to reproduce the material below that falls within their copyright:

The American Council on Education for the extracts from R. L. Thorndike (ed.): *Educational Measurement* (Second edition) and R. L. Linn (ed.): *Educational Measurement* (Third edition)

The American Psychological Association for the extract from the paper by S. A. Messick in *American Psychologist 30* .

Brooks/Cole Publishing Company for the table on page 30, adapted from M. J. Allen and W. M. Yen: *Introduction to Measurement Theory*

The Center for Applied Linguistics for the extract from the paper by J. B. Carroll in *Testing the English Proficiency of Foreign Students*

Educational and Psychological Measurement for the extracts from the paper by C. I. Mosier in Volume 7

Jay Haley for the extract from *Strategies of Psychotherapy*

The John Hopkins University Press for the figure on page 341, adapted from A. J. Nitko, 'Defining the criterion-referenced test' in R. A. Berk (ed.): *A Guide to Criterion-Referenced Test Construction*, and for the extract from the same paper

Language Learning, and the authors, for the table on page 196, from the paper by J. van Weeren and T. J. J. Theunissen in Volume 37

Newbury House Publishers for three figures (from J. A. Upshur, 'Context for language testing') in J. W. Oller and J. C. Richards: *Focus on the Learner*

Pergamon Press PLC for the extract from K. Johnson (ed.): *Communicative Syllabus Design and Methodology*

Psychometrika, and the authors, for the extract from the paper by K. K. Tatsuoka and M. M. Tatsuoka in Volume 52

Contents

Preface

This book has its origins in the close personal and collaborative relationship that Buzz Palmer and I have had for a good many years. We first hatched the idea of writing a book on language testing research somewhere between the 1981 'Illinois' study and the 1982 'Utah' study, at a time when we were both heavily committed to trying our best to incorporate what were then the still fairly new ideas about 'communicative competence' of people like Mike Canale, Merrill Swain, and Sandy Savignon into actual language tests, and to trying to find out if they were different from the kinds of language tests that were then most commonly used. The two studies that Buzz and I conducted together were a lot of hard work (neither of us may ever want to do another multitrait–multimethod study again!), but they provided a wealth of example tests and anecdotes that I have used with my classes of language testing students, and which also hopefully add a touch of both reality and comic relief to this book. More importantly, however, those studies forced us to face head-on some of the issues and problems that are the substance of this book, and to realize that addressing these will require the best ideas and tools that both applied linguistics and psychometrics have to offer. Buzz has provided me with frequent comments and suggestions as the book has taken form and he must share the credit for the inspiration and many of the ideas herein.

Much of what is in this book can also be traced to two individuals whose work has influenced my research interests, and indeed my career, in very fundamental ways. My first introduction to applied linguistics was Robert Lado's (1957) *Linguistics Across Cultures*, which was required reading for ESL Peace Corps volunteers in the mid-1960s. Even though this book was quite an eye-opener for a medieval English literature major during Peace Corps training, it wasn't until I was 'in the field', teaching ESL in a high school in the Philippines, that I began to appreciate its wisdom. Its real impact on my career, however, came a few years later, when I was drawn back to it, during graduate school, after having read John B. Carroll's

(1964) *Language and Thought.* It was Carroll's discussions of language acquisition research and cross-cultural research in psycholinguistics, along with Lado's discussion of contrasts across languages, that I found both exciting and challenging, and that piqued an interest that eventually led me to abandon medieval literary studies for dissertation research in second language acquisition.

It was not until after graduate school, when, as a Ford Foundation 'adviser', I found myself in charge of the development and administration of language tests at a national language center in Thailand, that my on-the-job learning led me to the library, where I first discovered that either Lado or Carroll had anything to do with language testing! During the next few years I was fortunate to have the opportunity to work with John Carroll on several occasions, on the development of language aptitude tests in Thai, and was always both awed and inspired by his encyclopedic knowledge, his brilliant insights, and his consummate craftsmanship. I continue to read his work with interest and to correspond with him on occasion to ask a question or pose a problem for his consideration. A great deal of whatever is useful in this book is a result of my contact with him and his work.

When I was trying to come up with a title for this book, it seemed that all the good titles had already been taken. There have been titles in language testing with 'issues' (for example, Oller 1983b; Alderson and Hughes 1981; Lowe and Stansfield 1988), 'current developments' (Hughes and Porter 1983), 'problems' (Upshur and Fata 1968; Interuniversitäre Sprachtestgruppe Symposium Proceedings: Culhane *et al.* 1981, 1984; Klein-Braley and Stevenson 1981; Kohonen *et al.* 1985; Lutjeharms and Culhane 1982), 'approaches' (Spolsky 1978a; Brindley 1986), 'directions' (Read 1981; Lee *et al.* 1985), 'concepts' (Brière and Hinofotis 1979a) and 'research' (Oller and Perkins 1980; Oller 1983b; Bailey *et al.* 1987). And while I'm not aware of any 'principles' or 'essentials' titles in language testing, I'm not convinced that what I have to offer is quite as certain as these terms would imply. The title I've chosen turns out to be a portmanteau of the titles of two seminal works in language testing that happen to have been published in the same year: 'Fundamental considerations in the testing for English language proficiency of foreign students' (Carroll 1961a) and *Language Testing* (Lado 1961). Thus, in solving my title problem, I also echo my debt to Lado and Carroll; hopefully what I've taken from them is returned in some small measure in the pages that follow.

Throughout the travail of writing this book, I have (sometimes) heeded the counsel, or head-bashing, if you will, of a group of individuals who have been my severest critics, and who have also aided and abetted me in this endeavor. Their written comments on various versions and parts of the manuscript have both kept me clearly attuned to fundamental issues, and pushed me to discuss areas that I might have wanted to avoid. They must therefore rightfully share the credit for what is good, and take their lumps as co-conspirators for whatever errors there are that came from them. Among those that should be thus implicated are Charles Alderson, Doug Brown, J. D. Brown, Larry Bouton, Gary Buck, Mike Canale, Gary Cziko, Fred Davidson, John de Jong, Antony Kunnan, Brian Lynch, John Oller, Sandy Savignon, Larry Selinker, Bernard Spolsky, Jack Upshur, and Swathi Vanniarajan. Comments from Gillian Brown on Chapters 4 and 5 were also very helpful. I am most grateful to Charles Alderson, John Carroll, John Clark, Bernard Spolsky, and Henry Widdowson, whose meticulous reading of the manuscript and insightful comments, from different perspectives, have improved it immensely. I would particularly like to thank Yukiko Abe-Hatasa, Buzz Palmer, Larry Selinker, and Jack Upshur for their comments and suggestions, based on their use of the book in manuscript form with their classes on language testing, and Sasi Jungsatitkul, who helped write the discussion questions. Finally, my sincerest gratitude goes to my own students, whose insights, questions, and comments have led me to sharpen my thinking on many issues, and to recognize (and admit) where I remain fuzzy and uncertain. I thank them also for patiently bearing the burden of helping me refine my presentation of these issues.

Writing this book has been challenging and rewarding in that it has given me the opportunity to work my way through some of the conundrums of language testing and to reach, if not solutions, at least a sense of direction and a strategy for research. It has also been a source of frustration, however, as I see the field moving at a pace beyond my ability to incorporate developments into the present discussion. Even as I write this preface, for example, I have received the manuscript of a 'state of the art' article on language testing from Peter Skehan, and from Liz Hamp-Lyons a review article of recent and forthcoming textbooks in applied linguistics research and language testing. These articles review recent work in language testing, and relate this to research in other areas of applied linguistics. Also in my mail is the list of titles of papers for the upcoming 11th Annual Language Testing Research Colloquium, which promise to report recent developments in a number of areas.

But while these developments may be a source of minor frustration to me, as I attempt to reach closure on this book, at the same time they give me cause for optimism. Language testers now have their own journal, *Language Testing*; three newsletters, *Language Testing Update*, the *AILA Language Testing News*, and the *IATEFL Testing SIG Newsletter*, and can count at least three major international conferences annually (the Language Testing Research Colloquium (LTRC) in North America, the Interuniversitäre Sprachtestgruppe (IUS) Symposium in Europe, and the Academic Committee for Research on Language Testing (ACROLT) Symposium in Israel), as well as several regional conferences, such as those in Estonia, Japan, and Thailand, which regularly focus on issues in language testing. What is most encouraging about these events and developments is that the concerns of language testing are drawing together a widening circle of applied linguists, language teachers, and psycho-metricians, who recognize the interrelatedness of their needs, interests, and areas of expertise, and whose collaboration can only advance our understanding of language ability and how we can most effectively and usefully measure it.

Savoy, Illinois
February 1989

1 Introduction

The aims of the book

In developing and using measures of language abilities, we are constantly faced with practical questions, 'What type of test should we use?', 'How long should the test be?', 'How many tests do we need to develop?', questions to which there are no clear-cut, absolute answers. Other questions are even more difficult to answer. For example, 'How reliable should our test be?', 'Are our test scores valid for this use?', and 'How can we best interpret the results of our test?' In addressing questions such as these, we inevitably discover that the answers depend upon a wide range of prior considerations. Since these considerations will vary from one test context to the next, an appropriate answer for one situation may be inappropriate for another. Thus, in developing and using language tests we are seldom, if ever, faced with questions to which there are right or wrong answers. Answering these questions always requires consideration of the specific uses for which the test is intended, how the results are to be interpreted and used, and the conditions under which it will be given.

This book is not a 'nuts and bolts' text on how to write language tests. Rather, it is a discussion of fundamental issues that must be addressed at the start of any language testing effort, whether this involves the development of new tests or the selection of existing tests. How we conceive of these issues will affect how we interpret and use the results of language tests. One objective of this book is thus to provide a conceptual foundation for answering practical questions regarding the development and use of language tests. This foundation includes three broad areas: (1) the context that determines the uses of language tests; (2) the nature of the language abilities we want to measure, and (3) the nature of measurement. This conceptual foundation is applicable to a wide range of general concerns in language testing, including diagnostic, achievement, and language aptitude testing. Furthermore, this foundation provides a

basis for addressing issues in the measurement of language proficiency, which presents some of the most complex and challenging
problems for language testing, problems to which much of the
discussion of this text is addressed.

A second objective of this book is to explore some of the problems
raised by what is perhaps a unique characteristic of language tests
and a dilemma for language testers – that language is both the
instrument and the object of measurement – and to begin to develop
a conceptual framework that I believe will eventually lead, if not to
their solution, at least to a better understanding of the factors that
affect performance on language tests. Unlike tests of other abilities or
areas of knowledge, where we frequently use language in the process
of measuring something else, in language tests, we use language to
measure language ability. What I believe this means is that many
characteristics of the instrument, or the method of observing and
measuring, will overlap with characteristics of the language abilities
we want to measure. In order to understand how these characteristics
interact, as I believe they do, and how they affect performance on
language tests, I believe we must develop a framework for describing
the characteristics of both the language abilities we want to measure
and of the methods we use to measure these abilities.

The climate for language testing

Language testing almost never takes place in isolation. It is done for a
particular purpose and in a specific context. A third objective of this
book is thus to relate language testing to the contexts in which it
takes place. Current research and development in language testing
incorporates advances in several areas: research in language acquisition and language teaching, theoretical frameworks for describing
language proficiency and language use, and measurement theory.[1]

Research in language acquisition and language teaching

As Upshur (1971) noted several years ago, there is an intrinsic
reciprocal relationship between research in language acquisition and
developments in language teaching on the one hand, and language
testing on the other. That is, language testing both serves and is
served by research in language acquisition and language teaching.
Language tests, for example, are frequently used as criterion
measures of language abilities in second language acquisition
research. Similarly, language tests can be valuable sources of

information about the effectiveness of learning and teaching. Language teachers regularly use tests to help diagnose student strengths and weaknesses, to assess student progress, and to assist in evaluating student achievement. Language tests are also frequently used as sources of information in evaluating the effectiveness of different approaches to language teaching. As sources of feedback on learning and teaching, language tests can thus provide useful input into the process of language teaching.

Conversely, insights gained from language acquisition research and language teaching practice can provide valuable information for designing and developing more useful tests. For example, insights about the effects of cognitive and personality characteristics on second language acquisition have led language testers to investigate the extent to which these factors also affect performance on various types of language tests (for example, Hansen and Stansfield 1981; Stansfield and Hansen 1983; Hansen 1984; Chapelle and Roberts 1986; Chapelle 1988). And more recently, language testers have begun discussing the idea that levels of second language ability may be related to developmental sequences that characterize second language acquisition (for example, Ingram 1985; Clahsen 1985; Brindley 1986; Pienemann *et al.* 1988). Bachman (1989a) reviews areas of interface between language testing and second language acquisition research, concluding that research in areas of common concern employing a wide range of research designs and methods is likely to advance knowledge in both fields. New views of language teaching practice can also inform language test development. Much of the development in 'communicative' language testing in the past decade, for example (see Morrow 1977, 1979; Harrison 1983; Seaton 1983; Criper and Davies 1988; Hughes, Porter, and Weir 1988; Alderson 1988) is derived directly from the 'communicative' view of language teaching espoused by applied linguists such as Widdowson, Johnson, Brumfit, Candlin, Wilkins, and Savignon.

Thus, advances in language testing do not take place in a vacuum; they are stimulated by advances in our understanding of the processes of language acquisition and language teaching. And developments in language testing can provide both practical tools and theoretical insights for further research and development in language acquisition and language teaching.

Language ability

A clear and explicit definition of language ability is essential to all language test development and use. Such a definition generally derives from either a language teaching syllabus or a general theory of language ability. Although much foreign/second language proficiency test development continues to be based on a skills and components framework such as those proposed by Lado (1961) and Carroll (1961a), many language testers now take a broader view of language ability. Oller, for example, has developed the notion of a 'pragmatic expectancy grammar' to characterize the abilities involved in appropriately 'mapping' aspects of discourse to the elements of the extralinguistic contexts in which language use takes place (Oller 1979b). Elsewhere, the terms 'communicative proficiency' (Bachman and Palmer 1982a), 'communicative language proficiency' (Bachman and Savignon 1986), and 'communicative language ability' (Bachman and Clark 1987; Bachman 1988) have been used to describe this broader view of language proficiency, whose distinguishing characteristic is its recognition of the importance of context beyond the sentence to the appropriate use of language. This context includes the discourse of which individual sentences are part and the sociolinguistic situation which governs, to a large extent, the nature of that discourse, in both form and function.[2]

Related to this broadened view of communicative language ability is the recognition that *communicative language use* involves a dynamic interaction between the situation, the language user, and the discourse, in which communication is something more than the simple transfer of information. This dynamic view of communication is reflected in the literature on communicative language teaching (for example, Johnson 1982; Savignon 1983) and interlanguage communication strategies (Færch and Kasper 1983), and has been included in frameworks of communicative competence (Hymes 1972b, 1982; Canale and Swain 1980; Canale 1983; Savignon 1972, 1983). This dynamic view of language use also underlies what Oller has called 'pragmatic mappings' between the elements of discourse and the extralinguistic context (Oller 1979b).

In response to these broader views of communicative language ability and communicative language use, much effort is being directed toward developing tests that not only measure a wide range of language abilities, including grammatical, discourse, sociolinguistic, and strategic competencies, but that are also 'authentic', in that they require test takers to interact with and process both the explicit linguistic information and the implicit illocutionary or functional meaning of the test material.

A different view of language ability, which informs the Interagency

Language Roundtable (ILR) oral interview (Lowe 1982, 1985) as well as the *ACTFL Proficiency Guidelines* (American Council on the Teaching of Foreign Languages 1986) and the oral interview test of language proficiency based on them, has gained considerable currency in the foreign language teaching profession. The various definitions of proficiency based on this view are derived, essentially, from the way the construct is defined operationally in the ILR and ACTFL scales. Lowe (1988), one of the major spokespersons for this view, defines proficiency as follows:

> proficiency equals achievement (ILR functions, content, accuracy) plus functional evidence of internalized strategies for creativity expressed in a single global rating of *general language ability* expressed over a wide range of functions and topics at any given ILR level. (emphasis added)
> (Lowe 1988: 12)

Lowe goes on to suggest that the two views of proficiency (the ILR/ACTFL view and that of 'communicative language ability' outlined above) may prove incompatible, claiming that the ACTFL view is a 'holistic, top-down view', while that of communicative language ability is 'an atomistic, bottom-up view of language ability'. (pp. 14–15).

Proponents of the ACTFL view have claimed that the 'Guidelines' can provide a basis for criterion-referenced testing and improved professional standards (Higgs 1982b). The renewed interest in language testing that these guidelines have generated is encouraging. Nevertheless, the way in which they define language proficiency has brought to the forefront questions about the relationship between test content, test method, and the validity of interpretations or uses that are made of test scores (Bachman and Savignon 1986; Bachman 1988a).

A common thread that runs through much recent writing in language testing is the belief that a precise, empirically based definition of language ability can provide the basis for developing a 'common metric' scale for measuring language abilities in a wide variety of contexts, at all levels, and in many different languages (Woodford 1978, 1981; B. J. Carroll 1980; Clark 1980; Brindley 1986). If such a scale were available, a rating of '1', for example, would always indicate the same level of ability, whether this were in listening, speaking, reading, or writing, for different contexts of language use, and even for different languages. Bachman and Clark (1987) state the advantages of a common metric as follows:

the obvious advantage of such a scale and tests developed from it is that it would provide a standard for defining and measuring language abilities that would be independent of specific languages, contexts and domains of discourse. Scores from tests based on this scale would thus be comparable across different languages and contexts.
(Bachman and Clark 1987: 28)

Such tests are of crucial interest for second language acquisition research and language program evaluation, where measures of language ability that can be used as criteria for comparing differences across age groups, varying native languages, and differing teaching methods are virtually nonexistent (Bachman 1989a). Such tests are equally important for use in making decisions about language competency, whether in the context of evaluating learner achievement in language programs, or for certifying the professional competence of language teachers.

Applications of measurement theory to language testing

Recently, we have seen major applications of advances in measurement theory to research and development in language testing. These applications have been primarily in four areas: construct validation, generalizability theory, item-response theory, and criterion-referenced testing.

Construct validation

Research into the relationships between performance on language tests and the abilities that underlie this performance (construct validation research) dates at least from the 1940s, with John B. Carroll's pioneering work (Carroll 1941). The interest of language testers in the construct validity of language tests was renewed in the 1970s by John Oller's 'unitary trait hypothesis', according to which language proficiency consists of a single unitary ability. By analyzing the relationships among scores from a wide variety of language tests, Oller believed he discovered a 'g-factor', which he interpreted as a unitary trait, 'general language proficiency'. Subsequent studies, however, disconfirmed the unitary trait hypothesis, and Oller himself eventually recognized that 'the strongest form of the unitary trait hypothesis was wrong' (Oller 1983a: 352). Nevertheless, Oller's work, as well as the research it stimulated, firmly established construct validation as a central concern of language testing research, and generated renewed interest in factor analysis as an analytic procedure. Other procedures have since been used to examine the construct validity of language tests, and these are discussed in greater detail in Chapter 7 below.

Generalizability theory

Generalizability theory (G-theory) provides a conceptual framework and a set of procedures for examining several different sources of measurement error simultaneously. Using G-theory, test developers can determine the relative effects, for example, of using different test forms, of giving a test more than once, or of using different scoring procedures, and can thus estimate the reliability, or generalizability, of tests more accurately. 'G-theory' has recently been used to analyze different sources of measurement error in subjective ratings of oral interviews and writing samples, and it is discussed in detail in Chapter 6.

Item response theory

Item response theory (IRT) is a powerful measurement theory that provides a superior means for estimating both the ability levels of test takers and the characteristics of test items (difficulty, discrimination). If certain specific conditions are satisfied, IRT estimates are not dependent upon specific samples, and are thus stable across different groups of individuals and across different test administrations. This makes it possible to tailor tests to individual test-takers' levels of ability, and thus to design tests that are very efficient in the way they measure these abilities. These characteristics are particularly useful for developing computer-adaptive tests, and item response theory is being used increasingly in the development and analysis of language tests. IRT also provides sample-free estimates of reliability, or precision of measurement. IRT is discussed in Chapter 6 below.

Criterion-referenced measurement

The measurement approach that has dominated research and development in language testing for the past twenty-five years is that of norm-referenced (NR) testing, in which an individual's test score is reported and interpreted with reference to the performance of other individuals on the test. The quintessential NR test is the 'standard-ized test' that has been tried out with large groups of individuals, whose scores provide 'norms' or reference points for interpreting scores.

In the other major approach to measurement, that of criterion-referenced (CR) testing, test scores are reported and interpreted with reference to a specific content domain or criterion level of performance. CR tests thus provide information about an individual's mastery of a given criterion domain or ability level. While the NR approach continues to dominate the field, language testers have advocated CR measurement in some contexts, and CR principles have recently been applied to the development of language achievement tests. Furthermore, because of problems associated with the NR interpretation of test scores, the CR approach has been proposed as a basis for developing language proficiency tests for both language program evaluation and for evaluating individual levels of ability. The CR approach is discussed more fully in Chapters 2, 6, and 8.

Research and development: needs and problems

The development and use of language tests involves an understanding, on the one hand, of the nature of communicative language use and language ability and, on the other, of measurement theory. Each of these areas is complex in its own right. Furthermore, there appear to be certain dilemmas involved in the application of current measurement models to tests that incorporate what we know about the nature of communicative language use. Language testers have thus been faced with increasingly complex problems, and have sought solutions to these problems in diverse ways.

The problems currently facing language testers have both practical and theoretical implications, and fall into two general areas. First is the problem of specifying language abilities and other factors that affect performance on language tests precisely enough to provide a basis for test development and for the interpretation and use of test scores. The second problem is determining how scores from language tests behave as quantifications of performance. That is, what are the scaling and measurement properties of tests of language abilities? Answering this question is particularly difficult because language tests may measure several distinct but interrelated abilities. Further complications arise if we would like to interpret scores from language tests as indicators of the degree of 'mastery' with reference to some externally defined domain or criterion level of ability, rather than as indices of the relative performance of different individuals.

Defining language abilities and characterizing test authenticity

All language tests must be based on a clear definition of language abilities, whether this derives from a language teaching syllabus or a general theory of language ability, and must utilize some procedure for eliciting language performance. As simplistic as this statement may seem, it turns out that designing a language test is a rather complex undertaking, in which we are often attempting to measure abilities that are not very precisely defined, and using methods of elicitation that themselves depend upon the very abilities we want to measure. This is the fundamental dilemma of language testing mentioned above: the tools we use to observe language ability are themselves manifestations of language ability. Because of this, the way we define the language abilities we want to measure is inescapably related to the characteristics of the elicitation procedures, or test methods we use to measure these abilities. Thus, one of the most important and persistent problems in language testing is that of defining language ability in such a way that we can be sure that the test methods we use will elicit language test performance that is characteristic of language performance in non-test situations.

Most current frameworks of language use are based on the concept of language as communication, and recognize the importance of the context, both discourse and sociolinguistic, in which language is used. Such frameworks are based on a wealth of information from naturalistic, observational studies. I believe that there is now sufficient empirical evidence about the nature of language use and the abilities that are involved in language use to begin the specification of a theoretical model of communicative language ability that will provide a basis for the development of both practical tests and of measures that can, in turn, provide the tools for the empirical investigation of this model.

A related concern has been with developing testing procedures that are 'authentic' (cf. *Language Testing 2*, 1, 1985), and attempts to characterize either authenticity in general, or the authenticity of a given test have been highly problematic. Language testers have used terms such as 'pragmatic' (Oller 1979b), 'functional' (B. J. Carroll 1980; Farhady 1980), 'communicative' (Morrow 1979; Wesche 1981; Canale 1983), 'performance' (for example, Jones 1979b, 1985a; Courchene and de Bagheera 1985; Wesche 1985) and 'authentic' (for example, Spolsky 1985; Shohamy and Reves 1985) to characterize the extent to which the tasks required on a given test are similar to 'normal', or 'real-life' language use. However, when we consider the great variety that characterizes language use – different contexts, purposes, topics, participants, and so forth – it is not at all clear how we might go about distinguishing 'real-life' from 'nonreal-life' language use in any meaningful way, so that attempts to characterize authenticity in terms of real-life performance are problematic. Related to this is the question of whether we can adequately reflect 'real-life language use' in language tests.

Another approach to defining authenticity in language test tasks is to adopt Widdowson's (1978) view of authentic language use as the interaction between the language user and the discourse. This notion is also implicit in Oller's (1979b) second pragmatic naturalness criterion: 'language tests . . . must require the learner to understand the pragmatic interrelationship of linguistic context and extralinguistic contexts' (Oller 1979b: 33). And while this is the approach I will advocate and expand upon in Chapter 8, it is also fraught with problems, not the least of which is the fact that different test takers are likely to interact *individually* in different ways with different test tasks. Some test takers, for example, may perceive a set of tasks as individual items and attempt to answer them one by one, while others may perceive them as a whole discourse, to be answered in relation to each other. Similarly, test takers may differ not only in the extent to which they are aware of and respond to the functional meaning of a given test item, but they may also have different expectations and different contexts, or what Douglas and Selinker (1985) call 'discourse domains', to which they relate that item. Since sociolinguists have been grappling with the protean nature of communicative language use in different contexts since Labov's work in the early 1970s, it is not surprising to find that variable responses to different test tasks pose a difficult problem for language testers.

Because of these problems, it is tempting simply to shrug off the question of authenticity as unimportant, as simply a matter of how the test 'appears' to the test taker. However, if authenticity is a function of the test taker's interaction with the test task, it will affect both the reliability and validity of test scores (Douglas and Selinker 1985; Oller 1986). Furthermore, the approach we take in defining authenticity is closely related to how we define language ability, and thus to how we interpret and use the results of language tests. Adequately characterizing authenticity and estimating its influence on test takers' performance is therefore one of the most pressing issues facing language testers, and constitutes a central theme of this book. I believe the key to solving this problem lies in specifying the characteristics of test tasks and test methods sufficiently well that we can begin to empirically examine test takers' performance on different types of test tasks.

Measurement concerns

A second set of problems derives from the limitations on measures of mental abilities in general, and of language abilities in particular. In this regard, we are concerned with the indirectness of our measures, the limited conditions under which we typically measure language ability, and the relatively restricted sample of performance that we obtain. Our primary concern is whether an individual's test performance can be interpreted as an indication of his competence, or ability to use language appropriately and effectively in *nontest* contexts.[3] Thus, the key measurement problem is determining the extent to which the sample of language use we obtain from a test adequately characterizes the overall potential language use of the individual. In considering this we are inevitably led to consider the question of whether the language use context of the test resembles so-called 'natural' or 'normal' nontest language use. And this, in turn, leads back to the problem of clearly describing 'natural' or 'authentic' language use.

Measurement assumptions

Our analyses and interpretations of test results are based on measurement theory, and the analytic procedures derived from this theory make specific assumptions about the nature of the abilities we test and the relationship between these abilities and scores on tests. One assumption that is fundamental to most current measurement models is that test scores are *unidimensional*, which means that the parts or items of a given test all measure the same, single ability. A related assumption of current measurement theory is that the items or parts of a test are *locally independent*. That is, we assume that an individual's response to a given test item does not depend upon how he responds to other items that are of equal difficulty.

However, from what we know about the nature of language, it is clear that virtually every instance of authentic language use involves several abilities. Listening to and comprehending a lecture, for example, requires, at least, knowledge about the sound system, lexicon and grammatical structure of the language, about the way discourse is organized, and about the sociolinguistic conventions that govern the lecturer's use of language. Furthermore, the very nature of language use is such that discourse consists of interrelated illocutionary acts expressed in a variety of related forms.

If language test scores reflect several abilities, and are thus not unidimensional, and if authentic test tasks are, by definition, interrelated, to what extent are current measurement models appropriate for analyzing and interpreting them? The potential dilemma thus faced by language testers is that tests designed to satisfy the measurement assumptions of unidimensionality and local independence may operate at cross purposes from maintaining the authenticity of the language tasks involved, while language tests involving authentic language use, on the other hand, may be incompatible with current measurement assumptions.

The effect of test method

A final problem related to measurement theory is that of determining the extent to which test performance is influenced by the particular test method used. Numerous studies have demonstrated that test method has a sizable influence on performance on language tests (for example, Clifford 1978, 1981; Bachman and Palmer 1981a, 1982a; Shohamy 1983b, 1984a). If we are to interpret test scores as indicators of language abilities, and not of how well an individual can take multiple-choice tests, for example, we clearly need to minimize the effects of test method.

Research and development: an agenda

In addition to addressing the problems just mentioned, language testers, as applied linguists, must respond to the practical need for more appropriate measures of language abilities for use in language acquisition and language attrition research, language program evaluation, and for making decisions about individuals' attained levels of competency with respect to various educational and employment requirements. I believe that most language tests currently available are inappropriate for these purposes because they are based on a model of language ability that does not include the full range of abilities required for communicative language use, and they incorporate norm-referenced principles of test development and interpretation.

To address both the practical needs and the theoretical problems of language testing, Bachman and Clark (1987) have called for the development of a theoretical framework of factors that affect performance on language tests, and for a program of empirical research into both the measurement characteristics of language tests based on such a theoretical framework and the validity of the framework itself. This research agenda has subsequently been seconded and expanded by other language testers as well (Clark and

Clifford 1988; Clark and Lett 1988). Thus, one of the major themes of this book is the characterization of these factors and how their effects influence the way we interpret and use test scores. These factors fall into four categories, as illustrated in Figure 6.1 in Chapter 6 (p. 165): communicative language ability, test method facets, personal attributes, and random factors.

The main thrust of my discussion of this theme is as follows. Some of the factors that affect scores on language tests are potentially within our control and some are not. Random factors, such as temporary fluctuations in test takers' physical condition or mental alertness, and breakdowns in equipment, are by their very nature unpredictable, and hence uncontrollable. The influence on language test performance of personal attributes, such as sex, age, native language and cultural background, background knowledge, and field independence are beginning to be better understood, but there are few contexts in which these can be practically controlled in the design and use of language tests. That leaves us with the character-istics, or 'facets', of the test method and communicative language ability, which, I argue, are two factors that we can and must attempt to control in the design and use of language tests. The frameworks developed in Chapters 4 and 5 of this book are presented as initial descriptions of these two sets of factors. They are also proposed as a starting place for a program of research and development which is discussed in greater detail in Chapter 8.

The issues discussed in this book are relevant to two aspects of language testing: (1) the development and use of language tests; and (2) language testing research. I believe that the fundamental goal of language test development is to assure that the information, or scores, obtained from language tests will be reliable, valid and useful. This means assuring that test performance is related to and appropriate for the particular interpretations and uses for which the test is intended. I believe the fundamental goals of language testing research, on the other hand, are (1) to formulate and empirically validate a theory of language test performance; and (2) to demon-strate the ways in which performance on language tests is related to communicative language use in its widest sense. It is my hope that this book will be useful for both these aspects of language testing.

Overview of the book

Each chapter in the book presents a set of related issues. Following the discussion of these issues is a summary, notes, suggestions for further reading, and discussion questions.

This chapter and the next two provide a general context for the discussion of language testing. In Chapter 2 the terms 'measurement', 'test', and, 'evaluation' are defined and the relationships among them are discussed. Also described are the properties of measurement scales and the different types of measurement scales that are commonly used in language testing. Next, the essential measurement qualities of tests – reliability and validity – are introduced. Several characteristics inherent to measures in the social sciences and the limitations these place on the interpretation and use of test scores are examined. Finally, a set of procedures for designing tests so as to minimize the effect of these limitations and maximize the reliability and validity of test scores is outlined. In Chapter 3 I discuss the various uses of language tests in educational programs, along with examples of different types of programs to illustrate these different uses. This is followed by a brief discussion of the research uses of language tests. Finally, a taxonomy for classifying different types of language tests is presented.

In Chapters 4 and 5 I present a theoretical framework for describing performance on language tests. In Chapter 4 I discuss the part of the framework that pertains to the language abilities we want to measure. 'Communicative language ability' is described as consisting of language competence, strategic competence, and psychophysiological mechanisms. In Chapter 5 I discuss the characteristics of the test methods we use to elicit language performance. These constitute facets of the testing procedure itself – the testing environment, the test rubric, the input the test taker receives, the response to that input, and the relationship between input and response. I suggest that this framework can be used both for describing the characteristics of existing language tests and for developing new language tests. I further propose that it provides a starting point for examining the reliability and validity of language tests and for formulating empirical hypotheses about the nature of performance on language tests.

Chapters 6 and 7 provide extensive discussions of the issues and problems related to demonstrating the reliability of test scores and the validity of test use. In Chapter 6 sources of error in test scores are discussed within the context of estimating the reliability of test scores. The classical true score measurement model is described and I discuss the approaches to reliability derived from it, including the assumptions, limitations and appropriate uses of these approaches. Next, some problems of the classical model are discussed. This is followed by discussions of the salient features of generalizability theory and item response theory as extensions of the classical model that address these problems. Next, I outline several approaches to estimating the reliability of criterion-referenced tests. I then discuss the effects of test method on test performance and how this affects our interpretation of test scores.

In Chapter 7 I discuss considerations in investigating the validity of the interpretations and uses we make of language test scores. I discuss the notion of validity as a unitary concept pertaining to a particular test interpretation or use. I then discuss the traditional approaches to validity – content, criterion, and construct – as parts of the process of validation that provide an evidential basis for the interpretation and use of language tests. Next, the topic of test bias is discussed, including brief discussions of some of the factors that research has shown to be potential sources of bias in language tests. Finally, I discuss validity issues related to the consequences and ethics of the use of language tests in educational systems and in society at large.

In the final chapter, I shed the mantle of objective discussant and take more of a proactive advocate's role, dealing with some persistent issues (and controversies) in language testing, and proposing an agenda for future research and development. I present what I perceive to be the pros and cons of two different approaches to defining language proficiency and authenticity in language tests, arguing that one, the 'interactional/ability' approach, provides a sounder foundation for the continued development of communicative language tests and for the validation of their use. I then argue for research and development of language tests guided by theoretical frameworks of communicative language ability and test method facets. I further argue that such development needs to be based on criterion-referenced principles of test design and interpretation, and propose an approach to the development of criterion-referenced scales of language ability that is not based on criteria of actual language performance or actual language users. Finally, I indulge in a bit of stock-taking and crystal ball gazing, urging language testers not to lose sight of either the applied linguistic or the psychometric side of language testing, and finding both excitement at the challenges that lie ahead and confidence in our ability to meet them.

Notes

1   Although many researchers distinguish language learning from language acquisition, I will use the term 'language acquisition'

in a nontechnical sense throughout this book to refer to the process of attaining the ability to use language.

2   The term 'language proficiency' has been traditionally used in the context of language testing to refer in general to knowledge, competence, or ability in the use of a language, irrespective of how, where, or under what conditions it has been acquired (for example, Carroll 1961a; Davies 1968b; Spolsky 1968; Upshur 1979; Oller 1979b; Rivera 1984). Another term that has entered the context of language testing, from linguistics via language teaching, is 'communicative competence', which also refers to ability in language use, albeit a broader view of such use than has been traditionally associated with the term 'language proficiency' (for example, Hymes 1972b; Savignon 1972, 1983; Canale and Swain 1980). Recently, the term 'proficiency' has come to be associated, in foreign language teaching circles, almost exclusively with a specific language testing procedure, the ACTFL/ILR Oral Proficiency Interview (Lowe 1983, 1985; Liskin-Gasparro 1984; American Council on the Teaching of Foreign Languages 1986).

The term 'proficiency' has thus acquired a variety of meanings and connotations in different contexts. Therefore, in order to forestall misinterpretation and, if possible, to facilitate the discussion of issues of concern to language testing, I want to clarify the usage that will be followed in this book. The term I prefer to use is simply 'language ability'. However, at times it is necessary to use the term 'language proficiency', and in such cases in this book it is essentially synonymous with 'language ability', or ability in language use.

3   It has become common practice to offer some sort of stylistic solution to the problems related to writing in a language which no longer has a neuter gender in its singular personal pronouns. One solution that I have decided against is the use of 'he or she' or 's/he', since this commits an almost equally grave infelicity, in my opinion, of dehumanizing the language. Another solution, particularly popular among male writers, it seems, is to offer a blanket disclaimer of sexism in language, and to then somehow justify the use of the masculine forms of pronouns on the basis of stylistic consistency. I find this approach personally unattractive, since it is inconsistent with my own beliefs about sexism in general. The approach I will use is to alternate between masculine and feminine forms (except, of course, when referring to specific persons whose sex is known). But rather than

accomplishing this alternation more or less at random, as happens in the human population, I will impose a sort of systematicity to this alternation, maintaining a given gender or combination of genders throughout a thematic section or extended example, and then switching this in the following section. I will, of course, make every attempt to avoid any sexual stereotyping.

2 Measurement

Introduction

In developing language tests, we must take into account considerations and follow procedures that are characteristic of tests and
measurement in the social sciences in general. Likewise, our
interpretation and use of the results of language tests are subject to
the same general limitations that characterize measurement in the
social sciences. The purpose of this chapter is to introduce the
fundamental concepts of measurement, an understanding of which is
essential to the development and use of language tests. These include
the terms 'measurement', 'test', and 'evaluation', and how these are
distinct from each other, different types of measurement scales and
their properties, the essential qualities of measures – reliability and
validity, and the characteristics of measures that limit our interpretations of test results. The process of measurement is described as a set
of steps which, if followed in test development, will provide the basis
for both reliable test scores and valid test use.

Definition of terms: measurement, test, evaluation

The terms 'measurement', 'test', and 'evaluation' are often used
synonymously; indeed they may, in practice, refer to the same
activity.[1] When we ask for an evaluation of an individual's language
proficiency, for example, we are frequently given a test score. This
attention to the superficial similarities among these terms, however,
tends to obscure the distinctive characteristics of each, and I believe
that an understanding of the distinctions among the terms is vital to
the proper development and use of language tests.

Measurement

Measurement in the social sciences is the process of quantifying the
characteristics of persons according to explicit procedures and rules.[2]

This definition includes three distinguishing features: quantification, characteristics, and explicit rules and procedures.

Quantification

Quantification involves the assigning of numbers, and this distinguishes measures from qualitative descriptions such as verbal accounts or nonverbal, visual representations. Non-numerical categories or rankings such as letter grades ('A, B, C . . .'), or labels (for example, 'excellent, good, average . . .') may have the characteristics of measurement, and these are discussed below under 'properties of measurement scales' (pp. 26–30). However, when we actually use categories or rankings such as these, we frequently assign numbers to them in order to analyze and interpret them, and technically, it is not until we do this that they constitute measurement.

Characteristics

We can assign numbers to both physical and mental characteristics of persons. Physical attributes such as height and weight can be observed directly. In testing, however, we are almost always interested in quantifying mental attributes and abilities, sometimes called traits or constructs, which can only be observed indirectly. These mental attributes include characteristics such as aptitude, intelligence, motivation, field dependence/independence, attitude, native language, fluency in speaking, and achievement in reading comprehension.

The precise definition of 'ability' is a complex undertaking. In a very general sense, 'ability' refers to being able to do something, but the circularity of this general definition provides little help for measurement unless we can clarify what the 'something' is. John B. Carroll (1983c, 1987a) has proposed defining an ability with respect to a particular class of cognitive or mental tasks that an individual is required to perform, and 'mental ability' thus refers to performance on a set of mental tasks (Carroll 1987a: 268). We generally assume that there are degrees of ability and that these are associated with tasks or performances of increasing difficulty or complexity (Carroll 1980, 1987a). Thus, individuals with higher degrees of a given ability could be expected to have a higher probability of correct performance on tasks of lower difficulty or complexity, and a lower probability of correct performance on tasks of greater difficulty or complexity.

Whatever attributes or abilities we measure, it is important to understand that it is these attributes or abilities and *not* the persons themselves that we are measuring. That is, we are far from being able to claim that a single measure or even a battery of measures can adequately characterize individual human beings in all their complexity.

Rules and procedures

The third distinguishing characteristic of measurement is that quantification must be done according to explicit rules and procedures. That is, the 'blind' or haphazard assignment of numbers to characteristics of individuals cannot be regarded as measurement. In order to be considered a measure, an observation of an attribute must be replicable, for other observers, in other contexts and with other individuals. Practically anyone can rate another person's speaking ability, for example. But while one rater may focus on pronunciation accuracy, another may find vocabulary to be the most salient feature. Or one rater may assign a rating as a percentage, while another might rate on a scale from zero to five. Ratings such as these can hardly be considered anything more than numerical summaries of the raters' personal conceptualizations of the individual's speaking ability. This is because the different raters in this case did not follow the same criteria or procedures for arriving at their ratings. Measures, then, are distinguished from such 'pseudo-measures' by the explicit procedures and rules upon which they are based. There are many different types of measures in the social sciences, including rankings, rating scales, and tests.[3]

Test

Carroll (1968) provides the following definition of a test:

> a psychological or educational test is a procedure designed to elicit certain behavior from which one can make inferences about certain characteristics of an individual.
> (Carroll 1968: 46)

From this definition, it follows that a test is a measurement instrument designed to elicit a specific sample of an individual's behavior. As one type of measurement, a test necessarily quantifies characteristics of individuals according to explicit procedures. What distinguishes a test from other types of measurement is that it is designed to obtain a specific sample of behavior. Consider the following example. The Interagency Language Roundtable (ILR) oral interview (Lowe 1982), is a test of speaking consisting of (1) a set of elicitation procedures, including a sequence of activities and sets of question types and topics; and (2) a measurement scale of language proficiency ranging from a low level of '0' to a high level of '5', on which samples of oral language obtained via the elicitation procedures are rated. Each of the six scale levels is carefully defined by an extensive verbal description. A qualified ILR interviewer might be able to rate an individual's oral proficiency in a given language according to the ILR rating scale, on the basis of several years' informal contact with that individual, and this could constitute a measure of that individual's oral proficiency. This measure could not be considered a test, however, because the rater did not follow the procedures prescribed by the ILR oral interview, and consequently may not have based her ratings on the kinds of specific language performance that are obtained in conducting an ILR oral interview.

I believe this distinction is an important one, since it reflects the primary justification for the use of language tests and has implications for how we design, develop, and use them. If we could count on being able to measure a given aspect of language ability on the basis of *any* sample of language use, however obtained, there would be no need to design language tests. However, it is precisely because any given sample of language will not necessarily enable the test user to make inferences about a given ability that we need language tests. That is, the inferences and uses we make of language test scores depend upon the sample of language use obtained. Language tests can thus provide the means for more carefully focusing on the specific language abilities that are of interest. As such, they could be viewed as supplemental to other methods of measurement. Given the limitations on measurement discussed below (pp. 30–40), and the potentially large effect of elicitation procedures on test performance, however, language tests can more appropriately be viewed as the best means of assuring that the sample of language obtained is sufficient for the intended measurement purposes, even if we are interested in very general or global abilities. That is, carefully designed elicitation procedures such as those of the ILR oral interview, those for measuring writing ability described by Jacobs *et al.* (1981), or those of multiple-choice tests such as the *Test of English as a Foreign Language* (TOEFL), provide the best assurance that scores from language tests will be reliable, meaningful, and useful.[4]

While measurement is frequently based on the naturalistic observation of behavior over a period of time, such as in teacher rankings or grades, such naturalistic observations might not include samples of behavior that manifest specific abilities or attributes. Thus a rating based on a collection of personal letters, for example, might not provide any indication of an individual's ability to write effective argumentative editorials for a news magazine. Likewise, a teacher's rating of a student's language ability based on informal interactive social language use may not be a very good indicator of how well that student can use language to perform various 'cognitive/ academic' language functions (Cummins 1980a). This is not to imply that other measures are less valuable than tests, but to make the point that the value of tests lies in their capability for eliciting the specific kinds of behavior that the test user can interpret as evidence of the attributes or abilities which are of interest.

Evaluation

Evaluation can be defined as the systematic gathering of information for the purpose of making decisions (Weiss 1972).[5] The probability of making the correct decision in any given situation is a function not only of the ability of the decision maker, but also of the quality of the information upon which the decision is based. Everything else being equal, the more reliable and relevant the information, the better the likelihood of making the correct decision. Few of us, for example, would base educational decisions on hearsay or rumor, since we would not generally consider these to be reliable sources of information. Similarly, we frequently attempt to screen out information, such as sex and ethnicity, that we believe to be irrelevant to a particular decision. One aspect of evaluation, therefore, is the collection of reliable and relevant information. This information need not be, indeed seldom is, exclusively quantitative. Verbal descriptions, ranging from performance profiles to letters of reference, as well as overall impressions, can provide important information for evaluating individuals, as can measures, such as ratings and test scores.

Evaluation, therefore, does not necessarily entail testing. By the same token, tests in and of themselves are not evaluative. Tests are often used for pedagogical purposes, either as a means of motivating students to study, or as a means of reviewing material taught, in which case no evaluative decision is made on the basis of the test results. Tests may also be used for purely descriptive purposes. It is

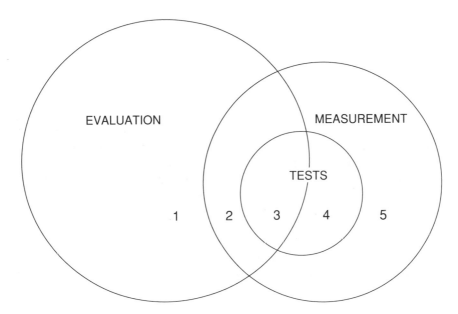

Figure 2.1 Relationships among measurement, tests, and evaluation

only when the results of tests are used as a basis for making a decision that evaluation is involved. Again, this may seem a moot point, but it places the burden for much of the stigma that surrounds testing squarely upon the test user, rather than on the test itself. Since by far the majority of tests are used for the purpose of making decisions about individuals, I believe it is important to distinguish the information-providing function of measurement from the decision-making function of evaluation.

The relationships among measurement, tests, and evaluation are illustrated in Figure 2.1. An example of evaluation that does not involve either tests or measures (area '1') is the use of qualitative descriptions of student performance for diagnosing learning problems. An example of a *non-test measure* for evaluation (area '2') is a teacher ranking used for assigning grades, while an example of a *test* used for purposes of evaluation (area '3') is the use of an achievement test to determine student progress. The most common non-evaluative uses of tests and measures are for research purposes. An example of tests that are not used for evaluation (area '4') is the use of a proficiency test as a criterion in second language acquisition research. Finally, assigning code numbers to subjects in second language research according to native language is an example of a *non-test measure* that is not used for evaluation (area '5'). In summary, then, not all measures are tests, not all tests are evaluative, and not all evaluation involves either measurement or tests.

Essential measurement qualities

If we are to interpret the score on a given test as an indicator of an individual's ability, that score must be both reliable and valid. These qualities are thus essential to the interpretation and use of measures of language abilities, and they are the primary qualities to be considered in developing and using tests.

Reliability

Reliability is a quality of test *scores*, and a perfectly reliable score, or measure, would be one which is free from errors of measurement (American Psychological Association 1985). There are many factors other than the ability being measured that can affect performance on tests, and that constitute sources of measurement error. Individuals' performance may be affected by differences in testing conditions, fatigue, and anxiety, and they may thus obtain scores that are inconsistent from one occasion to the next. If, for example, a student receives a low score on a test one day and a high score on the same test two days later, the test does not yield consistent results, and the scores cannot be considered reliable indicators of the individual's ability. Or suppose two raters gave widely different ratings to the same writing sample. In the absence of any other information, we have no basis for deciding which rating to use, and consequently may regard both as unreliable. Reliability thus has to do with the consistency of measures across different times, test forms, raters, and other characteristics of the measurement context.

In any testing situation, there are likely to be several different sources of measurement error, so that the primary concerns in examining the reliability of test scores are first, to identify the different sources of error, and then to use the appropriate empirical procedures for estimating the effect of these sources of error on test scores. The identification of potential sources of error involves making judgments based on an adequate theory of sources of error. Determining how much these sources of error affect test scores, on the other hand, is a matter of empirical research. The different approaches to defining and empirically investigating reliability will be discussed in detail in Chapter 6.

Validity

The most important quality of test interpretation or use is validity, or the extent to which the inferences or decisions we make on the basis of test scores are *meaningful, appropriate,* and *useful* (American Psychological Association 1985). In order for a test score to be a meaningful indicator of a particular individual's ability, we must be sure it measures that ability and very little else. Thus, in examining the meaningfulness of test scores, we are concerned with demonstrating that they are not unduly affected by factors other than the ability being tested. If test scores are strongly affected by errors of measurement, they will not be meaningful, and cannot, therefore, provide the basis for valid interpretation or use. A test score that is not reliable, therefore, cannot be valid. If test scores are affected by abilities other than the one we want to measure, they will not be meaningful indicators of that particular ability. If, for example, we ask students to listen to a lecture and then to write a short essay based on that lecture, the essays they write will be affected by both their writing ability and their ability to comprehend the lecture. Ratings of their essays, therefore, might not be valid measures of their writing ability.

In examining validity, we must also be concerned with the appropriateness and usefulness of the test score for a given purpose. A score derived from a test developed to measure the language abilities of monolingual elementary school children, for example, might not be appropriate for determining the second language proficiency of bilingual children of the same ages and grade levels. To use such a test for this latter purpose, therefore, would be highly questionable (and potentially illegal). Similarly, scores from a test designed to provide information about an individual's vocabulary knowledge might not be particularly useful for placing students in a writing program.

While reliability is a quality of test scores themselves, validity is a quality of test interpretation and use. As with reliability, the investigation of validity is both a matter of judgment and of empirical research, and involves gathering evidence and appraising the values and social consequences that justify specific interpretations or uses of test scores. There are many types of evidence that can be presented to support the validity of a given test interpretation or use, and hence many ways of investigating validity. Different types of evidence that are relevant to the investigation of validity and approaches to collecting this evidence are discussed in Chapter 7.

Reliability and validity are both essential to the use of tests.

Neither, however, is a quality of tests themselves; reliability is a quality of test scores, while validity is a quality of the interpretations or uses that are made of test scores. Furthermore, neither is absolute, in that we can never attain perfectly error-free measures in actual practice, and the appropriateness of a particular use of a test score will depend upon many factors outside the test itself. Determining what degree of relative reliability or validity is required for a particular test context thus involves a value judgment on the part of the test user.

Properties of measurement scales

If we want to measure an attribute or ability of an individual, we need to determine what set of numbers will provide the best measurement. When we measure the loudness of someone's voice, for example, we use decibels, but when we measure temperature, we use degrees Centigrade or Fahrenheit. The sets of numbers used for measurement must be appropriate to the ability or attribute measured, and the different ways of organizing these sets of numbers constitute *scales of measurement.*

Unlike physical attributes, such as height, weight, voice pitch, and temperature, we cannot directly observe intrinsic attributes or abilities, and we therefore must establish our measurement scales by definition, rather than by direct comparison. The scales we define can be distinguished in terms of four properties. A measure has the property of *distinctiveness* if different numbers are assigned to persons with different values on the attribute, and is *ordered in magnitude* if larger numbers indicate larger amounts of the attribute. If equal differences between ability levels are indicated by equal differences in numbers, the measure has *equal intervals*, and if a value of zero indicates the absence of the attribute, the measure has an *absolute zero point.*

Ideally, we would like the scales we use to have all these properties, since each property represents a different type of information, and the more information our scale includes, the more useful it will be for measurement. However, because of the nature of the abilities we wish to measure, as well as the limitations on defining and observing the behavior that we believe to be indicative of those abilities, we are not able to use scales that possess all four properties for measuring every ability. That is, not every attribute we want to measure, or quantify, fits on the same scale, and not every procedure we use for observing and quantifying behavior yields the same scale, so that it is necessary to use different scales of measurement, according to the characteristics of the attribute we wish to measure and the type of measurement procedure we use. Ratings, for example, might be considered the most appropriate way to quantify observations of speech from an oral interview, while we might believe that the number of items answered correctly on a multiple-choice test is the best way to measure knowledge of grammar. These abilities are different, as are the measurement procedures used, and consequently, the scales they yield have different properties. The way we interpret and use scores from our measures is determined, to a large extent, by the properties that characterize the measurement scales we use, and it is thus essential for both the development and the use of language tests to understand these properties and the different measurement scales they define. Measurement specialists have defined four types of measurement scales – *nominal, ordinal, interval,* and *ratio* – according to how many of these four properties they possess.[6]

Nominal scale

As its name suggests, a nominal scale comprises numbers that are used to 'name' the classes or categories of a given attribute. That is, we can use numbers as a shorthand code for identifying different categories. If we quantified the attribute 'native language', for example, we would have a nominal scale. We could assign different code numbers to individuals with different native language backgrounds, (for example, Amharic = 1, Arabic = 2, Bengali = 3, Chinese = 4, etc.) and thus create a nominal scale for this attribute. The numbers we assign are arbitrary, since it makes no difference what number we assign to what category, so long as each category has a unique number. The distinguishing characteristic of a nominal scale is that while the categories to which we assign numbers are distinct, they are *not ordered* with respect to each other. In the example above, although '1' (Amharic) is *not equal to* '2' (Arabic), it is neither greater than nor less than '2'. Nominal scales thus possess the property of distinctiveness. Because they quantify categories, nominal scales are also sometimes referred to as 'categorical' scales. A special case of a nominal scale is a *dichotomous scale,* in which the attribute has only two categories, such as 'sex' (male and female), or 'status of answer' (right and wrong) on some types of tests.

Ordinal scale

An ordinal scale, as its name suggests, comprises the numbering of different levels of an attribute that are ordered with respect to each other. The most common example of an ordinal scale is a ranking, in which individuals are ranked 'first', 'second', 'third', and so on, according to some attribute or ability. A rating based on definitions of different levels of ability is another measurement procedure that typically yields scores that constitute an ordinal scale. The points, or levels, on an ordinal scale can be characterized as 'greater than' or 'less than' each other, and ordinal scales thus possess, in addition to the property of distinctiveness, the property of ordering. The use of subjective ratings in language tests is an example of ordinal scales, and is discussed on pp. 36 and 44–5 below.

Interval scale

An interval scale is a numbering of different levels in which the distances, or intervals, between the levels are equal. That is, in addition to the ordering that characterizes ordinal scales, interval scales consist of equal distances or intervals between ordered levels. Interval scales thus possess the properties of distinctiveness, ordering, and equal intervals. The difference between an ordinal scale and an interval scale is illustrated in Figure 2.2.

In this example, the test scores indicate that these individuals are not equally distant from each other on the ability measured.[7] This additional information is not provided by the rankings, which might

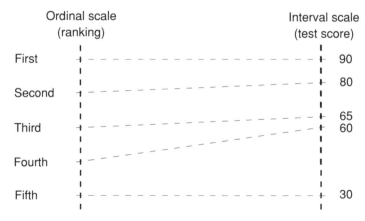

Figure 2.2   Comparison between ordinal and interval scales

be interpreted as indicating that the intervals between these five individuals' ability levels are all the same. Differences in approaches to developing ordinal and interval scales in language tests are discussed on pp. 36 and 44–5 below.

Ratio scale

None of the scales discussed thus far has an absolute zero point, which is the distinguishing characteristic of a ratio scale. Most of the scales that are used for measuring physical characteristics have true zero points. If we looked at a bathroom scale with nothing on it, for example, we should see the pointer at zero, indicating the absence of weight on the scale. The reason we call a scale with an absolute zero point a ratio scale is that we can make comparisons in terms of ratios with such scales. For example, if I have two pounds of coffee and you have four pounds, you have twice as much coffee (by weight) as I have, and if one room is ten feet long and another thirty, the second room is three times as long as the first.

To illustrate the difference between interval and ratio scales, consider the different scales that are used for measuring temperature. Two commonly used scales are the Fahrenheit and Celsius (centigrade) scales, each of which defines zero differently. The Fahrenheit scale originally comprised a set of equal intervals between the melting point of ice, which was arbitrarily defined as 32°, and the temperature of human blood, defined as 96°. By extending the scale, the boiling point of water was found to be 212°, which has since become the upper defining point of this scale. The Fahrenheit scale thus consists of 180 equal intervals between 32° and 212°, with 0° defined simply as 32 scale points below the melting point of ice. (The Fahrenheit scale, of course, extends below 0° and above 212°.) The Celsius scale, on the other hand, defines 0° as the melting point of ice (at sea level), and 100° as the boiling point of water, with 100 equal intervals in between. In neither the Fahrenheit nor the Celsius scale does the zero point indicate the absence of a particular characteristic; it does not indicate the absence of heat, and certainly not the absence of water or ice. These scales thus do not constitute ratio scales, so that if it was 50° Fahrenheit last night and 100° this noon, it is not the case that it is twice as hot now as it was last night. If we define temperature in terms of the volume of an 'ideal' gas, however, then the absolute zero point could be defined as the point at which gas has no volume. This is the definition of 0° that is used for the Kelvin, or absolute, scale, which is a ratio scale.

Each of the four properties discussed above provides a different type of information, and the four measurement scales are thus ordered, with respect to each other, in terms of the amount of information they can provide. For this reason, these different scales are also sometimes referred to as *levels of measurement*. The nominal scale is thus the lowest type of scale, or level of measurement, since it is only capable of distinguishing among different categories, while the ratio scale is the highest level, possessing all four properties and thus capable of providing the greatest amount of information. The four types of scales, or levels of measurement, along with their properties, are summarized in Table 2.1.

Property	Nominal	Ordinal	Interval	Ratio
		Type of scale		
Distinctiveness	+	+	+	+
Ordering	−	+	+	+
Equal intervals	−	−	+	+
Absolute zero point	−	−	−	+

Table 2.1   Types of measurement scales and their properties (after Allen and Yen 1979: 7)

Characteristics that limit measurement

As test developers and test users, we all sincerely want our tests to be the best measures possible. Thus there is always the temptation to interpret test results as absolute, that is, as unimpeachable evidence of the extent to which a given individual possesses the language ability in question. This is understandable, since it would certainly make educational decisions more clear-cut and research results more convincing. However, we know that our tests are not perfect indicators of the abilities we want to measure and that test results must always be interpreted with caution. The most valuable basis for keeping this clearly in mind can be found, I believe, in an understanding of the characteristics of measures of mental abilities and the limitations these characteristics place on our interpretation of test scores. These limitations are of two kinds: limitations in specification and limitations in observation and quantification.

Limitations in specification

In any language testing situation, as with any non-test situation in which language use is involved, the performance of an individual will be affected by a large number of factors, such as the testing context, the type of test tasks required, and the time of day, as well as her mental alertness at the time of the test, and her cognitive and personality characteristics. (See pp. 163–5 below for a discussion of the factors that affect language test scores.) The most important factor that affects test performance, with respect to language testing, of course, is the individual's language ability, since it is language ability in which we are interested.

In order to measure a given language ability, we must be able to specify what it is, and this specification generally is at two levels. At the theoretical level, we can consider the ability as a type, and need to define it so as to clearly distinguish it *both* from other language abilities and from other factors in which we are not interested, but which may affect test performance. Thus, at the theoretical level we need to specify the ability in relation to, or in contrast to, other language abilities and other factors that may affect test performance. Given the large number of different individual characteristics – cognitive, affective, physical – that could potentially affect test performance, this would be a nearly impossible task, even if all these factors were independent of each other. How much more so, given the fact that not only are the various language abilities probably interrelated, but that these interact with other abilities and factors in the testing context as well. At the operational level, we need to specify the instances of language performance that we are willing to interpret as indicators, or tokens, of the ability we wish to measure. This level of specification, then, defines the relationship between the ability and the test score, between type and token.

In the face of the complexity of and the interrelationships among the factors that affect performance on language tests, we are forced to make certain simplifying assumptions, or to *underspecify*, both in designing language tests and in interpreting test scores. That is, when we design a test, we cannot incorporate all the possible factors that affect performance. Rather, we attempt to either exclude or minimize by design the effects of factors in which we are not interested, so as to maximize the effects of the ability we want to measure. Likewise, in interpreting test scores: even though we know that a test taker's performance on an oral interview, for example, will be affected to some extent by the facility of the interviewer and by the subject matter covered, and that the score will depend on the consistency of the raters, we nevertheless interpret ratings based on an interview as indicators of a single factor – the individual's *ability* in speaking.

This indeterminacy in specifying what it is that our tests measure is a major consideration in both the development and use of language tests. From a practical point of view, it means there are virtually always more constructs or abilities involved in a given test performance than we are capable of observing or interpreting. Conversely, it implies that when we design a test to measure a given ability or abilities, or interpret a test score as an indicator of ability 'X', we are simplifying, or underspecifying the factors that affect the observations we make. Whether the indeterminacy is at the theoretical level of types, and language abilities are not adequately delimited or distinguished from each other, or whether at the operational level of tokens, where the relationship between abilities and their behavioral manifestations is misspecified, the result will be the same: our interpretations and uses of test scores will be of limited validity.

For language testing research, this indeterminacy implies that any theory of language test performance we develop is likely to be underspecified. Measurement theory, which is discussed in Chapter 6, has developed, to a large extent, as a methodology for dealing with the problem of underspecification, or the uncontrolled effects of factors other than the abilities in which we are interested. In essence, it provides a means for estimating the effects of the various factors that we have not been able to exclude from test performance, and hence for improving both the design of tests and the interpretation of their results.

Limitations in observation and quantification

In addition to the limitations related to the underspecification of factors that affect test performance, there are characteristics of the processes of observation and quantification that limit our interpretations of test results. These derive from the fact that all measures of mental ability are necessarily *indirect*, *incomplete*, *imprecise*, *subjective*, and *relative*.

Indirectness

In the majority of situations where language tests are used, we are interested in measuring the test taker's underlying competence, or ability, rather than his performance on a particular occasion. That is, we are generally not interested so much in how an individual performs on a given test on a given day, as in his ability to use language at different times in a wide range of contexts. Thus, even though our measures are necessarily based on one or more individual observations of performance, or behavior, we interpret them as indicators of a more long-standing ability or competence.[8]

I believe it is essential, if we are to properly interpret and use test results, to understand that the relationship between test scores and the abilities we want to measure is indirect. This is particularly critical since the term 'direct test' is often used to refer to a test in which performance resembles 'actual' or 'real-life' language performance. Thus, writing samples and oral interviews are often referred to as 'direct' tests, since they presumably involve the use of the skills being tested. By extension, such tests are often regarded, virtually without question, as valid evidence of the presence or absence of the language ability in question. The problem with this, however, is that the use of the term 'direct' confuses the behavioral manifestation of the trait or competence for the construct itself. As with all mental measures, language tests are *indirect* indicators of the underlying traits in which we are interested, whether they require recognition of the correct alternative in a multiple-choice format, or the writing of an essay. Because scores from language tests are indirect indicators of ability, the valid interpretation and use of such scores depends crucially on the adequacy of the way we have specified the relationship between the test score and the ability we believe it indicates. To the extent that this relationship is not adequately specified, the interpretations and uses made of the test score may be invalid.

Incompleteness

In measuring language abilities, we are never able to observe or elicit an individual's total performance in a given language. This could only be accomplished by following an individual around with a tape recorder 24 hours a day for his entire life, which is clearly an impossible task. That is, given the extent and the variation that characterize language use, it simply is not possible for us to observe and measure every instance of an individual's use of a given language. For this reason, our measures must be based on the observation of a part of an individual's total language use. In other words, the performance we observe and measure in a language test is a *sample* of an individual's total performance in that language.

Since we cannot observe an individual's total language use, one of our main concerns in language testing is assuring that the sample we do observe is representative of that total use – a potentially infinite set of utterances, whether written or spoken. If we could tape-record an individual's speech for a few hours every day for a year, we would have a reasonably representative sample of his performance, and we could expect a measure of speaking based on this sample to be very accurate. This is because the more representative our sample is of an individual's performance, the more accurate a representation of his total performance it will be. But even a relatively limited sample such as this (in terms of a lifetime of language use) is generally beyond the realm of feasibility, so we may base our measure of speaking on a 30-minute sample elicited during an oral interview. In many large-scale testing contexts, even an oral interview is not possible, so we may derive our measure of speaking from an even more restricted sample of performance, such as an oral reading of a text or a non-speaking test.

Just as large, representative samples yield accurate measures, the smaller and less representative are our samples of performance, the less accurate our measures will be. Therefore, recognizing that we almost always deal with fairly small samples of performance in language tests, it is vitally important that we incorporate into our measurement design principles or criteria that will guide us in determining what kinds of performance will be most relevant to and representative of the abilities we want to measure. One approach to this might be to identify the domain of relevant 'real-life' language use and then attempt to sample performance from this domain. In developing a test to measure how well students can read French literary criticism, for example, we could design our test so that it includes reading tasks that students of French literature actually perform in pursuing their studies.

A different approach would be to identify critical features, or components of language ability, and then design test tasks that include these. This is the approach that underlies so-called 'discrete-point' language tests, which tend to focus on components such as grammar, pronunciation, and vocabulary. However, this approach need not apply only to the formal features of language, or even to a single feature of language use. It might be of interest in a given situation, for example, to design a test that focuses on an individual's ability to produce pragmatic aspects of language use, such as speech acts or implicatures, in a way that is appropriate for a given context and audience.

The approach we choose in specifying criteria for sampling language use on tests will be determined, to a great extent, by how we choose to define what it is we are testing. That is, if we choose to define test content in terms of a domain of actual language use, we will need to specify criteria for selecting instances of performance from that domain. If, on the other hand, we choose to define test content in terms of components or abilities, we will need to specify criteria for test tasks that we believe require these abilities in their completion. In either case, our sample will be incomplete, albeit in different ways. Therefore, in interpreting individual test scores we must recognize that they are but estimates of ability based on incomplete samples of performance, and that both their reliability and the validity of their interpretation and use will be limited accordingly.

The notion of incompleteness also pertains to interpreting test results with reference to group performance. For example, if we wanted to know how a given student's writing ability compared with that of all other undergraduate college students in the United States, we might feel that we need to measure the writing ability of all such individuals. Since this is clearly not possible, we might instead try to measure the ability of a representative sample of college students. This is essentially the strategy followed in the development of standardized language tests, which are tried out with groups (samples) of individuals who are considered to be representative of the population of individuals for whom the test is intended. The performance of these individuals then becomes the 'norm' that provides a basis for interpreting the performance of subsequent test takers. Since norms are based on samples, the interpretation of scores on such tests depends, to a large extent, upon how representative the samples, or norm groups, are of the total population of test takers, so that scores on such tests must be understood as estimates, rather than as absolutes.

Imprecision

The accuracy or precision of our measurements is a function of both the representativeness and the number of tasks or units with which we define our scales. In measuring height, for example, we assume that the yardstick we use is a valid instance, or token, of the standard yardstick. The precision of our measurement of height with this yardstick will increase as we increase the number of units we use from feet to inches to fractions of inches. In measuring language abilities, where we are not dealing with direct physical comparisons, the units of our measurement scales must be defined, and precision, or reliability, becomes, in part, a function of how we define these units. The units that we use to define scales in language tests are most commonly of two kinds: levels or bands, such as in scales for rating compositions, and the number of tasks correctly completed, as in multiple choice tests.

In developing a rating scale, the points on the scale are typically defined in terms of either the types of language performance or the levels of abilities that are considered distinctive at different scale points. In order to be rated precisely, these scale points must be defined so as to clearly represent distinct levels, or bands. Assuming the levels can be distinctly defined, the more levels there are, the more precise our rating scale will, in theory, tend to be. However, in order for actual ratings made on the basis of our scale to be precise, it must also be possible for our raters, human beings, to clearly distinguish among all the different levels we have defined. Thus, even though we may define a rating scale with ten levels, we may find that our raters can only distinguish three broad levels, so that the ratings in fact comprise only a three-point scale. In such a case, to persist in using the ten-point scale would give a false impression of precision, not only to the raters, but to test users as well. However many levels we define, we are generally not able to demonstrate that the differences between different levels are equal, so that such rating scales most typically constitute ordinal scales. Thus, even though several approaches for obtaining interval scales from subjective ratings have been developed over the years (for example, Thurstone 1925, 1927a; Likert 1932; Guilford 1954), these procedures are seldom applied to the development of rating scales of language abilities.

The precision of scales defined by the number of tasks successfully completed will depend upon the *number* of tasks or 'items' that constitute the units of the scale, with larger numbers of items generally yielding more representative samples of performance. Equally important in the precision of such a scale is the *comparability* of these tasks, in terms of their difficulty relative to the ability of the test takers. We can determine the comparability of tasks, in terms of difficulty, from empirical data from trial administrations of the test. The precision of test scores will be lessened to the extent that the test includes tasks at levels of difficulty that are inappropriate for the ability level of the group being tested. For example, a test with all items at the same level of difficulty would not be a very accurate measure for individuals whose abilities are either greatly above or greatly below that level. Likewise, neither extremely easy nor extremely difficult items will provide very accurate measures for a group of individuals of relatively homogenous intermediate ability.

Lack of comparability of tasks in terms of abilities measured can affect the validity of the test. The less comparable the tasks or items are, in terms of the ability measured, the less valid the measure will be of a particular ability. For example, if the items in a test that is meant to measure knowledge of grammar are also heavily influenced (for the group being tested) by knowledge of vocabulary, then the validity of this test as a measure of grammar will be diminished. Determining the comparability of the tasks involves both subjective judgment and empirical evidence. We can judge the comparability of abilities on the basis of either a specific content domain, such as that specified in a course syllabus, or a theory of language proficiency, such as that proposed in Chapter 4, and the comparability of the tasks in terms of facets of the test method, as described in Chapter 5.

Because of the nature of language, it is virtually impossible (and probably not desirable) to write tests with 'pure' items that test a single construct or to be sure that all items are equally representative of a given ability. Likewise, it is extremely difficult to develop tests in which all the tasks or items are at the exact level of difficulty appropriate for the individuals being tested. Recent advances in item response theory and computer adaptive testing, however, have made it possible to administer certain types of language tests in a way that maximizes the 'fit' between the difficulty levels of items and the ability levels of test takers.

Subjectivity

As Pilliner (1968) noted, language tests are subjective in nearly all aspects. Test developers make subjective decisions in the design of tests and test writers make subjective decisions in producing test items. Furthermore, test takers make subjective judgments in taking tests, and, with the exception of objectively scored tests, scorers make subjective judgments in scoring tests. Language tests are based on either course syllabi or theories of language proficiency, both of which represent the subjective judgments of the individuals who devise them, and tests are therefore neither infallible nor exhaustive definitions of the abilities we may want to test. Furthermore, test developers subjectively select the specific abilities to be included in a given test. For these reasons, a test score should be interpreted as a reflection of a given test developer's selection of the abilities included in a given syllabus or theory.

The procedures by which we arrive at test scores are also determined subjectively. The decision to use an open-ended cloze test rather than a reading passage followed by multiple-choice questions, for example, is subjective, as is the setting of time limits and other administrative procedures. Finally, interpretations regarding the level of ability or correctness of the performance on the test may be subjective. All of these subjective decisions can affect both the reliability and the validity of test results to the extent that they are sources of bias and random variation in testing procedures.

Perhaps the greatest source of subjectivity is the test taker herself, who must make an uncountable number of subjective decisions, both consciously and subconsciously, in the process of taking a test. Each test taker is likely to approach the test and the tasks it requires from a slightly different, subjective perspective, and to adopt slightly different, subjective strategies for completing those tasks. These differences among test takers further complicate the tasks of designing tests and interpreting test scores.

Relativeness

The last limitation on measures of language ability is the potential relativeness of the levels of performance or ability we wish to measure. When we base test content on domains of language use, or on the actual performance of individuals, the presence or absence of language abilities is impossible to define in an absolute sense. The concept of 'zero' language ability is a complex one, since in attempting to define it we must inevitably consider language ability as a cognitive ability, its relationship to other cognitive abilities, and whether these have true zero points. This is further complicated with respect to ability in a second or foreign language by the question of whether there are elements of the native language that are either universal to all languages or shared with the second language. Thus, although we can all think of languages in which we know not a single word or expression, this lack of knowledge of the surface features of the language may not constitute absolute 'zero' ability. Even if we were to accept the notion of 'zero' language ability, from a purely practical viewpoint we rarely, even for research purposes, attempt to measure abilities of individuals in whom we believe these abilities to be completely absent.

At the other end of the spectrum, the individual with absolutely complete language ability does not exist. From the perspective of language history, it could be argued that given the constant change that characterizes any language system, no such system is ever static or 'complete'. From a cognitive perspective it might be argued that cognitive abilities are constantly developing, so that no cognitive ability is ever 'complete'. The language use of native speakers has frequently been suggested as a criterion of absolute language ability, but this is inadequate because native speakers show considerable variation in ability, particularly with regard to abilities such as cohesion, discourse organization, and sociolinguistic appropriateness. For these reasons, it seems neither theoretically nor practically possible to define either an absolutely 'perfect' level of actual language performance, or an individual with 'perfect' language ability.

In the absence of either actual language performance or actual individuals to serve as criteria for defining the extremes on a scale of language ability, all measures of language ability based on domain specifications of actual language performance must be interpreted as relative to some 'norm' of performance. This interpretation is typically determined by testing a given group of individuals and using their test performance to define a scale on which the performance of other individuals can be measured. One difficulty in this is finding a sample group of individuals that is representative of the population of potential test takers. Fortunately, principles and procedures for sampling have been developed that enable the test developer to identify and obtain a reasonably representative sample.

A much more complex issue is that of identifying the kind of language use that we choose to adopt as the norm to be tested. Given the number of varieties, dialects, and registers that exist in virtually every language, we must be extremely cautious in attempting to treat even 'native speakers' as a homogeneous group.[9] For example, there are many sample test items and exercises in Heaton's (1975) language testing book which native speakers of 'American English' are unable to answer correctly unless they happen also to know the appropriate forms in 'British English'. (The reverse might also be a problem if American textbooks were used in British schools.) And within each of these two varieties of English there is sufficient variation to require test developers to carefully screen test items for possible bias due to differences in dialects of test takers. In addition to differing norms across varieties of a given language, test developers must consider differences in norms of usage across registers. For example, a phrase such as 'it was the author's intent to determine the extent to which . . .' may be acceptable formal writing style, but would be inappropriate in most informal oral language use. Finally, test developers must consider differences between 'prescriptive' norms and the norms of actual usage. The distinctions between 'sit' and 'set' and between 'lay' and 'lie', for example, are rapidly disappearing in American English. Because of the variety of norms, both in terms of ability and in terms of language use, test users would be well advised to consider carefully whether the norms of language use operationally defined by a given test provide appropriate points of reference for interpreting the language test performance of the individuals they intend to test.

The other approach to defining language test content, that of identifying components, or abilities, provides, I believe, a means for developing measurement scales that are not dependent upon the particular domain of performance or language users. Such scales can be defined in terms of abilities, rather than in terms of actual performance or individuals, and thus provide the potential for defining absolute 'zero' and 'perfect' points. We will return to this in the next section.

However one chooses to define the standard for score interpretation, whether in terms of a 'norm group' (native-speaker or otherwise) of actual language users, or whether in terms of levels of language abilities, our interpretations and uses will be limited to these standards. If, for example, we choose native speakers of Castilian Spanish as our norm group, or standard for score interpretation, we cannot make valid inferences about individuals' ability to use other varieties of Spanish. Similarly, if we have chosen an absolute scale of 'grammatical competence' for our standard, we cannot make valid inferences about how a given test taker compares with, say, 'native speakers' of some variety of the language, without first establishing norms for these native speakers on our absolute scale.

Steps in measurement

Interpreting a language test score as an indication of a given level of language ability involves being able to infer, on the basis of an observation of that individual's language performance, the degree to which the ability is present in the individual. The limitations discussed above restrict our ability to make such inferences. A major concern of language test development, therefore, is to minimize the effects of these limitations. To accomplish this, the development of language tests needs to be based on a logical sequence of procedures linking the putative ability, or construct, to the observed performance. This sequence includes three steps: (1) identifying and defining the construct theoretically; (2) defining the construct operationally, and (3) establishing procedures for quantifying observations (Thorndike and Hagen 1977).

Defining constructs theoretically

Physical characteristics such as height, weight, and eye color can be experienced directly through the senses, and can therefore be defined by direct comparison with a directly observable standard. Mental abilities such as language proficiency, however, cannot be observed directly. We cannot *experience* grammatical competence, for example, in the same way as we experience eye color. We infer grammatical ability through observing behavior that we presume to be influenced by grammatical ability. The first step in the measurement of a given language ability, therefore, is to distinguish the construct we wish to measure from other similar constructs by defining it clearly, precisely, and unambiguously. This can be accomplished by determining what specific characteristics are relevant to the given construct.

Historically, we can trace two distinct approaches to defining language proficiency. In one approach, which I will call the 'real-life' approach, language proficiency itself is not defined, but rather, a domain of actual, or 'real-life' language use is identified that is considered to be characteristic of the performance of competent language users. The most well-developed exponents of this approach are the Interagency Language Roundtable (ILR) oral proficiency interview (Lowe 1982) and its close derivative, the ACTFL oral proficiency interview (American Council on the Teaching of Foreign Languages 1986). In this approach, a domain of language use is identified, and distinct scale points or levels are then defined in terms of this domain. The characteristics that are considered relevant for measuring language proficiency in this approach thus include virtually all the features that are present in any instance of language use, including both contextual features such as the relationship between the two interlocutors, specific content areas and situations, and features of the language system itself, such as grammar, vocabulary, and pronunciation. The following description of the 'advanced' level from the ACTFL scale illustrates this approach:

> Able to satisfy the requirements of everyday situations and routine school and work requirements. Can handle with confidence but not with facility complicated tasks and social situations, such as elaborating, complaining, and apologizing. Can narrate and describe with some details, linking sentences together smoothly. Can communicate facts and talk casually about topics of current public and personal interest, using general vocabulary.
> (American Council on the Teaching of Foreign Languages 1986:2)

As can be seen from this example, descriptions of scale levels in this approach include specific content areas and contexts, as well as features of language, that are considered relevant to the domain of language use that defines the performance to be sampled.

The other approach to defining language proficiency might be called the 'interactional/ability' approach. In this approach, language proficiency is defined in terms of its component abilities, such as those described in the skills and components frameworks of Lado (1961) and Carroll (1961a), the functional framework of Halliday (1976), or the communicative frameworks of Munby (1978) and Canale and Swain (1980), and in the research of Bachman and Palmer (1982a). For example, pragmatic competence might be defined as follows:

> the knowledge necessary, in addition to organizational com-
> petence, for appropriately producing or comprehending dis-
> course. Specifically, it includes illocutionary competence, or the
> knowledge of how to perform speech acts, and sociolinguistic
> competence, or the knowledge of the sociolinguistic conventions
> which govern language use.

Assuming that we have also defined other components of language ability, such as organizational, illocutionary, and sociolinguistic competence, this definition distinguishes pragmatic competence from organizational competence, and clearly specifies its component constructs.

Whichever approach is followed, domains of 'real-life' or component abilities, definitions must be clear and unambiguous. However, for test results to be useful, the definitions upon which the tests are based must also be acceptable to test users. That is, for a test of a given construct to be useful for whatever purpose, it is necessary that there be agreement on, or at least general acceptance of the theoretical definition upon which the test is based. No matter how clearly we might define strength of grip or hand size, for example, most of us would not regard these attributes as relevant to the definition of writing ability, and measures of these would thus not be accepted as valid measures of this construct.

Defining constructs operationally

The second step in measurement, defining constructs operationally, enables us to relate the constructs we have defined theoretically to our observations of behavior. This step involves, in essence, determining how to isolate the construct and make it observable. Even if it were possible to examine our subjects' brains directly, we would see little that would help us determine their levels of language ability. We must therefore decide what specific procedures, or operations, we will follow to elicit the kind of performance that will indicate the degree to which the given construct is present in the individual. The theoretical definition itself will suggest relevant operations. For example, in order to elicit language performance that would indicate a degree of pragmatic competence as defined above, we would have to design a test that would require the subject to process discourse and that would involve both the performance of illocutionary acts and adherence to sociolinguistic rules of appropriateness.

The context in which the language testing takes place also influences the operations we would follow. If, for example, we were interested in measuring the pragmatic competence of individuals whose primary language use is writing news reports, we would probably design a test that would require the subjects to perform illocutionary acts appropriately in this particular type of writing. Thus we might provide the test taker with a list of events and ask him to organize them in an appropriate sequence and to write a concise objective report based on them. Or for individuals who are planning to work as travel agents, we might design a test to determine how well they can respond to aural questions and obtain additional information, both in face-to-face situations and over the telephone. Thus the specific operations we use for making the construct observable reflect both our theoretical definition of the construct and what we believe to be the context of language use. These operations, or tests, become the operational definitions of the construct.

For an operational definition to provide a suitable basis for measurement, it must elicit language performance in a standard way, under uniform conditions. For example, ratings of oral proficiency based on samples of speech in which the type of task (such as informal greetings versus oral reading) is not controlled from one interview to the next cannot be considered adequate operational definitions because the language performance is not obtained under uniform conditions. Similarly, an oral interview in which the examiner simply carries on an unstructured conversation with the subject for 15 to 20 minutes is not an adequate operational definition because variations in the speech acts elicited, the subject matter discussed, or the levels of register required may be completely uncontrolled, not only from one test taker to the next, but from examiner to examiner.

Variations in testing procedures do, to some degree, characterize virtually all language tests. Our objective in developing tests, therefore, should be to specify, in our operational definitions, the features of the testing procedure in sufficient detail to assure that variations in test method are minimized, so that the specific performance elicited is an adequate sample of the language abilities that are being tested. The descriptive framework of test method facets presented in Chapter 5 is intended as a basis for specifying the features of testing procedures.

Quantifying observations

The third step in measurement is to establish procedures for quantifying or scaling our observations of performance. As indicated above, physical characteristics such as height and weight can be observed directly and compared directly with established standard scales. Thus, we need not define an inch every time we measure a person's height, because there exists, in the Bureau of Standards, a standard ruler that defines the length of an inch, and we assume that most rulers accurately represent that standard inch. In measuring mental constructs, however, our observations are indirect and no such standards exist for defining the units of measurement. The primary concern in establishing scales for measuring mental abilities, therefore, is defining the units of measurement. In rating a composition, for example, different raters might use, perhaps unconsciously, different units of measurement (percentages versus points on a scale of zero to five). While a given scale, if clearly defined, could provide a measure of the construct, there are obvious problems of comparability if different raters use different scales.

The units of measurement of language tests are typically defined in two ways. One way is to define points or levels of language performance or language ability on a scale. An example of this approach, with levels of language performance, is the ILR Oral Interview rating scale referred to above. In this scale, six main levels, from zero to five, are defined in terms of the context and content of language use, as well as in terms of specific components such as grammar, vocabulary, fluency, and pronunciation. Another scale, which has been developed for measuring writing ability, is that of Jacobs *et al.* (1981), in which different levels are defined for each of several different components, such as mechanics, grammar, organization, and content. In the context of language testing, this method of defining units of measurement generally yields scores that constitute an ordinal scale. That is, we cannot be sure that intervals between the different levels are equal. Vincent (1978), for example, demonstrated that the levels on the ILR (at that time called the Foreign Service Institute, or FSI) scale do not constitute equal intervals with respect to the amount of training required to move from one level to the next. Similarly, Adams (1980) and Clifford (1980) have suggested that the difference between levels two and three on the ILR Oral Interview is much greater than the difference between levels one and two. Because of this potential inequality of intervals, language test scores that are ratings should, in most cases, be analyzed using statistics appropriate for ordinal scales.[10]

Another common way of defining units of measurement is to count the number of tasks successfully completed, as is done in most multiple-choice tests, where an individual's score is the number of items answered correctly. We generally treat such scores as if they constitute an interval scale. However, to verify that the scores on a given test do in fact comprise an interval scale, we must define and select the performance tasks in a way that enables us to determine their relative difficulty and the extent to which they represent the construct being tested. The former determination can generally be made from the statistical analysis of responses to individual test items. The latter is largely a matter of test design and will depend on the adequacy of our theoretical definition of the construct.

Relevance of steps to the development of language tests

These general steps in measurement provide a framework both for the development of language tests and for the interpretation of language test results, in that they provide the essential linkage between the unobservable language ability or construct we are interested in measuring and the observation of performance, or the behavioral manifestation, of that construct in the form of a test score. As an example of the application of these steps to language test development, consider the theoretical definition of pragmatic competence we presented above. For measuring this construct in speaking, we might develop an oral interview with the following operational definition:

> The appropriate performance of speech acts in oral interview tasks consisting of short verbal question and answer exchanges, an oral presentation of familiar material, greetings and leave takings, as rated on the following scales by two interviewers:

0 Extremely limited vocabulary; no cohesion; poor organization

1 Small vocabulary; very little cohesion; poor organization

2 Vocabulary of moderate size; moderate cohesion; poor organization

3 Large vocabulary; good cohesion; good organization

4 Extensive vocabulary; excellent cohesion; excellent organization
(after Bachman and Palmer 1983a:3)

In a different context, the theoretical definition might be made operational in a different way. If, for example, we needed a measure for use with hundreds of students every six weeks, we might try to develop a multiple-choice test with the following operational definition:

The recognition of appropriately expressed speech acts in a written context consisting of two short (150 - 200 words) reading passages, each followed by ten five-choice multiple-choice questions. The score consists of the total number of questions answered correctly.

Thus, we might have two tests of the same construct: an oral interview yielding scores on a five-point ordinal scale and a 20-item multiple-choice test yielding scores on a 21-point (0 to 20) interval scale. This is illustrated in Figure 2.3.

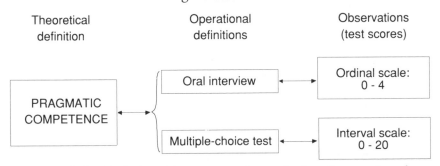

Figure 2.3   Relationships among theoretical and operational definitions and test scores

These steps in measurement are relevant to the development of achievement tests, where the learning objectives of the syllabus constitute the theoretical definitions of the abilities to be tested. In determining operational procedures for testing, both the context of learning and the teaching/learning activities employed need to be considered. By using testing techniques that are similar to activities used for learning, the test developer will minimize the possible negative bias of test method, since students will be expected to perform familiar tasks on the test. At the same time, this will maximize the positive 'washback' of testing procedures on teaching procedures. That is, using similar activities for testing and teaching will tend to reinforce the pedagogical usefulness of these activities. The use of a composition rather than a multiple-choice format for a final exam in a writing course, for example, might impress upon students the usefulness of writing activities for improving their writing skills. It should be noted, however, that the exclusive use of testing methods that are similar to teaching methods may result in tests that simply measure the extent to which students have learned to conform to instruction, and that ignore the important pedagogical question of whether they have generalized what has been taught to apply to other tasks and contexts.

In developing a language proficiency test, the test developer does not have a specific syllabus and must rely on a theory of language proficiency for providing the theoretical definitions of the abilities to be measured. For example, if an admissions officer needs to determine the extent to which applicants from a wide variety of native language backgrounds and language learning experiences will be able to successfully pursue an academic program in a second language, she may decide to measure their language ability. In this case, there is no specific syllabus on which to base theoretical definitions of the language abilities to be tested, so these will have to be derived from a general theory of language proficiency. Well-known examples of such tests of English as a foreign language are the *Test of English as a Foreign Language* (1987) and the *English Language Testing Service* test (Seaton 1981, 1983; Davies 1984).

Operational definitions of constructs in this kind of situation cannot be based on known learning activities, but should generally utilize testing techniques that can be assumed to be familiar to the majority of potential test takers. One could, of course, use a 'far out' approach simply to assure that familiarity with the testing procedure does not favor some test takers over others. This would raise a different problem, however, in that the 'far out' approach may seriously disadvantage all test takers. Utilizing familiar testing techniques does, to some extent, simplify the test developer's task, since this effectively narrows the range of techniques that must be considered. A potentially adverse effect of this, however, is the tendency for certain testing techniques to become institutionalized to the extent that they are perceived by test takers and test users alike as the only appropriate methods for testing language abilities. This institutionalized test 'appeal' in turn makes it difficult for test developers to introduce new testing procedures. One can see this exemplified to some extent in the recent history of multiple-choice tests for measuring language proficiency. This technique was initially rejected as artificial, superficial, and inappropriate for testing language abilities, but eventually became institutionalized to the extent that many test users were reluctant to accept not only relatively new techniques such as the cloze, but also more traditional methods such as the dictation, as potentially valid tests of language abilities. More recently, we have come full circle, and once again multiple-choice tests are being criticized as artificial and inappropriate, even though there are many situations in which the multiple-choice format is the most appropriate available.

Relevance of steps to the interpretation of test results

The steps in measurement discussed above also relate to virtually all concerns regarding the interpretation of test results. The first step, defining constructs theoretically, provides the basis for evaluating the validity of the uses of test scores. In the case where these abilities are defined in terms of a specific content area or domain, as in a course syllabus, we are interested in the extent to which the content of the test is a representative sample of that content domain. The definition of the content domain thus provides a means for examining the content relevance of the test. In the case of proficiency tests, our theory of language proficiency will provide the basis for examining construct validity, or the extent to which relationships among scores on tests of different constructs correspond to the relationships that are hypothesized by the theory.

The second step, defining constructs operationally, is also related to test validity, in that the observed relationships among different measures of the same theoretical construct provide the basis for investigating concurrent relatedness. For example, we would expect ratings of grammar based on a writing sample to correspond to scores on a multiple-choice test of grammar. The appropriateness of our operational definitions, or testing methods, will also affect the authenticity of the test tasks, and the way the test is perceived by test takers and test users. The cloze test, for example, which has demonstrated construct validity in specific testing contexts (Bachman 1982, 1985), is nevertheless perceived by many test takers as a highly artificial and 'untestlike' task.

Finally, the third step, how we quantify our observations, is directly related to reliability. The precision of the scales we use and the consistency with which they are applied across different test administrations, different test forms, different scorers, and with different groups of test takers will affect the results of tests. Consider, for example, the effect of having different speakers present listening comprehension test stimuli 'live' to different groups of test takers. Variations in the speed, volume, and clarity of presentation will affect students' performance, so that students who take the test with the most intelligible speaker will be unfairly advantaged and may perform better even though their listening comprehension ability may be comparable to that of students in other groups.

Summary

In this chapter a number of fundamental measurement terms and concepts have been presented. 'Measurement' and 'test' involve the quantification of observations, and are thus distinct from qualitative descriptions. Tests are a type of measurement designed to elicit a specific sample of behavior. 'Evaluation' involves decision making, and is thus distinct from measurement, which essentially provides information. Thus, neither measures nor tests are in and of themselves evaluative, and evaluation need not involve measurement or testing.

Four properties of measurement scales – distinctiveness, ordering, equal intervals and an absolute zero point – provide a basis for distinguishing four types of scales, or levels of measurement: nominal, ordinal, interval, and ratio.

Reliability and validity are the two essential qualities of measurement. Reliability is a quality of test scores, and pertains to the extent to which scores are free from measurement error, while validity, which is a quality of test interpretation and use, pertains to how meaningful, appropriate, and useful test results are for a particular purpose. The investigation and demonstration of reliability and validity necessarily involve both professional judgment and empirical research. While we need to take appropriate steps to maximize reliability and validity, these qualities are both relative, and the level that is deemed acceptable for each will be a function of factors in the specific language testing situation, such as the importance of the decision or the particular use or interpretation that is to be made of the test scores.

There are several characteristics of measures of ability that limit our interpretation and use of test scores and that must be considered in test development. Because of the complexity of and interactions among various components of language ability and factors in the testing procedure, it is not possible for us to specify all the factors that affect test performance. Therefore, in both the design of tests and the interpretation of test scores, we necessarily simplify, or underspecify the observations we make. Our interpretations of test scores are also limited because our observations of performance are indirect, incomplete, imprecise, subjective, and relative.

In order to minimize the effects of these limitations, and to maximize the reliability of test scores and the validity of test use, we should follow three fundamental steps in the development of tests: (1) provide clear and unambiguous theoretical definitions of the abilities we want to measure; (2) specify precisely the conditions, or operations that we will follow in eliciting and observing performance, and (3) quantify our observations so as to assure that our measurement scales have the properties we require. These steps in measurement provide the essential linkage between the abilities we want to measure on the one hand and observations of performance on the other, and thus form the basis for both test development and the interpretation and use of test scores.

Notes

1   Other terms that are also sometimes used as synonyms are 'assessment' and 'appraisal'. There appears to be no careful delineation of these two terms in the measurement literature, although they have been used in conjunction with impressionistic approaches to measurement (Cronbach 1984) and large-scale programs aimed at measuring a wide range of characteristics (Gronlund 1985). The distinction is sometimes made between 'examinations' and 'tests'. But, as Pilliner (1968) pointed out, there is no consensus on what the distinction is.

> Sometimes the distinction is made in terms of time allowed – a typical 'examination' lasts two, three, or more hours; a typical 'test' one half to one hour. . . . Or the distinction may be hierarchical. A university professor 'examines' his . . . students . . .; a primary school teacher 'tests' her nine-year-olds. Finally, the distinction may depend on whether assess-

ment is 'subjective' or 'objective'. In the first case, we have an 'examination'; in the second, a 'test'.
(Pilliner 1968:21–2)

Because of the generality and ambiguity of these terms, I consider them stylistic variants of 'evaluation' and 'test', and make no attempt to define them further.

2   In a broad sense, measurement in the social sciences is not limited to the attributes of persons. We can also measure, for example, the degree of consensus for a given language policy, the budgetary status of schools, the readability of texts, and the frequency of syntactic features in spoken discourse.

3   The word, 'measure', is itself systematically ambiguous, in that it functions as both a noun and a verb, each with different meanings. The noun is commonly used to refer to both the measurement procedure and the score yielded by that procedure. John Carroll (personal communication) has pointed out a further grammatical ambiguity, in that the verb 'measure' can take either of two objects: the entity being measured ('we measure a person') or the attribute ('we measure height'). Both are abridged forms, or transforms, of 'we measure a person for, or with respect to, height' or 'we measure the height of a person'.

4   This inclusion of subjective measurement procedures such as the oral interview and the composition in the category of tests is different from Raatz's (1981) argument that oral interviews are not tests, primarily because they are not objective. However, since the APA *Standards for Educational and Psychological Testing* (1985) explicitly includes as tests, measures such as 'structured behavior sample tests', which are subjective, and since many standard references on testing discuss subjective measures as tests (for example, Nitko 1983; Cronbach 1984; Gronlund 1985), there seems little reason to exclude oral interviews or other subjective measures as tests simply because they are not objective.

5   It should be noted that this decision-making view of evaluation is not universally held. See, for example, Stake (1978) and Eisner (1985) for different viewpoints.

6   See Allen and Yen (1979), Chapter 8, for a detailed discussion of scales of measurement. A more technical discussion is provided by Angoff (1971).

7   It should be noted that test scores do not automatically constitute an interval scale. Whether the scores on a given test

constitute an interval or only an ordinal scale can be determined by empirical analysis alone.

8 See Spolsky (1968) for a discussion of the distinction between competence and performance as it pertains to language testing.

9 For discussion of the problems of defining native speakers and native speaker norms, see Coulmas (1981a), Lantolf and Frawley (1985), Kachru (1985), and Paikeday (1985).

10 A number of approaches aimed at yielding both interval and ratio rating scales have been developed over the years, beginning with Thurstone's pioneering work (Thurstone 1925, 1927a, 1927b, 1928). For a detailed discussion of many such approaches to scale development, see Torgerson (1958) and Gulliksen (1950) Chapter 19.

Further reading

Several different views of evaluation can be found in the following: Popham (1969) (objectives-based evaluation); Stufflebeam (1973) (decision-oriented studies); Stake (1970) (client-centered studies). Tests, measures and evaluation are discussed in Gronlund (1985) Chapter 1. Two different approaches to defining language proficiency are presented in Carroll (1961a) and Canale (1983). General discussions of dictation, cloze tests, and oral interviews are provided in Cziko (1982) and Jones (1985a). An excellent discussion of operationalizing constructs as tests is provided in Davidson, Hudson, and Lynch (1985). Spolsky (1978b) is an interesting and useful historical overview of language testing.

Discussion questions

1. How do tests differ from evaluations? What functions do tests and evaluations perform? Do the functions overlap? In what way are they related?
2. Give some specific examples of the following:
    a. measures that are not tests
    b. measures that are not evaluative
    c. evaluation that does not involve measurement.
3. Considering the three distinguishing characteristics of measurement, which of the following would you regard as measures? Why or why not? If not a measure, how might you make it a measure?
    a. An essay test on the same topic is given independently to

Class A and Class B. The teacher in Class A evaluates the ideas expressed in the essays and gives grades of A through D. The teacher of Class B, on the other hand, counts grammatical mistakes and gives scores ranging from zero to 50.

b. Students are asked to complete a questionnaire designed to determine if they like or dislike the courses they are taking. For each course they can respond by checking one of the following:

Like very much
Like somewhat
So-so
Don't like much
Do not like at all

4. On what grounds are the following tests indirect, incomplete, imprecise, subjective, and relative measurement instruments?
   a. a one-hour 100-item multiple-choice test of grammar given as a test of proficiency in English grammar
   b. a 50-item completion test of writing
   c. a 130-word dictation test of listening comprehension.

5. How do reliability and validity considerations affect the interpretation of scores on language tests?

6. For each of the abilities below, write a theoretical definition and then two different operational definitions:
   a. ability to recognize and use the appropriate register
   b. ability to request information appropriately
   c. ability to understand the main idea of a paragraph.

7. Describe how you would apply the three steps of measurement to the development of achievement and proficiency tests. How are these steps different for the two types of tests? How are they the same?

3 Uses of language tests

Introduction

The single most important consideration in both the development of language tests and the interpretation of their results is the purpose or purposes the particular tests are intended to serve. The two major uses of language tests are: (1) as sources of information for making decisions within the context of educational programs; and (2) as indicators of abilities or attributes that are of interest in research on language, language acquisition, and language teaching. In educational settings the major uses of test scores are related to evaluation, or making decisions about people or programs. In order to justify the use of tests for educational evaluation, certain assumptions and considerations must be made regarding the usefulness and quality of the information which tests provide. An understanding of these assumptions and considerations, as well as of the different types of language tests and their roles in evaluation is therefore essential to the appropriate use of language tests. In the context of research, the interpretation of test results is of both theoretical and applied interest; such interpretations can assist in our understanding of the nature of language proficiency, and may have implications for language learning and language teaching.

Uses of language tests in educational programs

The fundamental use of testing in an educational program is to provide information for making decisions, that is, for evaluation. An educational program, in the broadest sense, is any situation in which one or more persons are engaged in teaching and learning. Educational programs, therefore, range in scope from individual tutoring to a single class, to a school, to a nation-wide program. Evaluation comprises essentially two components: (1) information, and (2) value judgments, or decisions. The information relevant to evaluation can be either qualitative (non-measurement) or quantitative (measurement). Qualitative information can be obtained from observations in a wide variety of ways, including performance checklists and observation schedules, as well as from narrative accounts of class performance of student self-reports (for example, Oskarsson 1978, 1988; Haughton and Dickinson 1988). Quantitative information can include measures such as class rank, teacher ratings, and self-ratings (for example, Oskarsson 1978; Bachman and Palmer 1981b, 1988; Davidson and Henning 1985; LeBlanc and Painchaud 1985), as well as tests.

Assumptions and considerations

The use of tests as a source of evaluation information requires three assumptions. First, we must assume that information regarding educational outcomes is essential to effective formal education. That is, we must consider accountability and feedback as essential mechanisms for the continued effectiveness of any educational program. Bachman and Savignon (1986) describe accountability as 'being able to demonstrate the extent to which we have effectively and efficiently discharged responsibility' and point out that 'without accountability in language teaching, students can pass several semesters of language courses with high grades and still be unable to use the language for reading or for conversing with speakers of that language' (p. 380). Feedback simply refers to information that is provided to teachers, students, and other interested persons about the results or effects of the educational program. A second assumption is that it is possible to improve learning and teaching through appropriate changes in the program, based on feedback. Without these assumptions there is no reason to test, since there are no decisions to be made and therefore no information required. Third, we must assume that the educational outcomes of the given program are measurable. This, of course, is a highly debatable assumption. At one extreme there is the view that any outcome that is learnable is measurable, while at the other extreme is the view that virtually no worthwhile educational objective can be adequately measured. I take the position that any outcome that can be defined can be measured, recognizing that many outcomes are very difficult to define and hence, to measure. It should be pointed out that while this discussion has focused on outcomes, the description and evaluation of the *processes* that are part of an educational program are equally important (Long 1984). However, since these processes are arguably even more complex than the outcomes, or 'products' of educational programs, they are more commonly described and evaluated on the basis of qualitative information.

In addition to these assumptions, we must also consider how much and what kind of testing is needed, as well as the quality of information provided by our tests. The amount and type of testing, if any, that is done depends upon the decisions that are to be made and the type of information that is needed to make the correct decisions. For example, if a classroom teacher must decide whether to proceed to the next lesson, he may need to find out if the class has mastered the objectives of the current lesson. Depending on how well he has been monitoring the class's performance, it may not be necessary for him to administer a test at all to make this decision. And if he does give a test, the type of test he gives will depend upon the type of information needed. In a conversation class, for example, it is unlikely that the teacher would find a paper-and-pencil test of much use.

A second consideration in using tests is the quality of the information that they must provide. In educational programs the decisions made are generally about people, and have some effect on their lives. It is therefore essential that the information upon which we base these decisions be as reliable and as valid as possible. Very few of us, for example, would consider the opinions of our students' friends and relatives to be reliable information for evaluating their classroom performance. Likewise, the students' performance in other classes, such as mathematics or geography, would not be a valid basis for evaluating their performance in a language class.

People frequently ask, 'How reliable should a test be?' or 'How valid should a test be?' While we must always strive to make our test scores as reliable as possible and to demonstrate that our uses of test scores are valid, the levels necessary for both of these qualities are relative, and depend upon the importance of the decisions to be made. In general, the more important the decision to be made, the greater the effort that should be expended in assuring that the test is reliable and valid. In every decision situation there is a certain probability for errors, and costs that are associated with those errors. The more important the decision, the greater the cost of making an error. If very important decisions are to be made about a large number of individuals, the costs associated with wrong decisions can be considerable. By maximizing the reliability and validity of the information provided by tests, we are reducing the probability of errors in the decisions we make, and hence the potential costs associated with those errors (Lord 1983). (The types of decision errors that can occur, and procedures for estimating the probability of their occurrence in the context of criterion-referenced tests are discussed in Chapter 6, pp. 214–20.)

At the same time, there are costs associated with assuring reliability and validity, even in classroom testing. Collecting the right kinds of information to estimate reliability, for example, and doing the necessary calculations, takes not only training, but time and effort. Similarly, the care that goes into designing and developing a test whose content is representative of a given course is a cost incurred in assuring content validity. In order to achieve very high levels of reliability and validity, we must carry out rigorous and extensive research and development, and this can be quite costly. In deciding how much time and effort to put into assuring reliability and validity, we need to consider the cost-effectiveness of such expenditures. That is, the costs associated with assuring reliability and validity should be offset by the potential reduction in costs associated with decision errors. If the costs associated with decision errors are minimal, then it would be wasteful to expend a great deal of time and effort to assure high levels of reliability and validity. On the other hand, if the potential costs of errors are great, it would be unethical not to make every effort to achieve the highest levels of reliability and validity possible.

If a classroom teacher, for example, errs and decides to move to the next lesson before the class is ready, the cost is the amount of time and effort wasted before the error is discovered. In this case, the cost may be minimal if the teacher is able to make the necessary adjustment quickly. Consider, on the other hand, a situation in which the results of a nation-wide examination are used to make university admission decisions about all high school graduates in an entire country. In this case, the cost of admitting students who eventually fail and drop out may be enormous, both in terms of the educational resources expended and the misdirection of the students' time and efforts, not to mention the amount of personal loss involved. And the costs of denying admission to students who would succeed in an academic program are equally high, when we consider the potential loss to the educational institutions and to society.

The classroom teacher in the example may, through minimal efforts, satisfy the levels of reliability and validity necessary for his needs, since the costs of making the wrong decision are relatively small and the decision can be easily reversed. In a nation-wide admissions testing program, however, the test developers and test users must make every possible effort to assure that the highest levels of reliability and validity are demonstrated, so as to minimize the risk of making wrong decisions that may be very costly to a large number of individuals, and that cannot be easily corrected. Thus, we need to strike an optimum balance between the costs of assuring reliability and validity and the potential costs associated with wrong decisions that might be made on the basis of our tests.

Types of decisions

Since the basic purpose of tests in educational programs is to provide information for making decisions, the various specific uses of tests can be best understood by considering the types of decisions to be made. These decisions are of two types: decisions about individuals, which we might call micro-evaluation, and decisions about the program, which we might call macro-evaluation (Bachman 1981).

Decisions about students

Selection (entrance, readiness)
The most frequently evaluated individuals in any educational program are the students. The first decision that may be made about students is whether or not they should enter the program. In many programs, such as in primary schools, entrance is nearly automatic with age, while other programs require a *selection*, or *entrance* test. If the purpose of this test is to determine whether or not students are ready for instruction, it may be referred to as a *readiness test*. One of the most common uses of language tests for making decisions regarding selection is in conjunction with measures of other abilities, such as grades from previous instruction, academic aptitude, and achievement. In many countries, for example, nation-wide university entrance examinations include a section testing a foreign language, in addition to tests of academic subjects such as mathematics, science, and history. Similarly, scores from the *Test of English as a Foreign Language* (TOEFL) are used by many colleges and universities in North America as a complement to other types of information such as grades, academic achievement tests, and letters of recommendation, for deciding which non-native English-speaking students to accept into academic programs.

Placement
In many language programs students are grouped homogeneously according to factors such as level of language ability, language aptitude, language use needs, and professional or academic specialization. In such programs, therefore, decisions regarding the placement of students into appropriate groups must be made. Probably the most common criterion for grouping in such programs is level of language

ability, so that placement tests are frequently designed to measure students' language abilities.

In designing a test for placement, the test developer may choose to base the test content either on a theory of language proficiency or on the learning objectives of the syllabus to be taken. In a situation where students enter the program from a wide variety of language backgrounds and prior language learning experience, and in which the syllabus to be followed encompasses the full range of competencies and skills of language proficiency, it may be quite difficult to specify a set of objectives clearly enough to provide a basis for test development. In this case, the test developer may choose to develop a test based on a theory of language proficiency and determine placement according to a norming procedure. If, on the other hand, the objectives of the program are clearly specified and sequenced, the test developer is more likely to develop a multi-level test based on the content objectives of the program. In this case, criteria for mastery can be set for each level of test content, making it possible to place students into levels according to the extent to which they have already acquired the competencies and skills included in the various levels of the program.

Another consideration in the development and use of tests for placement is the relative stability of enrollments in the different levels of a program from one term to the next. In situations where the proficiency levels of entering students vary considerably from one term to the next, this is a potential problem for placement and program administration. For example, if the program is relatively inflexible in its scheduling, perhaps because of limited space during certain times of the day, it may be necessary for the numbers of students enrolled in different levels to remain relatively stable from term to term. In this case, the test user could use a test that would enable her to place approximately the same numbers of students in different levels every term, assuming that the teachers would adjust their teaching to accommodate possible differences in levels of proficiency from term to term. A norm-referenced test (discussed below) would probably be best suited to this need. If, however, the program can easily adjust its timetable to accommodate large changes in the numbers of students enrolled at different levels from term to term, the test user might use a test whose cut-offs for placement do not change from one term to the next, and reassign teachers to adjust for the differences in numbers. A criterion-referenced test (discussed below) would probably be best suited to this situation. I would hasten to note that I am not offering either of these choices as a recommended procedure, for either placement or program management, but simply as examples to illustrate this consideration.

Diagnosis

Information from language tests can be used for diagnosing students' areas of strength and weakness in order to determine appropriate types and levels of teaching and learning activities. Thus, virtually any language test has some potential for providing diagnostic information. A placement test can be regarded as a broad-band diagnostic test in that it distinguishes relatively weak from relatively strong students so that they can be provided learning activities at the appropriate level. Similarly, a readiness test differentiates students who are ready for instruction from those who are not. A detailed analysis of student responses to the questions on placement and readiness tests can also provide more specific information about particular areas of weakness. When we speak of a diagnostic test, however, we are generally referring to a test that has been designed and developed specifically to provide detailed information about the specific content domains that are covered in a given program or that are part of a general theory of language proficiency. Thus, diagnostic tests may be either theory or syllabus-based.

Progress and grading

Feedback on the effectiveness of student learning is generally of interest to both teachers and the students themselves. This information is useful to the teacher for *formative evaluation*, that is, for providing continuous feedback to both the teacher and the learner for making decisions regarding appropriate modifications in the instructional procedures and learning activities (Nitko 1988). For example, if new material is being introduced at an inappropriate rate, either so slowly that students lose interest, or so quickly that students cannot comprehend it, the effectiveness of learning is likely to decrease. Teachers also need to make decisions about when to move on to another unit of instruction. If subsequent units assume mastery of the objectives of the current unit, the teacher must be assured that students have mastered these objectives before moving on. Such information can also be helpful to individual students, in that it can identify areas of strength and weakness and perhaps suggest alternative learning activities. In most language programs formative evaluation decisions are made largely on the basis of qualitative feedback the students and teacher obtain in the process of learning and teaching. Many classroom teachers also give short tests or quizzes at the end of each instructional unit or group of units to provide additional information on student progress. Such testing is often facilitated by the inclusion, in published materials, of unit tests. These tests, or quizzes, which are based on the content of the course, are referred to as *achievement* or *attainment tests*. Tests that are used to determine whether or not students have mastered the course content are called *mastery tests*.

One decision about individual students that is seldom based solely on qualitative information is the *summative evaluation* of student progress, typically in the form of grades or marks, at the end of an instructional course (Nitko 1988). In most cases grades are assigned on the basis of performance on tests in addition to classroom performance. In a typical program, for example, the final grade in the course might be determined by a weighted average of mid-term and final examinations, class quizzes and teacher ratings of classroom performance. While the specific types of tests used for making decisions regarding progress and grades may vary greatly from program to program, it is obvious that the content of such tests should be based on the syllabus rather than on a theory of language proficiency. That is, they will all be achievement tests.

Decisions about teachers

We also need to make decisions about teachers in most educational programs. The decision to hire a given individual as a teacher, for example, will depend on a wide range of information, some of which may be obtained from tests. If teachers are not native speakers of the target language, we may wish to obtain information about their language proficiency by means of a proficiency test. It is particularly important, in this regard, to recognize that the proficiency required of a language teacher may be both quantitatively and qualitatively different from that of the students. A language teacher must be proficient in not only the complete range of language abilities (grammatical, textual, illocutionary, and sociolinguistic competence), but must also command a wide variety of pedagogically oriented communication strategies and metalinguistic competencies (for example, knowledge of syntactic forms or categories of speech acts) that will enable her to talk with her students about language in a way that will be instructionally useful. Thus, the language tests that are used for students may not be sufficient for evaluating teachers' communicative language ability.

Decisions about programs

Information from language tests can also be useful in making decisions about programs. In developing a new program, for example, we will be concerned with evaluating specific components in terms of their appropriateness, effectiveness, and efficiency, so as to make improvements that will maximize these characteristics. The performance of students on achievement tests can provide an indication of the extent to which the expected objectives of the program are being attained, and thus pinpoint areas of deficiency. Thus, for purposes of the formative evaluation of programs, where the focus is on providing information that will be useful for making decisions about a program while it is under development, achievement tests that are based on the content of the syllabus are appropriate (Scriven 1967; Millman 1974; Baker 1974a, 1974b; Bachman 1981).

If, on the other hand, we are interested in summative evaluation of programs, in which the focus is on whether our program is better than other comparable programs, or whether it is the 'best' program currently available, achievement tests by themselves will be of limited use. This is because such tests will provide no information about whether the students have learned skills and abilities beyond those stated as program objectives, or whether mastery of the objectives is sufficient for the students' communicative needs (Bachman 1989c). Consider, for example, a program focusing on oral language use. Performance in an oral interview test might be sufficient information to determine whether the program had been successful in terms of students' mastery of the program's objectives. If, however, the interview were limited entirely to situations and topics related to the course itself, the results from this test might be of little use in evaluating whether students who had successfully completed the course could generalize their achievement to the use of oral language in situations outside of the classroom. For purposes of summative evaluation, therefore, it is often necessary to obtain measures of language proficiency in addition to information on student achievement of syllabus objectives.

Illustrative examples

In 'Context for language testing', Upshur (1973) discussed the educational context of language testing with examples of different types of programs. In his first example, reproduced as Figure 3.1, students enter the program, undergo instruction, and leave. There are

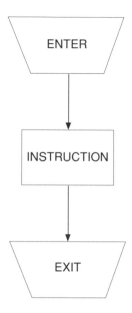

Figure 3.1   Program 1 (Upshur 1973)

no decisions to be made, and consequently no need for tests in this program.

There are two major problems with such a program, however. First, there is no indication of whether or not the program is appropriate for all those who enter. It may be, for example, that the program is too advanced for some and too elementary for others. Second, there is no feedback about whether or not students learn. Another program, illustrated in Figure 3.2 (p. 64), requires at least one decision, that is a decision about who exits the program after instruction, as indicated by the diamond.

In this program, information from the test provides feedback on student learning, thus solving the second problem of Program 1. The kind of test that would be appropriate in this situation would be an achievement test. The introduction of this exit criterion, however, creates another problem. What happens to students who are not successful in achieving the objectives of the course? According to the diagram, students who cannot pass the exit test must continue taking the course until they succeed. There is no provision for them to exit in any other way. This program also fails to address the problem of program appropriateness.

A third program, illustrated in Figure 3.3 (p. 65), provides a solution to the problem of program appropriateness.

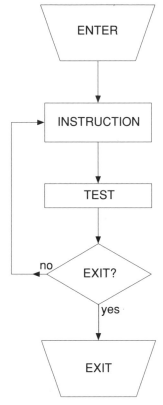

Figure 3.2   Program 2 (Upshur 1973)

In this program a decision regarding who is exempt from the course is made on the basis of information from a test. This represents only a partial solution to the entrance problem, however, since students for whom the course is too advanced may still enter the program. Following instruction, students take the test again (or a parallel form), to determine if they may exit the program. In this program, a single test serves two purposes: screening for exemption and determination of mastery. In this kind of situation, an achievement test based on the objectives of the course is clearly appropriate. Although this program provides for selection of appropriate students and feedback regarding achievement, it still provides no means for students who do not learn to exit the program.

A more complex program is shown in Figure 3.4 (p. 66), as an example of a multi-level program with several different types of decisions to be made. This provides an illustration of the variety of uses

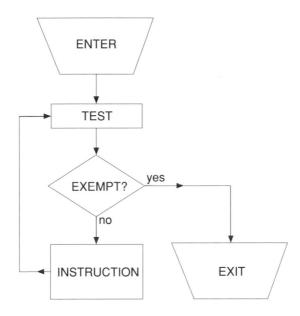

Figure 3.3   Program 3 (Upshur 1973)

of tests in an educational program. The initial decisions of selection and placement in this program are made on the basis of a test. If students are too low for the program, they do not enter, and if their test performance indicates that they have mastered the objectives of the course, they are exempt. Those students for whom the program is appropriate are then placed into one of three levels of instruction. At the end of each level of instruction, students take an achievement test to determine whether they progress to the next higher level. If they pass the test, they progress, and if not, they are given remedial work that might be determined by the areas of weakness identified in the achievement test. Thus, the achievement test serves two purposes: determining progress and diagnosing student weaknesses.

In this program, rather than being tested again after the remedial component, students automatically progress to the next level. It would be possible, of course, to test students again after the remedial component, and then provide additional remedial work in the areas in which they are still deficient. However, in most programs there are limits to the time and resources that can be provided, and in this example the program can only provide two opportunities for students to master the objectives: the regular instructional program and one remedial component. In this case, we would hope that the

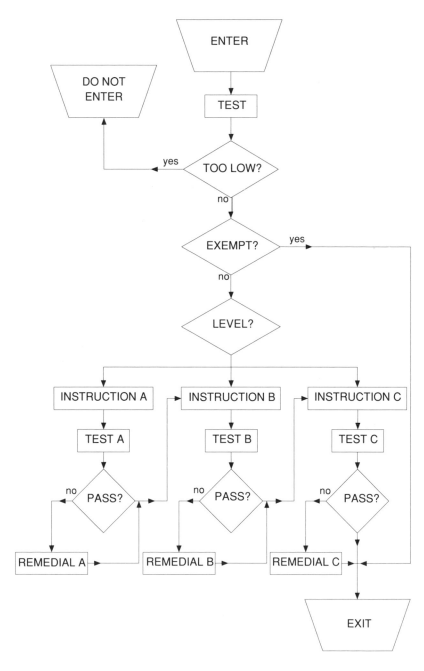

Figure 3.4   Program 4

remedial work would focus on the students' deficiencies and employ learning activities and teaching methods that are particularly well suited to individual students' learning styles. An alternative approach would be to have the student simply repeat the regular course of instruction. However, this approach assumes that the failure to achieve the objectives is due largely to the student's inadequacies, rather than to those of the instructional program. The provision of effective remedial instruction with subsequent progress to the next level also provides a means for students who are not successful in the regular course to make progress and eventually exit the program.

In this program, then, several different types of decisions need to be made, and these are made primarily on the basis of information from tests. One approach to developing tests for this program would be to develop achievement tests. The placement test could be a multi-level achievement test based on the objectives of all three levels, while the tests at the end of each level would focus on the objectives of that level. In some situations, where incoming students may vary widely in their backgrounds, it might be more appropriate to base the placement test on a general theory of language proficiency, while still basing the progress tests on the objectives of the course.

This program is not intended as a 'model' program to be emulated, but rather serves to illustrate a wide range of uses of tests in an educational program. This program could be altered in a number of ways to meet different needs and situations. For example, a slightly simpler program, but with the same types of decisions to be made, might have students take the multi-level achievement placement test, or a parallel form, at the end of each level of instruction. In this way, even greater flexibility could be built into the program, since it might be possible for students who make outstanding progress to skip from Level A to Level C, or to exit the program after Level B.

Programs such as those described in these examples, then, illustrate the fundamental consideration regarding the use of tests in educational programs: the amount and type of testing we do depends on the number and kinds of decisions to be made. Considerations regarding the qualities of these tests, that is, reliability and validity, will be discussed in greater detail in Chapters 6 and 7.

Research uses of language tests

As operational definitions of theoretical constructs, language tests have a potentially important role in virtually all research, both basic and applied, that is related to the nature of language proficiency, language processing, language acquisition, language attrition, and language teaching. The question of whether language proficiency is a single unitary competence or whether it is composed of distinct component traits is one which has been of considerable interest to language testing researchers for several years (Oller 1976, 1979b; Oller and Hinofotis 1980; Bachman and Palmer 1981a; Carroll 1983a), and which also has implications for the theory of language acquisition and for language teaching. It is now generally agreed that language proficiency is not a single unitary ability, but that it consists of several distinct but related constructs in addition to a general construct of language proficiency (Oller 1983a).

Much current research into the nature of language proficiency has now come to focus on identifying and empirically verifying its various components (for example, Farhady 1980; Bachman and Palmer 1982a; Allen *et al.* 1983; Sang *et al.* 1986). Of particular interest in this regard are models of communicative competence, which have provided the theoretical definitions for the development of tests of constructs such as sensitivity to cohesive relationships, discourse organization, and differences in register (for example, Genesee *et al.* 1975; Cohen and Olshtain 1980; Ontario Ministry of Education 1980; Wesche 1981; Swain 1985). Such tests in turn provide the basis for verifying (or falsifying) these theoretical models. This research involves the construct validation of language tests, which is discussed further in Chapter 7.

Language tests can also be used in research into the nature of language processing. Responses to language tests can provide a rich body of data for the identification of processing errors and their explanation, while language testing techniques can serve as elicitation procedures for collecting information on language processing. In the investigation of how individuals process information in a reading passage, for example, the cloze would seem to have a great deal of potential. Through careful observation and analysis of subjects' response patterns, such as the order in which they complete the blanks and the changes they make in their answers as they work through the passage, we may begin to be able to test some of the hypotheses that are suggested by various theories of reading. An area related to this is the investigation of the process of test taking itself (for example, MacKay 1974; Cohen and Aphek 1979; Cohen 1984, forthcoming; Grotjahn 1986).

A third research use of language tests is in the examination of the nature of language acquisition. Studies of language acquisition often require indicators of the amount of language acquired for use as criterion or dependent variables, and these indicators frequently include language tests. Several studies have used tests of different components of communicative language ability as criteria for examining the effect of learner variables such as length of residence in country, age of first exposure to the target language, and motivational orientation on language acquisition (for example, Purcell 1983; Bachman and Palmer 1983b; Fouly 1985; Bachman and Mack 1986). Language tests are also sometimes used as indicators of factors related to second language acquisition, such as language aptitude and level of proficiency in the native language. Gardner *et al.* (1983, 1985b), for example, used measures of attitudes, motivational intensity, and prior language achievement to examine a model of language acquisition.

Although language attrition, or loss, is not simply the reverse of language acquisition, many of the same factors that have been examined with respect to language acquisition are also hypothesized to affect language attrition, and language tests also have a role to play in this area of research. Oxford (1982) and Clark (1982), for example, both discuss the role of language tests in research on language attrition, as well as considerations for their use in such research. Furthermore, it is clear from both Gardner's (1982) review of the research on social factors in language retention and his own research on attrition (for example, Gardner *et al.* 1985a) that language tests play a vital role in such research.

A fifth area of research in which language tests play an important role is in the investigation of effects of different instructional settings and techniques on language acquisition. Measures of language proficiency were essential components of several large-scale foreign language teaching method evaluation studies that were conducted in the 1960s (for example, Smith 1970; Levin 1970; Lindblad and Levin 1970), as well as the more recent large-scale study of bilingual proficiency conducted by the Modern Language Centre of the Ontario Institute for Studies in Education (Allen *et al.* 1982, 1983; Harley *et al.* 1987). Language tests have also provided criterion indicators of language ability for studies in classroom-centered second language acquisition (for example, the research reviewed and discussed in Chaudron 1988), and for research into the relationship between different language teaching strategies and aspects of second language competence (for example, Sang *et al.* 1986).

Features for classifying different types of language test

Language test developers and users are frequently faced with questions regarding what type of test would be most appropriate for a given situation, and in discussions of language testing one often hears questions such as, 'Should we use a norm-referenced test or an achievement test?' or 'Should we use both a diagnostic and a proficiency test in our program?' Such uses of labels for describing test types often raise more questions than they answer. How are norm-referenced tests different from achievement tests? Cannot proficiency tests be used for diagnosis? Questions like these imply comparisons that are like the proverbial question, 'Which are better, apples or oranges?' in which objects that are similar in some ways and different in others are compared according to a criterion they do not share ('appleness' or 'orangeness'). To clarify the use of such terms, language tests can be classified according to five distinctive features: the purpose, or use, for which they are intended; the content upon which they are based; the frame of reference within which their results are to be interpreted; the way in which they are scored, and the specific technique or method they employ.

Intended use

Any given language test is typically developed with a particular primary use in mind, whether it be for an educational program or for research. In research, language tests are used to provide information for comparing the performances of individuals with different characteristics or under different conditions of language acquisition or language teaching and for testing hypotheses about the nature of language proficiency. In educational settings, however, language tests provide information for making a wide variety of decisions. One way of classifying language tests, therefore, is according to the type of decision to be made. Thus we can speak of *selection*, *entrance*, and *readiness* tests with regard to admission decisions, *placement* and *diagnostic* tests with regard to identifying the appropriate instructional level or specific areas in which instruction is needed, and *progress*, *achievement*, *attainment*, or *mastery* tests with respect to decisions about how individuals should proceed through the program, or how well they are attaining the program's objectives. While it is generally best to develop a specific test for each different type of decision, this is not always necessary, and greater efficiency of testing can sometimes be achieved by developing a test for more than one specific purpose, with the understanding that the validity of each separate use must be adequately demonstrated.

Content

As indicated in Chapter 2, the 'content' of language tests can be based on either a theory of language proficiency or a specific domain of content, generally as provided in a course syllabus. We can refer to theory-based tests as *proficiency tests*, while syllabus-based tests are generally referred to as *achievement tests*. Whether or not the specific abilities measured by a given proficiency test actually differ from those measured by a given achievement test will depend, of course, on the extent to which the theory upon which the proficiency test is based differs from that upon which the syllabus is based. For example, a language proficiency test based on a theory of grammatical competence is likely to be quite similar to an achievement test based on a grammar-based syllabus, but quite different from an achievement test based on a notional-functional syllabus These relationships are illustrated in Figure 3.5.

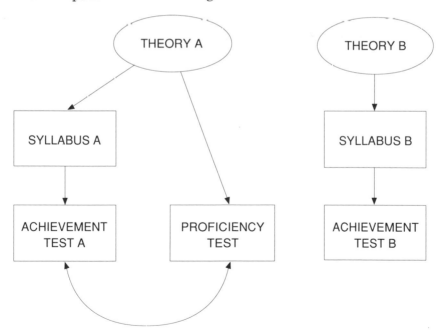

Figure 3.5 Relationships among theory, syllabus, and test content

Language aptitude tests are also distinguished according to content. Like language proficiency tests, language aptitude tests are theory-based, but the theory upon which they are based includes abilities that are related to the acquisition, rather than the use of language. The theory of language aptitude, as described by Carroll (1958, 1981), hypothesizes that cognitive abilities such as rote memorization, phonetic coding, and the recognition of grammatical analogies are related to an individual's ability to learn a second or foreign language, and together constitute language aptitude. This theory has been operationally defined in measures such as the *Modern Language Aptitude Test* (Carroll and Sapon 1959) and the *Pimsleur Language Aptitude Battery* (Pimsleur 1966).

Frame of reference

The results of language tests can be interpreted in two different ways, depending on the frame of reference adopted. When test scores are interpreted in relation to the performance of a particular group of individuals, we speak of a norm-referenced interpretation. If, on the other hand, they are interpreted with respect to a specific level or domain of ability, we speak of a criterion- or domain-referenced interpretation. Tests that are developed to permit these different interpretations are called norm-referenced and criterion-referenced tests.

Norm-referenced tests

Norm-referenced (NR) tests are designed to enable the test user to make 'normative' interpretations of test results. That is, test results are interpreted with reference to the performance of a given group, or norm. The 'norm group' is typically a large group of individuals who are similar to the individuals for whom the test is designed. In the development of NR tests the norm group is given the test, and then the characteristics, or norms, of this group's performance are used as reference points for interpreting the performance of other students who take the test. The performance characteristics, or norms, most typically used as reference points are the mean $\bar{x}$, or average score of the group, and the standard deviation s, which is an indicator of how spread out the scores of the group are.

If the NR test is properly designed, the scores attained will typically be distributed in the shape of a 'normal' bell-shaped curve. A perfectly normal distribution of scores has certain statistical characteristics that are known and constant. In a normal distribution, for example, we know that 50 per cent of the scores are below the mean, or average, and 50 per cent are above. We also know that 34 per cent of the scores are between the mean and one standard deviation above (+1s) or below (−1s) the mean, that 27 per cent are between one and two standard deviations from the mean (13.5 per cent above and 13.5 per cent below), and that only 5 per cent of the scores will be as far away as two or more standard deviations from the mean. These characteristics are illustrated in Figure 3.6.

We can use these known characteristics for interpreting scores of individuals on NR tests. For example, the mean of the *Test of English as a Foreign Language* (TOEFL) is about 512 and the standard deviation is about 66 (Test of English as a Foreign Language 1987). Thus, a score of 578 on the TOEFL is about one standard deviation above the mean (512 + 66 = 578). This score indicates that the individual is well above average with reference to the norm group and, more precisely, that his performance is equal to or greater than that of 84 per cent of the students in the norm group.

In other cases, NR test results are interpreted and reported solely with reference to the actual group taking the test, rather than to a separate norm group. Perhaps the most familiar example of this is what is sometimes called 'grading on the curve', where, say, the top ten per cent of the students receive an 'A' on the test and the bottom ten per cent fail, irrespective of the absolute magnitude of their scores.

In order to provide the most easily interpretable results, NR tests are designed to maximize the distinctions among the individuals in a

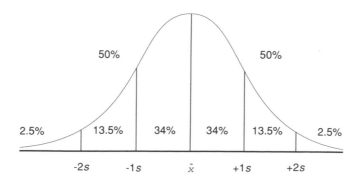

Figure 3.6   Some characteristics of normal distribution

given group. Such tests are also sometimes referred to as 'psycho-metric' tests since most theoretical models of psychometrics, or psychological measurement, are based on the assumption of a normal distribution and maximizing the variations among individuals' scores (Cziko 1981).

The quintessential NR test is the *standardized test*, which has three characteristics (Gronlund 1985). First, standardized tests are based on a fixed, or standard content, which does not vary from one form of the test to another. This content may be based on a theory of language proficiency, as with the *Test of English as a Foreign Language*, or it may be based on a specification of language users' expected needs, as is the case with the *English Language Testing Service* test (Seaton 1981, 1983; Criper and Davies 1988; Alderson 1988). If there are alternate forms of the test, these are carefully examined for content equivalence. Second, there are standard procedures for administering and scoring the test, which do not vary from one administration of the test to the next. Finally, standardized tests have been thoroughly tried out, and through a process of empirical research and development, their characteristics are well known. Specifically, their measurement properties have been examined, so that we know what type of measurement scale they provide, that their reliability and validity have been carefully investigated and demonstrated for the intended uses of the test, that their score distribution norms have been established with groups of individuals similar to those for whom the test is intended, and that if there are alternate forms of the test, these are equated statistically to assure that reported scores on each test indicate the same level of ability, regardless of the particular form of the test being used.

Criterion-referenced tests

Criterion-referenced (CR) tests are designed to enable the test user to interpret a test score with reference to a criterion level of ability or domain of content. An example would be the case in which students are evaluated in terms of their relative degree of mastery of course content, rather than with respect to their relative ranking in the class. Thus, all students who master the course content might receive an 'A', irrespective of how many students achieve this grade. The primary concerns in developing a CR test are that it adequately represent the criterion ability level or sample the content domain, and that it be sensitive to levels of ability or degrees of mastery of the different components of that domain.

The necessary condition for the development of a CR test is the specification of a level of ability or domain of content (Glaser 1963; Glaser and Nitko 1971; Nitko 1984). It is important to point out that it is this *level of ability or domain of content* that constitutes the criterion, and *not* the setting of a cut-off score for making decisions. The definition of a criterion level or domain and the setting of a cut-off score for a given decision are two quite distinct issues. It is quite possible to develop and use a CR test without explicitly setting a cut-off score. A good example of this would be a diagnostic test that is used to identify specific areas within a content domain where individuals might benefit from further instruction, without necessarily evaluating them as masters or non-masters. Here the implicit categories are 'might benefit from instruction' and 'probably would not benefit from further instruction'. It is equally possible to set a cut-off score for making decisions on the basis of the distribution of scores from a NR test, without reference to a content domain. For example, if we wanted to be highly selective, we could set the cut-off score for entrance into a program at two standard deviations above the mean.

From the discussion above about test content, it is clear that achievement tests based on well-defined domains can satisfy the condition of domain specification for CR tests. Of current research interest is the question of whether language proficiency tests can also be developed so as to provide CR scores (Bachman and Savignon 1986; Bachman and Clark 1987). Much has been written recently about the advantages of CR, or 'edumetric' language tests (Cziko 1981), as well as of a 'common metric' for measuring language ability (for example, Woodford 1978, 1981; B. J. Carroll 1980; Clark 1980; Bachman and Clark 1987; Bachman 1989b), and this will be discussed in greater detail in Chapter 8.

The two primary distinctions between NR and CR tests are (1) in their design, construction, and development; and (2) in the scales they yield and the interpretation of these scales. NR tests are designed and developed to maximize distinctions among individual test takers, which means that the items or parts of such tests will be selected according to how well they discriminate individuals who do well on the test as a whole from those who do poorly. CR tests, on the other hand, are designed to be representative of specified levels of ability or domains of content, and the items or parts will be selected according to how adequately they represent these ability levels or content domains. And while NR test scores are interpreted with reference to the performance of other individuals on the test, CR test scores are interpreted as indicators of a level of ability or degree of mastery of the content domain. These differences between NR and CR tests have particularly important consequences for how we estimate and interpret the reliability. This involves technical considerations that are discussed at length in Chapter 6 (pp. 209–20).

Despite these differences, however, it is important to understand that these two frames of reference are not necessarily mutually exclusive. It is possible, for example, to develop NR score interpretations, on the basis of the performance of appropriate groups of test takers, for a test that was originally designed with reference to a criterion level of proficiency or content domain. Similarly, it is sometimes useful to attempt to scale a NR test to an existing CR test (for example, Carroll 1967).

Scoring procedure

As Pilliner (1968) pointed out, 'subjective' tests are distinguished from 'objective' tests entirely in terms of scoring procedure. All other aspects of tests involve subjective decisions. The test developer uses the best information at hand (for example, curriculum content or theory of language) to subjectively determine the content to be covered, while the test writers make subjective decisions about how best to construct the test items. Tests are also subjective in the taking, since test takers must make subjective decisions about how best to answer the questions, be they essays or multiple-choice.

In an *objective test* the correctness of the test taker's response is determined entirely by predetermined criteria so that no judgment is required on the part of scorers. In a *subjective test*, on the other hand, the scorer must make a judgment about the correctness of the response based on her subjective interpretation of the scoring criteria. The multiple-choice technique is the most obvious example of an objective test, although other tests can be scored objectively as well. Cloze tests and dictations, for example, can be scored objectively by providing scorers with scoring keys that specify exactly which words are acceptable and which are not. Tests such as the oral interview or the written composition that involve the use of rating scales are necessarily subjectively scored, since there is no feasible way to 'objectify' the scoring procedure.

Testing method

The last characteristic to be considered in describing a test is the specific testing method used. Given the variety of methods that have been and continue to be devised, and the creativity of test developers, it is not possible to make an exhaustive list of the methods used for language tests. One broad type of test method that has been discussed widely by language testers is the so-called 'performance test', in which the test takers' test performance is expected to replicate their language performance in non-test situations (for example, Jones 1985a, 1985b; Wesche 1985). The oral interview and essay are considered examples of performance tests. However, these, as well as virtually all of the more commonly used methods, such as the multiple-choice, completion (fill-in), dictation, and cloze are not themselves single 'methods', but consist of different combinations of features: instructions, types of input, and task types. Test method 'facets' such as these provide a more precise way of describing and distinguishing among different types of tests than do single category labels, and are discussed in detail in Chapter 5.

Summary of classification features

I believe the classification scheme described above provides a means for a reasonably complete description of any given language test, and that descriptions of language tests that refer to only a single feature are likely to be misunderstood. By analogy, describing a given speech sound as a 'fricative' does not provide sufficient information for a phonologist to identify it. And even if we describe its other features by calling it the broad-grooved post-palatal fricative of English (/ʃ/, <sh>), this does not tell us whether a given instance of this sound is used as an expression of amazement or as a request for silence.

While the above features for classifying language tests are distinct, there are some areas of overlap. First, the terms 'achievement', 'attainment', and 'mastery' may refer to both the type of content upon which the test is based and the type of decision to be made. This is not inconsistent, since achievement assumes the attainment or mastery of specific objectives. Second, although there is no necessary connection between test content and frame of reference, the results of proficiency and aptitude tests, because of the way in which these constructs have been defined in the past, have been interpreted only in relation to some reference group. Achievement tests, on the other hand, are generally criterion-referenced. I say 'generally' because it is fairly common, particularly in tests of language arts for native speakers, for language tests based on the contents of specific textbooks or course materials to be normed with relevant groups by level, such as year in school.

Rigorous definitions such as 'a norm-referenced multiple-choice test of achievement in grammar for the purpose of placement' are unlikely to replace shorter descriptions such as 'a multiple-choice grammar test' or 'a grammar test for placement' in common usage. I believe, however, that an awareness of the different features that can be used to describe tests may help clarify some misconceptions about the ways in which specific tests differ from each other and facilitate better communication among test users about the characteristics of the tests they use. More importantly, it is these features that determine, to a large extent, the approaches we take in investigating and demonstrating reliability and validity.

Summary

The main point of this chapter is that the most important consideration in the development and use of language tests is the purpose or purposes for which the particular test is intended. By far the most prevalent use of language tests is for purposes of evaluation in educational programs. In order to use language tests for this purpose, we must assume that information regarding educational outcomes is necessary for effective formal education, that appropriate changes or modifications in the program are possible, and that educational outcomes are measurable. The amount and type of testing that we do will depend upon the decisions that need to be made. Since the decisions we make will affect people, we must be concerned about the quality – reliability and validity – of our test results. In general, the more important the decision, in terms of its impact upon individuals and programs, the greater assurance we must have that our test scores are reliable and valid.

In educational programs we are generally concerned with two types of decisions. Decisions about individuals include decisions about entrance, placement, diagnosis, progress, and grading. Decisions about programs are concerned with characteristics such as the appropriateness, effectiveness, or efficiency of the program.

Language tests also have a potentially important use in several areas of research. The information obtained from language tests can assist in the investigation of the very nature of language proficiency, in examining how individuals process language, in the study of language acquisition and attrition, and in assessing the effects of different instructional methods and settings on language learning.

Different types of language tests can be distinguished according to five features: use (selection, entrance, readiness, placement, diagnosis, progress), the content upon which they are based (achievement, proficiency, aptitude), the frame of reference for interpreting test results (norm, criterion), the scoring procedure (subjective, objective), and specific testing method (for example, multiple-choice, completion, essay, dictation, cloze).

Further reading

Nitko (1989) provides an excellent discussion of the issues related to the design and uses of tests in educational programs. More extensive discussions of criterion-referenced tests can be found in Popham (1978) and Nitko (1984). A thorough coverage of the technical issues in criterion-referenced testing is provided in Berk (1980, 1984a). Cziko (1981) discusses the differences between norm-referenced ('psychometric') and criterion-referenced ('edumetric') language tests. Pilliner (1968) describes several different types of tests and discusses these with reference to reliability and validity. Bachman (1981) discusses various types of decisions to be made in formative program evaluation, and makes some suggestions for the types of tests to be used. Bachman (1989b) discusses some of the advantages of using criterion-referenced proficiency tests for both formative and summative program evaluation, and describes some of the considerations in the development and use of such tests.

Discussion questions

1. What are the major characteristics of norm-referenced (NR) and criterion-referenced (CR) tests? How would scores from the following tests typically be interpreted (NR or CR)?
   achievement test
   diagnostic test
   entrance test
   placement test
   progress test
   Under what conditions could scores from these tests be interpreted in both ways?
2. What uses do achievement tests have for formative and summative program evaluation?
3. What decisions do we make about individual students? What types of tests are used to provide information as a basis for these decisions? Can we use one test for all these decisions?
4. Are the decisions that we make in educational programs all of equal importance? Make a list of six different types of decisions

that need to be made in educational programs and rank them from most important to least important. What factors did you consider in this ranking (for example, number of students affected, impact on students' careers, impact on teacher's career)?

5.   How is the relative importance of the decisions to be made related to the qualities of reliability and validity?

4 Communicative language ability

Introduction

Performance on language tests is affected by a wide variety of factors, and an understanding of these factors and how they affect test scores is fundamental to the development and use of language tests. Although language testing specialists have probably always recognized the need to base the development and use of language tests on a theory of language proficiency (for example, Carroll 1961a, 1968; Lado 1961), recently they have called for the incorporation of a theoretical framework of what language proficiency is with the methods and technology involved in measuring it (Upshur 1979; Henning 1984; Bachman and Clark 1987). The frameworks presented in this chapter and the next constitute an initial response to this call, and reflect my conviction that if we are to develop and use language tests appropriately, for the purposes for which they are intended, we must base them on clear definitions of both the abilities we wish to measure and the means by which we observe and measure these abilities.

In this chapter I describe *communicative language ability* in a way that I believe provides a broad basis for both the development and use of language tests, and language testing research. This description is consistent with earlier work in communicative competence (for example, Hymes 1972b, 1973; Munby 1978; Canale and Swain 1980; Savignon 1983; Canale 1983), in that it recognizes that the ability to use language communicatively involves both knowledge of or competence in the language, and the capacity for implementing, or using this competence (Widdowson 1983; Candlin 1986).[1] At the same time, I believe the framework presented here extends earlier models, in that it attempts to characterize the processes by which the various components interact with each other and with the context in which language use occurs.

I do not presume to present this framework as a complete theory of language abilities; books, indeed entire libraries have been written on specific aspects of this. I expect that those who become interested in measuring specific language abilities will also become familiar with the relevant research literature, and that, as test development and use proceed, will themselves contribute to that research.

This framework is, however, presented as a guide, a pointer, if you will, to chart directions for research and development in language testing. As research progresses, it is likely that changes will be made in the framework itself to reflect our growing knowledge. And while this framework is based largely on research in linguistics and applied linguistics, it has evolved through empirical research in language testing (Bachman and Palmer 1982a). The model presented here is thus a result of refinement on the basis of empirical evidence, illustrating, I believe, its utility for guiding and informing empirical research in language testing.

Language proficiency and communicative competence

An earlier framework for describing the measurement of language proficiency was that incorporated in skills and components models such as those proposed in the early 1960s by Lado (1961) and Carroll (1961b, 1968). These models distinguished skills (listening, speaking, reading, and writing) from components of knowledge (grammar, vocabulary, phonology/ graphology), but did not indicate how skills and knowledge are related. It was not clear whether the skills were simply manifestations of the knowledge components in different modalities and channels, or whether they were qualitatively different in other ways.[2] For example, does reading differ from writing only in that it involves interpretation rather than expression? If that were so, how can we account for the fact that although few of us can write with the sophistication and elegance of T. S. Eliot or William Faulkner, we can read and comprehend such writers?

A more serious limitation of the skills/components model was its failure to recognize the full context of language use – the contexts of discourse and situation. Halliday's (1976) description of language functions, both textual and illocutionary, and van Dijk's (1977) delineation of the relationship between text and context, clearly recognize the context of discourse. Hymes (1972b, 1973, 1982) further recognizes the sociocultural factors in the speech situation. What has emerged from these ideas is an expanded conception of language proficiency whose distinguishing characteristic is its recognition of the importance of context beyond the sentence to the appropriate use of language. This context includes both the discourse, of which individual utterances and sentences are part, and the sociolinguistic situation which governs, to a large extent, the nature of that discourse, in both form and function.

Along with this recognition of the context in which language use takes place has come a recognition of the dynamic interaction between that context and the discourse itself, and an expanded view of communication as something more than the simple transfer of information. Thus, Hymes (1972b) describes language use as follows:

> the performance of a person is not identical with a behavioral record. . . . It takes into account the interaction between competence (knowledge, ability for use), the competence of others, and the *cybernetic and emergent properties of events themselves.* (emphasis added)
> (Hymes 1972b:283)

Similarly, Savignon (1983) characterizes communication as:

> dynamic rather than . . . static. . . . It depends on the negotiation of meaning between two or more persons. . . . [It] is context specific. Communication takes place in an infinite variety of situations, and success in a particular role depends on one's understanding of the context and on prior experience of a similar kind.
> (Savignon 1983:8–9)

Kramsch's (1986) discussion of communicative interaction echoes these notions:

> Interaction always entails negotiating intended meanings, i. e., adjusting one's speech to the effect one intends to have on the listener. It entails anticipating the listener's response and possible misunderstandings, clarifying one's own and the other's intentions and arriving at the closest possible match between intended, perceived, and anticipated meanings.
> (Kramsch 1986:367)

Recent formulations of communicative competence thus provide a much more inclusive description of the knowledge required to use language than did the earlier skills and components models, in that they include, *in addition to* the knowledge of grammatical rules, the knowledge of how language is used to achieve particular communicative goals, and the recognition of language use as a dynamic process.

A theoretical framework of communicative language ability

Communicative language ability (CLA) can be described as consisting of both knowledge, or competence, and the capacity for implementing, or executing that competence in appropriate, contextualized communicative language use. This is essentially how Candlin (1986) has described communicative competence:

> the ability to create meanings by exploring the potential inherent in any language for continual modification in response to change, negotiating the value of convention rather than conforming to established principle. In sum, . . . a coming together of organized knowledge structures with a set of procedures for adapting this knowledge to solve new problems of communication that do not have ready-made and tailored solutions.
> (Candlin 1986:40)

The framework of CLA I propose includes three components: language competence, strategic competence, and psychophysiological mechanisms. Language competence comprises, essentially, a set of specific knowledge components that are utilized in communication via language. Strategic competence is the term I will use to characterize the mental capacity for implementing the components of language competence in contextualized communicative language use. Strategic competence thus provides the means for relating language competencies to features of the context of situation in which language use takes place and to the language user's knowledge structures (sociocultural knowledge, 'real-world' knowledge). Psychophysiological mechanisms refer to the neurological and psychological processes involved in the actual execution of language as a physical phenomenon (sound, light). The interactions of these components of CLA with the language use context and language user's knowledge structures are illustrated in Figure 4.1.

Language competence

Recent frameworks of communicative competence have included several different components associated with what I will call *language competence*. In describing a theoretical framework for specifying an individual's communicative competence in a second language, Munby (1978) includes 'linguistic encoding' (the realization of language use as verbal forms), 'sociocultural orientation' (contextual appropriacy and communicative needs), 'sociosemantic

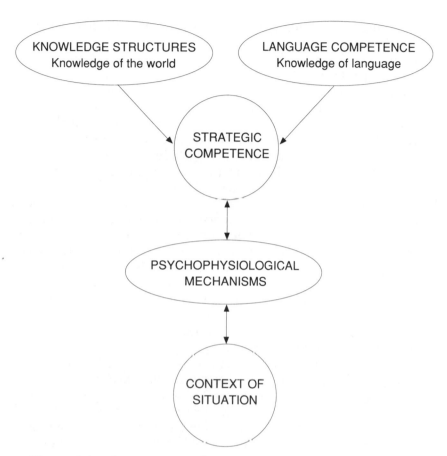

Figure 4.1   Components of communicative language ability in communicative language use

basis of linguistic knowledge', and 'discourse level of operation'. Canale and Swain (1980), examining the theoretical bases of language teaching and language testing, distinguish 'grammatical competence', which includes lexis, morphology, sentence-grammar semantics, and phonology, from 'sociolinguistic competence', which consists of sociocultural rules and rules of discourse, while Canale (1983) makes a further distinction between sociolinguistic competence (sociocultural rules) and 'discourse competence' (cohesion and coherence). Finally, Hymes (1982), in a far-reaching description of 'linguistic competence', includes 'resource grammar' (features that are part of the formal code), 'discourse grammar' (features typically associated with style, such as informality and politeness), and 'performance style' (idiosyncratic features of individual language use).

Attempts to empirically validate these various components have not been conclusive. Allen *et. al.* (1983), for example, developed measures of grammatical competence (morphology and syntax), discourse competence (cohesion and coherence), and sociolinguistic competence (sensitivity to register). The factor analysis of their test scores failed to support the factorial distinctness of these particular components. Bachman and Palmer (1982a), on the other hand, found some support for the distinctness of components of what they called 'communicative proficiency'. They developed a battery of language tests that included grammatical competence (morphology and syntax), pragmatic competence (vocabulary, cohesion, and organization), and sociolinguistic competence (sensitivity to register, naturalness, and cultural references). The results of their study suggest that the components of what they called grammatical and pragmatic competence are closely associated with each other, while the components they described as sociolinguistic competence are distinct.

The description of language competence presented here builds upon these empirical findings by grouping morphology, syntax, vocabulary, cohesion, and organization under one component, organizational competence. 'Pragmatic competence' is redefined to include not only elements of Bachman and Palmer's sociolinguistic competence, but also those abilities related to the functions that are performed through language use. Language competencies can thus be classified into two types: organizational competence and pragmatic competence. Each of these, in turn, consists of several categories. The components of language competence are illustrated in Figure 4.2. This 'tree' diagram is intended as a visual metaphor and not as a theoretical model, and as with any metaphor, it captures certain features at the expense of others. In this case, this diagram represents the hierarchical relationships among the components of language competence, at the expense of making them appear as if they are separate and independent of each other. However, in language use these components all interact with each other and with features of the language use situation. Indeed, it is this very interaction between the various competencies and the language use context that characterizes communicative language use. In the last part of this chapter, a model of how these competencies may interact in language use is presented in the discussion of strategic competence.

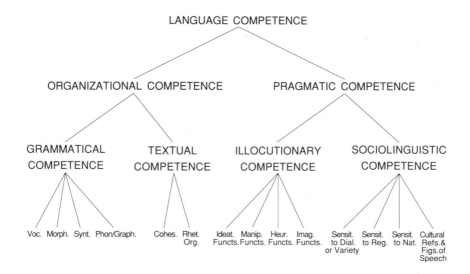

Figure 4.2   Components of language competence

Organizational competence

Organizational competence comprises those abilities involved in controlling the formal structure of language for producing or recognizing grammatically correct sentences, comprehending their propositional content, and ordering them to form texts. These abilities are of two types: grammatical and textual.

Grammatical competence

Grammatical competence includes those competencies involved in language *usage*, as described by Widdowson (1978). These consist of a number of relatively independent competencies such as the knowledge of vocabulary, morphology, syntax, and phonology/ graphology. These govern the choice of words to express specific significations, their forms, their arrangement in utterances to express propositions, and their physical realizations, either as sounds or as written symbols. Suppose, for example, a test taker is shown a picture of two people, a boy and a taller girl, and is asked to describe it. In so doing, the test taker demonstrates her lexical competence by choosing words with appropriate significations (*boy*, *girl*, *tall*) to refer to the contents of the picture. She demonstrates her knowledge of morphology by affixing the inflectional morpheme (-er) to 'tall'. She demonstrates her knowledge of syntactic rules by putting the words in the proper order, to compose the sentence 'The girl is taller than the boy'. When produced using the phonological rules of English, the resulting utterance is a linguistically accurate represent-ation of the information in the picture.

Textual competence

Textual competence includes the knowledge of the conventions for joining utterances together to form a text, which is essentially a unit of language – *spoken or written* – consisting of two or more utterances or sentences that are structured according to rules of cohesion and rhetorical organization. Cohesion comprises ways of explicitly marking semantic relationships such as reference, sub-situation, ellipsis, conjunction, and lexical cohesion (Halliday and Hasan 1976), as well as conventions such as those governing the ordering of old and new information in discourse. Rhetorical organization pertains to the overall conceptual structure of a text, and is related to the *effect* of the text on the language user (van Dijk 1977:4). Conventions of rhetorical organization include common methods of development such as narration, description, comparison, classification, and process analysis (McCrimman 1984). We teach some of these organizational conventions formally in expository writing classes when we show students how to order information in a paragraph: topic sentence, first primary support sentence, secondary support sentences, second primary support sentence . . . conclusion, or transition sentence. Other conventions for organizing discourse may not be taught formally at all, however, either because they are not fully understood or because they are simply too complex to teach.

Textual competence is also involved in conversational language use. Indeed, much of the work in discourse analysis that takes conversation as its primary point of departure deals with compon-ents of textual competence (for example, Sinclair and Coulthard 1975; Coulthard 1977; Hatch 1978; Larsen-Freeman 1980; Richards and Schmidt 1983b). Conventions involved in establishing, maintain-ing, and terminating conversations have been discussed in terms of 'maxims' (Grice 1975), 'conversation rules' (Hatch and Long 1980), 'conversational routines' (Coulmas 1981b), and 'conversational competence' (Richards and Sukwiwat 1983). These conventions, such as attention getting, topic nomination, topic development and conversation maintenance (Hatch 1978) appear to be ways in which interlocutors organize and perform the turns in conversational discourse, and may be analogous to the rhetorical patterns that have been observed in written discourse.

What this work on the analysis of conversational language use reveals, I believe, is a rich variety of devices for marking cohesive relationships in oral discourse, and for organizing such discourse in ways that are maximally appropriate to the language use context and maximally efficient in achieving the communicative goals of the interlocutors. And while many of these conventions have analogues in written discourse, it is obvious that conversational interchange, by its interactive or reciprocal nature, gives rise to or necessitates devices for organizing discourse that are unique to this genre of discourse. Nevertheless, rather than considering these conventions as a separate component of communicative language ability, I believe they can be best described in terms of the abilities associated with textual competence.

Pragmatic competence

The abilities discussed thus far pertain to the organization of the linguistic signals that are used in communication, and how these signals are used to refer to persons, objects, ideas, and feelings. That is, they concern the relationships among signs and their referents. Equally important, in communicative language use, are the relationships between these signs and referents on the one hand, and the language *users* and the *context* of communication, on the other. The description of these latter relationships constitutes the domain of *pragmatics*, which van Dijk (1977) has described as follows:

> pragmatics must be assigned an empirical domain consisting of CONVENTIONAL RULES of language and manifestations of these in the production and interpretation of utterances. In particular, it should make an independent contribution to the analysis of the conditions that make utterances ACCEPTABLE *in some situation for speakers of the language.* (emphasis added)
> (van Dijk 1977:189–90)

Van Dijk distinguishes two aspects of pragmatics: (1) the examination of the 'pragmatic conditions' that determine whether or not a given utterance is acceptable to other users of the language as an act, or the performance of an intended function; and (2) the characterization of the conditions that determine 'which utterances are successful in which situations' (p. 190). Pragmatics is thus concerned with the relationships between utterances and the acts or functions that speakers (or writers) intend to perform through these utterances, which can be called the *illocutionary force* of utterances, and the characteristics of the context of language use that determine the *appropriateness* of utterances. The notion of pragmatic competence presented here thus includes illocutionary competence, or the knowledge of the pragmatic conventions for performing acceptable language functions, and sociolinguistic competence, or knowledge of the sociolinguistic conventions for performing language functions appropriately in a given context.

Illocutionary competence

Speech acts

The notion of illocutionary competence can be introduced by reference to the theory of speech acts. A sentence such as 'It's cold in here', for example, may function as an assertion about the physical atmosphere in a room, as a warning not to bring the baby in, or as a request to turn on the heater. Each of these is a different speech act. Searle (1969) distinguishes three types of speech act: utterance acts, propositional acts, and illocutionary acts. An *utterance act* is simply the act of saying something. A *propositional act* involves referring to something or expressing a predication about something. An *illocutionary act* is the function (assertion, warning, request) performed in saying something. The meaning of an utterance can thus be described in terms of its propositional content (reference and predication) and its illocutionary force (intended illocutionary act). Austin (1962) and Searle (1969) also include, in their discussions of meaning, *perlocutionary acts*, or the effect of a given illocutionary act on the hearer.[3]

To illustrate these different speech acts, imagine a context in which I wish to get someone to leave. To accomplish this, I use my illocutionary competence, which indicates that a simple statement can function as a request. (I will also use my sociolinguistic competence, discussed below, to determine which of several possible statements is the most appropriate in this specific context.) If I say, 'I would like you to leave', I am performing a propositional act in producing a sentence which is both grammatically well-formed and has propositional content, or signification. My ability to perform this propositional act derives from my grammatical competence. If the person I am addressing understands the signification of the utterance, interprets the illocutionary force of the act as a request (as it was intended to be interpreted), and carries out the request, the performance of the speech act has the consequence, or perlocutionary effect, of his leaving. This perlocutionary effect is, of course, dependent upon the grammatical and illocutionary competencies of both me and my interlocutor, but it also depends upon non-language competency factors, such as the other person's willingness and ability to comply.

There are a number of general strategies by which a speaker can signal his intent in performing an illocutionary act. He can signal his intent directly by announcing its illocutionary force ('I request that you leave now'). He may also signal his intent by using an appropriate syntactic form, such as the imperative in 'Leave!' In this case, the general intention of the speaker is clear (the act is a directive of some sort), but the specific illocutionary force is not, for the imperative could be interpreted by a listener as an order, a command, or a warning.

Another strategy available to the speaker is to be less direct. This consists of using a sentence type whose form is not generally associated with the given illocutionary act, and whose interpretation depends very heavily on the circumstances under which the act is performed. For example, the speaker could use a declarative sentence to state why the hearer should act: 'I can hardly stand your company any more.' Or he could be even less direct, and simply state, 'It's nearly midnight.' The less direct the speaker is in signaling the illocutionary force he intends, the more dependent its interpretation will be on the way it is said, and the context in which it is said. (The choice from among several alternative utterances of differing degrees of directness will thus be a function of both the speaker's illocutionary competence, and his sensitivity to the characteristics of the specific context, which is part of sociolinguistic competence, discussed below.)

Fraser and Nolan (1981) have described eighteen strategies for requesting, illustrating the wide range of directness in requests that is possible in English. Sixteen of these strategies do not entail the use of the word 'request'. The following five examples from their list provide some indication of the complexity of language use:

(1) By announcing the intent to perform the act
    ('I *request* that you help me.')
(2) By using an imperative sentence, which conveys the intent
    ('Please help me.')
(3) By expressing a consequence of the hearer's acting
    ('If you help me, I'll buy you a new comic book.')
(4) By asking if the hearer has the ability to act
    ('Can/could/can't/couldn't you . . . help me?')

(5) By asking if the hearer has a reason for (not) acting
       ('Why are (aren't) you helping me?')
(Fraser and Nolan 1981: 101)

Illocutionary competence is used both in expressing language to be
taken with certain illocutionary force and in interpreting the
illocutionary force of language. An extension of the example above
illustrates what is intended and interpreted when one uses language
over and above what is understood when one employs only the
organizational competencies associated with usage.

A: It's nearly midnight!
B: It's raining cats and dogs.
A: Thanks a lot!

Employing grammatical competence, one could determine that the
forms of these three utterances are grammatically accurate and that
their propositional meanings match a mental image: two people, one
of whom appears upset, in a room, a violent thunderstorm outside.
Employing illocutionary competence, one interprets the three sentences by assigning to each an illocutionary force (recognizing each as
a particular illocutionary act or collection of acts). The illocutionary
forces of the three utterances (request, refusal, sarcastic rebuttal) are
clarified by the addition of the words in parentheses.

A: It's nearly midnight! (Please leave.)
B: (No, I won't leave because) it's raining cats and dogs.
A: Thanks a lot (for nothing)!

Language functions
The previous section has introduced the distinction between form
and function in language use through the discussion of speech acts.
However, to account for this distinction as it relates to both the
expression of language (speech, writing) and its interpretation
(listening, reading), we need to consider a broader framework of
functions that we can accomplish through language use. The
description of language functions provided here is drawn, to a large
extent, from Halliday (1973, 1976), although it extends to adult
language use several of the functions he has described in the context
of child language acquisition. Furthermore, the functions described
here are grouped into four macro-functions: ideational, manipulative, heuristic, and imaginative.

By far the most pervasive function in language use is the *ideational*
function, by which we express meaning in terms of our experience of
the real world (Halliday 1973:20). This includes the use of language

to express propositions or to exchange information about knowledge or feelings. For example, language is used ideationally to present knowledge in lectures or scholarly articles. It is also ideationally used to express feelings, as when one pours out one's emotions to a good friend or in a diary, with or without any intention of eliciting advice or help.

The *manipulative* functions are those in which the primary purpose is to affect the world around us. One such function is the *instrumental* function with which we use language to get things done. For example, we may get someone, including ourselves, to do something by forming or uttering suggestions, requests, orders, commands, or warnings. We may accomplish other things by saying what we intend to do, as, for example, with offers, promises, or threats. The *regulatory* function is used 'to control the behavior of others – to manipulate the persons and, with or without their help, the objects in the environment' (Halliday 1973:18). In addition, this function is performed in formulating and stating rules, laws, and norms of behavior. The *interactional* function of language is its use to form, maintain, or change interpersonal relationships. Any act of interpersonal language use involves two levels of message: context and relationship. Haley (1963) makes this point:

> When any two people meet for the first time and begin to establish a relationship, a wide range of behavior is possible between them. They might exchange compliments or insults or sexual advances or statements that one is superior to the other, and so on. As the two people define their relationship with each other, they work out what type of communicative behavior is to take place in this relationship. Every message they interchange by its very existence either reinforces this line or suggests a shift in it to include a new kind of message. In this way, the relationship is mutually defined by the presence or absence of messages interchanged by the two people. (Haley 1963:6–7)

Phatic language use, such as in greetings, ritual inquiries about health, or comments on the weather, is primarily interactional in function. Its propositional content is subordinate to the relationship maintaining function.

The *heuristic* function pertains to the use of language to extend our knowledge of the world around us, and occurs commonly in such acts as teaching, learning, problem solving, and conscious memorizing. Teaching and learning may be either formal, as in an academic setting, or informal, as in self-study. The use of language in problem solving is exemplified in the writing of papers in which one goes through the processes of invention, organization, and revision. The use of language to aid the conscious retention of information is exemplified in the memorization of facts, words, formulae, or rules. It is important to note that this function also pertains to the use of language for the purpose of extending one's knowledge of language itself, that is, for acquiring or learning a language. For example, when a language teacher points to a book on a table and says, 'The book is on the table', he is not conveying information. That is, he is not performing an ideational function, but rather a heuristic function of illustrating the meaning of the preposition 'on' in English.

The *imaginative* function of language enables us to create or extend our own environment for humorous or esthetic purposes, where the value derives from the way in which the language itself is used. Examples are telling jokes, constructing and communicating fantasies, creating metaphors or other figurative uses of language, as well as attending plays or films and reading literary works such as novels, short stories, or poetry for enjoyment.

While these have been discussed as distinct functions, clearly most instances of language use fulfill several functions simultaneously. Such is the case when a teacher makes an assignment (*ideational, manipulative,* and *heuristic* functions) in an amusing way (*imaginative* function), or when one reads a magazine article for enjoyment (*imaginative* function) and in so doing acquires useful information (*heuristic* function). Furthermore, although language functions have been discussed as if they occurred in individual, unconnected utterances, it should be emphasized that the majority of language use involves the performance of multiple functions in connected utterances, and it is the connections among these functions that provide coherence to discourse.

Sociolinguistic competence

While illocutionary competence enables us to use language to express a wide range of functions, and to interpret the illocutionary force of utterances or discourse, the appropriateness of these functions and how they are performed varies from one language use context to the next, according to a myriad of sociocultural and discoursal features. Sociolinguistic competence is the sensitivity to, or control of the conventions of language use that are determined by the features of the specific language use context; it enables us to perform language functions in ways that are appropriate to that context. Without attempting to identify and discuss the features of the language use situation that determine the conventions of language use, I will discuss the following abilities under sociolinguistic competence: sensitivity to differences in dialect or variety, to differences in register and to naturalness, and the ability to interpret cultural references and figures of speech.

Sensitivity to differences in dialect or variety
In virtually every language there are variations in use that may be associated with language users in different geographic regions, or who belong to different social groups. These regional and social varieties, or dialects, can be characterized by different conventions, and the appropriateness of their use will vary, depending on the features of the language use context. An example of the way different contexts require the use of different varieties of English is that of a Black student who indicated that she would not consider using Black English in class, where 'Standard American English' would be appropriate. On the other hand, she would probably be understood as either affected and pretentious or joking, were she to use Standard American English in informal conversations with Black friends. Sensitivity to differences in dialect or variety of language is thus an important part of sociolinguistic competence.

Sensitivity to differences in register
Halliday, McIntosh, and Strevens (1964) used the term 'register' to refer to variation in language use within a single dialect or variety.[4] They distinguished differences in register in terms of three aspects of the language use context: 'field of discourse', 'mode of discourse', and 'style of discourse' (pp. 90–4). The field of discourse may consist simply of the subject matter of the language use, as in lectures, discussions, or written expositions; it may also refer to the entire language use context, as in the registers of playing football, planting trees, or computer 'hacking'. Variations in register also occur as a function of differences between modes of discourse – spoken and written. Anyone who has attempted to capture 'genuine' dialogues in writing, or to present a written paper 'conversationally' can attest to the differences between written and spoken registers.

Another term that has been used to describe the features or conventions that characterize the language used within a particular area or for specific functions is 'discourse domain'. Swales (1987), for instance, discusses entries in philatelic catalogues and the language used in written mail requests for reprints of papers or articles as examples of domains that characterize discourse communities. The discourse domain in which language use occurs, whether it be spoken, as in lectures or job interviews, or written, as in business letters, job announcements, or scholarly papers, will determine the register of language use, including the specific functions and organizational features that are appropriate to that register. And just as the use of a particular dialect or variety is associated with membership in a speech community, using the register of a particular discourse domain can establish one's membership in a 'discourse community'. How often, for example, do we seek out people at large parties with whom we can 'talk shop'? Likewise, we very quickly feel like an outsider when we cannot participate in a given domain of discourse.

The following test item from Bachman and Palmer (1982d) provides an example of sensitivity to discourse domain (that of love letters):

In the blanks below, write the appropriate *greeting* and *ending*:

Dear Madam,

I've been thinking about you all day, and can hardly wait to hold you in my arms again. I'll be waiting for you under the apple tree.

Further affiant sayeth not,

George

(Some of the responses of advanced non-native speakers of American English to this question, such as, 'To the Loved One', and 'Cheers', suggest that this is a relatively esoteric area of language competence, to say the least!)

The third of Halliday, McIntosh and Strevens' dimensions for characterizing variations in register is 'style of discourse, which refers to the relations among the participants' (p. 92). The classic discussion of style is still Joos (1967), who distinguished five different levels of style, or register, in language use: frozen, formal, consultative, casual, and intimate. These five styles are characterized primarily in terms of the relationships that obtain between the participants in the language use context, so that the use of the inappropriate style can be interpreted as presumptuous or even rude. Consider, for example, the inappropriate familiarity of the salesperson who telephones people at random from numbers in the telephone directory, and says something like, 'Hi, Lyle, this is Herb from All-American Storm Windows. How are you tonight? That's just great. Say, you know winter is just around the corner, and I was just calling to let you know that . . .'

Sociolinguistic competence thus involves sensitivity to variations in register, since the illocutionary force of utterances virtually always depends on the social contexts in which they are used. These variations occur in both highly formalized language use, as in greetings, introductions, or leave takings, and in extended language use, as when we use more elaborate syntactic structures and cohesive devices in formal writing, or when we sustain a conversation in a regional dialect with childhood friends and family members.

Sensitivity to naturalness

A third aspect of sociolinguistic competence is that which allows the user to either formulate or interpret an utterance which is not only linguistically accurate, but which is also phrased in what Pawley and Syder (1983) call a *nativelike way*, that is, as it would be by speakers of a particular dialect or variety of a language who are native to the culture of that dialect or variety. For example, consider the interpretation of the second line of the following exchange:

A: Why are you yelling?
B: Because I have much anger with him.

While this example merely sounds strange, or archaic, non-naturalness of language use can also affect interpretability. Compare, for example, 'I wish you wouldn't do that' with 'I would feel better by your not doing that', or 'I have my doubts' with 'I have several doubts'.

Ability to interpret cultural references and figures of speech

The final aspect of sociolinguistic competence to be dealt with here is that which allows us to use and interpret cultural references and figures of speech. Many of these will be incorporated, with set meanings, into the lexicon of any language, and can thus be considered part of lexical, or vocabulary, competence. Nevertheless, knowledge of the extended meanings given by a specific culture to particular events, places, institutions, or people is required whenever these meanings are referred to in language use. For example, to interpret the following exchange, the language user would have to know that 'Waterloo' is used linguistically to symbolize a major and final defeat with awful consequences for the defeated:

A: I hear John didn't do too well on his final exam.
B: Yeah, it turned out to be his Waterloo.

Knowledge of only the referential meaning of the place name without knowing what the name connotes in American and British English would not allow the correct interpretation of the second utterance.

Similarly, interpreting figurative language involves more than simply knowledge of referential meaning. For example, the correct interpretation of hyperboles such as, 'I can think of a million good reasons for not smoking' and clichés like 'It's a jungle out there', require more than a knowledge of the signification of the words and grammatical structures involved, while similes such as Faulkner's 'the sound of tires on the hot tar was like the tearing of new silk', and metaphors like Eliot's 'The river sweats Oil and tar', invoke images far beyond those of the concrete objects to which they refer. Although individuals from different cultural backgrounds will, no doubt, be able to attach meaning to figures of speech, the conventions governing the use of figurative language, as well as the specific meanings and images that are evoked are deeply rooted in the culture of a given society or speech community, which is why I have included them as part of sociolinguistic competence.

To summarize, language competence comprises two types of competence, organizational and pragmatic. Organizational competence includes the knowledge employed in creating or recognizing grammatically correct utterances, in comprehending their propositional content, and in organizing them to form oral or written texts. Pragmatic competence includes the types of knowledge which, *in addition to* organizational competence, are employed in the contextualized performance and interpretation of socially appropriate illocutionary acts in discourse. These competencies include the knowledge of language functions, of sociolinguistic rules of appropriateness, and of cultural references and figurative language.

Strategic competence

As mentioned above, one characteristic of recent frameworks of communicative competence is the recognition of language use as a dynamic process, involving the assessment of relevant information in the context, and a negotiation of meaning on the part of the language user. This dynamic view of communication is also reflected in the literature on interlanguage communication strategies. There have been essentially two approaches to defining communication strategies: the 'interactional' definition and the 'psycholinguistic' definition (Færch and Kasper 1984).

The interactional definition, as stated by Tarone (1981), characterizes a communication strategy as 'the mutual attempt by two interlocutors to agree on a meaning in situations where the requisite meaning structures do not seem to be shared' (p. 288). Tarone includes both linguistic and sociolinguistic rule structures in her notion of meaning structure, and considers communication strategies distinct from this meaning structure. In their review of the literature, Færch and Kasper (1984) observe that an interactional view of communication strategies is too narrow in scope, since it only applies to 'the negotiation of meaning as a joint effort between two interlocutors' (p. 51), while much communicative language use, such as reading novels or writing textbooks, involves only one individual, with no feedback from a second interlocutor. Tarone (1981) does, however, describe another type of strategy, the *production strategy*, as 'an attempt to use one's linguistic system efficiently and clearly, with a minimum of effort' (p. 289). Like communication strategies, production strategies are distinct from the language user's language competence. Unlike communication strategies, however, they 'lack the interactional focus on the negotiation of meaning' (ibid.).

Recent frameworks of communicative competence that have incorporated the notion of strategies have generally accepted the interactional definition. Thus, Canale and Swain (1980), citing the research on communication strategies, include strategic competence as a separate component in their framework of communicative competence. They describe strategic competence as providing a *compensatory* function when the linguistic competence of the language users is inadequate:

Strategic competence . . . will be made up of verbal and nonverbal communication strategies that may be called into action to compensate for breakdowns in communication due to perform-ance variables or to insufficient competence.
(Canale and Swain 1980:30)

Canale (1983) has extended this definition of strategic competence to include both the compensatory characteristic of communication strategies and the enhancement characteristic of production strategies:

Strategic competence: mastery of verbal and nonverbal strategies both (a) to compensate for breakdowns in communication due to insufficient competence or to performance limitations and (b) to enhance the rhetorical effect of utterances.
(Canale 1983:339)

While these definitions provide some indication of the function of strategic competence in facilitating communication, they are limited in that they do not describe the mechanisms by which strategic competence operates. I would also note that these definitions include non-verbal manifestations of strategic competence, which are clearly an important part of strategic competence in communication, but which will not be dealt with in this book.

In an attempt to provide a more general description of strategies of communication, Færch and Kasper (1983) have described a 'psycho-linguistic' model of speech production. Drawing on the work of cognitive psychologists such as Miller *et al.* (1960) and Clark and Clark (1977), they describe a model of speech production that includes a planning phase and an execution phase. The planning phase consists of communicative goals and a planning process, the product of which is a plan. Communicative goals consist of (1) an actional element, associated with speech acts; (2) a modal element associated with the role relationship holding between the inter-actants; and (3) a propositional element, associated with the content of the communicative event (p. 24). Færch and Kasper further describe the planning process as an interaction of three components: the communicative goal, the communicative resources available to the individual, and the assessment of the communicative situation (p. 27). The execution phase of Færch and Kasper's model consists of 'neurological and physiological processes' that implement the plan, resulting in language use.

Færch and Kasper's model is intended only to explain the use of communication strategies in interlanguage communication. How-ever, I view strategic competence as an important part of all communicative language use, not just that in which language abilities are deficient and must be compensated for by other means, and would therefore extend Færch and Kasper's formulation to provide a more general description of strategic competence in communicative language use. I include three components in strategic competence: assessment, planning, and execution.

Assessment component

The assessment component enables us to (1) identify the information – including the language variety, or dialect – that is needed for realizing a particular communicative goal in a given context; (2) determine what language competencies (native language, second or foreign language) are at our disposal for most effectively bringing that information to bear in achieving the communicative goal; (3) ascertain the abilities and knowledge that are shared by our interlocutor; and (4) following the communication attempt, evaluate the extent to which the communicative goal has been achieved. The importance of assessing our interlocutor's capabilities has been underscored by Corder (1983):

> The strategies adopted by speakers, of course, depend upon their interlocutors. What we attempt to communicate and how we set about it are determined not only by our knowledge of the language but also by our current assessment of our interlocutor's linguistic competence and his knowledge of the topic of discourse.
> (Corder 1983: 15)

The process of assessment can be illustrated by the following example. When I lived in Bangkok, it was frequently a major undertaking to explain to dinner guests how to reach my house. After having struggled to give directions on several occasions, I eventually discovered, through the process of assessment, that it was necessary to first determine what part of the city the person would be coming from. This was learned at great embarrassment after I had sent many a hungry dinner guest off in the wrong direction, assuming that they would be coming to my house the same way I usually did. Being able to extract this information necessitated determining the most effective and appropriate forms and structures (in both English and Thai) to do so over the phone without sounding impolite or eccentric. Even the most polite attempt to convey such information was of little avail, however, if the person I had invited had little sense of direction or was unfamiliar with the major districts of the city. In such cases, the conversation rather quickly turned from giving directions to attempting to ascertain some landmark we both knew. Once this was determined, a new set of directions could be provided. In summary, the information I needed to effectively attain my communicative goal was the part of the city the person was coming from, and the bulk of the conversation frequently involved ascertaining what geographical knowledge of the city my intended dinner guest and I shared.

Planning component

The planning component retrieves relevant items (grammatical, textual, illocutionary, sociolinguistic) from language competence and formulates a plan whose realization is expected to achieve the communicative goal. In the case of a monolingual speech context, relevant items will be drawn from the native language (L_1) competence, while in a bilingual, second, or foreign language use context, the items may be retrieved from the native language, from the language user's interlanguage rule system (L_i), or from the second or foreign language (L_2). In the example above, I retrieved the appropriate forms of address and the questioning routines I had learned specifically for the occasion, and formulated a plan for utilizing them to acquire the information needed. Depending on how the conversation evolved, other items would be retrieved and other plans formulated.

This description of the assessment and planning components in communicative language use is similar to Johnson's 1982 characterization of the processes involved in communication:

> There are at least three processes which [a listener] must undertake if he is to fulfill his role as interactant. Firstly, he must 'scan' [the speaker's] utterance to extract . . . its pragmatic information . . . [which is] that part of the total information conveyed which contributes to the information required by the speaker. It is, in short, information which the listener wants to receive. . . . [The listener] approaches the task of listening comprehension prepared to search for certain pieces of information in his interactant's words. Once this information comes, it has to be assessed according to the speaker's aim, and this is the second process which [the listener] must undertake. . . . [The listener] compares, then, what he is told with what he wants to know, identifies any mismatch and then − as a third process − formulates his next utterance.
> (Johnson 1982:149)

It is exactly these characteristics of communicative language use that I associate with strategic competence. As indicated above, communication involves a dynamic interchange between context and discourse, so that communicative language use is not characterized simply by the production or interpretation of texts, but by the relationship that obtains between a text and the context in which it occurs. The interpretation of discourse, in other words, requires the ability to utilize available language competencies to assess the context for relevant information and to then match this information to information in the discourse. It is the function of strategic competence to match the new information to be processed with relevant information that is available (including presuppositional and real world knowledge) and map this onto the maximally efficient use of existing language abilities.

Execution component

Finally, the execution component draws on the relevant psychophysiological mechanisms to implement the plan in the modality and
channel appropriate to the communicative goal and the context. The
interactions among the components of strategic competence, language competencies, and the language use context are illustrated in
Figure 4.3 below, which represents an extension of Færch and
Kasper's model (1983: 25).

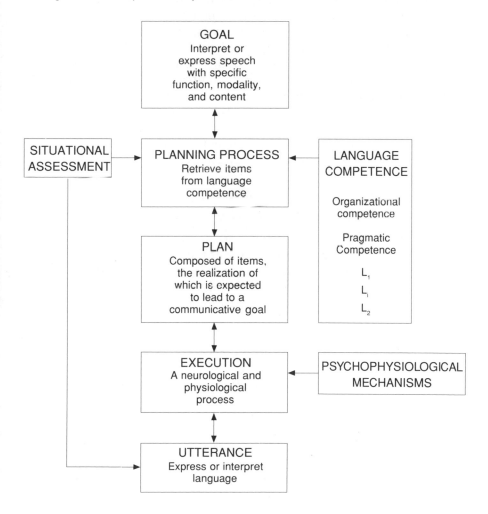

Figure 4.3   A model of language use

In comprehending, or interpreting, the same processes – assessment, planning, and execution – are involved. In attending a lecture, for example, our communicative goal may be to better understand a given area of knowledge. In assessing the situation, we consider the topic, what we know about the speaker, the likely audience, and our own knowledge and abilities, and form expectations regarding the utterances we will have to interpret and our likelihood of being able to comprehend them. This assessment may be quite deliberate, as in the case of a classroom lecture, and we may actually make conscious preparations, such as reading an assigned article, to better achieve our communicative goal. In other cases, our assessment may be less premeditated, and we may need to make on-the-spot adjustments. For example, if we find that the lecturer's speech is heavily accented, we will need to employ competencies associated with interpreting non-native speech. If we are lacking these, we may find the lecture incomprehensible, and fail in our communicative goal. Recent research into the role of schemata in reading (for example, Carrell 1982, 1986) provides, I believe, further exemplification of the role of plans and resultant expectations in receptive language use.

The influence of strategic competence on language test performance

At this point we may well wonder about the extent to which strategic competence affects scores on language tests. Suppose that two non-native speakers of a language were to take three tests: a test of usage, a test of contextualized receptive performance in which the scores are influenced in part by practical outcomes, and a test of productive oral performance. Suppose we find that the two subjects' scores are the same on the first two tests but different on the third. When we analyze tapes of the third test, we find that the more effective test taker made use of more of the various different ways of performing illocutionary acts than did the second, and that her propositions made more references to relevant objects in the environment.

We ask the less effective test taker why she did not try all of the different ways of performing the required illocutionary acts that the more effective test taker used, and why she did not make reference to relevant objects in the environment to get her message across. She replies, 'I just didn't think of them at the time', or 'I didn't notice the objects in the environment', or 'It didn't seem worth the effort.'

In such a case we might characterize the more effective language user as more willing and adept at making use of what she knew was available in order to perform a function using language, but we would be reluctant to say that the two speakers' *language* competence differed. In other words, we would consider both persons to have the same control of the rules of usage and use, but to differ in their willingness to exploit what they knew and their flexibility in doing so. And while this example deals with the generality of strategic competence for non-native speakers, I believe it applies to native speakers as well.

Some types of test tasks may measure strategic competence, almost by design. In tests of reading comprehension, for example, it is common practice to include questions requiring inference. I believe that correctly answering such questions requires strategic competence, in that the test taker must recognize what information outside the discourse itself is relevant to answering the question, and then must search for that information in his memory.

There would also appear to be some types of language test tasks that are particularly susceptible to the effects of test takers' strategic competence, in that they can successfully complete such tasks by utilizing their strategic competence to compensate for deficiencies in other competencies. An example of such a test is the picture description test described by Palmer (1972, 1981), in which the test taker is required to describe a picture as quickly as possible in order to enable the examiner to distinguish the picture described from a number of similar pictures. As a test of organizational competence, it should require the examinee to employ a variety of vocabulary items. In fact, the subject matter of the pictures was selected with this in mind. However, Palmer (1981) noticed that some subjects with obviously small vocabularies described the pictures in terms of their placement on the page, in terms of how dark or light they are, or how big or small. These subjects appear to have adopted the strategy of ignoring the propositional content of the pictures and communicating instead about the nonverbal visual code (the lines and shapes) used to represent them. In tests such as these, it may well be that performance is affected more by strategic competence than by the specific language ability the test was originally intended to measure.

The type of scoring used can also be expected to influence the effect of strategic competence on test performance. If a test is scored solely on the basis of the practical effect of the language performance, the potential contribution of strategic competence may be high. Consider, for example, a test in which an examinee is required to write a set of instructions describing how to perform some task, such as preparing a scattergram: drawing two intersecting axes and labeling them, and entering a small set of data correctly. Suppose the test is scored *only* on the extent to which the scattergram drawn by the examiner matches that shown to the examinee, and that the examinee is informed that this is the criterion for correctness. An examinee willing to use what she knows to be simplified and perhaps ungrammatical structures might nevertheless be able to write a set of understandable instructions adequate for the task. On the other hand, an examinee not willing to do so might spend an inordinate amount of time in attempting to produce linguistically accurate sentences, and not complete the task. The same test scored partly on the basis of different criteria, say the range of structures used and the accuracy with which they are used, might reward the strategically adept examinee – the one willing to use simple and ungrammatical language – to a lesser degree.

Can we measure strategic competence?

I have argued that strategic competence influences language perform-ance in that there do appear to be language users who make better use of their language competence in performing various functions. Similarly, some types of language test tasks seem to involve strategic competence to a greater degree than do others. However, rather than considering strategic competence solely an aspect of *language* competence, I consider it more as a general ability, which enables an individual to make the most effective use of available abilities in carrying out a given task, whether that task be related to communic-ative language use or to non-verbal tasks such as creating a musical composition, painting, or solving mathematical equations.

And it is here that we begin to enter the realm of general cognitive abilities, or intelligence, which is beyond the scope of this book. Oller (1983a) has hypothesized that what he calls 'a general factor of language proficiency', that involves 'the process of "pragmatic mapping" of utterance forms . . . into the contexts of experience' (p. 356) 'is the principal function of intelligence' (p. 355). John B. Carroll, on the other hand, (personal communication) holds that intelligence, while not totally independent, is distinct from language abilities. I would agree that it may be inaccurate to identify strategic competence with intelligence. At the same time, to simply dismiss strategic competence as a general ability whose effects on language test performance we cannot measure is to beg the question. Determining the effects of various abilities on test performance is ultimately an empirical question – that of construct validation. It is therefore my hope that the formulation of strategic competence presented here will prove useful for generating hypotheses about test performance, and for designing tests that will enable us to examine these hypotheses through empirical research.

Psychophysiological mechanisms

Thus far I have discussed those competencies that I believe are part of communicative language ability. In order to fully characterize language use, however, it is also necessary to consider the psychophysiological mechanisms that are involved in language use. These are essentially the neurological and physiological processes that Færch and Kasper (1983) include in their discussion of the execution phase of language use. Thus, we can distinguish the visual from the auditory channel and the productive from the receptive mode. In receptive language use, auditory and visual skills are employed, while in productive use the neuromuscular skills (for example, articulatory and digital) are employed. For instance, in the example on pp. 87–8 above, the test taker correctly used her linguistic competence to form the sentence, 'The girl is taller than the boy.' She also used her visual skill to gain access to the non-linguistic information in the picture, her auditory skill to gain access to the information in the administrator's instructions, and her articulatory skill to pronounce the words correctly and to provide appropriate stress and intonation.

Summary

In this chapter, a framework for describing communicative language ability as both knowledge of language and the capacity for implementing that knowledge in communicative language use has been proposed. Communicative language ability consists of language competence, strategic competence, and psychophysiological mechanisms. Language competence includes organizational competence, which consists of grammatical and textual competence, and pragmatic competence, which consists of illocutionary and sociolinguistic competence. Strategic competence is seen as the capacity that relates language competence, or knowledge of language, to the language user's knowledge structures and the features of the context in which communication takes place. Strategic competence performs assessment, planning, and execution functions in determining the most

effective means of achieving a communicative goal. Psychophysiological mechanisms involved in language use characterize the channel
(auditory, visual) and mode (receptive, productive) in which competence is implemented.

This framework is presented as one part of a theory of factors that
affect performance on language tests. The second part of this theory,
a description of the characteristics of test methods that affect
performance on language tests, will be described in the next chapter.

Notes

1   Although words that refer to various aspects of using language
    have been quite clearly defined over the years, there appears to
    be some disagreement in their interpretation. Thus, at the risk of
    adding to this confusion, I will try to indicate exactly how I
    understand and use these words. I use *knowledge* and *compet-
    ence* more or less synonymously, to refer to entities which we
    may hypothesize to be in the minds of language users.
    Furthermore, I use *competence* in Hymes's (1972b) sense, and
    do not limit this to 'linguistic competence', as originally defined
    by Chomsky (1965). The terms *trait* and *construct* are more
    precise synonyms for *knowledge* and *competence*. The term
    ability includes both knowledge or competence and the capabil-
    ity for implementing that competence in language use – the
    'ability to do X'. I consider *communicative language ability*
    to provide a more inclusive definition of *proficiency* than has
    been defined in the context of oral language testing (for
    example, American Council on the Teaching of Foreign
    Languages 1986; Liskin-Gasparro 1984; Lowe 1985, 1986).
    The terms *use* and *perform* (and their noun counterparts) are
    more or less synonymous, referring to the execution, or
    implementation of abilities. *Use* and *perform* thus subsume a
    wide range of terms such as, *listen, speak, read, write, produce,
    interpret, express, receive, understand,* and *comprehend,* which
    themselves have more specific meanings.
2   Carroll (1968) discusses 'linguistic performance abilities', such
    as speed and diversity of response, complexity of information
    processing, and awareness of linguistic competence, but con-
    siders these as essentially outside the construct of language
    proficiency. These will be touched on in the discussion of test
    method factors in Chapter 5.
3   Searle (1969) points out that not all illocutionary acts have

perlocutionary effects associated with them, and argues that perlocutionary effects cannot be considered part of illocutionary acts.

4 A comprehensive discussion of register is given in Besnier (1986).

Further reading

The framework described by Canale and Swain (1980) is seminal to research on communicative competence. This paper includes an excellent review of the research related to the four main components of the framework: grammatical, discourse, sociolinguistic, and strategic competence. Widdowson's (1978) distinctions between usage and use and between text and discourse provide a basis for understanding the relationship between the organizational and illocutionary aspects of language competence. Hymes (1972b) develops the notion of sociolinguistic appropriateness, distinguishing between what is possible, what is feasible, what is appropriate, and what is actually done, in communicative language use. Halliday (1976) discusses the outlines of his theory of functional grammar. Hymes (1972b, 1982) and van Dijk (1977) provide extensive analyses of the features that constitute the context of language use. Richards and Schmidt (1983b) provide extensive examples that illustrate the role of strategic competence in conversation. Richards and Sukwiwat (1983) discuss the effects of transferring native language (Thai) conversational conventions to conversational dis course in a second language (English). Finegan and Besnier (1988) provide excellent discussions of dialects (Chapter 12), and registers (Chapter 13).

Discussion questions

1. Does every native speaker have the same degree of communic-ative language ability? On what competencies are native speakers most likely to be the same?
2. In what aspects of communicative language ability are native speakers most likely to differ? What competencies arise as a result of being in the speech community? Which are a result of education?
3. Discuss the propositional, illocutionary, and perlocutionary acts in the following utterances:
    a. 'There isn't enough sugar in my coffee.'

     b. 'Do you have the time?'
     c. 'I want to speak to the manager!'
     d. 'Trick or treat?'
     e. 'Smoking causes lung cancer, heart disease, emphysema, and may complicate pregnancy.'

4. Is an order of acquisition or learning of language competencies implied by the proposed framework? Must some be mastered before others can be learned? Can some be mastered independently without mastering others?

5. Describe how you might measure an individual's strategic competence in language use.

6. Discuss the roles of language competence and strategic competence in the following exchange between a native speaker (NS) of English and a learner of English (L) (Færch and Kasper 1983:20):

NS: . . . what do you read at home . . . what do you er
L: mmmm . . . er historie
    . . .
NS: do you have history lessons in school
L: . . . kings
NS: when you learn about er I don't know . . . old kings
L: oh yes I have that . . .
NS: but you like reading books about history
L: er this history . . . you know . . . er young histories . . . er
NS: aha
L: not not with this old things you know kings or . . . all that . . .
NS: do you mean . . . recent . . . in more recent years like that
L: er . . . a history is . . . maybe on a boy . . . girl and . . . er young people life and . . . yer
NS: oh you mean a story . . . just a story about people . . . not not

5   Test methods

Introduction

In Chapter 4 a framework for characterizing those abilities that are of interest in language tests was described. That framework provides a means for characterizing the traits, or constructs, that constitute the 'what' of language testing. However, we know that test performance is also affected by the characteristics of the methods used to elicit test performance. Some test takers, for example, may perform better in the context of an oral interview than they would sitting in a language laboratory speaking into a microphone in response to statements and questions presented through a pair of earphones. And individuals who generally perform well in oral interviews may find it difficult to speak if the interviewer is someone they do not know. Some test takers find a cloze test intimidating, and do poorly, while at the same time performing well on a test consisting of the completion of individual sentences, or a multiple-choice test based on a reading passage. 'Live' versus recorded presentation of aural material, personality of examiner, filling in the blanks in isolated sentences as opposed to completing blanks in a text, and the amount and type of text to be processed, are but a few examples of the ways in which the methods we employ in language tests can vary. These characteristics, or 'facets', of test methods constitute the 'how' of language testing, and are of particular importance for designing, developing, and using language tests, since it is these over which we potentially have some control. These test method facets are the primary focus of this chapter.

One way to conceive of a language test is as a means for controlling the context in which language performance takes place. From this perspective, the characteristics of the test method can be seen as analogous to the features that characterize the context of situation, or the speech event, as this has been described by linguists (for example, Firth 1957; Hymes 1964, 1972a; Labov 1972; van Dijk 1977; Brown and Yule 1983). Firth (1957), for example, described the 'context of situation', which he considered the central construct in the study of language, as a 'group of related categories at a different level from grammatical categories but rather of the same abstract nature' (Firth 1957:182). Firth's categories included the verbal and non-verbal actions of the participants, the relevant objects, and the effect of the verbal action. Hymes (1972a) argues that the language used in different speech events is determined, to a large extent, by the components of the context in which they take place – components such as the participants (sender and receiver), the setting, the topic, and the purpose. Similarly, Labov (1972) discusses variation in language use in terms of correlations between linguistic features, or variables, and nonlinguistic variables, such as the speaker, addressee, audience, setting and so forth, in the social context.

The characteristics of test methods can be seen as restricted or controlled versions of these contextual features that determine the nature of the language performance that is expected for a given test or test task. Some of these features are essentially 'givens' in many testing situations. For example, the primary, if not the sole purpose of most language test performance is to demonstrate one's ability in the language of interest, while the roles of the participants are generally, though not necessarily, restricted to those of superior examiner and subordinate test taker. I say 'not necessarily', because one objective of the test developer might be to design test tasks that generalize across a range of language use contexts, adjusting the characteristics of these test tasks in such a way that they retain the essential features of language use contexts, but in focused, idealized form. Thus, in addition to demonstrating a certain level of writing ability, it may be possible for a composition, for example, to serve some communicative purpose, or for the interlocutors in an oral interview to assume roles more in keeping with those typical of non-test language use contexts. The particular way test method facets are designed and controlled, and the correspondence between these and the features of language use contexts will have a direct effect on the 'authenticity' of the test and test tasks. In general, one would expect that the closer the correspondence between the characteristics of the test method and the essential features of language use contexts, the more 'authentic' the test task will be for test takers. The questions of what precisely authenticity in language tests is and how to best achieve it are complex ones, and I will return to these in greater detail in Chapter 8.

Given what is known about the role of contextual features in language use in general, it is not surprising to find that aspects of the test method, which provide much of the context of language tests, affect performance on language tests. Numerous research studies (for example, Clifford 1978, 1981; Brütsch 1979; Bachman and Palmer 1981a, 1982a; Shohamy 1983b, 1984a) have demonstrated that the methods we use to measure language ability influence performance on language tests. Bachman and Palmer (1981a), for example, found that scores from self-ratings loaded consistently more highly on method factors than on specific trait or ability factors, and that translation and interview measures of reading loaded more heavily on method than on trait factors. Similarly, Bachman and Palmer (1982a) found that scores from both self-ratings and oral interviews consistently loaded more heavily on test method factors than on specific trait factors. A similar effect of elicitation procedure on language learners' interlanguage systems has been noted by Douglas (1986), who provides several examples of how language use varies as a function of context.

Performance on language tests thus varies as a function both of an individual's language ability and of the characteristics of the test method. Furthermore, the effects of different test methods themselves are likely to vary from one test taker to another. Not every test taker, for example, will be equally adept in oral interview tests; and while one person might perform very well on a multiple-choice test of reading, another may find such tasks very difficult. As a possible explanation for this variation in performance across different testing situations, Douglas (1986) has suggested that communicative language ability itself may vary from one test task to another (p. 158), and proposes that 'our communicative competence paradigm needs to be evaluated in terms of its ability to deal with variation in production of target forms in different interactional situations' (p. 159). I believe the assessment function of strategic competence, as described in Chapter 4, provides a mechanism for explaining this variability. That is, the manner in which language ability is implemented as a plan for execution will vary, depending on how a given test task is presented, and the test taker's assessment of the specific test task and of the language use required by the task.

Test performance is also affected by individual attributes that are not part of test takers' language ability. These may include test takers' cognitive and affective characteristics, their 'real world knowledge', and factors such as their age, sex, native language, educational and socio-economic background. Measurement specialists and language testers alike have tended to consider factors such as these as potential sources of test bias, and they are discussed in Chapter 7. At the same time, these individual attributes may interact with aspects of the methods used in any given test, so that individuals with different backgrounds and personalities may perform differentially on different types of language tests. Several researchers, for example, have found higher correlations between the cognitive style or ability, field independence, and performance on cloze tests than between field independence and other types of language tests (for example, Hansen and Stansfield 1981; Stansfield and Hansen 1983; Hansen 1984; Chapelle 1988).

Another set of individual characteristics that is of interest to test developers and users is related to the amount and type of preparation or prior experience with a given test among test takers. These characteristics are sometimes referred to as 'test-wiseness', and include a variety of general strategies related to efficient test taking, such as the conscious pacing of one's time, reading questions before the passages upon which they are based, and ruling out as many alternatives as possible in multiple-choice items and then guessing among the ones remaining. In general, such strategies should facilitate the test-taking process by reducing the effect on performance of unfamiliarity with features of a given test method. This same purpose is served by provision of careful instructions with examples as part of the test itself.

In addition to such general strategies, there may be differences in test takers' preparation for specific tests. One of the primary differences between the *Test of English as a Foreign Language* (TOEFL) and the *Certificate of Proficiency in English* (CPE), for example, is that individuals who take the CPE have almost always taken a course whose syllabus is based upon the CPE, while individuals who take the TOEFL may or may not have had any prior preparation for this test. At one level, this may mean that the CPE is more of an achievement test, while the TOEFL is more of a proficiency test, as these have been defined in Chapter 3 (p. 71). From a test development point of view, however, what this means is that the developers of the CPE can make a number of assumptions about test takers' familiarity with the procedures and tasks included in the test, that the developers of the TOEFL cannot. These differences in assumptions about test takers' prior familiarity with the test and the testing procedures are reflected, to a large extent, in differences in the explicitness of the instructions of these two tests, with the instructions for the TOEFL generally being more explicit than those for the CPE (Bachman, Davidson, and Lynch 1988).

Because of what is known about the effects of test methods on test performance, I believe it is necessary, in order to more fully understand variation in language test performance, to develop a framework for delineating the specific features, or 'facets' of test method. This use of the term 'facet' for specific aspects of test method is consistent with Guttman's (1970) discussion of facet design and analysis, which he has proposed as a basis for test design. In addition, aspects of test method can be treated as 'facets' in the examination and analysis of reliability, within the framework of generalizability theory (Cronbach *et al.* 1972), which is discussed in Chapter 6. Finally, both Guttman and Cronbach would appear to consider the delineation of test method facets as essential to the investigation of construct validity (Guttman 1980). A discussion of facet theory is beyond the scope of this book; interested readers can find discussions in the works noted at the end of this chapter.[1] Suffice it here to say that the principles of facet design have informed the framework of test method facets described below, and that I believe facet theory to have important applications in the design and use of language tests.

Much of the research mentioned above has dealt with test methods as if they were monolithic wholes. Bachman and Palmer (1982a), for example, examined the following test methods: 'oral interview', 'writing sample', 'multiple-choice', and 'self-rating', while Allen *et al.* (1983) treated 'oral production', 'multiple-choice', and 'written production' as distinct test methods. The problem with such a holistic approach to describing test methods can be demonstrated by considering some examples. There are a number of specific testing procedures, such as the oral interview, elicited imitation, and reading aloud, that might be included under an 'oral production' method. And within each of these procedures one can find variations. Oral interviews, for example, can vary in length, elicitation procedure, the specific tasks required (for example, answering yes-no questions, offering a supported opinion), the number of participants, and so forth. Similar 'sub-methods' can be delineated within the 'written production' method (for example, filling in the blanks, sentence completion, composition), and variations can be described within these sub-methods. Bachman and Palmer's (1982d) 'writing sample' method, for example, included several different writing tasks, such as the description of a picture, providing appropriate greetings and closings to various types of correspondence, and a comparison and contrast essay. Similarly, their self-rating measure included three different types of items (Bachman and Palmer 1981b, 1988). And in even as well-defined a procedure as the multiple-choice we find variation in item format (for example, matching, complete the missing information, direct question), length, and task specification (for example, select correct answer, select 'best' answer, identify or select incorrect part).

Clearly, then, there are a large number of test method facets, many of which have gone uninvestigated. Thorndike (1951), Stanley (1971), and Feldt and Brennan (1988), for example, in their discussions of sources of variation in test scores do not include a category of 'test method'. All of these writers do, however, list several factors that I would consider to be either aspects of test method itself, or to vary as a function of test method. Stanley (1971), for example, mentions 'stable response sets', 'item types', 'comprehension of the specific test task', 'momentary "set" for a particular test', 'conditions of testing', and 'interaction of personality, sex, or race of examiner with that of examinee' (Stanley 1971: 364). Similarly, Feldt and Brennan (1988) mention 'situational factors' in the environment of test takers, and 'instrumental variables', related to inconsistencies in the performance of electronic or mechanical equipment that may be utilized in testing, and in the degree to which test tasks adequately sample the abilities of different individuals (Feldt and Brennan 1988: 107). Measurement specialists who have written about test method have discussed several general aspects of test method: range of tasks, stimuli, or situations included in the test, instructions that describe the test taker's task, the type of response expected, and how responses are evaluated (for example, Cronbach 1971, 1984; Popham 1978, 1984).

A framework of test method facets

There have been a number of descriptions of the characteristics of language testing methods over the years. Savard (1968) and Mackey (1968), for example, proposed classification schemes that would be useful for cataloguing language tests. Carroll (1968) provided an extensive treatment of test method facets in language tests in which he described tasks required in individual language test items. Carroll discussed four general types of language test tasks, which he distinguished largely in terms of differences in their stimulus and response characteristics. Cohen (1980) also discusses factors such as the item stimulus and response formats, the tested response behavior, and scoring procedures as 'distinctive elements' of a test.

A similar framework has been described by Clark (1972), who discusses 'test modalities'. Clark uses the term *stimulus* for 'any spoken, written (including printed) or otherwise presented materials to which the student attends in the test situation and which represent or convey the testing task at issue' (p. 27). He further distinguishes stimulus modalities in terms of whether they are presented in writing or speech, or pictorially, and if presented in writing or speech, in terms of language – foreign or native. Clark defines a *response* as 'any physical activity on the part of the student in reaction to the stimulus materials', and categorizes them into two types: ' "free" – in which the student makes a spoken or written response – and "multiple-choice" – in which he simply selects an answer from among two or more alternatives' (p. 27). Clark characterizes 'free' responses according to whether they consist of speech or writing, and whether they are in the foreign or the native language.

Weir (1983), drawing on the work of Munby (1978), Morrow (1977, 1979), and Hawkey (1982), presents a different framework of categories for describing what he calls 'communicative test events'. This framework includes 'general descriptive parameters of communication', such as activities, setting, and dialect; 'dynamic communication characteristics', such as realistic context, relevant information gap, and normal time constraints; and 'task dimensions', such as the amount of communication involved, functional range, and referential range.

The framework of test method facets that I present in this chapter is an extension and recasting, to a large extent, of Carroll's and Clark's taxonomies, incorporating more recent views of the nature of language. Thus, where Carroll speaks of 'linguistic complexity' as a characteristic of test tasks, I refer to the 'nature of the language'. Where both Carroll and Clark use the term 'stimulus', I use 'input', to avoid the negative connotations the former term has acquired in language teaching over the years, and to underscore its potential *function*, as the term 'input' has recently been defined with reference to language learning and teaching (Krashen 1982). At the same time, many of the dimensions in Weir's framework have analogues in the test method facets presented here. Thus, Weir's parameter of 'setting' is a part of my 'test environment,' while his 'relevant information gap' would appear to be a function in part, at least, of the degree of contextualization.

I present this framework of test method facets not as a definitive statement or exhaustive list, but rather as a guide for empirical research that I hope will lead to a better understanding of the extent to which these facets affect performance on language tests, and to the discovery of additional facets not included.[2] The five major categories of test method facet are: (1) the testing environment; (2) the test rubric; (3) the nature of the input the test taker receives; (4) the nature of the expected response to that input, and (5) the relationship between input and response. These categories of test method facets are listed in Figure 5.1.

Testing environment

Test takers might be expected to perform differently under differing environmental conditions. Bowen (1978), for example, found that although scores on repeated administrations of an integrative grammar test under differing conditions were highly correlated with each other, average levels of performance differed significantly across administrations. *Testing environment* includes the facets: (1) familiarity of the place and equipment used in administering the test; (2) the personnel involved in the test; (3) the time of testing, and (4) physical conditions. The *place* of testing may be either familiar or unfamiliar, and one might expect a familiar place to be less threatening than an unfamiliar one. Test takers tested with familiar *equipment* such as paper and pencils or tape recordings might perform better than those tested with unfamiliar equipment, such as computers. Tests administered by familiar *personnel* may be conducive to better performance than those administered by unfamiliar personnel, and test takers might perform differently when examined by a superior, a peer, or a subordinate. In addition, research indicates that the number of individuals involved in interactive tests, such as an oral interview, can affect test takers' perceptions of the test, and thus, presumably, their performance (for example, Brütsch 1979; Shohamy 1982; Scott 1986). The *time of testing* may affect test performance, with test takers performing better or worse on a test given early in the day, for example, than on one given just after a heavy noon meal or late in the day. Finally, test takers might perform differently under different *physical conditions*. One aspect of this is the presence of noise in the environment. Other physical characteristics of the test environment include facets such as temperature, humidity, seating arrangement, and lighting.

Test rubric

The *rubric* of the test consists of the facets that specify how test takers are expected to proceed in taking the test. These include the test organization, time allocation, and instructions.

1 FACETS OF THE TESTING ENVIRONMENT

Familiarity of the place and equipment
Personnel
Time of testing
Physical conditions

2 FACETS OF THE TEST RUBRIC

Test organization
Salience of parts
Sequence of parts
Relative importance of parts

Time allocation

Instructions
Language (native, target)
Channel (aural, visual)
Specification of procedures and tasks
Explicitness of criteria for correctness

3 FACETS OF THE INPUT

Format
Channel of presentation (aural, visual)
Mode of presentation (receptive)
Form of presentation (language, nonlanguage, both)
Vehicle of presentation ('live', 'canned', both)
Language of presentation (native, target, both)
Identification of problem (specific, general)
Degree of speededness

Nature of language
Length
Propositional content
  Vocabulary (frequency, specialization)
  Degree of contextualization (embedded/ reduced)
  Distribution of new information (compact/ diffuse)
  Type of information (concrete/abstract, positive/negative, factual/counter-factual)
  Topic
  Genre
Organizational characteristics
  Grammar
  Cohesion
  Rhetorical organization
Pragmatic characteristics
  Illocutionary force
  Sociolinguistic characteristics

4 FACETS OF THE EXPECTED RESPONSE

Format
Channel (aural, visual)
Mode (productive)
Type of response (selected, constructed)
Form of response (language, nonlanguage, both)
Language of response (native, target, both)

Nature of language
Length
Propositional content
  Vocabulary (frequency, specialization)
  Degree of contextualization (embedded/ reduced)
  Distribution of new information (compact/ diffuse)
  Type of information (concrete/abstract, positive/negative, factual/counter-factual)
  Topic
  Genre
Organizational characteristics
  Grammar
  Cohesion
  Rhetorical organization
Pragmatic characteristics
  Illocutionary force
  Sociolinguistic characteristics

Restrictions on response
Channel
Format
Organizational characteristics
Propositional and illocutionary characteristics
Time or length of response

5 RELATIONSHIP BETWEEN INPUT AND RESPONSE

Reciprocal
Nonreciprocal
Adaptive

Figure 5.1   Categories of test method facet

Test organization

The majority of language tests consist of a collection of parts, which may be either individual items or questions, or sub-tests which may themselves consist of individual items. The salience of these parts, how they are sequenced, and their relative importance can be expected to affect test takers' performance.

Salience of parts

The test taker's perception of the test, and hence his performance, may be affected by both the salience of the parts as distinct entities and by the descriptions of these parts that are provided by the test developer. In tests in which the parts consist of individual items, for example, test takers may adopt differing response strategies, depending on a number of factors, such as their perception of the relative difficulty of the different items, how they are instructed to respond, and the amount of time allocated.

Some tests consist of a number of separate sub-tests. (Another way to view this is to consider the test itself to be a battery of tests.) In many tests these different sub-tests are explicitly identified with labels and brief statements describing what the sub-test is intended to measure. In the multiple-choice part of Bachman and Palmer's (1982c) *Test of Communicative Competence in English*, for example, the sub-tests are identified by separate labels, 'Test A' through 'Test J', and the instructions of each subtest begin with a statement of the ability tested. Test A, for example, is identified as 'a test of how well you [the test taker] can recognize correct grammar', while Test E is 'a test of how well you [the test taker] can recognize a well-organized English paragraph', and Test J is a test 'of how well you [the test taker] can recognize natural English'. In other tests, the descriptive information is provided in the label, such as 'listening comprehension', 'reading comprehension', and 'composition', as well as by different input formats, as in the *Certificate of Proficiency in English* (University of Cambridge Local Examinations Syndicate 1987). At the other end of this continuum of salience are tests in which the different parts are not explicitly marked at all. The parts of the ILR oral interview, for example – warm-up, level check, probe, and wind-down – are not explicitly marked, and are not intended to be noticed at all by the test taker (Lowe 1982).

Sequence of parts

The sequence in which the different parts are presented may also influence test takers' performance. In tests which are designed to measure level of ability ('power tests'), the parts are typically of differing degrees of difficulty, and ordered from easy to difficult. In tests aimed primarily at measuring an individual's rate of perform-ance ('speeded tests'), on the other hand, items will be of nearly the same level of difficulty, and may be ordered more or less at random. In either case, the sequence in which items are presented in a test reflects, to some degree, the test designer's intention, and introduces an element of control on the test takers' responses. However, different individuals respond differentially to this control. Some individuals may answer items in the sequence presented, while others may not. That is, some test takers may move systematically through the test, answering the items in sequence, irrespective of how easy they find them or of how much time they spend on them, while others may adopt a strategy of going through the test several times, answering only the items they are absolutely certain of the first time, successively answering items that they find more and more difficult, and leaving any that they feel they simply cannot answer until the last, at which time they may attempt to guess the correct answer. In observing hundreds of individuals take cloze tests over the years, for example, I have noticed that these two strategies clearly stand out, even though test takers are explicitly instructed that they should read the entire passage through before attempting any answers, and that they need not fill in the blanks in the order in which they occur. I would hypothesize that for this type of test, test takers who skip around are likely to achieve higher scores than those who rigorously move through the passage, filling in the gaps in the order in which they occur.

In tests that consist of separate sub-tests, test takers may not be given the opportunity of answering them in the order in which they choose. This is particularly true for standardized tests, in which sub-parts may actually be timed separately, as with the *Test of English as a Foreign Language*, and the *Certificate of Proficiency in English*. If the sub-tests are relatively independent of each other, the sequence of presentation may be a less important influence on test performance than it is in tests in which the sub-tests are interrelated, as in the *Ontario Test of English as a Second Language* (Wesche *et al.* 1987; Wesche 1987) and the *English Language Testing Service* (Seaton 1983; Criper and Davies 1988; Alderson 1988).

In computer-adaptive tests, the order in which items are presented is a function of the test taker's responses. Thus, if the test taker misses a given item, the next item to be presented will be slightly easier, while correct responses will lead to the presentation of progressively more difficult items. In this method of sequencing test items, not only do test takers have no direct choice over the sequence in which items are presented, but test takers at different ability levels are likely to take different items, or the same items in different sequences. Furthermore, a given test taker might be presented different items in different orders upon retaking the test.

Relative importance of parts

The parts of a test are not always weighted equally, with reference to the test taker's total score. If the test score is the sum of the individual part scores, the relative importance, or weight, of any given part to the total score will be a function of how much test takers' scores on that part vary and the degree to which their scores on that part are correlated with their scores on the other parts that make up the test. A part in which nearly everyone receives the same score, and which is highly correlated with the other parts of the test, for example, will contribute relatively little to the total test score. A part with a wide range of scores, and that is *not* correlated very highly with the other parts of the test will contribute considerably to the total test score. Since this relative weighting is a function of the way the test scores themselves are distributed, rather than of the relative importance accorded by the test developer, it is referred to as 'self-weighting'. This 'self-weighting' applies not only to scores on sub-tests, but also to item scores that may be added to yield a test score. The relative importance of individual scores, either sub-test or item, that are added to make a total, or composite score, are always self-weighting as a function of how much they vary and the degree to which they are correlated with the other scores that are added to make the total score. Therefore, the test developer must consider the self-weighting of the parts when designing a test whose parts are intended to be weighted in a particular way.

Test performance may be affected to the extent that the test taker is aware of the relative importance of the parts of the test. In many cases the test taker is not aware of the weighting of the parts of the test, and hence may assume that all are weighted equally. If, however, the relative importance of the parts is made explicit, such as through explicit statements or through time allocations, test takers might be expected to tailor their test-taking strategies to maximize their opportunity to do well on the parts that are the most important.

Time allocation

The amount of time allocated for the test or its parts is likely to affect test performance. In some tests, the time limit is such that not all test takers can manage to answer all the items or parts of the test. In 'speeded tests' such as these, test scores are partly a function of the test taker's level of ability and partly a function of the speed or rate at which she can complete the test. In other tests, sufficient time is allocated for all, or the vast majority of test takers to attempt every item. In 'power tests' such as these, the test score will be primarily a function of the test taker's level of ability. Test users need to be aware of these differences in what speed and power tests measure, and, wherever appropriate, use a test format and time allocation that distinguishes level of ability from speed, or rate of performance. In addition to variation in the overall allocation of time, the input of the test can vary in the speed with which it is presented, and this is discussed below under facets of the input.

Instructions

Test *instructions* play a crucial role in test takers' performance, since their performance depends, to a great extent, on how well they understand the conditions under which the test will be taken, the procedures to be followed and the nature of the tasks they are to complete. Madsen (1982), for example, mentions unclear or inaccurate instructions and inadequate time allocation as sources of test anxiety, and hence, influences on test performance. Facets of instructions include: (1) language; (2) channel; (3) the specification of procedures and tasks, and (4) the explicitness of the criteria for correctness.

Language and channel
The *language* in which the instructions are presented might be the test taker's native language or the language being tested (target language), or both. The instructions might be presented in either the aural or visual *channel*, or both. That is, in some tests the test takers may read along while listening as the instructions are presented to them aurally.

Specification of procedures and tasks
The instructions generally specify both the procedures to be followed in taking the test and the nature of the test taker's tasks. Procedures include the way in which test takers are to respond, such as whether responses are to be marked on the test itself or on a separate answer sheet, whether they should circle or check the alternative they choose, how they should fill in missing blanks, how they are to record their spoken response into a microphone, and so on. The instructions can also identify the different parts of the test, the order

in which they are to be completed, their relative importance, and the amount of time allocated to each.

The instructions will also generally specify the tasks the test taker is expected to complete. This task specification will indicate both the type of response required (selection, construction) and the form the response is expected to take (language, nonlanguage, native/target language). In general, the more complex the task required and the less familiar it is to the test takers, the greater the burden carried by the instructions to specify clearly what is expected of the test taker. A person who has never taken a multiple-choice test, for example, may not understand the format unless the instructions are clearly stated. Performance may also be facilitated by the use of sample test items that illustrate what the test taker is required to do. We could expect test takers to perform better when they clearly understand the task that is required of them.

Explicitness of criteria for correctness

The *criteria for correctness* may be quite clear, as in a multiple-choice test of grammar, in which there is only one grammatically correct choice. In other tests the criteria may be rather vague, as in a writing test in which the test taker is simply told to make her composition clear and well organized. In cases where scoring procedures and criteria for correctness are clear and explicit, the test taker's knowledge of these can be expected to affect her test performance directly. It is useful, I believe, to distinguish the effects of different scoring criteria on test *scores* from their direct effect on test *performance*. Thus, even though different criteria for correctness are likely to affect test scores, if these criteria are not explicit and hence not known to test takers, the difference is not likely to affect their test performance directly. For example, using different criteria for correctness – exact versus acceptable words – in a cloze test clearly affects individual test scores (for example, Oller 1972; Alderson 1979a, 1980). However, this difference in scoring criterion is not likely to affect test takers' performance unless they are informed of which criterion is to be used. In this chapter I am concerned primarily with the effects of scoring criteria on performance; the effect of different scoring criteria on test scores is discussed in Chapter 6.

In Chapter 4 (pp. 105–6) an example was given of how differing criteria for correctness might affect the test taker's test-taking strategy, and hence his performance. In multiple-choice tests it is common practice for instructions to state whether or not a correction for guessing will be used, often in the form of a statement such as, 'your score on the test will be the number of questions you answer correctly; there will be no penalty for guessing'. The intent of such an instruction is generally to encourage test takers to rule out as many of the incorrect options as they are able, and only then to make their best (i.e., at least partially knowledgeable) guess among the remaining alternatives. The scoring criteria given in the instructions to writing tests are also likely to affect test performance. If grammatical correctness is stated as a scoring criterion, for example, some test takers may simply avoid attempting to use structures they are not sure of. Other scoring criteria, on the other hand, may be less inhibiting. In one of the writing tasks used by Bachman and Palmer (1982d), for example, test takers were shown a picture and instructed to 'write about (describe) the picture, in as much detail as possible. You will be graded on your vocabulary, including *how much* you write without repeating.'

There are also measures in which there is no 'correct' answer.[3] Measures of attitudes toward various aspects of language, language instruction, and members of a given speech community, or of motivation for learning a language, for example, ask individuals to respond in a way that reflects their personal feelings, perceptions, or ways of thinking (for example the scales developed by Gardner and Lambert 1972) Similarly, self-ratings of language ability are aimed at eliciting responses that individuals believe characterize their level of ability or what they can do with language (for example, Oskarsson 1978; Bachman and Palmer 1981b, 1988; von Elek 1985; Davidson and Henning 1985; LeBlanc and Painchaud 1985). In measures such as these, if it can be reasonably assumed that the respondents in a particular testing situation have no reason to dissimulate their true perceptions, their responses would *de facto* be considered correct.

Input and expected response

The characteristics of the input and the expected response are two additional sets of facets that affect performance on language tests. *Input* consists of the information contained in a given test task, to which the test taker is expected to respond. The response is slightly more complex, in that a distinction needs to be made between the expected response and the test taker's actual response (Cohen 1980). We can specify the expected response through our test design, and can attempt to elicit it through appropriate instructions, task specification, and input. The expected response is thus part of the test method.

The actual response, however, is a function not only of the test method, but of factors beyond the test developer's control, not the least of which is the language ability to be measured. Despite our best efforts to provide clear instructions and precise task specifications, test takers do not always respond in ways we expect. In a writing task, for example, a test taker's response might be an acceptable sample of discourse, but entirely off the topic presented in the instructions and input. A difference such as this presents problems in interpretation and scoring. Is the difference due to lack of clarity or to ambiguity in the instructions or input? Is the topic or the task inappropriate for the test taker? Has the test taker avoided the topic to conceal an inadequacy in language ability? Or has the test taker misunderstood the language of the writing task, because of low ability in reading?

Questions such as these illustrate the fact that the nature of the expected response is based on the assumption that the test taker will be submissive to the context control introduced by the specific test task. The problem in interpretation and scoring is determining whether the actual response is a reflection of the test taker's assertion of 'normal' language processing or of incompetence. Which is more fair (to all test takers, including those who responded as expected), to score the response as a sample of written discourse, ignoring the fact that it is off the topic, or to penalize the test taker for not responding as expected? Depending on what is the cause of the discrepancy between expected and actual response, and how we decide to score the actual response, either the reliability or the validity of the test taker's score, or both, may be compromised.[4] The qualitative analysis of actual responses, along with that of test takers' self-reports can help clarify questions such as these. Such analyses can also provide a wealth of additional information, including insights into both the adequacy and appropriateness of the test instructions and tasks, the test takers' strategies of test taking and their levels of language ability (cf., for example, Cohen 1984, forthcoming; Grotjahn 1986). The analysis of actual responses and of test takers' self-reports is thus an important part of test development, as it can lead to more appropriate specification of tasks and expected responses.

Input and expected response constitute two distinct sets of test method facets. Nevertheless, because of the similarities between input and expected response characteristics, as well as the interaction between them, I will discuss them together. The facets of input are two-fold: format and nature of language. In addition to these two facets, expected response facets include the types and degree of restrictions on response.

Input format

The input format includes the *channel, mode, form, vehicle,* and *language* of presentation, the *identification of the problem,* and the *degree of speededness.*

Channel and mode of presentation

The input may be presented either aurally or visually, in the receptive mode, while the expected response may be either oral or written, and is in the productive mode. The input channel in a listening comprehension test, for example, would be aural, while the expected response channel could be either visual or oral, depending, for example, on whether the test taker marks the correct choices on multiple-choice questions, or responds by speaking. Some tests may use both aural and visual channels for input, as in a listening test in which a text is presented aurally and questions are presented in writing. It is also conceivable that a test could employ both oral and visual response channels, as in a test in which the test taker listens to a lecture and is then required to produce both a written précis and a spoken summary.

Form of presentation

The presentation can consist of a language sample, as in a reading comprehension test in which the test taker reads a passage written in the target language. It might also consist of nonlanguage material, as in a test in which the test taker sees only pictures, or a physical action such as standing up or sitting down. The presentation could also consist of a combination of language and nonlanguage material, as in a test consisting of reading passages along with tables and graphs that the test taker must interpret. Finally, it could consist of rules, as would be the case if the test taker read a descriptive rule and had to determine whether the rule was correct or incorrect.

Vehicle of presentation

If the form of presentation consists of language and the input channel is aural, we need to further distinguish 'live' human input from 'canned' human input, as in a tape recording. This distinction would seem to be identical to that made by Clark (1979) in characterizing 'direct' and 'semi-direct' tests of speaking ability.

Language of presentation

If the input consists of language, it can be in either the target language or in the test taker's native language. A multiple-choice test in which the stem and alternatives are in the target language is an example of the former, while a translation test in which the test taker is given selections in her native language to translate into the target language is an example of the latter. Research in EFL reading comprehension tests suggests that test takers perform significantly better when questions about a reading passage in the target language are presented in their native language (Shohamy 1984a).

Identification of the problem

In some input formats, the problem is clearly identified, focusing the test taker's attention on a specific, limited amount of material to be evaluated. The 'problem' may be identified in a number of ways, such as underlining, deletions, or instructions calling attention to a particular form. One of the characteristics of 'discrete-point' tests, which attempt to measure specific components of language ability separately, is this precise identification of the problem. 'Editing' tasks, on the other hand, can vary considerably in the degree of specificity with which the problem is identified, from tasks that require the test taker to correct the errors identified in underlined words or phrases in a text, to tasks in which test takers must both identify and correct an unspecified number of errors in a given text. In some 'integrative' tests, such as the oral interview, composition, or dictation, the problem areas may not be identified at all.

Degree of speededness

The input may be perceived as speeded if it is presented at a rate that calls the test taker's attention to speed as a factor in performance. An obvious example is a speed reading test. Another example would be a listening comprehension test in which the test taker is scored on how quickly he can formulate a reply to the meaning of the input. The perception of speededness may vary from one test taker to another. Palmer (1981), for example, administered an oral production test using pictures as stimuli and assigned scores according to the amount of time it took test takers to communicate correctly the unique content of one picture from a set of four pictures. He found that test takers who perceived the test as speeded avoided long, grammatically correct sentences, in order to quickly convey the correct information in an almost telegraphic style.

This aspect of speededness pertains to the test taker's *perception* of the importance of speed in her completion of the test tasks. Clearly, for test takers whose language abilities are weak, any test involving the processing of language at even moderate speed is likely to be difficult. This difficulty and perception of speededness may lead to guessing, or compensatory test taking strategies, as in Palmer's (1981) picture description test described above, or even the complete lack of response to the test task. However, I distinguish between speed of processing, which is a factor in test performance, as it is in non-test language use, and speededness, which may be an artificial condition of the test task.

Format of expected response

The format of the expected response includes the *type of response*, the *form of the response*, and its *language*.

Type of expected response

One type of expected response is what Popham (1978) refers to as the 'selected' response, which characterizes multiple-choice tests. This can involve simply selecting the correct answer from among several alternatives, or the identification of an incorrect alternative, as in a sentence with several different words or phrases underlined, only one of which is incorrect. In other tests, this response type may require the actual location of a problem or error from among a wide range of 'alternatives', as in a text editing task.

The second expected response type is the 'constructed response' (Popham 1978), in which the response consists of the production of a language sample in response to the input material. Such language production may be highly structured, as in tests that elicit single sentence or phrasal responses, such as the *Bilingual Syntax Measure* (Burt *et al.* 1975) and the *Ilyin Oral Interview* (Ilyin 1972). In some tests, on the other hand, the response is fairly unstructured. Examples of such tests are the *ILR Oral Interview* (Lowe 1982), the *Oral Interview Test of Communicative Proficiency in English* (Bachman and Palmer 1983a), and the writing tasks described by Jacobs *et al.* (1981). Research supports the intuitive hypothesis that constructed response types will generally be more difficult than selected response types (for example, Samson 1983; Shohamy 1984a).

Both selected and constructed responses can involve metalanguage, in which the test taker uses language to describe the characteristics of the *language* of the input. Constructed metalinguistic responses typically consist of a description or analysis of the language itself, such as the statement of a generalization or rule about the organizational (grammatical, textual) structure or an analysis of the illocutionary force of the input material. Metalinguistic responses are generally limited to tests that are intended to measure the test taker's conscious understanding of the characteristics of language, as might be appropriate for students of linguistics or applied linguistics, or for language teachers.

Form of expected response
The form that the response is expected to take may be language, nonlanguage or both. Selected responses, for example, typically require only a nonverbal response, such as making a mark on a piece of paper. Constructed responses, on the other hand, will generally consist of language, but may also consist of nonlanguage material, as in a test in which test takers draw a picture or complete a chart, based on input material, or of physical actions, as in a test in which test takers respond to commands such as 'Stand up!', 'Open the window!', or 'Walk across the room and throw your toothbrush in the wastebasket!'

Language of expected response
If the constructed response is expected to consist of language, it may be in the native language, as in tests requiring the test taker to translate target language input material, or in the target language.

Nature of language input and expected response

When the form of the input or response is language, that language can be characterized by its *length, propositional content, organizational characteristics*, and *illocutionary characteristics*. It is largely these characteristics of language that determine the comprehensibility of the input, whether this is in the aural or visual channel. In a listening test, for example, these characteristics will affect the degree to which the test taker comprehends the input of the test, while in a reading test, it is these characteristics that will determine, by and large, the readability of the input text.[5]

Length
Input and responses that consist of language samples may vary in length from a single word, to a sentence, to an extended piece of discourse. While length in itself may not be a critical facet affecting performance, the longer the language sample, the greater the potential effects of the other characteristics discussed below.

Propositional content
Propositional content can be described with reference to the characteristics of the information in the context and in the discourse: *vocabulary, degree of contextualization, distribution of information, type of information, topic*, and *genre*.

Vocabulary

The vocabulary used in the input and response can vary in a number of ways. Without discussing this in great detail, we might expect that the less frequent the vocabulary used in the input, the more difficult the task will be. Vocabulary can also vary in terms of its domain of usage, so that items in which the vocabulary is highly specialized, such as that associated with technical registers and slang, might be expected to be relatively more difficult than those in which the vocabulary is less specialized.

The vocabulary of the test input may also include cultural references and figures of speech, depending on the group of individuals to be tested and the purpose of the test. With beginning level students, for example, it may not be appropriate to include very many of these, while at more advanced levels, these features, which often characterize particularly effective communicative language use, may be of considerable interest to the test user.

Degree of contextualization

Cummins (1983) has described the notion of 'context embeddedness' as one characteristic that differentiates typical non-academic inter- active language use from academic language use. Context-embedded language use is that which is supported by a wide range of meaningful linguistic, paralinguistic, and situational cues in the context. To put it another way, language use that occurs in a context rich with familiar or known information that is relevant to the information expressed in the discourse is context-embedded. This notion of relevant contextual information is similar to what Brown and Yule refer to as 'activated features of context', which con- stitute 'those aspects of the context that are directly reflected in the text, and which need to be called upon to interpret the text' (Brown and Yule 1983: 75). The degree to which the discourse is contextualized can be expressed in terms of the ratio of familiar, relevant 'contextual' information to the new information in the discourse:

$$\text{Degree of contextualization} = \frac{\text{contextual information}}{\text{new information in discourse}}$$

Context-embedded language use thus involves discourse in which there is a *high* ratio of contextual information to new information, while context-reduced language use involves discourse in which there is a *low* ratio of contextual to new information.

Contextual information may be of three types: (1) that which is supplied directly by the immediate physical context; (2) that whose recall is prompted by the information in the input language, and (3) that developed in the input discourse itself. In face-to-face interactive language use the language users have access to information that is communicated nonverbally, such as through gestures and facial expressions. An oral interviewer, for example, may communicate her interest in words and also in her facial expression, gestures, or posture. In language use that is not interactive between persons, nonverbal information may be provided through various graphic figures, or line drawings, as in tests that require the test taker to describe the events depicted in a sequence of cartoons. Relevant information may also be available in the immediate physical environment, as in an oral interview in which the test taker is asked to describe the objects in the room.

Language use can also be contextualized with respect to inform-ation whose recall is prompted by information in the discourse. For example, in a writing test, the test taker may be asked to write about a topic that the tester presupposes he will know or be able to recall, such as comparing and contrasting some feature of his native country with a comparable one in a foreign country. Another example would be a reading comprehension test in which the subject matter of the input is presupposed to be familiar to the test taker. Recent research in reading has demonstrated that prior knowledge of content, or content schemata, has an effect on both native and foreign or second language reading (for example, Steffensen *et al.* 1979; Berkowitz and Taylor 1981; Johnson 1981; Carrell 1987). The effect of prior knowledge of content on performance on reading comprehension tests has also been demonstrated in a number of studies (for example, Chacevych *et al.* 1982; Alderson and Urquhart 1985a, 1985b). With respect to degree of contextualization, then, tests in which contextual information is provided by the test taker's content schemata would appear to be highly context-embedded.

The language of the test input, however, is not always context-embedded. In designing and writing language test tasks, we necessarily make assumptions, or presuppositions, about the relevant information the test takers bring to the task. When these presuppos-itions are inappropriate for a particular group of test takers, the result can be test tasks that are context-reduced. An example of this might be a reading test in which the passages contain fairly technical information and concepts not familiar to the test takers. In a great deal of written discourse, particularly academic or scientific dis-course, the author presupposes the knowledge of certain information on the part of the reader. To the extent that the reader has this knowledge and is able to recall it, the discourse will be context-embedded. If, however, the reader either does not have this information or is not able to recall it, the discourse may be context-reduced, and more demanding to interpret.

We can also develop context-reduced tasks by design, as is typically the case when we attempt to minimize the possible effects of differences in prior knowledge among a group of test takers. Thus, in developing listening comprehension tasks for language proficiency tests, for example, it is common practice to either select or write texts that are of a relatively esoteric but non-technical nature, so that no group of test takers will be favored by prior knowledge of the content. Because of its importance as an influence on language test performance, and because it is a facet that is particularly amenable to design and control, the content area, or topic, of the test language is discussed as a separate facet below.

Finally, relevant contextual information may be found in the discourse itself. An example of this would be a reading test consisting of an unlabeled map of a city and a text that describes the city, in which the test taker is required to answer questions based on information in both. Similarly, in an oral interview, the discourse that evolves during the course of the interview provides an ever increasing pool of contextual information that is available for interpretation of subsequent utterances. Brown and Yule (1983) refer to this information as 'co-text', and argue that this provides an expanding context that affects the way an individual interprets the discourse: 'any sentence other than the first in a fragment of discourse, will have the whole of its interpretation forcibly constrained by the preceding text' (p. 46). Similarly, Krashen (1985) refers to the cumulative build-up of contextual information in reading as the 'first few pages effect', citing anecdotal reports by intermediate second language students that in reading a novel 'they find the first few pages of a new author's work hard going. After this initial difficulty, the rest of the book goes more easily' (Krashen 1985: 73).

The amount of context in the input will affect the extent to which the test taker is able to interpret and respond to the propositional content of the discourse. Thus, the more context-embedded the input is, the more likely the test taker will be able to respond to its propositional content. At the same time, the degree of contextualization of a given input is likely to vary from one test taker to another. This is because the test taker's ability to interpret and respond to the propositional content of the input will be a function not only of the amount of context in the input itself, but also of the amount of relevant information she is able to activate, or of her 'presuppositional pool', which Venneman (1975) describes as information 'constituted from general knowledge, from the situative context of the discourse, and from the completed part of the discourse itself' (Venneman 1975: 314, quoted in Brown and Yule 1983: 79).

The degree of contextualization is also a consideration with respect to the relationship between the expected and actual response. Here we need to consider both the relevance of the information in the actual response to that in the input and the newness of the information provided in the actual response. This is particularly critical in tests in which the response involves the production of a relatively unstructured language sample. Responses that lack relevance, either to the input material or to contextual information, may have an effect on the testing procedure itself. In an oral interview, for example, if the test taker produces answers that are irrelevant to the questions asked, the examiner will most likely have to alter the elicitation procedure in an effort to continue the discourse. Similarly, writing samples that are not relevant to the topic or task required by the test may make it difficult to apply the intended criteria for scoring.

Responses are 'new' if they supply information that is not known and that cannot be predicted from the context. This characteristic is related to the notion of an 'information gap' found in most definitions of communication (for example Johnson 1982; Cherry 1957). That is, communication takes place when 'new' information is provided that fills in the complementary gaps in the amount of information possessed by the communicators.

Distribution of new information
This facet characterizes the distribution of the new information that must be processed and manipulated in order for the test taker to successfully complete a given test task. Discourse in which new information is distributed over a relatively short space or time may be called *compact*, while discourse with new information distributed over a relatively long space or time may be called *diffuse*. For example, in a group oral interview consisting of fairly rapid exchanges, with each of the participants speaking one or two sentences in turn, the new information in each utterance is likely to be compact. Listening to a lecture and then summarizing its content, on the other hand, requires keeping in mind information from the

beginning, the middle and the end, and the relevant information is thus diffuse.

We might hypothesize that input in which the information is either highly compact or highly diffuse will be relatively difficult to process. With highly compact input, the test taker may have very little opportunity to negotiate meaning, or may have to negotiate meaning very quickly, and such performance will be very demanding of his competence. An example of this might be a highly speeded listening comprehension test in which test takers have little time to consider their answer to a question before the next question begins. Input in which the information is highly diffuse may also be very demanding, in that it requires the test taker to encode information, hold it in memory and then recall it for subsequent processing. Examples of this would be a task that required summarizing a lengthy report, or one in which the test taker has to answer questions based on a lecture.

Input in which the test taker has adequate opportunity to negotiate meaning, either through interaction or through repeating or slowing down the input, is neither compact nor diffuse. An oral interview conducted at 'normal' conversational speed, for example, provides ample opportunity for the test taker to interact with the interviewer in a way that enables her to interpret the information in the discourse and relate it to information in the context. Similarly, in a reading test with an ample time allotment, the test taker can read at his own pace, and reread sections that he finds difficult. Input in which the distribution of information is neither highly compact nor highly diffuse would thus not be expected to place undue demands on the competence of the test taker in either interpreting or responding. This suggests that one way in which we might attempt to 'probe' the test taker's highest level of ability would be to make the information more compact. This may be partly what characterizes that part of some oral interviews in which the examiner does try to push the test taker beyond his 'comfort zone' with respect to content, speed of speech, and so forth.

Type of information
The type of information in input and expected response can be classified along three dimensions: concrete/abstract, positive/negative, and factual/counterfactual. We generally think of *abstract* information as that whose mode of representation is primarily symbolic or linguistic, whereas *concrete* information is capable of representation in other than linguistic modes, such as visual, auditory, tactile, or

kinesthetic. Consider the abstract statistical concept 'standard deviation'. It can be represented linguistically as 'the square root of the sum of the squared differences from the mean divided by the number of cases', or in abbreviated form, using mathematical symbols:

$$s = \sqrt{\frac{\Sigma\,(x - \bar{x})^2}{n}}$$

It is more difficult to represent this concept visually (as a labeled diagram of a normal curve) or in other modes. Other abstract concepts such as 'honesty' can be visualized, but this nearly always takes the form of a parable or story which one associates with honesty. Static visualization of abstract concepts appears to exist primarily in cultural stereotypes such as Rodin's 'Thinker' as a visualization of the abstract concept of 'thinking'.

In contrast, the concrete concept 'Harley-Davidson motorcycle' can be represented in many modes. It can be represented linguistically ('a two-wheeled, 45 degree V-twin vehicle'), kinesthetically (the feeling of the G-forces transmitted through it in a high-speed banked turn), olfactorily (the smell of the oil), auditorally (the crack of the exhaust), and visually (its low, extended lines). We might hypothesize that input consisting of abstract information will be more demanding of the test taker than will input containing largely concrete information.

Information can also vary in terms of the degree to which it is negative. Information that includes no explicit negative elements or markers can be considered to be positive, as in 'Fred and I have agreed to meet at the airport at 10 o'clock.' Information presented with negative markers can vary in both the level and number of elements negated. The sentences, 'I didn't want John to go to the store', and 'I wanted John not to go to the store', for example, both include a single negative element, but differ in the level of negation, with the matrix sentence containing the negative element in the former, while in the latter, the embedded sentence carries the negative element. The sentence, 'I didn't expect him not to understand', on the other hand, contains two negative elements, one in the matrix sentence and one in the embedded sentence. It could be hypothesized that the more negative information contained in the input, the more difficult it will be to process.

Counterfactual information is that which includes assertions about conditions which are possible or probable in some alternative world, but not in the known, factual world (van Dijk 1977:79).

Counterfactual sentences typically take the form of conditionals, such as, 'If I won the lottery I would retire', and 'If cows could jump over the moon, dogs might laugh', and differ in the degree of similarity they imply between the alternative world and the factual world. A possible world in which I won the lottery would be quite similar to the actual world, in that most of the laws of nature would still hold. The possible world in which cows fly and dogs laugh, however, would be quite different from the factual world. We might hypothesize that counterfactual information would be more difficult to process than factual information, and that counterfactuals in which there are great dissimilarities between the factual and possible worlds would be more difficult to interpret than those in which the factual and possible worlds are quite similar.

Topic
The topic of a given piece of discourse is generally understood as 'what it is about'; it is the subject matter of the discourse. The topic of the input in the majority of language tests is determined by the test writer, who typically chooses topics that she feels will be interesting and relevant to test takers and at the same time neutral with respect to potential differences in their background knowledge. In tasks that require a constructed response, the topic of the response is expected to match, or be relevant to that of the input. For example, in a test in which a test taker listens to a short lecture followed by a question about the content of the lecture and is required to give a short spoken answer, the individual's answer may be evaluated on its relevance to the topic of the lecture and question in addition to, or instead of, its formal accuracy. As indicated above, with respect to the relationship between new information in the response and information in the input, responses in which the topic is unrelated to the topic of the input may make it difficult to score the response according to the criteria set by the test writer.

In tests in which there is a reciprocal or interactive relationship between input and response (discussed below), it is possible for the topic of the discourse to be determined jointly by the test administrator and the test taker. In the oral interview test of communicative proficiency developed by Bachman and Palmer (1983a), for example, in preparation for a 'formal' presentation that is part of the interview, the examiner and the candidate go through a list of possible topics and determine which is best suited to the candidate's interests and knowledge.

Studies such as those cited above have documented the fact that the topic of input has a substantial effect on test takers' performance.

In tests of reading comprehension this is sometimes referred to as 'passage effect'. If the subject matter of the input is familiar to some test takers and not others, these individuals may have an unfair advantage, resulting in better performance. Clearly, we want to avoid this as a source of 'test bias'. On the other hand, we also want the subject matter to be interesting and relevant to test takers. The problem this creates for test writers is that of avoiding either extreme. That is, in the attempt to avoid possible bias, test writers may select topics that are very general or innocuous, and thus entirely unengaging to test takers. One the other hand, topics that are expected to be engaging because they are interesting and relevant may be biased in favor of some test takers for that very reason. One possible solution to this problem is the presentation of a fairly large number of topics, which could reduce the likelihood of serious bias.

Genre

Hymes (1972a) uses the term 'genre' to refer to a component of speech that has identifiable 'formal characteristics that are traditionally recognized', giving as examples the categories of 'poem, myth, tale, proverb, riddle, curse, prayer, oration, lecture, commercial, form letter, and editorial' (Hymes 1972a: 65). According to Coulthard (1977), a genre is one type of stylistic structure for organizing sentences and utterances into larger units such as greetings, farewells, and prayers (Coulthard 1977: 37). Brown and Yule (1983) suggest that genres may differ in their formal characteristics such as paragraph structure, thematic sequence, the stereotypical ordering of events in time, and the distribution of sentence types and pronominal forms. They also indicate that differences in genres affect how individuals interpret discourse:

> we pay attention to those salient features which are constitutive of the type of genre, and expect that the peripheral features will be as they have been in the past. Obviously there will be types of occasions which have not occurred within our past experience. We have cultural stereotypes which suggest that such occasions are difficult for us ... because we do not know the appropriate responses.
> (Brown and Yule 1983: 63).

It could be argued that particular types of language tests (for example, multiple-choice, cloze, dictation) themselves constitute genres, and that these activate certain expectations in test takers familiar with them, thus facilitating the task of test taking for these individuals, while making the task more difficult for test takers not familiar with the particular type. In addition, if the language of the input in a given test is characteristic of a genre that is unfamiliar to the test taker, we would hypothesize that tasks that depend on the interpretation of that input would be relatively difficult. Unfamiliarity with the characteristics of a given genre may also make the expected response more difficult. Consider, for example, the relative difficulty of composing a letter of complaint to a toy manufacturer, in response to a prompt in a writing test, for a high school student and for an adult who has several children. Similarly, an oral role play requiring interviewees to negotiate with an airline official for a free hotel room because of a late flight arrival is likely to be easier for test takers who are experienced travelers than for those who have traveled very little by air.

Organizational characteristics

Organizational competence was described in Chapter 4 (pp. 87–9) as comprising those abilities that are related to controlling the formal organization of language. This formal organization is a characteristic of the discourse of both the input and the response, and is of three types: grammar, cohesion, and rhetorical organization. In general, the longer the language sample, the greater the need to incorporate organizational characteristics to make it interpretable. Thus input material consisting of a list of words and a list of meanings to be matched with the words involves very little organization, while a test requiring test takers to answer questions based on a lecture presented orally, or to summarize the propositional content in a reading passage, will involve the full range of organizational characteristics.

The input material in tests that require a constructed response is generally accurately organized, in terms of grammar, cohesion and rhetorical organization. The examiner's questions in an oral interview, for example, are most likely to be within the norms of grammar and cohesion for semi-formal spoken discourse. Likewise with many tests requiring a selection response, as in a reading comprehension test in which the test taker must choose the best answer from among several possible answers, based on a reading passage, the material is organized in terms of grammar, cohesion, and rhetorical structure.

However, input material in tests that require a selected response may include errors involving one or more organizational characteristics. An example of input involving grammatical errors is a multiple-choice item in which several words in a sentence are underlined, one of which is ungrammatical. The following test item is an example of input involving errors in both cohesion and rhetorical organization (Bachman and Palmer 1982c). In this item the test taker is asked to choose the paragraph that is the best organized.

(1) The king of Ruritania declared war on Utopia because its dictator had sent him a highly insulting letter. Moreover, the Ruritanian farmers needed more land, and besides, the dictator had called the king a cowardly fool in the letter.

(2) The dictator of Utopia sent a highly insulting letter to the king of Ruritania, calling him a cowardly fool. Moreover, the Ruritanian farmers needed more land. Therefore, the king of Ruritania declared war on Utopia for these two reasons.

(3) The dictator of Utopia thought the king of Ruritania was a cowardly fool. He sent the king a highly insulting letter to tell him so. The Ruritanian farmers needed more land. For these three reasons, the king of Ruritania declared war on Utopia.

(4) The king of Ruritania declared war on Utopia for two reasons. First, the Utopian dictator had sent the king a highly insulting letter, calling him a cowardly fool. Second, the Ruritanian farmers needed more land.

(5) The dictator of Utopia sent a highly insulting letter to the king of Ruritania, calling him a cowardly fool. The king therefore declared war on Utopia. A second reason for the war was that the Ruritanian farmers needed more land.
(Bachman and Palmer 1982c:E2)

Pragmatic characteristics

Illocutionary force
The input and response can also be characterized in terms of their illocutionary force, or the language functions performed. As noted by Searle (1969), the function performed by any 'exam question' is not to elicit information, but rather to find out if the examinee knows something (p. 66). Input consisting of a language sample thus performs the 'primary' function of requesting a response and could, in this somewhat trivial sense, be regarded as functional.

More important, however, is the extent to which the input performs language functions in addition to the manipulative function that is inherent in the test. At one extreme are 'nonfunctional' tests in which neither the input nor the response performs any illocutionary act. An obvious example is a multiple-choice test of grammar in which the input material in the stem and choices serves solely as a medium for focusing the test taker's attention on the grammatical form of the language, and in which the response is simply a mark on a piece of paper. At the other end of the spectrum are tests in which both the input and the response involve the performance of a variety of language functions. An example of this is a well conducted oral interview in which the examinee is involved in the conversation to the extent that he virtually forgets the formal organizational characteristics of the discourse.

Determining the functionality of a given test task is problematical, in that the degree of functionality depends on the interaction between the test taker and the task material. (In this sense, functionality is essentially what Widdowson (1978) has called 'authenticity'.) A given task may be functional for some test takers and not for others. Consider the following example, in which test takers are asked to complete a portion of a two-line dialogue:

'I have a psychology exam tomorrow and need to study. I wonder where my textbook is.'

'I haven't seen it, but you   borrow mine if you like.'

The utterances in this dialogue perform several functions. The first utterance functions both as a statement of fact and a request, while the second is both a factual statement and an offer of assistance. However, in order to complete this item correctly, the test taker need respond only to the formal context that requires the modal 'may' (or 'can'), without any consideration of the illocutionary force of the utterance. It is possible, of course, that some test takers may be aware of the different functions performed, and consider these in formulating their response. Thus, the extent to which test takers are aware of and respond to the functions performed by input is likely to vary from individual to individual, and gauging the functionality of test tasks such as the example above, which do not require the interpretation of illocutionary force for correct completion, is virtually impossible to do on the basis of content alone.

An additional complexity is that input varies from nearly 'unifunctional' to multifunctional. Simple, short instructions for constructing a diagram, for example, might be entirely manipulative in function, while a poem to be read and reacted to might be primarily imaginative. In an oral interview, on the other hand, the input might perform a variety of functions, including requesting information (manipulative), presenting propositions or opinions (ideational), and telling a joke (imaginative).

Sociolinguistic characteristics
The last set of facets by which the language of the input and response are characterized are sociolinguistic characteristics, which consist of (1) dialect or variety; (2) register; and (3) naturalness. Since it is these sociolinguistic characteristics of language use that are most directly linked to the context in which language use takes place, these features in both the input and expected response will be determined, by and large, by factors in the testing situation, such as the characteristics of the target language to be tested, the group of individuals being tested, and the abilities to be tested.

Dialect or variety   While there may be instances in which we need to test an individual's ability to use different dialects or varieties of a given language appropriately, in the majority of language testing situations the target language to be measured is in some sense regarded as a 'standard' dialect or variety. The discussion of the reasons for a given dialect's or variety's coming to be considered a standard by a given group of language users is far beyond the scope of this book.[6] Suffice it to say that these reasons are largely geographical, social, political, economic, and historical. In designing, developing, and using language tests we obviously need to be sensitive to these factors, and avoid using tests in which the dialect or variety of input is inappropriate for the testing situation. That is, we need to make every effort to ensure that the dialect or variety of language of both the input and the expected response is appropriate to the language use context in which test takers are most likely to find themselves using the language, or which is recognized by language educators as the most appropriate variety. For example, to the extent that the dialect of language used and taught in schools is different from students' native regional or social dialects, it may be inappropriate for the language of tests used in schools to be characterized by features of these dialects. With respect to English, there are many countries with local varieties of English, and developers and users of language tests in these countries need to be sure that the language of the test is consistent with local educational policy, if the results of the test are to be used for making decisions within the school system. Thus, it may be that for some test purposes, the local variety of English is most appropriate, while for other purposes, either British or American English may be more appropriate. In India, for example, it may be appropriate to use Indian English as the test language in some contexts and British English in others.

In testing second or foreign language proficiency, the variety of language used in the test needs to be appropriate to the needs of the learners. Thus, for American college students studying Spanish, it may be that a variety of Spanish spoken in Latin America is appropriate, while Castilian Spanish might be more appropriate for students of Spanish in England. In testing English as a foreign language, the variety of English used in the test may be determined by the test developer's perception of the target variety that is most appropriate to test takers' needs, so that the *Test of English as a Foreign Language* includes American English in its input, while the *Certificate of Proficiency in English* includes British English.

Even though the issues related to dialect and variety are extremely volatile, both politically and socially, in many language testing contexts, the question of the dialect or variety of the language of input is often either simply not considered, or a choice is made on the basis of inaccurate or incomplete information. This is particularly true of languages such as French, Spanish or English, which exist in several major varieties in different parts of the world, and about which there seems to be considerable controversy regarding which variety, if any, is to be considered the 'standard'.

Register As with dialect and variety, the register of test language needs to be appropriate to the context and needs of test takers. In many tests, particularly those designed to be used in educational settings, the register of input and expected response is rather formal. The language of reading comprehension tests, for example, is appropriately in a formal written register. In other settings, a more informal register of test language may be appropriate. When the register of the test language is not entirely appropriate to the register of the target language use context, however, the test results may provide misleading information for making educational decisions about individuals, as has been documented by Cummins (1980b).

Since the use of the register that is appropriate to a situation is an essential component of communicative language use, in many situations it is necessary to measure the ability to use more than one register. One example of how this might be done in a test of writing was provided on page 96 in Chapter 4, while in a multiple-choice format, an error–recognition task could be used, in which the test taker is asked to identify the word or phrase that is not appropriate to the particular item. In this latter case, the language of the input would then vary, so as to establish the register of the context in each item. In their oral interview, Bachman and Palmer (1983a) specify that the two interviewers are to assume different roles, one formal and the other informal, so as to establish appropriate contexts for assessing test takers' ability to use these two registers appropriately.

Restrictions on expected response

Virtually all language use, even in situations which might be characterized as 'authentic' or 'natural', is restricted in various ways by the context or situation. Upon meeting a colleague on the way to class, for example, we are usually not free to utter whatever may come into our head, but are restricted both in the illocutionary act we perform (greeting), and in the register we use (formal, informal).

The language used in language tests is sometimes characterized as 'non-natural', or 'non-normal', or relatively 'artificial'. One way to characterize artificiality of language use is in terms of the extent to which variation in the language use of the expected response is inappropriately restricted. Five types of such restrictions can be distinguished: (1) restrictions on the channel; (2) restrictions on the format; (3) restrictions on organizational characteristics; (4) restrictions on propositional and illocutionary characteristics; and (5) restrictions on the time or length of the response.

Restrictions on channel
Language use takes place under a wide variety of conditions. Conversations are carried out face-to-face, in quiet rooms, and on noisy streets. Phone conversations take place out of visual contact over clear lines and over static-filled circuits. Speeches are attended in quiet halls with excellent sound amplification equipment and in noisy parks. In fact, many types of language use normally take place under less than ideal conditions. Consider, for example, announcements of arrivals and departures in airports and train stations, or conversations with taxi drivers, which usually occur in a noisy vehicle with a two-way radio blaring in the background and with neither participant able to see the face of the other. One would expect such conditions to have some effect on the performance of the participants.

In many language testing situations, such interference in the channel does not occur and, therefore, cannot influence the performance of the participants. Consider an oral interview administered in a quiet room in a face-to-face situation, in which the candidate is required to simulate a phone conversation, with the examiner playing the role of a friend (Bachman and Palmer 1983a). Though phones are provided, they are not hooked up, and the examinee and examiner are permitted to see each other. Under these conditions, there is restriction on normal interference found in the channel. At the other extreme, variability can be restricted by adding interference to the channel, as in the well-known 'noise test' experiments in which differing degrees of controlled hiss ('white noise') were added to various types of input material to measure language proficiency in listening (Spolsky *et al.* 1968, Spolsky *et al.* 1972; Gradman and Spolsky 1975).

Restrictions on format
The type and form of the response will be determined by the specification of the task set by the test. In some tests the format is highly restricted, as in selection or identification response types, while in other tests the format may be fairly unrestricted, as in a composition test requiring the production of a writing sample.

Restrictions on organizational characteristics

Restrictions on grammatical forms
In all language use the grammatical forms used to encode messages are selected according to the inclinations of the user, consistent with the contextual demands of the situation. In production, the language user selects the forms she may feel are appropriate for performing a given illocutionary act, while in reception, she has no advance warning of what forms will be encountered other than what can be predicted from her knowledge of the natural redundancies and restrictions on normal use.

Restrictions on form at the word level are common in language testing. The most obvious example is the multiple-choice vocabulary item in which test takers are required to deal with the meanings of a specific pair of words, without the opportunity to express the equivalent meaning in their own words. Restrictions on form at the sentence level occur in tests such as the *Bilingual Syntax Measure* (Burt *et al.* 1975), where the materials are designed to elicit particular structures and thus restrict variability.

Restrictions on the organization of discourse
A relatively high level of restriction on language performance is in the organization of discourse. An example of such a restriction would be requiring that a student follow a specific rhetorical pattern, such as comparing and contrasting two things, or arguing for or against a given proposition. Another example is the oral interview role play

discussed above, in which the subject is told to pretend to call up a close friend and converse with him on the telephone. In this particular role play, the organization is restricted by instructing the subject to do four things: first, inquire about the friend's health and the health of the members of his family; second, find out what the friend had been doing; third, suggest that the two of them do something together that evening; and finally, make plans for how to get where they have decided on going (Bachman and Palmer 1983a). This organizational restriction tends to be very demanding, since it is difficult for a speaker to keep in mind an outline he is supposed to follow and at the same time determine what to insert into the outline.

Turn taking, one aspect of rhetorical organization in conversational language use, can also be restricted by externally imposed rules rather than by having the turn taking emerge from the interaction between the language users. An example of this is an oral communication test involving pictures (Palmer 1972). In this test each problem, or discourse unit, consists of the examinee's asking exactly three questions of the examiner in order to determine which of four similar pictures the examiner has in mind. Thus, each dialogue consists of six turns ordered as follows: question, answer, question, answer, question, answer. Each turn ends when a single question or answer has been produced. Without this restriction the test taker might well adopt a rather different pattern of turn taking, if given the general problem of determining which of four pictures the examiner has in mind.

Many language testing situations restrict the performance at an even higher level, that of the selection of the speech event itself, such as a discussion, a debate, or writing a composition. Indeed, test takers are often required to participate in a particular speech event when they have little interest in doing so. While it may be the case that such a test could reinforce whatever negative attitudes test takers may already have, it is not clear to what extent this level of restriction in language tests could be considered artificial. This is because this type of restriction occurs fairly frequently, both in the context of formal language learning and outside the classroom in 'natural' language performance.

Restrictions on propositional and illocutionary characteristics
Restrictions may also apply to the propositional content and illocutionary force of language use. Consider the meaning of the following utterance: 'How many children do you want to have?' The propositional content is an inquiry about a specific individual's

preference as to family size, and one function performed by this utterance is a request for information. Another function, however, is likely to be an interpersonal relationship defining function. Consider the illocutionary force of this question, were it to be posed unexpectedly by a young man on his first date with a young woman. His intention might well be to increase the intimacy of the relationship, that is, to define it, from his perspective, as one close enough to permit the discussion of prospective family size. The effect, of course, might be to break up the relationship, if the woman were not at all interested in either getting that serious or in having children. In language tests involving open-ended role plays, the selection of propositional content and illocutionary acts may be relatively unrestricted. However, some test takers may realize that they are merely going through the motions of communicating, and this realization may restrict the relationship-defining function of their performance.

A language test totally restricting variability in propositional content while still allowing some variability in illocutionary force could be constructed by giving a test taker private, written instructions to express a specific proposition in such a way as to perform one of two illocutionary acts. For example, he might be instructed to express the propositional content, 'How many times have you missed class this semester?' with the illocutionary force of a complaint, as opposed to that of a request for information. The examiner could be told in advance what proposition to expect but not what illocutionary force to expect. In this test, the propositional content of the message would be completely restricted, yet some variability would be allowed in the illocutionary force.

Frequently, language tests restrict the illocutionary force of responses. For example, picture description tests in which the examinee is allowed only to describe what is in a given picture in order to allow the examiner to distinguish between the picture described and a number of other similar pictures (Palmer 1972) totally restrict the illocutionary force of the examinee's responses, yet allow a fair amount of variability in propositional content.

Restrictions on time or length of response

Language use is always constrained, to some degree, by time or length. We are all familiar with the brevity necessitated by the cost of international long distance telephone calls, the anxiety of having to 'fill up' a 50-minute period on a program, or the luxury of 'whiling away' a summer's afternoon with an elderly aunt or uncle. In testing situations, administrative considerations almost inevitably place additional restrictions on time or length.

In summary, there are five different areas in which restrictions can be placed on expected responses in language testing situations. Whenever artificial restrictions are imposed, some of the variability encountered in 'normal' language performance is likely to be lost, and some of the authenticity as well.

As the studies cited above indicate, there has been considerable research into the effects of differences in specific input or expected response facets on language test performance. In addition, several studies have examined differences in what are essentially input-expected response units. Pike (1979), for example, found variations in correlations among thirteen different multiple-choice question formats, while Clark and Swinton (1980) found variations in both correlations and item characteristics among eleven speaking test question types. In both of these studies, item or question formats were treated as units, rather than as different combinations of input and expected response facets. Research into self-ratings also indicates difference in performance as a function of input and expected response. LeBlanc and Painchaud (1985), for example, found that self-rating questions whose input content was closely related to test takers' language use needs and situations were more highly correlated with language proficiency test scores than were those that were stated in abstract terms. Bachman and Palmer (1988) found that self-relating questions that ask test takers to judge how difficult various aspects of language use are for them appear to be better indicators of specific language abilities than are questions that ask how well they can use various aspects of language.

Relationship between input and response

The relationships between input and response in language tests can be classified into three types: *reciprocal*, *nonreciprocal*, and *adaptive*.

Reciprocal input and response

Reciprocal language use can be defined as the use of language by one individual to produce an effect in another individual through the reduction of uncertainty with knowledge of results. This definition contains a number of components. The term 'language' focuses on the verbal (spoken or written), as opposed to the non-verbal (for example, gestures, pictures) components of discourse. The phrases

'one individual' and 'another individual' make explicit the requirement that at least two parties – a sender and a receiver – be involved.
The phrase 'to produce an effect' indicates that the language use has
a communicative goal, or illocutionary intention. The phrase
'reduction of uncertainty' characterizes the means by which the
communicative goal is effected, that is, by means of a change in
information at the disposal of the receiver. One of the distinguishing
characteristics of reciprocal language use, then, is *interaction*, the
fact that the language used by the sender at any given point in the
communicative exchange affects subsequent language use. Finally,
'with knowledge of results' makes explicit the second distinguishing
characteristic of reciprocal language use, the presence of *feedback*.
An example of reciprocal language use is the short dialogue in
Chapter 4 (p. 92), in which two parties were involved. Each
performed illocutionary acts to affect the other. There was in each
case a reduction of uncertainty. And each speaker had knowledge of
the results of his utterance on the other. Reciprocal language use is
illustrated in Figure 5.2.

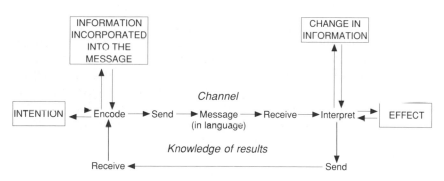

Figure 5.2 A model of reciprocal language use

Nonreciprocal input and response

Nonreciprocal language use is that in which there is no interaction
between language users, that is, in which continual give and take
between two or more individuals does *not* take place. In nonreciprocal language use, therefore, there is no feedback, and the language
used does not affect subsequent language use. In reading a book, for
example, the reader is seldom able to give feedback to the author,
and the text of the book will not change, irrespective of whether or
not the reader finds certain statements objectionable or of questionable accuracy and notes this in the margins, or needs to stop and look

up a word in a dictionary. Other examples of nonreciprocal language use include letter writing, reading, listening to lectures, watching movies, and talking to oneself. Nonreciprocal language use is illustrated in Figure 5.3.

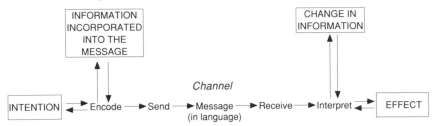

Figure 5.3   A model of nonreciprocal language use

Reciprocal tests or test tasks are those in which the test taker's response affects subsequent input, and in which the test taker receives feedback on the relevance and correctness of his answer. An example would be a well-conducted oral interview, in which there is continual interaction between input and response. Nonreciprocal test tasks, on the other hand, are those in which both interaction and feedback are missing, as in a cloze or dictation test. If we consider the wide range of language test types in current use – multiple-choice, cloze, dictation, composition, and tape-mediated tests of speaking, to mention some of the more popular ones – it is clear that many, if not the majority, are nonreciprocal. However, this is not to imply that such tests are necessarily less valid, reliable, or useful than tests that are reciprocal. On the contrary, inasmuch as language use in general is often nonreciprocal, as in reading books and newspapers or listening to radio and television programs, such tests constitute entirely legitimate approaches to testing language abilities.

Just as language tests can restrict the nature of the expected response, they can also restrict the relationship between input and expected response. An example of a restriction to nonreciprocal language use is a listening comprehension test in which the test taker listens to a conversation between two persons and is then asked, by a third person, a question about that conversation. In this case the test taker is unable to interact with either the participants in the conversation or the third person who asks him a direct question, and receives no feedback on the relevance of his answer.

Adaptive input and response

The relationship between input and response is adaptive if the input is influenced by the response, but without the feedback that characterizes a reciprocal relationship. In an adaptive, or 'tailored' test, the particular tasks presented to the test taker are determined by her responses to previous tasks. An individual taking an adaptively administered multiple-choice test, for example, typically begins with an item that is of medium difficulty. If she answers this item correctly, the next item presented will be slightly more difficult. If she misses that item, the next item presented will be slightly easier, and so on. In most adaptive tests, the test taker is not aware of the correctness of her responses, nor that subsequent tasks are determined by these responses. And herein lies the difference between adaptive and reciprocal tests. Adaptive tests do not involve the feedback or reduction of uncertainty through knowledge of results that characterizes reciprocal language tests. An oral interview, for example, is reciprocal to the extent that both the examiner and the examinee negotiate meaning. Since this negotiation of meaning necessarily involves a certain amount of unpredictability, the examiner's input will vary as a function of the examinee's responses, and such an interview will also be adaptive. The adaptive administration of multiple-choice items described above, however, is not reciprocal, since the test taker may be totally unaware of the effect of her responses on the selection of test items, and receives no feedback on the correctness of her answers. Thus, reciprocal tests are necessarily adaptive. In adaptive tests, however, the reduction of uncertainty may involve only the test administrator, so that not all adaptive tests are reciprocal. This distinction is important, since the absence of interaction that characterizes adaptive tests may be a factor that influences some test takers' perceptions of authenticity, and hence the way they respond to test items. The characteristics that distinguish reciprocal, nonreciprocal and adaptive relationships between input and response are summarized in Table 5.1.

Relationship between input and response	Feedback: knowledge of relevance or correctness of response	Interaction: response affects subsequent input
Reciprocal	+ (present)	+ (present)
Adaptive	− (absent)	+ (present)
Nonreciprocal	− (absent)	− (absent)

Table 5.1   Distinguishing characteristics of relationships between input and response

One of the most promising and challenging areas of research and development in language testing is that of computer adaptive testing, or the application of computers and related technology to the design, administration, and analysis of tests. There has been considerable work in this area to date (for example, Stansfield 1986a; Larson 1987; Henning 1987) and I will return to this topic in Chapter 8.

Applications of this framework to language testing

The applications of this framework to language testing are potentially in four areas: (1) the description of existing language tests; (2) the design of new tests; (3) the validation of language tests, and (4) the formulation of hypotheses for language testing research.

The description of language tests

Test users are frequently faced with the need to compare and evaluate different tests with respect to their possible utility for a given testing need. If we want to assess prospective students' level of language ability in order to make the appropriate placement into a language program, for example, we may wish to determine if an appropriate test is available for use, rather than developing one of our own. In other situations, we may be interested in finding a test that will be useful for assessing achievement in a language program.

While the information about test tasks that is typically provided in test manuals by test developers may be adequate descriptions of their own tests, this information is often not sufficient to permit detailed comparison of two or more tests, or the comparison of a test with the content and learning tasks included in a language program. This is because test developers are under no particular constraints to describe their tests in terms of either each other's test descriptions or specific course syllabi. In situations such as these, a common framework such as that provided in this chapter could be very useful for describing and comparing the types of tasks included in two similar tests or in a test and a language program.

An example of such a comparative description of different language tests is that done as part of the Cambridge-TOEFL Comparability Study (Bachman, Kunnan, Vanniarajan, and Lynch 1988; Bachman, Davidson, and Lynch 1988; Bachman, Davidson, Lynch, and Ryan 1989; Bachman, Davidson, Ryan, and Choi 1989). This study was aimed at examining the comparability, in the broadest sense, of the EFL proficiency test batteries developed by the Educational Testing Service on the one hand, and the University of Cambridge Local Examinations Syndicate, on the other. One aspect of the study was the comparison of the tasks required in the two sets of tests. For this comparison, two types of measures were used: (1) frequency of occurrence of various elements, and (2) subjective ratings by experienced language testers of the items or parts of the different tests on scales that corresponded to the test method facets in the framework presented in this chapter.

Bachman, Kunnan, Vanniarajan, and Lynch (1988) counted frequencies of occurrence of different characteristics of input in the reading comprehension parts on one form of the *Test of English as a Foreign Language* (TOEFL) and one form of the *Certificate of Proficiency in English* (CPE). Among their findings, they reported that on the average the CPE reading passages were longer than were TOEFL reading passages, both in terms of number of words and number of clauses. Another contrast was found in the types of sentences used in reading passages and stems of vocabulary items: while both the TOEFL and CPE reading passages contained high percentages (60 and 68, respectively) of complex sentences, stems of TOEFL vocabulary items contained only 43 per cent complex sentences, as opposed to the CPE's 84 per cent. With respect to illocutionary acts, the CPE reading passages were found to include a much wider variety of speech acts than did the reading passages of the TOEFL.

Using subjective ratings of experienced language testers, Bachman, Davidson, and Lynch (1988) found considerable differences between the structure sections on one form of the TOEFL and one form of the *First Certificate in English* (FCE) in several facets of rubric: relative importance of parts, specification of procedures and tasks, and explicitness of criteria for correctness. They also found that the TOEFL structure items contained higher proportions of abstract (68 and 22 per cent, respectively) and negative information (22 versus 8 per cent) than did items in the comparable part of the FCE, while neither test contained much counterfactual information. Finally, while raters judged 58 per cent of the TOEFL items to be 'academic', 30 per cent 'technical', and 23 per cent 'American culture' in topic, none of the FCE items were rated as being in these categories.

Language test design

As indicated in Chapter 3, an essential step in the development of language tests is operationalizing the constructs that we want to measure. In many testing programs, test writers work from a table of specifications, so as to ensure that different items and forms of the test are equivalent in content, or that the content of the test adequately represents the content of a syllabus. Clearly, the more detailed the table of specifications, the easier it should be to assure such equivalences in content. But while tables of specifications are often quite detailed in terms of the components of ability to be tested, they often fail to specify the facets of the test tasks with similar precision. For example, a table of specifications for a test of English grammar might contain an extensive and detailed list of the specific structures to be covered, but may say little about the test method facets, other than to indicate that a four-choice multiple-choice format is to be used.

Proponents of criterion-referenced testing have long advocated an extension of the traditional table of specifications to a detailed set of descriptions or procedures for generating individual test tasks or items. Several approaches, including 'item forms' (Hively *et al.* 1973), 'amplified objectives' (Popham 1974), and 'test specifications' (Popham 1984), have achieved fairly widespread use among practitioners.[7] One feature that these approaches have in common is that in addition to specifying the ability or learning objective to be tested, the attributes of both the stimulus and response are described in detail. In a recent application of this approach to the development of language tests, Griffin *et al.* (1988) have demonstrated that the detailed specification of item characteristics, in addition to the 'objective' of the item, can provide a basis for relating patterns of test performance more closely to teaching and learning sequences in language programs. I believe that the framework of test method facets described in this chapter provides a basis for the further refinement of this approach to language test design and development.

In addition to providing a detailed basis for the description of different tests for purposes of selection, and for the design of specific language tests, the framework of test method facets described here may provide language testers with an appropriate means of codifying and describing, at a very useful level of detail, the tests they are developing, using, or researching, for purposes of improved and more standardized communication within the field of language testing itself.

The validation of language tests

The process of test validation will be discussed in detail in Chapter 7. One of the main points that is made there is that a detailed description of the aspects of the test method is as essential to the validation process as is that of the abilities to be measured. The validation of language tests must therefore be based on a detailed description of both the abilities to be measured and the facets of the test methods. This is true of any type of language test, be it achievement or proficiency, norm- or criterion-referenced. An example of the application of the frameworks presented above to language test validation is the study reported by Bachman, Davidson, Ryan, and Choi (1989) in which the content and task analysis of the *Test of English as a Foreign Language, Test of Written English, Speaking Proficiency in English Assessment Kit*, the *Certificate of Proficiency in English*, and the *First Certificate in English* was done as a first step in investigating the comparability of these tests. Similar approaches have been followed by other language testing researchers. Grotjahn (1986), for example, has discussed 'logical task analysis' as a basis for making predictions and testing hypotheses relevant to validation research, while Perkins and Linnville (1987) discuss 'construct definition' as an approach to construct validation. Both of these approaches involve describing characteristics of test tasks or items, and promise to enrich the research in the validation of language tests.

The formulation of hypotheses for language testing research

As stated in Chapter 1, one of the goals of language testing research is to investigate the factors that affect performance on language tests. Considerable research has already demonstrated that test methods affect performance on language tests, and much of this has examined the effects of specific facets, either by themselves, or as they interact with other facets.

An example of this is the research which has examined a wide range of facets in the cloze test, such as deletion ratio (for example, Oller 1975; Alderson 1979b), type of deletion (for example, Ohnmacht and Fleming 1974; Bachman 1982, 1985), type of response (for example, Jonz 1976), scoring criterion (for example, Darnell 1970; Oller 1972), organization of passage (for example, Ramanauskas 1972; Cziko 1978), passage content (for example, Bormuth 1964; Klein-Braley 1981), and discourse organization (for example, Chavanachart 1984). It is this investigation of a variety of facets that has enriched our understanding of the cloze as a technique for language testing, and which illustrates, I believe, the usefulness of examining specific facets of a single test method. Research on other methods such as the oral interview (for example, the papers in Clark 1978a; Shohamy 1983a, 1983b; Scott and Madsen 1983) illustrates the same point.

In Chapter 2 (p. 25) it was pointed out that when test performance is unduly affected by factors other than the ability being measured, the meaningfulness or validity of score interpretations will be lessened. The effects of both the test method and the interaction between test takers' individual characteristics and the methods used in language tests may reduce the effect on test performance of the language abilities we want to measure, and hence the interpretability of test scores. For this reason, it is important to understand not only the nature and extent of these effects, but also to control or minimize them. As research into the effects on test performance of personal attributes and test method facets progresses, test developers will have better information about which characteristics interact with which test method facets, and should be able to utilize this information in designing tests that are less susceptible to such effects, that provide the greatest opportunity for test takers to exhibit their 'best' performance, and which are hence better and fairer measures of the language abilities of interest.

Summary

In addition to the abilities we want to measure, the test methods that we use have an important effect on test performance. If we consider the variety of testing techniques that are used in language tests, and the ways in which these techniques vary, it is obvious that test methods vary along a large number of dimensions. If we are to understand the ways in which test methods influence test performance, therefore, it is necessary to examine the various dimensions, or facets, of test methods.

In this chapter I have described a framework for characterizing the facets of test method that affect performance on language tests. These facets can be grouped into five sets. The *testing environment* includes the extent to which the test taker is familiar with the place and the equipment used for administering the test, the personnel, both administrators and other test takers, involved in the test, the time of testing and conditions of the test administration. The *test rubric* includes the test organization, time allocation, and instructions. Instructions can be characterized in terms of the language (native, target) in which they are presented, whether they are presented aurally or in writing, or both, the clarity with which the test procedures and test tasks are specified, and the explicitness of the criteria for correctness.

Input and *expected response* share some common facets, and the ways in which they can be related to each other provide a means for distinguishing three general types of test methods. *Input* can be characterized in terms of whether it is presented in the auditory or visual channel, or both, whether it consists of language or non-language material, or both, whether it is presented 'live' or by some artificial means, how precisely the problem is identified, the degree of speededness, and the nature of the language employed.

Expected response facets include channel, type of response (selected or constructed), form of response (language, nonlanguage or both), the nature of the language used, and the degree and types of restrictions that are placed on the response. Even though all language use is restricted in many ways by the context in which it takes place, the degree of *artificial* restriction imposed by the test on the expected response may affect the 'naturalness' and hence the authenticity of the test task. For both input and response, the nature of the language used can be characterized in terms of its length, the degree of contextualization (embedded, reduced), the distribution of inform-ation (compact, diffuse), the type of information (abstract/concrete, negative/positive, factual/counterfactual), the topic, the genre, its organizational characteristics (grammar, cohesion, rhetorical organization), and its illocutionary and sociolinguistic characteristics.

The *relationship between input and expected response* can be reciprocal, in which there is an interactive negotiation of meaning, nonreciprocal, in which there is no interaction between input and response, and adaptive, in which the input is affected by the test taker's response, but without feedback to the test taker.

The frameworks described here and in Chapter 4 have been presented as a means for describing performance on language tests, and I would reiterate that they are intended as a guide for both the development and use of language tests and for research in language testing. These frameworks provide the applied linguistic foundation that informs the discussions in the remainder of the book. In Chapter 6 they are used to distinguish sources of variation in test scores, as a means of investigating their reliability, in Chapter 7 they are shown to provide a basis for the investigation of test validity, and in Chapter 8 they provide a basis for discussing the authenticity of language tests.

Notes

1   Nontechnical discussions of facet theory are given by Canter (1983, 1985b) and Brown (1985).
2   There are several aspects of discourse that have been mentioned

in connection with processing difficulty, which might find their place in a framework of test method facets. G. Brown (1989), for example, discusses the number of participants involved, the salience of the features distinguishing between the participants, the simplicity and symmetry of spatial structures, the simplicity and sequencing of temporal structures, and the intentionality of discourse as factors that affect the conceptual difficulty in processing texts.

3 Cronbach (1984) discusses such tests as 'tests of typical performance', as opposed to 'tests of maximum performance', in which explicit criteria for a good performance must be given (pp. 28–33).

4 Henning (1987) discusses this difference between the expected response and the actual response as a potential threat to what he calls 'response validity' (p.92).

5 A wide range of factors, such as 'vocabulary load', 'syntactic complexity', 'syntactic density', 'level of information', 'information structure', and 'topic progression', to mention a few, has been discussed in the vast literature on readability. A consideration of this research is far beyond the purview of this book. However, it is my belief that the majority of these can be characterized, as they pertain to language tests, by the facets described in this framework.

6 Finegan and Besnier (1988) Chapter 15 provide an excellent discussion of standard varieties, their characteristics, and the factors that determine their status. Greenbaum (1985) and Kachru (1986) provide fuller discussions of standard varieties of English.

7 Roid (1984) provides a useful review of criterion-referenced item writing procedures.

Further reading

Stanley (1971) provides a list of possible sources of variation in test scores. Popham (1978) discusses components of test specifications that include some of the facets of test method discussed in this chapter. Canter (1985a) includes a collection of papers on the theory and application of facet theory in the social sciences. Of particular interest are Canter's personal anecdotal history of the development of facet theory (Canter 1985b), Brown's introductory-level discussion of facet theory (Brown 1985), and Canter's discussion of how to conduct facet research (Canter 1985c). Carroll (1968) discusses 'linguistic performance variables' and outlines a 'taxonomy of language test tasks'. Cohen (1980), in Chapter 3, 'The process of test taking', provides an extensive discussion of the factors that may cause test takers' actual responses to differ from test developers' expected responses.

Discussion questions

1. Considering the effects of testing environment on test performance, should we or should we not set the environment so that it affects performance as little as possible? What might be done to minimize the potential negative effects of testing environment?

2. What information should be included in test instructions so that they are clearly understood by test takers? Give some examples.

3. Suppose you knew that your answer to an in-class essay examination was going to be evaluated in terms of grammatical correctness, cohesion, and organization, in addition to its content. Would this affect the way you wrote your answer? If yes, how?

4. Discuss the restrictions on response that are imposed in an oral interview.

5. Consider a test that consists of two parts: Part I, in which test takers are required to write answers to questions such as 'Where do you come from?' and 'What is your hobby?' and Part II, in which the answers to the questions in Part I are to be used in writing a paragraph about themselves. Is this test reciprocal? Adaptive? What test method facets might affect performance on this test?

6 Reliability

Introduction

A fundamental concern in the development and use of language tests is to identify potential sources of error in a given measure of communicative language ability and to minimize the effect of these factors on that measure. We must be concerned about errors of measurement, or unreliability, because we know that test performance is affected by factors other than the abilities we want to measure. For example, we can all think of factors such as poor health, fatigue, lack of interest or motivation, and test-wiseness, that can affect individuals' test performance, but which are not generally associated with language ability, and thus not characteristics we want to measure with language tests. However, these are but some of the more obvious sources of measurement error. In addition to factors such as these, which are largely unsystematic and hence unpredictable, the test method facets discussed in Chapter 5 are potential sources of error that can be equally detrimental to the accurate measurement of language abilities. When we minimize the effects of these various factors, we minimize measurement error and maximize reliability. In other words, the *less* these factors affect test scores, the *greater* the relative effect of the language abilities we want to measure, and hence, the reliability of language test scores.

When we increase the reliability of our measures, we are also satisfying a necessary condition for validity: in order for a test score to be valid, it must be reliable. Many discussions of reliability and validity emphasize the differences between these two qualities, rather than their similarities. But instead of considering these as two entirely distinct concepts, I believe both can be better understood by recognizing them as complementary aspects of a common concern in measurement – identifying, estimating, and controlling the effects of factors that affect test scores. The investigation of reliability is concerned with answering the question, 'How much of an individual's test performance is due to measurement error, or to factors other than the language ability we want to measure?' and with minimizing the effects of these factors on test scores. Validity, on the other hand, is concerned with the question, 'How much of an individual's test performance is due to the language abilities we want to measure?' and with maximizing the effects of these abilities on test scores. The concerns of reliability and validity can thus be seen as leading to two complementary objectives in designing and developing tests: (1) to minimize the effects of measurement error, and (2) to maximize the effects of the language abilities we want to measure.

The investigation of reliability involves both logical analysis and empirical research; we must *identify* sources of error and *estimate* the magnitude of their effects on test scores. In order to identify sources of error, we need to distinguish the effects of the language abilities we want to measure from the effects of other factors, and this is a particularly complex problem. This is partly because of the interaction between components of language ability and test method facets, which may make it difficult to mark a clear 'boundary' between the ability being measured and the method facets of a given test. In an oral interview, for example, whether we consider a particular topic of a conversational interaction to be part of the test taker's ability to speak the language effectively or a part of the topic facet of the test method will depend upon how we want to interpret the test taker's score. If we want to make inferences about the test taker's ability to speak on a wide variety of topics, then a specific topic might be considered part of the test method, and hence a potential source of error. If, on the other hand, we want to measure the test taker's ability to speak in this particular topic domain, then the topic could reasonably be considered part of the ability. The way we identify sources of error is thus clearly a function of the inferences or uses we want to make of the test score, which again demonstrates the relationship between reliability and validity.

Identifying sources of error is also complicated by the effects of other characteristics, such as sex, age, cognitive style, and native language, which may also be difficult to distinguish from the effects of the language abilities we want to measure. While research has provided insights into the relationships among factors such as these and language acquisition, their effects on test performance have only recently begun to be investigated. Clearly identifying and distinguishing the various factors that are potential sources of error of measurement on a given test is thus crucial to the investigation of reliability. When we look at the other side of the coin, so to speak, and ask 'How much of an individual's performance is due to the language ability we want to measure (as opposed to sources of error)?' we can see that this is also essential to the examination of validity, which will be discussed in Chapter 7.

Estimating the magnitude of the effects of different sources of error, once these sources have been identified, is a matter of empirical research, and is a major concern of measurement theory. Just as there are many potential sources of measurement error, numerous approaches to estimating or quantifying the size of their effects on test scores have been developed. And just as the sources of error may involve complex interactions, and affect different individuals differentially, the procedures required to adequately estimate the reliability of a given test score are necessarily complex. The purpose of this chapter, however, is not to provide a basis for actually conducting these analyses, but rather to present the rationale and logic that underlies them, as a basis for their appropriate utilization and interpretation in the development and use of language tests.

In this chapter I will discuss measurement error in test scores, the potential sources of this error, the different approaches to estimating the relative effects of these sources of error on test scores, and the considerations to be made in determining which of these approaches may be appropriate for a given testing situation. I will begin by considering the factors that affect test scores as sources of variation, within the framework of norm-referenced tests. Then classical 'true score' measurement theory will be described, as well as how this model can be used to define error in language test scores, how these definitions of error are related to different ways of estimating reliability, and the limitations of this model. While developments in modern measurement theory – generalizability theory and item response theory – provide more powerful tools for test development and interpretation, estimates of reliability based on the classical true score model are still useful in many practical testing contexts, particularly in classroom testing. Furthermore, an understanding of the classical model will facilitate an understanding of modern measurement theory, in that the latter has evolved from the classical model, largely in response to its limitations. Next, I will discuss generalizability theory, which is a powerful extension of the classical true score model that permits the simultaneous estimation of the effects of multiple sources of error in language test scores. This is followed by a discussion of the use of reliability estimates from both classical true score theory and generalizability theory to compute the standard error of measurement, and of the use of this statistic in the interpretation and reporting of individual test scores. Next, I present a brief overview of item response theory, which provides a basis for estimates of measurement error that are not dependent upon particular samples of individuals, and for examining differential measurement error at different ability levels. I then discuss the different approaches to estimating the reliability of criterion-referenced tests and the use of these estimates in score interpretation. Finally, the effects of factors such as test length and amount of variation in scores on estimates of reliability are discussed, as well as the different effects of systematic measurement error, including that due to test method facets.

Factors that affect language test scores

Measurement specialists have long recognized that the examination of reliability depends upon our ability to distinguish the effects (on test scores) of the abilities we want to measure from the effects of other factors. That is, if we wish to estimate how reliable our test scores are, we must begin with a set of definitions of the abilities we want to measure, and of the other factors that we expect to affect test scores (Stanley 1971: 362). Thus, both Thorndike (1951) and Stanley (1971) begin their extensive treatments of reliability with general frameworks for describing the factors that cause test scores to vary from individual to individual. These frameworks include general and specific *lasting* characteristics, general and specific *temporary* characteristics, and systematic and chance factors related to test administration and scoring. General frameworks such as these provide a basis for the more precise definition of factors that affect performance on tests of specific abilities.

The frameworks described in Chapters 4 and 5 are intended specifically for use in examining factors that affect scores on *language* tests. The framework of communicative language ability presented in Chapter 4 provides a basis for stating hypotheses about the ways in which specific abilities determine how a given individual performs on a given test and, consequently, the score he receives on that test. In a test of sensitivity to register, for example, we would expect that the students who perform the best and receive the highest scores would be those with the highest level of sociolinguistic competence. In other words, we would like to infer that a high score on a language test is determined or caused by high communicative language ability, and a theoretical framework defining this ability is thus necessary if we want to make inferences about ability from test scores.

However, performance on language tests is also affected by factors other than communicative language ability. These can be grouped into the following broad categories: (1) test method facets, as discussed in Chapter 5; (2) attributes of the test taker that are not considered part of the language abilities we want to measure, and (3) random factors that are largely unpredictable and temporary. Test method facets are *systematic* to the extent that they are uniform from one test administration to the next. That is, if the input format facet is multiple-choice, this will not vary, whether the test is given in the morning or afternoon, or whether the test is intended to measure grammatical or illocutionary competence. (As we will see later, the *effects* of test method facets on test performance may be the same for all individuals taking the test, or may vary from individual to individual.)

Attributes of individuals that are not related to language ability include individual characteristics such as cognitive style and knowledge of particular content areas, and group characteristics such as sex, race, and ethnic background. These attributes, like test method facets, are also systematic in the sense that they are likely to affect a given individual's test performance regularly. If an individual's field dependence, for example, affects his performance on one cloze test, it is likely to affect his performance on any cloze test. And knowledge of economics is likely to affect an individual's performance on any test in which economics is included as propositional content. Both of these categories that can have systematic effects on test performance are potential sources of error in our measurement of language abilities.

In addition to these systematic sources of error, an individual's test score will be affected to some degree by *unsystematic*, or *random* factors. These include unpredictable and largely temporary conditions, such as his mental alertness or emotional state, and uncontrolled differences in test method facets, such as changes in the test environment from one day to the next, or idiosyncratic differences in the way different test administrators carry out their responsibilities. The limitations on observation and quantification discussed in Chapter 2 – incompleteness of language sample and imprecision of the scales – constitute another source of error. To the extent that an individual's test score is affected by test method facets, attributes other than the abilities we want to measure, and random factors, any inference we make about his level of language ability on the basis of his test score will be in error to some degree.

The effects of these various factors on a test score can be illustrated

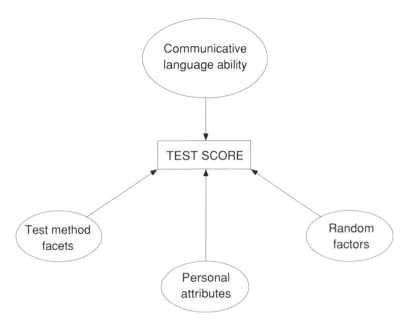

Figure 6.1   Factors that affect language test scores

as in Figure 6.1. In this type of diagram, sometimes called a 'path diagram', rectangles are used to represent *observed variables*, such as test scores, ovals to represent *unobserved variables*, or hypothesized factors, and straight arrows to represent hypothesized causal relationships.

The result of the effects of all these factors is that whenever individuals take a language test, they are not all likely to perform equally well, and so their scores vary. If we consider the total amount of variation in the scores of different individuals on a given test, we might think of different proportions of that variation being due to the different factors discussed above. This is because the different factors will affect different individuals differently. Just as individuals vary in their level of language ability, so they will vary in the extent to which they are affected by different methods of testing. Some individuals, for example, may do very well on a multiple-choice test but perform poorly on a composition test. Or it may be the case that members of one racial or ethnic group may do better or worse on a given test than do members of other groups. Or, some test takers may be well rested and mentally alert on the day of the test while others may have stayed up too late preparing for the test and consequently not be able to perform at their highest level of ability.

I would reiterate that our primary interest in using language tests is to make inferences about one or more components of an individual's communicative language ability. A major concern in the design and development of language tests, therefore, is to minimize the effects of test method, personal attributes that are not part of language ability, and random factors on test performance. Similarly, the interpretation and use of language test scores must be appropriately tempered by our estimates of the extent to which these scores reflect factors other than the language abilities we want to measure. Random factors and test method facets are generally considered to be sources of measurement error, and have thus been the primary concern of approaches to estimating reliability. Personal attributes that are not considered part of the ability tested, such as sex, ethnic background, cognitive style and prior knowledge of content area, on the other hand, have traditionally been discussed as sources of test bias, or test invalidity, and these will therefore be discussed in Chapter 7.

Two statistical concepts that will be useful in discussing reliability are 'mean' and 'variance'. The mean, symbolized by $\bar{x}$, is the arithmetic average of the scores of a given group of test takers. The variance, symbolized by s^2, is a statistic that characterizes how much individual scores vary from the group mean. (The variance is equal to the square of the standard deviation, discussed on pp. 72–3 above.) Subscripts such as x, t, or e will be used to indicate specific types of variance. The symbol s^2_x for example, will be used to refer to the variance in observed test scores.

Classical true score measurement theory

When we investigate reliability, it is essential to keep in mind the distinction between unobservable abilities, on the one hand, and observed test scores, on the other. As mentioned in Chapter 2, the language abilities we are interested in measuring are abstract, and thus we can never directly observe, or know, in any absolute sense, an individual's 'true' score for any ability. This can only be estimated on the basis of the score actually obtained on a given test of that ability. Therefore, any attempt to estimate the reliability of a set of test scores must be based on a model that specifies the hypothesized relationships between the ability measured and the observed scores on the test.

True score and error score

Classical true score (CTS) measurement theory consists of a set of assumptions about the relationships between actual, or observed test scores and the factors that affect these scores. The first assumption of this model states that an observed score on a test comprises two factors or components: a *true score* that is due to an individual's level of ability and an *error score*, that is due to factors other than the ability being tested.[1] This assumption can be represented in the formula

$$x = x_t + x_e \qquad [1]$$

where x is the observed score, x_t is the true score, and x_e the error score. This is illustrated in Figure 6.2.

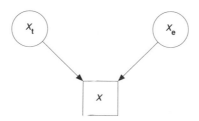

Figure 6.2   True score and error score as factors affecting an observed score

Similarly, we can characterize the variance of a set of test scores as consisting of two components:

$$s^2_x = s^2_t + s^2_e \qquad [2]$$

where s^2_x is the observed score variance, s^2_t is the true score variance component, and s^2_e is the error score variance component.

   A second set of assumptions has to do with the relationship between true and error scores. Essentially, these assumptions state that error scores are unsystematic, or random, and are uncorrelated with true scores.[2] Without these assumptions it would not be possible to distinguish true scores from error scores. These assumptions constitute the CTS model's definition of measurement error as that variation in a set of test scores that is unsystematic or random. In summary, the CTS measurement model defines two sources of variance in a set of test scores: the true score variance, which is due to differences in the ability of the individuals tested, and measurement error, which is unsystematic, or random.

Parallel tests

Another concept that is part of CTS theory is that of *parallel tests*. In order for two tests to be considered parallel, we assume that they are measures of the same ability, that is, that an individual's true score on one test will be the same as his true score on the other. But since we never actually know the true scores for a given test, how are we to know if two tests are parallel? The answer to this question is provided by the way parallel tests are defined in classical measurement theory: two tests are parallel if, for every group of persons taking both tests, (1) the true score on one test is equal to the true score on the other, and (2) the error variances for the two tests are equal. From this definition we can derive an operational definition: parallel tests are two tests of the same ability that have the same means and variances and are equally correlated with other tests of that ability. Thus two tests, X and X', giving scores x and x', can be considered parallel if the following conditions are met:

$$\bar{x} = \bar{x}' \qquad [3]$$
$$s^2{}_x = s^2{}_{x'} \qquad [4]$$
$$r_{xy} = r_{x'y} \qquad [5]$$

Here r_{xy} and $r_{x'y}$ are the correlations between the scores from a third test Y and the tests X and X' respectively, where Y is any other test of the same ability. In practice, although we virtually never have strictly parallel tests, we treat two tests as if they were parallel if the differences between their means and variances are not statistically significant. This can be determined by using the appropriate tests of significance, such as the F ratio for variances and the z test or t test for means.[3] Such tests are generally referred to as 'equivalent' or 'alternate' forms.[4]

Reliability as the correlation between parallel tests

The definitions of true score and error score variance given above ([2]) are abstract, in the sense that we cannot actually observe the true and error scores for a given test. These definitions thus provide no direct means for determining the reliability of observed scores. That is, since we never know what the true or error scores are, we cannot *know* the reliability of the observed scores. In order to be able to *estimate* the reliability of observed scores, therefore, we must define reliability operationally in a way that depends only on observed scores, and for this we employ the operational definition of parallel tests. Recall that in parallel tests the true score on one is equal to the true score on the other. Furthermore, the error scores of both tests are assumed to be random, and will be uncorrelated. Because of the effect of the random error scores, the correlation between observed scores of parallel tests will be less than perfect. The smaller the effect of the error scores, the more highly the parallel tests will be correlated. Thus, if the observed scores on two parallel tests are highly correlated, this indicates that effects of the error scores are minimal, and that they can be considered reliable indicators of the ability being measured. This is illustrated in Figure 6.3.

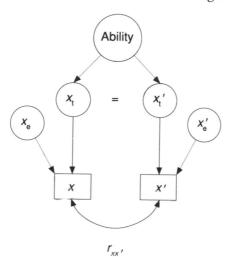

Figure 6.3   Correlations between true and observed scores on parallel tests

From this we can derive a definition of reliability as the correlation between the observed scores on two parallel tests, which we can symbolize as $r_{xx'}$. It is this definition that provides the basis for all estimates of reliability within CTS theory.

Fundamental to this operational definition of reliability is the assumption that the observed scores on the two tests are experimentally independent. That is, an individual's performance on the second test should not depend on how she performs on the first. If the individual's performance on the first test does influence her performance on the second, then we cannot infer that the correlation between the observed scores is due to the influence of a common ability, as illustrated in Figure 6.4.

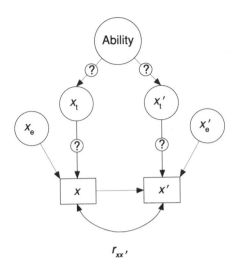

*Figure 6.4   Correlations between parallel tests that are not
experimentally independent*

Reliability and measurement error as proportions of observed score variance

Given the means of estimating reliability through computing the correlation between parallel tests, we can derive a means for estimating the measurement error, as well. If an individual's observed score on a test is composed of a true score and an error score, the greater the proportion of true score, the less the proportion of error score, and thus the more reliable the observed score. In looking at a set of test scores of many individuals, we can say that the greater the proportion of true score variance in these scores, the more reliable those scores. Thus, one way of defining reliability is as the proportion of the observed score variance that is true score variance, which can be represented as follows:

$$r_{xx'} = s^2_t/s^2_x \qquad [6]$$

Since the proportions of true score variance and error score variance add up to one, we can express the proportion of error variance as the complement of reliability:

$$s^2_t/s^2_x + s^2_e/s^2_x = 1$$

$$s^2_e/s^2_x = 1 - s^2_t/s^2_x \qquad [7]$$

$$(s^2_t/s^2_x = r_{xx'})$$

$$s^2_e/s^2_x = 1 - r_{xx'} \qquad [8]$$

This leads to the definition of error score variance in terms of the total score variance and reliability:

$$s^2_e = s^2_x (1 - r_{xx'}) \qquad [9]$$

This definition is particularly important, since estimates of error variance are more directly applicable to interpreting test scores than are estimates of reliability. This is because reliability estimates provide information about sets of scores, while estimates of error variance can be used to interpret individual test scores.

In summary, reliability is defined in the CTS theory in terms of true score variance. Since we can never know the true scores of individuals, we can never know what the reliability is, but can only estimate it from the observed scores. The basis for all such estimates in the CTS model is the correlation between parallel tests. Our estimates of reliability thus depend upon the extent to which the tests satisfy both the assumptions regarding parallel tests and the assumptions of the model regarding the relationship between true and observed scores.[5]

I would also repeat my earlier point that even though we often speak of the reliability of a given test, strictly speaking, reliability refers to the test *scores*, and not the test itself. Furthermore, since reliability will be a function not only of the test, but of the performance of the individuals who take the test, any given estimate of reliability based on the CTS model is limited to the sample of test scores upon which it is based. Thus, even though the manual for a standardized test will provide information about the reliability of scores obtained with given norm groups, we must always estimate the reliability of the scores of the specific groups with whom we may want to use the test. Some of the different approaches to estimating reliability in the CTS model are discussed in the following section.

Sources of error and approaches to estimating reliability

In any given test situation, there will probably be more than one source of measurement error. If, for example, we give several groups of individuals a test of listening comprehension in which they listen to short dialogues or passages read aloud and then select the correct answer from among four written choices, we assume that test takers' scores on the test will vary according to their different levels of listening comprehension ability. At the same time, there will be some variation in students' scores due to differences in how they feel the day of the test, in the way the passages are read (for example, clarity, volume, speed) to the different groups, the content of the different passages, how much time was provided for the test takers to answer, and so forth. As discussed above, these sources of variation are sources of measurement error.

Within the CTS model, there are three approaches to estimating reliability, each of which addresses different sources of error. *Internal consistency* estimates are concerned primarily with sources of error from within the test and scoring procedures, *stability* estimates indicate how consistent test scores are over time, and *equivalence* estimates provide an indication of the extent to which scores on alternate forms of a test are equivalent. The estimates of reliability that these approaches yield are called *reliability coefficients*.

Internal consistency

Internal consistency is concerned with how consistent test takers' performances on the different parts of the test are with each other. Inconsistencies in performance on different parts of tests can be caused by a number of factors, including the test method facets discussed in Chapter 5. Performance on the parts of a reading comprehension test, for example, might be inconsistent if passages are of differing lengths and vary in terms of their syntactic, lexical, and organizational complexity, or involve different topics. Similarly, performance on different items of a multiple-choice test that includes items with different formats – some with blanks to be completed and others with words underlined that may be incorrect – may not be internally consistent. Thus, if the questions in a listening comprehension test, for example, measured this ability or its component parts with varying degrees of consistency, the scores would not be very reliable indicators of this ability.

Split-half reliability estimates
One approach to examining the internal consistency of a test is the *split-half* method, in which we divide the test into two halves and then determine the extent to which scores on these two halves are consistent with each other. In so doing, we are treating the halves as parallel tests, and so we must make certain assumptions about the equivalence of the two halves, specifically that they have equal means and variances. In addition, we must also assume that the two halves are independent of each other. That is, that an individual's

performance on one half does not determine how he performs on the other. This assumption does not mean that the two halves will not be correlated with each other, but rather that the correlation will be due to the fact that they are both measuring the same trait or ability, and not to the fact that performance on one half depends upon performance on the other. In other words, there might be two interpretations for a correlation between the halves: (1) they both measure the same trait, and (2) individuals' performance on one half depends on how they perform on the other. In order to interpret the relationship between the halves as an indication that they both measure the same ability, or that they both have the same true score variance, we must be able to rule out the second interpretation. Hence, the assumption that the halves are independent of each other.

A convenient way of splitting a test into halves might be to simply divide it into the first and second halves. The problem with this, however, is that most language tests are designed as 'power' tests, with the easiest questions at the beginning and the questions becoming progressively more difficult. In tests such as these, the second half would obviously be more difficult than the first, so that assumption of equivalence would not be satisfied.

Another way would be simply to split the test into random halves, that is, to assign items to halves at random. In general, one way of assigning a set of unordered items to different groups at random is to simply assign every other one to one group. We do this when we ask students to 'count off' in order to separate them into different groups. This is the basis for the *odd–even* method, in which all the odd-numbered items are grouped together into one half and all the even-numbered items into another. This approach is particularly applicable to tests in which the items are designed to measure the same ability and to be independent of each other, such as is typical of multiple-choice tests of grammar or vocabulary in which the items 'stand alone'.[6] In tests such as these, we assume that a random (odd–even) selection of items will yield two tests that are equivalent and independent of each other.

In many cases, however, splitting the test into equivalent halves is problematic, since a random method of splitting the test is not applicable. Consider, for example, a multiple-choice test in which different items are designed to measure different abilities, such as might be the case in a classroom achievement test that is intended to measure several different learning objectives. In this case, a random (for example, odd–even) method may yield halves that are not equivalent in content, and it may be preferable to divide the test into two halves by design, based on the content of the items, rather than at random, to assure that they are comparable in content. In this case, one must be particularly careful to assure that the two halves thus obtained are also equivalent.

A more serious problem is posed by tests in which the items are not independent of each other, such as is typical of multiple-choice reading tests with sets of items based on the same passage, and of cloze or dictation tests. Here the problem of clearly identifying the language ability measured by individual items is much more difficult than with 'stand alone' multiple-choice items. If we could assume that all the items in the test measure the same language ability, then we might be justified in using an odd–even method for splitting the items. The assumption that the two halves are independent of each other is much more problematic, since it is well known that many of the items in cloze tests are dependent on the context beyond the clause (Chihara *et al.* 1977; Bachman 1982, 1985; Chavez-Oller *et al.* 1985) and that whether an individual answers a given item correctly may well depend upon whether he has answered other items correctly. Thus, an odd–even split may yield halves consisting of items that are not independent and in which the halves are consequently not independent. In cases such as these, where we are not sure that the items are measuring the same ability or that they are independent of each other, the test–retest and parallel forms methods, discussed below, are more appropriate for estimating reliability. However, in situations where it is not possible to retest individuals, or to administer equivalent forms, and some estimate of internal consistency is the only means of examining the reliability of the test, we must make every attempt to split the test into halves in such a way as to maximize their equivalence and their independence.[7]

The Spearman–Brown split-half estimate

Once the test has been split into halves, it is rescored, yielding two scores – one for each half – for each test taker. In one approach to estimating reliability, we then compute the correlation between the two sets of scores. This gives us an estimate of how consistent the *halves* are, however, and we are interested in the reliability of the whole test. In general, a long test will be more reliable than a short one, assuming that the additional items correlate positively with the other items in the test. In the split-half method, we have reduced the test by half, and we must therefore correct the obtained correlation for this reduction in length. The most commonly used formula for this is a special case of the Spearman–Brown prophecy formula (Spearman 1910; Brown 1910), which yields a split-half reliability coefficient:[8]

$$r_{xx'} = \frac{2r_{hh'}}{1 + r_{hh'}} \qquad [10]$$

where $r_{hh'}$ is the obtained correlation between the two halves of the test. Two assumptions must be met in order to use this method. First, since we are in effect treating the two halves as parallel tests, we must assume that they have equal means and variances (an assumption we can check). Second, we must assume that the two halves are experimentally independent of each other (an assumption that is very difficult to check). That is, that an individual's performance on one half does not affect how he performs on the other.

The Guttman split-half estimate
Another approach to estimating reliability from split-halves is that developed by Guttman (1945), which does not assume equivalence of the halves, and which does not require computing a correlation between them. This split-half reliability coefficient is based on the ratio of the sum of the variances of the two halves to the variance of the whole test:

$$r_{xx'} = 2\left(1 - \frac{s^2_{h1} + s^2_{h2}}{s^2_x}\right) \qquad [11]$$

where s^2_{h1} and s^2_{h2} are the variances of the two halves. Since this formula is based on the variance of the total test, it provides a direct estimate of the reliability of the whole test. Therefore, unlike the correlation between the halves that is the basis for the Spearman–Brown reliability coefficient, the Guttman split-half estimate does *not* require an additional correction for length.

Reliability estimates based on item variances
In estimating reliability with the split-half approach, there are many different ways in which a given test could be divided into halves. Since not every split will yield halves with exactly the same characteristics in terms of their equivalence and independence, the reliability coefficients obtained with different splits are likely to vary, so that our estimates of reliability will depend greatly on the particular split we use. One way of avoiding this problem would be to split the test into halves in every way possible, compute the reliability coefficients based on these different splits, and then find the average of these coefficients. For example, in a four-item test, the three possible splits would be: (1) items 1 and 2 in one half and items 3 and 4 in the other; (2) 1 and 3, 2 and 4; (3) 1 and 4, 2 and 3. This

approach soon becomes impractical, however, beyond a very small set of items, since the number of reliability coefficients to be computed increases geometrically as a function of the number of items in the test. Thus, while with four items there are only three possible splits and three coefficients to compute, with eight items there are 35 possible splits and 595 coefficients to compute.[9] With a relatively short test of only 30 items we would have to compute the coefficients for 77,558,760 combinations of different halves!

Kuder–Richardson reliability coefficients
Fortunately, there is a way of estimating the average of all the possible split-half coefficients on the basis of the statistical character-istics of the test items. This approach, which was developed by Kuder and Richardson (1937), involves computing the means and variances of the items that constitute the test. The *mean* of a dichotomous item (one that is scored as either right or wrong) is the proportion, symbolized as p, of individuals who answer the item correctly. The proportion of individuals who answer the item incorrectly is equal to $1 - p$, and is symbolized as q. The *variance* of a dichotomous item is the product of these two proportions, or pq. The reliability coefficient provided by Kuder–Richardson formula 20 (KR–20), which is based on the ratio of the sum of the item variances to the total test score variance, is as follows:

$$r_{xx'} = \frac{k}{k-1} \left(1 - \frac{\Sigma pq}{s^2_x} \right) \qquad [12]$$

where k is the number of items on the test, Σpq is the sum of the item variances, and s^2_x is the total test score variance. As with split-half approaches, the Kuder–Richardson formula makes certain assump-tions, specifically, that the items are of nearly equal difficulty and independent of each other.[10] If it happens that the items are of equal difficulty, the reliability coefficient can be computed by using a formula that is both easier to compute and that requires less information. This formula, Kuder–Richardson formula 21 (KR–21), is as follows:

$$r_{xx'} = \frac{ks^2_x - \bar{x}(k - \bar{x})}{(k-1)s^2_x} \qquad [13]$$

This formula will generally yield a reliability coefficient that is lower than that given by KR–20.[11] Like the Guttman split-half coefficient, the Kuder–Richardson formulae are based on total score variance, and thus they do *not* require any correction for length.

Coefficient alpha
Both the Guttman split-half estimate and the Kuder–Richardson formulae estimate reliability on the basis of ratios of the variances of test components – halves and items – to total test score variance.[12] Cronbach (1951) developed a general formula for estimating internal consistency which he called 'coefficient alpha', and which is often referred to as 'Cronbach's alpha':

$$\alpha = \frac{k}{k-1}\left(1 - \frac{\Sigma s^2_i}{s^2_x}\right) \qquad [14]$$

where k is the number of items on the test, Σs^2_i is the sum of the variances of the different parts of the test, and s^2_x is the variance of the test scores. In the case of dichotomous items, Σs^2_i will be the sum of the item variances, Σpq, in formula [12]. If the parts are two halves, Σs^2_i will be the sum of the two halves, $s^2_{h1} + s^2_{h2}$ in formula [11], and the expression $k/(k-1)$ will reduce to a value of two. It can thus be shown that all estimates of reliability based on the analysis of variance components can be derived from this formula and are special cases of coefficient alpha (for example, Stanley 1971; Cronbach *et al.* 1972; Cronbach 1984).

In summary, the reliability of a set of test scores can be estimated on the basis of a single test administration only if certain assumptions about the characteristics of the parts of the test are satisfied. In using the Spearman–Brown split-half approach, we must assume that the two halves are equivalent and independent of each other, while with the Guttman split-half, we need only assume that the halves are independent of each other. In the Spearman–Brown approach the reliability is *underestimated* to the extent that the halves are not equivalent. For both, the reliability is *overestimated* to the extent that the halves are not independent of each other. The Kuder–Richardson estimates based on item variances assume that the items in the test are equivalent and independent of each other. As with the split-half estimates, the Kuder–Richardson formulae *underestimate* reliability when the items are not equivalent, and *overestimate* when the items are not independent of each other. The assumptions that must be satisfied in applying these estimates of internal consistency and the effects of violating these assumptions are summarized in Table 6.1. In cases where either of the assumptions is violated, as may be true for cloze and dictation tests, one of the other approaches (parallel forms or test–retest) to reliability discussed below should be used.

Two approaches to estimating internal consistency have been discussed. On the one hand we have an estimate based on

Estimate	Assumption		Effect if assumption is violated	
	Equivalence	Independence	Equivalence	Independence
Spearman–Brown	yes	yes	underestimate	overestimate
Guttman	no	yes	—	overestimate
Kuder–Richardson	yes	yes	underestimate	overestimate

Table 6.1   Assumptions for internal consistency reliability estimates, and effects of violating assumptions

correlation (the Spearman–Brown split-half estimate), and on the other, estimates which are based on ratios of the variances of parts of the test – halves or items – to total test score variance (the Guttman split-half, the Kuder–Richardson formulae, and coefficient alpha). While these two approaches have been demonstrated to be statistically equivalent if all relevant assumptions of parallel tests and the measurement model are met (for example, Stanley 1971), they do represent essentially different approaches in their logic. Furthermore, these two approaches generalize to the other methods for estimating reliability within the classical model discussed below. In general, we will see that the variables that are correlated (different ratings, separate administrations of the same test, parallel forms) in the first approach also provide the basis for examining variance ratios in the second approach.

Rater consistency

In test scores that are obtained subjectively, such as ratings of compositions or oral interviews, a source of error is inconsistency in these ratings. In the case of a single rater, we need to be concerned about the consistency within that individual's ratings, or with *intra-rater* reliability. When there are several different raters, we want to examine the consistency across raters, or *inter-rater* reliability. In both cases, the primary causes of inconsistency will be either the application of different rating criteria to different samples or the inconsistent application of the rating criteria to different samples.

Intra-rater reliability
When an individual judges or rates the adequacy of a given sample of language performance, whether it is written or spoken, that judgment will be based on a set of criteria of what constitutes an 'adequate' performance. If the rater applies the same set of criteria consistently in rating the language performance of different individuals,

this will yield a reliable set of ratings. That is, assuming that the language samples themselves are error free, individuals' true scores will be determined to a large extent by the set of criteria by which their performance is judged.

In any rating situation, effects due to sequencing may introduce inconsistency into either the rating criteria themselves or the way in which they are applied. In reading through a set of compositions, for example, a rater may begin by paying little attention to grammar, focusing primarily on cohesion, organization, and content. However, if the papers are full of grammatical errors, the rater may unconsciously begin paying more attention to them, so that these begin to affect her ratings. In this case, the criteria themselves may change, so that students whose papers were scored first may receive higher scores, even though their papers are not different, with respect to grammatical accuracy, from those that were scored later.

The sequence of scoring can also affect the consistency with which the rating criteria are applied. Suppose, for example, we interview and rate 20 individuals in one day, with little time in between individuals. As the day wears on, and one interview fades into another, we may unconsciously relax our ratings, so that even though we may still be rating individuals on the same components, say, grammar and pronunciation, they sound better and better. Or if we have two or three very weak individuals in a row, even though the next person is average, we may give him a very high rating, simply because of the contrast between his performance and that of the individuals who preceded him. This ordering effect can also work in the opposite direction, if we have several very good individuals followed by an average one.

In order to examine the reliability of ratings of a single rater, we need to obtain at least two independent ratings from this rater for each individual language sample. This is typically accomplished by rating the individual samples once and then re-rating them at a later time in a different, random order. Once the two sets of ratings have been obtained, the reliability between them can be estimated in two ways. One way is to treat the two sets of ratings as scores from parallel tests and compute the appropriate correlation coefficient (commonly the Spearman rank-order coefficient) between the two sets of ratings, interpreting this as an estimate of reliability. In this approach it is essential that the test user determine the extent to which the two sets of ratings constitute parallel tests. This is because a high positive correlation can be obtained even though the two sets of ratings are quite different, as long as the rank orders of the ratings are similar. For example, if the first set of ratings were 1, 2, and 3 while the second set were 3, 4, and 5, respectively, for the same individuals, the correlation would be +1.00. However, since the two sets of ratings do not have equal means ($\bar{x}_A = 2$, $\bar{x}_B = 4$) they cannot be considered parallel tests, and the correlation cannot be considered an estimate of reliability.

Another approach to examining the consistency of multiple ratings is to compute a coefficient alpha, treating the independent ratings as different parts. If one rater assigns two independent ratings to every individual in a group, a combined rating for each individual can be obtained by adding, or summing, the two ratings for that individual. We can then compute the variance s^2_r for each rating, as well as the variance s^2_{r+r} for the summed ratings. To estimate the reliability of such ratings, we then compute coefficient alpha:

$$\alpha = \frac{k}{k-1}\left(1 - \frac{s^2_{r1} + s^2_{r2}}{s^2_{r1\ +\ r2}}\right) \qquad [15]$$

where s^2_{r1} and s^2_{r2} are the variances of two ratings and $s^2_{r1\ +\ r2}$ is the variance of the summed ratings. Since there are two ratings in this case, $k/(k-1)$ reduces to a value of two, as in the Guttman split-half formula.

Inter-rater reliability

Ratings given by different raters can also vary as a function of inconsistencies in the criteria used to rate and in the way in which these criteria are applied. If, for example, we gave a group of essays to five different raters and simply asked them to rate the essays, we would be likely to obtain very different results from the different raters. One source of inconsistencies may be that while some of the raters use grammatical accuracy as the sole criterion for rating, some may focus on content, while others look at organization.

And even if you asked them all to rate on the same component, say, grammatical accuracy, there are likely to be differences in the way the raters interpret this. One rater may simply count the number of grammatical mistakes and divide by the total number of words, to arrive at a percentage as his rating. Others may decide to use rating scales, but may use different numbers of scale points. Finally, if you told them all to rate the papers on a scale from one to ten, there may still be inconsistencies in how the raters interpret this scale, so that one rater's '9' might be another's '5'.

In examining inter-rater consistency, we can use essentially the same approaches as were discussed above with intra-rater consistency. We can compute the correlation between two different raters and interpret this as an estimate of reliability. When more than two raters are involved, however, rather than computing correlations for all different pairs, a preferable approach is that recommended by Ebel (1979), in which we sum the ratings of the different raters and then estimate the reliability of these summed ratings by computing a coefficient alpha (formula [14]), where k is the number of raters, s^2_i is the variance of the ratings for a given rater, Σs^2_i is the sum of the variances of different raters' ratings, and s^2_x is the variance of the summed ratings (Ebel 1979: 282–4). (Note that where $k = 2$ this formula is equal to formula [15].)

A major practical advantage of internal consistency estimates of reliability is that they can be made on the basis of a single test administration. However, as indicated above, there are situations in which the assumptions they require are not satisfied. Furthermore, in many testing situations there are sources of error that are related to factors outside the test itself, such as differences in the conditions of test administration, or in the test takers themselves, that are not addressed by internal consistency estimates. Such is the case in situations where the same test may be given more than once, or where alternate forms of a test are used. For these reasons, other ways of estimating reliability are needed.

Stability (test-retest reliability)

As indicated above, for tests such as cloze and dictation we cannot appropriately estimate the internal consistency of the scores because of the interdependence of the parts of the test. There are also testing situations in which it may be necessary to administer a test more than once. For example, if a researcher were interested in measuring subjects' language ability at several different points in time, as part of a time–series design, she would like to rule out the possibility that changes in observed test scores were a result of increasing familiarity with the test. This might also be the concern of a language program evaluator who is interested in relating changes in language ability to teaching and learning activities in the program. In situations such as these, reliability can be estimated by giving the test more than once to the same group of individuals. This approach to reliability is called the 'test–retest' approach, and it provides an estimate of the stability of the test scores over time.

In this approach, we administer the test twice to a group of individuals and then compute the correlation between the two sets of scores. This correlation can then be interpreted as an indication of how stable the scores are over time. The primary concern in this approach is assuring that the individuals who take the test do not themselves change differentially in any systematic way between test administrations. That is, we must assume that both practice and learning (or unlearning) effects are either uniform across individuals or random. Practice effects may occur if certain individuals remember some of the items or feel more comfortable with the test method, and consequently perform better on the second administration of the test. If, on the other hand, there is a considerable time lapse between test administrations, some individuals' language ability may actually improve or decline more than that of others, causing them to perform differently the second time. In either case, these systematic changes will be a source of inconsistency in test scores.

These two sources of inconsistency — differential practice effects and differential changes in ability — pose a dilemma for the test–retest approach, since providing a relatively *long* time between test administrations will tend to minimize the practice effects, while providing greater opportunity for differences in learning. Giving the test twice with *little* time between, on the other hand, minimizes the effects of learning, but may enhance practice effects. For this reason, there is no single length of time between test administrations that is best for all situations. In each situation, the test developer or user must attempt to determine the extent to which practice and learning are likely to influence test performance, and choose the length of time between test and retest so as to optimize reduction in the effects of both. It should be noted here that a more serious problem inherent in this approach is that test–retest differences due to practice effect — test method facets — are fundamentally different from test–retest differences that are due to changes in ability. That is, the former are clearly due to factors other than the ability being tested, and hence can legitimately be treated as error. Differences due to changes in ability, however, might more appropriately be interpreted as a function of test takers' 'true scores'. This problem with classical measurement theory is discussed below.

Equivalence (parallel forms reliability)

Another approach to estimating the reliability of a test is to examine the equivalence of scores obtained from alternate forms of a test. Like the test–retest approach, this is an appropriate means of estimating the reliability of tests for which internal consistency estimates are either inappropriate or not possible. It is of particular interest in testing situations where alternate forms of the test may be actually used, either for security reasons, or to minimize the practice effect. In some situations it is not possible to administer the test to all examinees at the same time, and the test user does not wish to take the chance that individuals who take the test first will pass on information about the test to later test takers. In other situations, the test user may wish to measure individuals' language abilities frequently over a period of time, and wants to be sure that any changes in performance are not due to practice effect, and therefore uses alternate forms. In either case, the test user must be able to assume that the different forms of the test are equivalent, as described above, particularly that they are at the same difficulty level and have similar standard deviations.

In order to estimate the reliability of alternate forms of a given test, the procedure used is to administer both forms to a group of individuals. Since administering two alternate forms to the same group of individuals will necessarily involve giving one form first and the other second, there is a possibility that individuals may perform differently because of the order in which they take the two forms. That is, they may do better on the second form they take because of the practice effect of having taken the first, thus confounding the relative equivalence of the forms with the test-retest effect. One way to minimize the possibility of an ordering effect is to use a 'counterbalanced' design, in which half of the individuals take one form first and the other half take the other form first. This is illustrated in Table 6.2, for a test with Form A and Form B.

	First	Second
Half I	Form A	Form B
Half II	Form B	Form A

Table 6.2   An example of 'counterbalanced' test design

The means and standard deviations for each of the two forms can then be computed and compared to determine their equivalence, after which the correlation between the two sets of scores (Form A and Form B) can be computed. This correlation is then interpreted as an indicator of the equivalence of the two tests, or as an estimate of the reliability of either one.

Summary of classical true score approaches to reliability

The three approaches to estimating reliability that have been developed within the CTS measurement model are concerned with different sources of error. The particular approach or approaches that we use will depend on what we believe the sources of error are in our measures, given the particular type of test, administrative procedures, types of test takers, and the use of the test. *Internal consistency* estimates are concerned with sources of error such as differences in test tasks and item formats, and inconsistencies within and among scorers. Estimates of *equivalence* also examine inconsistencies, not within a single form, but across different forms of a test. Finally, *stability* estimates are concerned with inconsistencies that may arise as a function of time, such as random changes in individuals' health or state of mind, or changes in administration procedures, such as differences in temperature, lighting, timing, and audibility of administrators' voices.

As a matter of procedure, we generally attempt to estimate the internal consistency of a test first, since if a test is not reliable in this respect, it is not likely to be equivalent to other forms or stable over time. This is because measurement error is random and therefore not correlated with anything. Thus, the greater the proportion of measurement error in the scores from a given test, the lower the correlation of those scores with other scores will be. If there are other possible sources of error in our testing situation, we proceed to other approaches, either stability or equivalence or both. Thus, in order to investigate all relevant sources of error for a given test, we may need to develop alternate forms and provide for multiple administrations.

Suppose, for example, that we need to develop an oral interview that will measure individuals' listening comprehension and speaking skills for use in admitting and placing students into a language program. This test will also be given periodically to determine if students are ready to begin job training that will be conducted in the target language. This job training will involve listening to descriptions and explanations, and following instructions given by several different trainers, as well as responding verbally to their questions. We must interview new students for admission and placement every two weeks, as well as at the end of each unit of instruction to determine if they are ready to begin job training. In order to minimize practice effects, we will need several alternate sets of interview questions. We will also need to use several different interviewers. In this situation, therefore, we need to be concerned with three possible sources of error – inconsistency of questions, lack of equivalence of different sets of questions, and lack of consistency among inter-viewer/raters.

We might begin by developing a set of interview questions and examining their internal consistency. This could be done by administering the same set of questions to a group of interviewees and estimating the reliability of their responses to the different questions. Assuming the internal consistency of the items is accept-able, we could then proceed to develop alternate sets and also estimate their internal consistency. We might then give these alternate sets to a group of students and estimate their equivalence. Finally, to estimate the consistency of different interviewers, we would investigate the inter-rater reliability.

Problems with the classical true score model

In many testing situations these apparently straightforward pro-cedures for estimating the effects of different sources of error are complicated by the fact that the different sources of error may interact with each other, even when we carefully design our reliability study. In the previous example, distinguishing lack of equivalence from interviewer inconsistency may be problematic. Suppose we had four sets of questions. In an ideal situation, we might have each interviewer administer all four sets of questions and give four separate ratings based on these sets to each test taker. With six interviewers this would give us 24 ratings for each test taker. We could compute a coefficient alpha for the ratings based on the four sets of questions and interpret this as an estimate of equivalence reliability. Similarly, we could interpret the coefficient alpha for the ratings of the different raters as indicators of inter-rater reliability.

In this design, however, there are potential sources of error that cannot be investigated within the CTS model. Suppose, for example, that one of the interviewers consistently rated the lowest test takers higher out of sympathy, or that one set of questions favored individuals who had greater familiarity with the subject matter, or that all of the interviewers liked one set of questions better than they did the others. Because interactions such as these will have differential effects, across questions and raters, *both* our equivalent forms and our inter-rater reliability estimates will be misleading. If all interviewers consistently give higher ratings with one set of questions, for example, this will tend to increase inter-rater reliability estimate, completely obscuring an important source of error variance – the interaction between interviewers and one of the sets of questions.

The problem of correctly identifying and estimating the relative effects of different sources of error is even more serious when it is not possible to carefully control the administration of tests according to an experimental design. In the majority of testing contexts, assigning students to groups at random, administering tests at the same time under the same conditions to all groups, and assuring that retests are administered at exactly the same intervals to all groups, are practical impossibilities. But without random assignment, differences among groups may confound our estimates of reliability. For example, if some groups are already quite familiar with the test method and therefore benefit less from the practice of the first administration of the test than do other groups, the test–retest correlations will be lowered. Likewise if some groups find it easier to remember certain content areas than do other groups. There may also be an interaction between ability and test form if the highest ability group does not perform the best on all forms, or if the weakest group performs better than other groups on some forms.

One problem with the CTS model, then, is that it treats error variance as homogeneous in origin. Each of the estimates of reliability discussed above addresses one specific source of error, and treats other potential sources either as part of that source, or as true score. Equivalent forms estimates, for example, do not distinguish inconsistencies between the forms from inconsistencies within the forms. In estimating the equivalence of forms, therefore, any inconsistencies among the items in the forms themselves will lower our estimate of equivalence. Thus, if two tests turn out to have poor equivalence, the test user will not know whether this is because they are not equivalent or whether they are not internally consistent, unless he examines internal consistency separately.

In test–retest estimates, lasting changes in ability, which should be interpreted as true score variance, may be treated as error variance. For example, if some individuals' ability increases between test administrations while other individuals' ability remains about the same, this will result in a low estimate of stability. This is particularly a problem when assessing test–retest reliability in an educational setting where students are hopefully acquiring greater language ability, but in all probability doing so at different rates. Uniform but temporary improvements due to practice effect, on the other hand, may contribute to our estimate of true score variance. Thus, if all students' performance is equally improved the second time they take a test, simply because of short-term memory effects, this may result in a high test–retest correlation, suggesting that the test is a stable indicator of their language ability. In the classical model, therefore, different sources of error may be confused, or confounded with each other and with true score variance, since it is not possible to examine more than one source of error at a time, even though performance on any given test may be affected by several different sources of error simultaneously.

A second, related problem is that the CTS model considers all error to be random, and consequently fails to distinguish systematic error from random error. Factors other than the ability being measured that *regularly* affect the performance of some individuals and not others can be regarded as sources of systematic error or test bias. One source of systematic error—that associated with test method—has been extensively studied, and this factor will be discussed at length below (pp. 223–6). Other sources of test bias range from cultural content to psychological task set to the effects of guessing, or what Carroll (1961b) called 'topastic error'. The subject of test bias in general has been dealt with extensively in the measurement literature, and several sources of bias in language tests have also been investigated. These are discussed in detail in Chapter 7.

Generalizability theory

A broad model for investigating the relative effects of different sources of variance in test scores has been developed by Cronbach and his colleagues (Cronbach *et al.* 1963; Gleser *et al.* 1965; Cronbach *et al.* 1972). This model, which they call generalizability theory (G-theory), is grounded in the framework of factorial design and the analysis of variance.[13] It constitutes a theory and set of procedures for specifying and estimating the relative effects of different factors on observed test scores, and thus provides a means for relating the uses or interpretations to be made of test scores to the way test users specify and interpret different factors as either abilities or sources of error.

G-theory treats a given measure or score as a sample from a hypothetical universe of possible measures.[14] When we interpret a test score we generalize from a single measure to a universe of measures. In other words, on the basis of an individual's performance on a test we generalize to her performance in other contexts. The more reliable the sample of performance, or test score, is, the more generalizable it is. Reliability, then, is a matter of generalizability, and the extent to which we can generalize from a given score is a function of how we define the universe of measures. And the way we define a given universe of measures will depend upon the universe of generalization – the decisions or inferences we expect to make on the basis of the test results.

The application of G-theory to test development and use takes place in two stages. First, considering the uses that will be made of the test scores, the test developer designs and conducts a study to investigate the sources of variance that are of concern or interest. This involves identifying the relevant sources of variance (including traits, method facets, personal attributes, and random factors), designing procedures for collecting data that will permit the test developer to clearly distinguish the different sources of variance, administering the test according to this design, and then conducting the appropriate analyses. On the basis of this *generalizability study* ('G-study'), the test developer obtains estimates of the relative sizes of the different sources of variance ('variance components').

Depending on the outcome of this G-study, the test developer may revise the test or the procedures for administering it, and then conduct another G-study. Or, if the results of the G-study are satisfactory (if sources of error variance are minimized), the test developer proceeds to the second stage, a *decision study* ('D-study'). In a D-study, the test developer administers the test under operational conditions, that is, under the conditions in which the test will be used to make the decisions for which it is designed, and uses G-theory procedures to estimate the magnitude of the variance components.[15] These estimates provide information that can inform the interpretation and use of the test scores.

The application of G-theory thus enables test developers and test users to specify the different sources of variance that are of concern for a given test use, to estimate the relative importance of these different sources simultaneously, and to employ these estimates in the interpretation and use of test scores. G-theory can thus be seen as an extension of CTS theory, since it can examine the different sources of error variance discussed above (inconsistency, instability, lack of equivalence). Or, to look at it from another perspective, the CTS model is a special case of G-theory in which there are only two sources of variance: a single ability and a single source of error.

Universes of generalization and universes of measures

When we want to develop or select a test, we generally know the use or uses for which it is intended, and may also have an idea of what abilities we want to measure. In other words, we have in mind a *universe of generalization*, a domain of uses or abilities (or both) to which we want test scores to generalize. But within any given universe of generalization, there is likely to be a wide range of possible tests that could be used. In developing a test for a given situation, therefore, we need to ask what types of test scores we would be willing to accept as indicators of the ability to be measured for the purpose intended. That is, we need to define the *universe of possible measures* that would be acceptable for our purposes.[16]

Consider, for example, a situation in which we need to develop a test for use in placing large numbers of students into a course in listening comprehension. Because of the large number of students to be tested, and constraints on time and facilities, it will be necessary to limit the total testing time to 20 minutes per student. After reviewing the different ways in which we might try to measure this ability, we decide that we would be willing to accept, as a measure of listening comprehension, a score derived from any of three testing techniques – a multiple-choice test score, a dictation test score, or a rating of listening comprehension based on an oral interview. Furthermore, within these testing techniques, we might want to specify certain limitations. We could indicate, for example, that passages for the multiple-choice and dictation tests should be non-technical and from several different content areas, and that the multiple-choice questions, if presented in written form, should not be so extensive as to require reading comprehension, or that the interviews should cover a variety of language functions and contain a wide range of question types.

In specifying these different aspects of acceptable measures, we are, in effect, identifying various samples within a universe of possible measures that are relevant to this particular testing context – the universe of generalization. This universe can be defined in terms of specific characteristics, or *facets*, and the different *conditions* that may vary within each facet. Thus, the facets and conditions we specify define a given universe or set of possible measures. The facets and conditions for the example above are illustrated in Table 6.3. In this example, testing technique is a facet that has three conditions: multiple-choice, dictation, oral interview. Within the multiple-choice and dictation there is the facet of passage content, with economics, history, and physics as conditions, while within the oral interview is the facet of rater, with three conditions, Wayne, Susan, and Molly.

CONDITIONS / FACETS	Multiple-choice			Dictation			Oral interview		
Testing technique	Multiple-choice			Dictation			Oral interview		
Passage content	Economics	History	Physics	Economics	History	Physics			
Rater							Wayne	Susan	Molly

Table 6.3   Example of facets and conditions defining a universe of possible measures

Since we need a test that can be given in 20 minutes, our G-study would need to provide information that would permit us to choose *one* of the three conditions within the facet of testing technique. In order to do this we would use the information obtained from our G-study to determine the comparability of scores obtained from the different techniques, or the extent to which we can generalize across techniques. Within the multiple-choice and dictation tests, we would need to determine that passage content does not affect test takers' scores differentially. Or to put it another way, we would have to be sure that a test score based on the economics passage would generalize to performance on other passages. Finally, we would want to assure generalizability of ratings across raters, which is a facet within the oral interview technique. In developing the test and testing procedures, therefore, we would conduct a G-study to investigate the extent to which the test score is generalizable across the different conditions within each of the facets that define the universe of possible measures for this particular testing context.

Populations of persons

In addition to defining the universe of possible measures, we must define the group, or *population of persons* about whom we are going to make decisions or inferences. The way in which we define this population will be determined by the degree of generalizability we need for the given testing situation. If we intend to use the test results to make decisions about only one specific group, then that group defines our population of persons. In many testing situations, however, we are interested in generalizing beyond a particular group. This is true any time we intend to use a test with more than one group, as is often the case with entrance or placement tests that are used over a period of time with several groups of applicants. This is also the case with norm-referenced tests that will be used with a variety of different groups. In cases such as these, the characteristics of the population of persons need to be defined so that test users will know to which groups the results of the test will generalize. Some typical characteristics are age, level of language ability (for example, beginning, intermediate, advanced), and language use characteristics (for example, academic, vocational, professional).

Universe score

If we could obtain measures for an individual under all the different conditions specified in the universe of possible measures, his average score on these measures might be considered the best indicator of his ability. A *universe score* x_p is thus defined as the mean of a person's scores on all measures from the universe of possible measures (this universe of possible measures being defined by the facets and conditions of concern for a given test use). The universe score is thus the G-theory analog of the CTS-theory true score. The variance of a group of persons' scores on all measures would be equal to the universe score variance s^2_p, which is similar to CTS true score variance in the sense that it represents that proportion of observed score variance that remains constant across different individuals and different measurement facets and conditions.

The universe score is different from the CTS true score, however, in that an individual is likely to have different universe scores for different universes of measures. If, for example, we define a universe of measures with only two facets – difference in test occasions and equivalence of forms – universe scores thus defined will not generalize to a universe defined in terms of only one facet – consistency of items. Or, in terms of CTS-theory, true score estimates of stability and equivalence are likely to be different from those of internal consistency. In the example above, if we limit our universe of listening comprehension measures to ratings on oral interviews, and only examine these, we cannot be sure that individuals will have equivalent universe scores on multiple-choice and dictation tests. Likewise, if we define our population of persons as 'all freshmen at American colleges and universities', the test results of individuals in this population are not likely to generalize to a population of elementary school children. This conceptualization of generalizability makes explicit the fact that a given estimate of generalizability is limited to the specific universe of measures and population of persons within which it is defined, and that a test score that is 'True' for all persons, times, and places simply does not exist.

Generalizability coefficients

The G-theory analog of the CTS-theory reliability coefficient is the generalizability coefficient, which is defined as the proportion of observed score variance that is universe score variance:

$$\rho^2_{xx'} = \frac{s^2_p}{s^2_x} \qquad [16]$$

where s^2_p is universe score variance and s^2_x is observed score variance, which includes both universe score and error variance. We can also define different proportions of observed score variance that are due to error variances associated with the different facets in our universe of measures. Thus, in the listening comprehension example above, we might define error variance due to testing technique as s^2_{test}/s^2_x and the error due to passage content as $s^2_{passage}/s^2_x$.

Estimation

The source of variance in which we are most interested is that which is due to differences in persons, specifically differences in the ability being measured. It is the variance due to differences in persons' ability that constitutes the universe score variance, s^2_p, used in estimating the generalizability coefficient. Other sources of variance (facets of the universe of measures) that are included in any given G-study, and how they are interpreted, will depend upon the specific testing context. In order to estimate the relative effect of these different sources of variance on the observed scores, it is necessary to obtain multiple measures for each person under the different conditions for each facet. Thus, the number of measures needed per person will be equal to the product of the number of conditions in the different facets.[17]

One statistical procedure that can be used for estimating the relative effects of different sources of variance on test scores is the analysis of variance (ANOVA).[18] To illustrate the logic of this procedure, consider our earlier example of an oral interview with different question forms, or sets of questions, and different interviewer/raters (pp. 184–5). We can represent the variance in test scores in terms of the different facets in our G-study design:

$$s^2_x = s^2_p + s^2_f + s^2_r \qquad [17]$$

where: s^2_x is the variance in all the test scores

s^2_p is the universe, or person score variance

s^2_f is the variance due to differences in question forms

s^2_r is the variance due to differences in raters

However, these sources of variance may interact with each other, so that some test takers might do better with a particular form or rater, or certain raters may give higher ratings when using a particular question form, for example. We therefore need to include, as additional sources of variance, the interactions between persons and facets (persons by forms, s^2_{pf}, persons by raters s^2_{pr}), between the two facets (s^2_{fr}), and that between persons, forms, and raters, s^2_{pfr}. Finally, there will be some residual variance (s^2_e) that is not accounted for by the sources in the design.

There are thus several sources of variance, or *variance components*, in this design. Using ANOVA, we could obtain estimates for all the variance components in the design: (1) the main effects for persons, raters, and forms; (2) the two-way interactions between persons and raters, persons and forms, and forms and raters, and (3) a component that contains the three-way interaction among persons, raters, and forms, as well as for the residual, or random variance. This analysis would enable us to estimate the relative effects of the different variance components in which we are interested. If we found that the variance component for persons by forms (s^2_{pf}) was significantly large, this would indicate that at least one question form was biased for or against individuals of either high or low ability. Likewise, a significant variance component for persons by raters (s^2_{pr}) would indicate biased raters. If the variance component for forms by raters (s^2_{fr}) was significant, this would suggest that the raters rated more highly with some question forms than with others. We would probably regard these as sources of error that need to be examined so as to eliminate them from the interview.

If none of these interactions was significantly large, we could then examine other potential sources of error: the variance components for question forms and raters. If we found that the variance component for forms (s^2_f) was significantly large, this would be an indication that the interviewees performed better on some sets of questions than on others, or that the four sets were not equivalent. In this case we would examine the four sets of questions to try to determine why they were not equivalent. Similarly if we found that the variance component for raters (s^2_r) was significantly large, we would attempt to determine what factors might have caused the raters to rate differently. Finally, we could interpret the variance component for persons (s^2_p) as the variance due to differences in individual interviewees' abilities, that is, differences in their universe scores. Hopefully, we would find this variance component to be the largest, since this corresponds to universe score variance. In this way, the generalizability study would provide us with specific information about magnitude of various sources of variance in a set of test scores.

If we wanted to obtain an estimate of the reliability of the ratings in our example, we could compute a generalizability coefficient by dividing the universe score variance, s^2_p, by the total variance in all 24 measures (four forms, six raters), s^2_x:

$$\rho^2_{xx'} = \frac{s^2_p}{s^2_x} \qquad \begin{matrix}[18]\\(= [16])\end{matrix}$$

This generalizability coefficient is an estimate of the proportion of the total score variance that is accounted for by the universe score variance, taking into consideration all the sources of error that have been included in the G-study design, both systematic (forms, raters, 2-way interactions, 3-way interaction) and random (residual).

Recall that the CTS-theory approach to this problem would be either to compute correlations among scores on the four forms and among the different raters, or to compute alpha coefficients to estimate the equivalent forms and inter-rater reliabilities. The problem with this was that it would not account for possible interactions. It would, however, provide separate estimates based on different sources of error. If separate coefficients of generalizability corresponding to specific sources of error were of interest, these could also be obtained from the ANOVA results. We would first compute the proportion of variance for the specific error component by dividing the variance component for that error by the observed score variance. Subtracting this from one would then give us the proportion of observed score variance that is universe score variance, or the generalizability coefficient corresponding to that particular source of error variance. Generalizability coefficients for the various sources of error in the above example would be as follows:

Inter-rater generalizability coefficient:

$$1 - \frac{s^2_r}{s^2_x} \qquad [19]$$

Equivalent forms generalizability coefficient:

$$1 - \frac{s^2_f}{s^2_x} \qquad [20]$$

Forms by raters generalizability coefficient:

$$1 - \frac{s^2_{fr}}{s^2_x} \qquad [21]$$

Persons by forms generalizability coefficient:

$$1 - \frac{s^2_{pf}}{s^2_x} \qquad [22]$$

Persons by raters generalizability coefficient:

$$1 - \frac{s^2_{pr}}{s^2_x} \qquad [23]$$

We could also compute a generalizability coefficient for the residual variance component, but since this is considered to be random, it will be of little practical use in helping us design our interview, except if the random variance component turns out to be very large, in which case we may have to design another G-study to help us identify what the major source of error is.

Two recent studies that illustrate the practical application of G-theory to the development and use of language tests are Bolus *et al.* (1982) and van Weeren and Theunissen (1987). Van Weeren and Theunissen were interested in determining the relative effects of differences in items and raters as sources of error in a test of pronunciation. In a study with Dutch secondary school students of French and German, they administered tests of French and German pronunciation. Each test consisted of a passage in either French or German that included items that were common pronunciation problems for native Dutch-speaking students. Each student was required to read aloud a passage in the language he had studied, and these oral readings were recorded on tape. Each item in each recording was then rated by several different raters who were all qualified teachers of the language, either French or German. The G-study design for each language included two facets: items and raters. For the French test, there were 40 items and 15 raters, while for the German test there were 24 items and 14 raters. On the basis of their sample, they computed variance components for each test, and then used these to estimate generalizability coefficients for different lengths of tests and different numbers of raters. Their results are summarized in Table 6.4 below:

	French		German	
	1 rater	2 raters	1 rater	2 raters
20 random items	.58	.66	.27	.38
30 random items	.66	.73	.35	.47
40 random items	.72	.78	.41	.53
40 fixed items	.86	.92	.51	.67

*Table 6.4   Generalizability coefficients
(van Weeren and Theunissen 1987)*

This table presents generalizability coefficients estimated for 20, 30, and 40 random items, that is, for items selected at random from a 'possible' universe of pronunciation items, and for 40 items exactly like the ones actually included, or for 40 'fixed' items. Generalizability coefficients are also given for one and two presumably 'random' raters from a possible universe of raters, for each length of test.

These results illustrate several advantages of G-theory over classical test theory. First, G-theory can be used to estimate the effect of changing both the number of items and the number of raters, thus enabling the test developer to determine the most feasible means for maximizing reliability within given administrative constraints. In the case of the French test, increasing the number of items has approximately the same effect on reliability as adding a second rater, so that if time constraints do not permit the tester to use a large number of items, a second rater should be used to increase reliability. If a second rater cannot be used, then the test should be lengthened to increase reliability. With the German test, on the other hand, adding a second rater would be much more effective in increasing reliability than would lengthening the test, thus giving the tester less flexibility in adjusting the testing procedure to increase reliability.

G-theory can also provide comparable reliability estimates for tests of differing lengths with differing numbers of raters. Thus, although there were 40 items in the French test, with 15 raters, and 24 items with 14 raters for the German test, generalizability coefficients were estimated for 20, 30, and 40 items with one and two raters, for both tests. This is comparable to the Spearman–Brown prophecy formula in classical test theory, but is much more powerful, in that increases in generalizability due to changes in several facets can be estimated simultaneously.

In summary, G-theory provides a model for examining reliability that is potentially more powerful than the CTS model. The application of G-theory enables the test developer or user to distinguish and explicitly examine different sources of error that are ambiguous in the CTS model, and to examine sources of error – interactions – that are confounded and cannot be investigated at all in the CTS model. It also makes it possible for the test user to estimate the relative effects of several sources of variance in a single study and to use these estimates to determine the most feasible option for increasing reliability in a given testing situation.

The most important application of G-theory to the development and use of tests is that it provides a logical framework for systematically identifying and empirically examining those sources of measurement error that are relevant to the uses for which the test is intended. It thus helps assure that the test developer relates the investigation of reliability to actual test conditions, and enables the test user to better judge the extent to which the test is likely to yield comparable results under other conditions and with other persons.

Standard error of measurement: interpreting individual test scores within classical true score and generalizability theory

The approaches to estimating reliability that have been developed within both CTS theory and G-theory are based on group performance, and provide information for test developers and test users about how consistent the scores of *groups* of individuals are on a given test. However, reliability and generalizability coefficients provide no direct information about the accuracy of *individual* test scores. That is, they give us information about the consistency in the relative standing of the individuals in a group across different halves, items, raters, times of administration, and forms, but say nothing about how much we might expect an individual's score to vary across these same components. It makes sense to say, for example, that 85 per cent of the variance among a given set of test scores is true or universe score variance ($r_{xx'} = .85$), but it would be meaningless to say that 85 per cent of a person's score is true score. If a person scored 67 on such a test, would this mean that her true score is 57? Or that we are 85 per cent sure that 67 is her true score? Or that we would expect her to score 67 on the test 85 per cent of the time? Unfortunately, none of these is correct; indeed, neither reliability nor generalizability coefficients can themselves be used directly to interpret individual test scores. For this, we need some indicator of how much we would expect an individual's test scores to vary, given a particular level of reliability. The most useful indicator for this purpose, within CTS theory and G-theory, is called the *standard error of measurement.*

If our tests were perfectly reliable, observed scores would always be equal to true scores. That is, if a test taker were to take a perfectly reliable test many times, without practice effect and without undergoing any changes herself, she would always obtain the same score, and this would equal her true score. However, our tests are *not* perfectly reliable, and errors of measurement – error scores – cause observed scores to vary from true scores. Since error scores are assumed to be random, with a mean equal to zero, some of these error scores will be positive, causing the test taker's score to be higher than her true score, some will be negative, causing her observed score to be lower than her true score, and some will be equal to zero, in which case the test taker's obtained scores will equal her true score. For example, if an individual's composition were scored by a rater who is inconsistent, and thus happens to score her test paper more leniently than usual, this could cause her observed score to be higher than her true score. On the other hand, if a test taker stayed up late the night before the test, and consequently was not as alert as usual, this could well cause her observed score to be lower than her true score.

What we are really looking at, when we investigate the amount of measurement error in individual test scores, are differences between test takers' obtained scores and their true scores. If a hypothetical test taker were to take a test a large number of times, we would expect some of her obtained scores to be different from her true score. If the test were highly reliable, very few of the obtained scores would differ from the true score, and these would not differ by much. If the test were taken a very large number (hundreds) of times, (and the test taker did not change from one test administration to the next) we would expect the obtained scores to form a normal distribution, whose mean would be equal to the test taker's true score. From the definition of true and error score (formula [1], p. 167) we can see that the difference between an obtained score and the true score is equal to the error score ($x - x_t = x_e$), so that differences among the hypothetical test taker's obtained scores would be solely a function of differences in their error scores. Thus, the standard deviation of the hypothetical distribution of obtained scores would be equal to the standard deviation of the error scores. The more reliable the test is, the closer the obtained scores will cluster around the true score mean, resulting in a smaller standard deviation of errors; the less reliable the test, the greater the standard deviation. Because of its importance in the interpretation of test scores, the standard deviation of the error scores has a name: the *standard error of measurement* (SEM). If we could give a test to an individual hundreds of times, we could compute both her expected true score – the mean of the observed scores – and the SEM.

Of course, it is not generally possible for an individual to take a test such a large number of times, and even if it were, the test taker would inevitably change from one test administration to the next. Therefore, we cannot actually estimate an individual's true score this way. However, we can use the theorems of the classical measurement model to estimate the SEM from the obtained scores of a given group of test takers. This SEM can then be used to describe how close the obtained score of individuals in this group are to their true scores.

Recall that in classical measurement theory, error variance can be defined as a function of the total score variance and the reliability coefficient:

$$s^2_e = s^2_x (1 - r_{xx'}) \qquad [24]$$
$$(= [19])$$

where s^2_e is the error variance, s^2_x is the variance of the observed scores, and $r_{xx'}$ is the reliability coefficient. The same relationship holds for G-theory, substituting the appropriate generalizability coefficient for the reliability coefficient. If we work through the algebra, we can derive a formula for estimating the SEM directly from the coefficient of reliability (or generalizability) and the standard deviation of the observed scores:

$$s^2_e = s^2_x (1 - r_{xx'})$$

Taking the square root of both sides of the equation yields a formula for s_e, which is an estimate of the SEM.

$$s_e = s_x \sqrt{1 - r_{xx'}} \qquad [25]$$

If the standard deviation of a test were 15, for example, and its reliability were estimated as .85, then the estimated SEM, by formula [25], would be 5.81, or, rounded to the nearest whole number, approximately six score points.

This estimate of the SEM indicates how far a given obtained score is from its true score, and thus provides a means for estimating the accuracy of a given obtained score as an indicator of an individual's true score. We can do this by using the estimate of the SEM to define the upper and lower limits of an interval, or band, around the obtained score. Since both CTS theory and G-theory assume that error scores are normally distributed and uniform for all test takers, at all levels of ability, we can use the constant percentages associated with the normal distribution to determine the probability that the individual's true score will fall within this band. (See pp. 72–3 for a discussion of the percentages under the normal distribution.) Since the SEM is the standard deviation of the error scores, we know that there is a 68 per cent probability that the true score will fall within one SEM of the obtained score. If, for example, the estimated SEM of a given test were four, and an individual obtained a score of 67, we could say that there is about a 68 per cent probability that her true score is between 63 and 71 (67 ± 4). Or, to put it another way, we would be about 68 per cent confident that her true score is between 63 and 71. Because this interval defines the level of confidence we have in estimating the true score from the observed score, it is called a *confidence interval*. The confidence intervals for this example are illustrated in Figure 6.5.

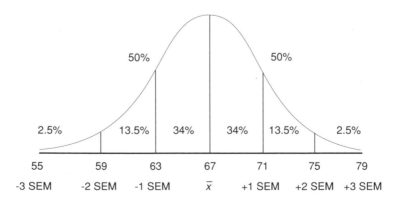

Figure 6.5 Illustration of SEM confidence intervals

If we wanted to be even more confident in our estimation, we could set the interval to *two* SEMs of the obtained score, and be about 95 per cent confident that the true score is between 59 and 75.

One very useful application of the SEM is in the reporting of band scores. A band score, or band interpretation, is a straightforward application of the confidence intervals discussed above. A *band score* is the score range around an observed score that is defined by a given confidence interval of the SEM. Thus, in the example above, the 68 per cent band score for an observed score of 67 is 63–71, while the 95 per cent band score is 59–75.

When only the obtained scores on tests are reported, there is often a tendency to treat them as accurate indicators of the abilities the tests were designed to measure. This may result in the over-interpretation of small or chance differences in observed scores as indicating actual differences in the abilities measured. This is particularly problematic for tests which report very high coefficients of reliability. However, since the estimated standard deviation of the differences between raw scores and true scores (the SEM) is a function of *both* the standard deviation of the test scores themselves and their reliability, reporting high reliability coefficients, without accompanying band score interpretations, can be misleading. Consider, for example, two individuals who scored 500 and 520 on a test whose reported standard deviation and reliability are 100 and .96 respectively. Without a band interpretation, a test user might consider this difference large enough to warrant different decisions for the two test takers. However, when we consider that the estimated SEM of this test is 20 points ($100 \times \sqrt{1 - .96}$), and that these two observed scores actually have overlapping band scores (480–520, 500–540), we realize that there is a 68 per cent chance that this difference in observed scores is due to measurement error.

The SEM thus provides a means for applying estimates of reliability to the interpretation and use of individuals' observed test scores. Its primary advantage is that it makes test users aware of how much variability in observed scores to expect as a result of measurement error. Suppose, in the example above, that a cut-off score for admission to a program had been set at 520. Without considering the SEM and its associated band interpretations, one test taker would be admitted and the other would not. Consideration of the band score, however, might lead to a different outcome. If the administrator of the program wanted to be reasonably (68 per cent) certain not to erroneously deny admission to potentially successful students, she might decide to accept students with scores as low as 500 (within one

SEM of 520). If she wanted to be very (95 per cent) certain that she did not miss any potentially successful students, she could accept students with scores as low as 480, or two SEMs below the cut-off. If, on the other hand, the program administrator were more concerned with minimizing errors in the other direction – admitting students who were not likely to succeed – she would be less likely to accept students whose obtained scores were much below the cut-off.

From this example, it should be clear that the extent to which one wishes to take into account score variations that are due to measurement error will depend on the nature of the particular use that will be made of the test score. In addition, the degree of confidence one wishes to have will be a function of the seriousness of the decisions to be made. Thus, if the decisions to be made are relatively minor, that is, can be easily changed if wrong, and affect a relatively small number of individuals, then the 68 per cent confidence interval or band interpretation is probably sufficiently stringent. If, on the other hand, the decisions to be made will have major consequences for test takers, then the more conservative 95 per cent or 99 per cent (± three SEMs) confidence intervals may be required to minimize the chance of decision errors.

As a matter of caution, it should be noted that although the estimation of the SEM is objective, the inferences about true scores that can be made on the basis of confidence intervals are complex, and require a number of assumptions that may or may not be justified in any given testing situation. These are essentially the assumptions that underlie the particular approach used to estimate reliability, as well as the general assumptions of CTS theory and G-theory. Nevertheless, because of its usefulness in interpreting individual test scores, the SEM is actually of more practical interest to test users than is the coefficient of reliability upon which it is based.

Item response theory

A major limitation to CTS theory is that it does not provide a very satisfactory basis for predicting how a given individual will perform on a given item. There are two reasons for this. First, CTS theory makes no assumptions about how an individual's level of ability affects the way he performs on a test. Second, the only information that is available for predicting an individual's performance on a given item is the index of difficulty, p, which is simply the proportion of individuals in a group that responded correctly to the item. Thus, the only information available in predicting how an individual will answer an item is the average performance of a group on this item. However, it is quite obvious that an individual's level of ability must also be considered in predicting how she will perform on a given item; an individual with a high level of ability would clearly be expected to perform better on a difficult item that measures that ability than would a person with a relatively low level of the same ability.

Because of this and other limitations in CTS theory (and G-theory, as well), psychometricians have developed a number of mathematical models for relating an individual's test performance to that individual's level of ability.[19] These models are based on the fundamental theorem that an individual's expected performance on a particular test question, or item, is a function of *both* the level of difficulty of the item and the individual's level of ability. Such models are generally referred to as 'item response' models, and the general theory upon which they are based is called 'item response' theory (IRT). (Another common term that is used for this theory is 'latent-trait' theory.)

The unidimensionality assumption

Item response theory is based on stronger, or more restrictive assumptions than is CTS theory, and is thus able to make stronger predictions about individuals' performance on individual items, their levels of ability, and about the characteristics of individual items. In order to incorporate information about test takers' levels of ability, IRT must make an assumption about the number of abilities being measured. Most of the IRT models that are currently being applied make the specific assumption that the items in a test measure a single, or *unidimensional* ability or trait, and that the items form a *unidimensional* scale of measurement. IRT models also make the technical assumption of local independence, referred to in Note 6.

Item characteristic curves

In addition to these general assumptions, each specific IRT model makes specific assumptions about the relationship between the test taker's ability and his performance on a given item. These assumptions are explicitly stated in the mathematical formula, or *item characteristic curve* (ICC), that characterizes this relationship.[20] These ICCs are the cornerstones of IRT models, in that they express the assumed relationship between an individual's probability of passing a given item and his level of ability. Different IRT models can be characterized in terms of differences in their general form, and in the types of information, or parameters, about the characteristics of the item itself that they use in expressing the ICC. The form of the ICC is determined by the particular mathematical model on which it is based.[21] The types of information about item characteristics may include: (1) the degree to which the item discriminates among individuals of differing levels of ability (the 'discrimination' parameter a); (2) the level of difficulty of the item (the 'difficulty' parameter b), and (3) the probability that an individual of low ability can answer the item correctly (the 'pseudo-chance' or 'guessing' parameter c). The ICC for a given item is considered to be fully defined when its general form is specified and when the parameters for the given item are known. One of the major considerations in the application of IRT models, therefore, is the estimation of these item parameters.

One IRT model that incorporates information on all three of the above parameters to describe the ICC, the three-parameter model, will be used to illustrate briefly the characteristics of ICCs. This model specifies that the relationship between the level of ability and the probability of a correct response is non-linear, and that it is a function of all three of the parameters mentioned above. This relationship can be presented graphically for individual items, as in Figure 6.6.

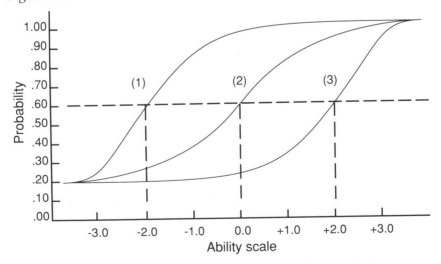

Figure 6.6   Examples of 3-parameter item characteristic curves

The scale of ability, which in this example has a mean of zero and a standard deviation of one, is represented along the horizontal axis, while the probability of a correct response, which ranges theoretically from zero to one, is represented on the vertical axis. ICCs for three items, (1), (2), and (3), are represented. First, we can see that the pseudo-chance parameter c is the same (p = .20) for all three items. In this model, this parameter defines the lower bound ('asymptote') of the ICC. Next, consider the difficulty parameter, b, which is defined as the level of ability at which the probability of a correct response is halfway between the pseudo-chance parameter and one, which in this example is .60. Item (1), with a difficulty parameter equal to -2.0, is the easiest item, while item (3), with a difficulty parameter of $+2.0$, is the most difficult. That is, individuals who are quite low (two standard deviations below the mean) in ability level have a 60 per cent probability of answering item (1) correctly, while individuals who are one standard deviation below the mean ability and above are virtually certain to get the item correct. For item (3), on the other hand, only individuals whose ability level is well above (one standard deviation) the mean ability have a probability greater than chance of answering the item correctly.

These items also vary in terms of the discrimination parameter, a, which is proportional to the slope of the ICC at the point of the difficulty parameter. The steeper the slope, the greater the discrimination parameter. Thus, item (2), which has the gentlest slope, has the lowest discrimination. That is, there is very little change in the probability of a correct response as a function of differences in ability. Items (1) and (3), on the other hand, have much steeper slopes, and discriminate much more effectively between individuals at different ability levels.

Two other IRT models that are fairly common are the two-parameter model, in which it is assumed that individuals of low ability will have virtually no probability of a correct response, so that the pseudo-chance parameter is effectively set equal to zero, and the one-parameter, or Rasch model, in which the discrimination of all the items is assumed to be equal, and it is also assumed that there is no guessing. A discussion of the relative merits and limitations of these various models is well beyond the scope of this book. It is worth noting, however, that although the three-parameter model is used for development and analysis of the *Test of English as a Foreign Language*, the majority of IRT applications to language testing to date have utilized the Rasch model (for example, Davidson and Henning 1975; Griffin 1985; Henning *et al.* 1985; Madsen and

Larson 1986; Pollitt and Hutchinson 1987; Larson 1987; Madsen 1987; Adams *et al.* 1987; Henning 1987).

Ability score

Recall that neither CTS theory nor G-theory provides an estimation of an individual's level of ability. Both approach this indirectly through the use of the standard error of measurement for establishing a confidence interval around the observed score, within which we can be reasonably sure the true or universe score will fall. Furthermore, these confidence intervals for estimating true or universe scores are based on the performance of a given group, so that the confidence intervals for individuals with high, intermediate, and low ability are the same. One of the advantages of IRT is that it provides estimates of individual test takers' levels of ability. These ability scores (commonly symbolized by the Greek letter theta, 'θ') can be estimated in the process of fitting the observed item responses to an IRT model.

Hambleton and Swaminathan (1985) have described a typical procedure for estimating ability scores. First, the test developer collects a set of observed item responses from a relatively large number of test takers. After an initial examination of how well various models fit the data, an IRT model is selected. Then, through an iterative procedure, parameter estimates are assigned to items and ability scores to individuals, so as to maximize the agreement, or 'fit' between the particular IRT model and the test data (Hambleton and Swaminathan 1985: 53–4). Because of the complexities of the computations involved in these estimations, they generally can be performed only through the use of computer programs.[22]

If the general IRT assumptions are met and if the particular IRT model fits the data, three major advantages accrue from the use of IRT models. First, assuming a large number of items that measure the same trait, an individual's ability estimate is independent of the particular set of items that are taken. Second, assuming a large population of test takers, the item parameter estimates are independent of the particular sample of test takers upon whose responses they are based. These two properties have important implications for practical testing applications, particularly for tailored testing, equating different test forms, and identifying test bias, applications that are beyond the scope of this discussion. A third advantage, however, is directly relevant to the topic of reliability, and is discussed below.

Precision of measurement

There are a number of limitations on both CTS theory and G-theory with respect to estimating the precision of measurement, only two of which will be discussed here.[23] First, estimators of both reliability and generalizability, and the standard errors of measurement associated with them, are sample dependent, so that scores from the same test administered to different groups of test takers may differ in their reliabilities. A second limitation is that error variance is treated as homogeneous across individuals, so that estimates of reliability or generalizability are based on group, rather than individual performance. That is, measurement error is assumed to be the same for individuals whose test performance is excellent, poor, or average, so that a low score on a test is regarded as just as reliable an indicator of ability as an average score.

Item information function

These limitations on the CTS theory and G-theory approaches to precision of measurement are addressed in the IRT concept of *information function*. The *item information function* refers to the amount of information a given item provides for estimating an individual's level of ability, and is a function of both the slope of the ICC and the amount of variation at each ability level. In general, the steeper the slope of the ICC and the smaller the variation, the greater the information function. Thus, a given item will have differing information functions at different levels of ability. That is, a difficult item will provide very little information at low levels of ability, since virtually all individuals at these levels will get the item wrong. Similarly, an easy item that high ability individuals uniformly answer correctly will not provide much information at this ability level. Thus, the information function of a given item will be at its maximum for individuals whose ability is at or near the value of the difficulty parameter.

These characteristics can be illustrated by considering the information functions for the three test items whose ICCs were shown in Figure 6.6. Assuming that the amount of variation in these items at each ability level is the same, their information function will differ primarily as a function of differences in their slopes and their difficulty parameters. The information functions for these three items are illustrated in Figure 6.7. In this example, item (1) has a very high information function, which is at its maximum at −2.0 on the ability

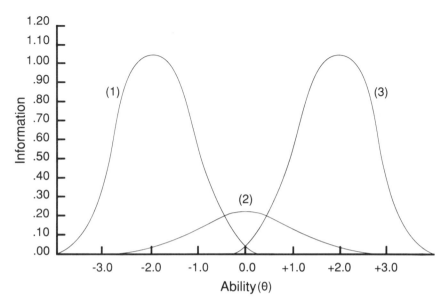

Figure 6.7   Examples of item information functions

scale. This item, then, provides the most information about differences in ability at the lower end of the ability scale. Item (3), on the other hand, which also has a very high information function, provides the most information about differences in ability at the high end of the ability scale. In contrast to these two items, item (2) provides relatively little information at any point on the ability scale.

Test information function

The *test information function* (TIF) is the sum of the item information functions, each of which contributes independently to the total, and is a measure of how much information a test provides at different ability levels. The TIF is the IRT analog of CTS theory reliability and the standard error of measurement, and offers two important advantages over these indicators of precision of measurement. Since the standard error of the ability estimates at a given ability level are inversely related to the TIF, it provides estimates of measurement errors *at each ability level*. An additional advantage is that the TIF is independent of the particular sample of individuals upon whose responses it is based. This is because the TIF is a function of the individual item information functions, each of which is based on ICCs that are sample independent. The TIF is thus generalizable across different samples of individual test takers.

IRT offers many important advantages over CTS theory, both in terms of ability and item parameter estimates that are sample independent, which are very useful properties for practical applications such as tailored testing, test equating, and identifying item bias, and in terms of its increased power in estimating the precision of measurement. These advantages are possible because of the stronger assumptions made by IRT models. But while these assumptions make more powerful predictions possible, they place greater restrictions on the applications of IRT to practical testing problems, and a greater burden of responsibility on both test developers and test users to assure that the IRT assumptions are met, and that the particular IRT model selected provides an adequate fit to the test data to be analyzed.

Modern measurement theory has developed beyond the classical true score model. Nevertheless, there remain many testing situations in which the number of test takers is too small, or limitations on available resources preclude designing studies that would permit the use of either generalizability theory or item response theory for estimating test reliability. In the majority of classroom testing situations, for example, teachers have neither the time nor the resources to design G-studies or to compute IRT item and ability parameters. Furthermore, most decisions at the class level are made on a day-to-day basis, and hence can be quickly changed if necessary. One fundamental consideration in the investigation of reliability that was mentioned earlier is that this must be cost effective. That is, the time and resources that go into investigating reliability and minimizing measurement error must be justified by the amount of information gained and the usefulness of that information, given the types and level of decisions to be made. I believe that estimating reliability and applying such estimates to the interpretation and use of test scores is an essential part of testing, in all contexts, from the classroom to nationwide programs. Thus, in situations that may not permit the use of G-theory or IRT, estimating reliability through classical approaches is a far better alternative than failing to investigate the effects of measurement error at all because these more powerful approaches are not possible.

Reliability of criterion-referenced test scores

All of the approaches to reliability discussed thus far have been developed within frameworks that operationally define level of ability (true score, universe score, IRT ability parameter, θ) as an average of an indefinitely large number of measures. That is, an individual's observed score on a given test is interpreted in relation to an estimate of what his average score would be if we were able to obtain a large number of measures of that ability. Similarly, an individual's performance can be interpreted with reference to the average performance of other individuals on the test, specifically, how far above or below the group average he is. This, of course, is the definition of a norm-referenced (NR) test score. In order for scores on such tests to be interpretable, they must be clearly distinct from each other. Thus, tests that are intended to provide NR score interpretations are designed and developed to maximize inter-individual score differences, or score variance.

In the criterion-referenced (CR) interpretation of test scores, on the other hand, an individual's ability is defined not in terms of the average performance of a group of individuals, but in terms of his successful completion of tasks from a set or domain of criterion tasks, or his performance with reference to a criterion level that defines the ability in question. In CR test interpretation, test scores provide information not about an individual's relative standing in a given group, but about his relative 'mastery' of an ability domain. Thus, tests intended to provide CR score interpretations are designed and developed to be maximally representative of the criterion ability.

As a consequence of the way ability is defined operationally in classical true score theory, reliability estimates are highly dependent upon the amount of variability in test scores. This can be demonstrated by considering the extreme case in which there is no variance in test scores, such as would happen if all individuals answered all test items correctly. In this case, as has been noted by Cziko (1981), classical correlational approaches to reliability (split-half, equivalence, stability) would yield estimates of zero. This is also true for estimates based on variance components, such as KR-20 and the Guttman split-half.[24]

In many situations where CR tests are used, we find very little variation in test scores. Suppose, for example, that we have developed an achievement test based on specific course objectives. If we give this test to beginning language learners at the start of the course, we would expect them to obtain uniformly low scores, while it is likely, if instruction has been effective, that most students would obtain slightly higher scores, with little variation among them, if we gave them the test again after a period of, say, two weeks. By the end of the course, if instruction had been equally effective for all students, we would expect students to obtain uniformly high scores, again with little variation among them. If we estimated the internal consistency of each set of scores using KR-20, we would probably obtain disappointingly low reliability coefficients. And if we computed the correlations between the first two sets of scores, this would probably give a very low estimate of stability, since there is likely to be very little variance in either the test or the retest scores. At the same time, it is intuitively obvious that in this example, the achievement test scores may accurately reflect changes in the students' relative mastery of the content objectives. Thus, the problem with using classical NR estimates of reliability with CR test scores is that such estimates are sensitive primarily to inter-individual variations, which are of little interest in CR interpretation.

Because of the differences in score interpretation, CR and NR tests are typically used in different decision contexts. NR test scores are most useful in situations in which comparative decisions, such as the selection of individuals for a program, are to be made. CR test scores, on the other hand, are more useful in settings where making 'absolute' decisions regarding mastery or nonmastery (or degree of mastery) of the ability domain is the primary concern (Cronbach *et al.* 1972). NR test situations are those in which we are interested in making comparisons among individuals and groups with reference to the performance of other individuals or groups. CR test situations, on the other hand, are those in which we are interested in comparisons between an individual's or a group's level of ability and a level of ability that defines 'mastery' of the ability domain, or in changes in individuals' levels of ability, with reference to a criterion domain or level of ability, over time.

In language testing, the most common CR test situations are those that occur in educational programs and language classrooms, in which decisions such as progress or assigning grades must be made. In situations such as these, achievement tests are most commonly used. There are, however, two specific types of decisions, involving certification and minimum competency, in which proficiency tests are more typically used.

Aspects of reliability in CR tests

Although NR reliability estimates are inappropriate for CR test scores, it is *not* the case that reliability is of no concern in such tests. On the contrary, consistency, stability, and equivalence are equally important for CR tests. However, they take on different aspects in the CR context, and therefore require different approaches to both estimation and interpretation. Indeed, some measurement specialists who have developed procedures for estimating these qualities in CR tests have rejected the term 'reliability coefficient' in favor of others such as 'agreement index' (Berk 1984c) and 'dependability co-efficient' (Kane and Brennan 1980). The concept of reliability applies to two aspects of criterion-referenced tests: the accuracy of the obtained score as an indicator of a 'domain' score, and the consistency of the decisions that are based on CR test scores.

Dependability of domain score estimates

One approach to CR test development is to specify a well-defined set of tasks or items that constitute a domain, with any given test viewed as a sample of items or tasks from that particular domain.[25] In this approach to CR test development, the analogue to CTS theory 'true score' and the G-theory 'universe score', is the 'domain score', which is an individual's level of mastery of the given domain, or the score he could be expected to obtain if he were tested on all the items in the domain.

In order for an individual's observed score on a given test to be interpreted as a dependable indicator of his domain score, we must be sure that the given sample of items or tasks is representative of that domain.[26] Assume, for example, that we have defined a number of abilities that constitute the domain of reading comprehension, and that we have generated a large number of items that we believe measure these abilities. If we take a sample of, say, 30 items from this pool of items, can we assume that these specific items are all equally representative of the domain? This question pertains to the internal consistency of items drawn from a criterion domain, and is analogous to internal consistency in NR tests. Another question is whether two different samples of 30 items each are equally representative of the domain, which is analogous to equivalent forms reliability in NR tests. If the samples of items are highly consistent and if different sets of items are equivalent, then observed scores should be dependable indicators of domain scores.

Domain score dependability index

One approach to estimating the dependability of scores on domain-referenced tests involves a direct application of G-theory to estimate the proportion of observed score variance that is domain score variance (Kane and Brennan 1980; Brennan 1984). This approach yields a coefficient Φ which Brennan (1984) calls a 'general purpose index of dependability of domain-referenced interpretations'. This coefficient is generally computed from the variance components as part of G- and D-studies, and this requires considerable computation. Recently however, J. D. Brown (1989) has derived a formula for Φ that is relatively simple to compute, and requires only the number of persons who took the test, the number of items on the test, the mean and standard deviation of the proportion scores (the mean and standard deviation divided by the number of items, respectively), and the norm-referenced KR–20 for the test. Brown's formula thus provides a practical means for estimating the dependability of an obtained score on a domain-referenced test as an indicator of an individual's domain score.

Criterion-referenced standard error of measurement

Several different methods for estimating the dependability of observed scores as indicators of domain scores have been developed.[27] Most of them involve the estimation of a standard error of measurement (SEM). Recall that in the NR interpretation, the SEM is the standard deviation of the error scores, that is, of the differences between observed and true scores, and that the estimate of this SEM, the s_e, is a function of both the reliability and the standard deviation of the obtained test scores (cf. pp. 197–202). In the CR interpretation, the SEM is the standard deviation of the differences between the observed score and the *domain* score, and it is thus not a function of the relative differences between observed scores and the mean score of a given group.

An individual-specific estimate of the criterion-referenced SEM is the $SE_{meas}(x_i)$, which is computed as follows (Berk 1984c):

$$SE_{meas}(x_i) = \sqrt{\frac{x_i(n - x_i)}{n - 1}} \qquad [26]$$

where x_i is the observed test score for a given individual and n is equal to the number of items on the test.[28] Such estimates of the SEMs for individual test takers can be used to compute individual band scores. If, for example, an individual scored 25 on a 30 item CR test, his $SE_{meas}(x_i)$ would equal 2.28, which, rounded to the nearest whole number, would yield a 68 per cent band score of 23–27 (25 ± 2) and a 95 per cent band score of 21–29 (25 ± 4).[29] The advantages of this estimate of the SEM for CR tests are that it is easy to calculate and interpret and that it provides an unbiased estimate of error based on an infinite or finite domain of items (Berk 1984b). The disadvantages are that individual estimates will be lower for extremely high or low scores, and higher for scores around the mean, and that calculations are tedious, since a separate estimate must be calculated for each observed test score. Nevertheless, the $SE_{meas}(x_i)$ is the appropriate estimate for computing a band score for the cut-off score (Berk 1984b).

A group-specific estimate of the SEM, the $s(d_p)$, can be computed by finding the mean of $SE_{meas}(x_i)$s for a given group of test takers. However, this estimate is strongly affected by test length and variation in individual abilities and it can thus be misleading when applied to highly skewed or bimodal distributions, in which case it will tend to overestimate the SEMs for the extreme high or low scores and underestimate the SEMs of scores near the mean (Berk 1984b). It is therefore most appropriately applied to long tests in which test takers are relatively homogeneous in their levels of ability.

Dependability of mastery/nonmastery classifications

In many language testing contexts, it may be necessary or desirable to distinguish individuals who are minimally competent in or at a 'mastery' level of a given language ability from those who are not.[30] In such contexts, 'mastery/nonmastery' classification decisions about individuals are often made in terms of a predetermined level of 'mastery', or 'minimum competence', which may correspond to an observed 'cut-off' score on a CR test. For example, the decision to advance an individual to the next unit of instruction, or to permit him to graduate from a language program, might be contingent upon his scoring at least 80 per cent on an achievement test. In other situations, certification of proficiency or minimum competency in a language might be awarded only if test takers obtain a minimum level of mastery, as indicated by a predetermined cut-off score on a language proficiency test.

As with any decision, there is a chance that mastery/nonmastery classification decisions will be in error, and such errors will result in certain costs, in terms of lost time, misallocated resources, and so forth. Because of the costs associated with errors of classification, it is extremely important that we be able to estimate the probability that the mastery/nonmastery classifications we make will be correct. Estimating this probability involves taking into consideration the fact that a correct decision will be a function not only of errors of measurement in the observed scores, but also of the specific observed score that is selected as a cut-off score. Thus, the dependability of mastery/nonmastery classifications will be different for different 'cut-off' scores.

Cut-off score

There are many different approaches to setting cut-off scores, and a complete discussion of these is beyond the scope of this text.[31] However, an appreciation of the difference between mastery levels and cut-off scores, as well as familiarity with the types of mastery/ nonmastery classification errors and their relative seriousness, is relevant to both determining the most appropriate cut-off score and estimating the dependability of classifications based on a given cut-off score, and a brief overview of these will be presented.

Mastery level and cut-off score

Mastery level for a given language ability can be understood as the *domain score* that is considered to be indicative of minimal competence (for a given purpose) in that ability. This distinction between the domain score that corresponds to minimum competency, or mastery, and its corresponding observed, cut-off score is important, since the cut-off score, as with any observed score, will be subject to measurement error as an indicator of the domain score at mastery level, and this measurement error will be associated with errors in mastery/nonmastery classifications that are made on the basis of the cut-off score.

Classification errors

Whenever we make a mastery/nonmastery classification decision, there are two possible types of errors that can occur. A 'false positive' classification error occurs when we classify the test taker as a master when his domain score is in fact below the cut-off score. If, on the other hand, we incorrectly classify him as a nonmaster when his domain score is above the cut-off, we speak of a 'false negative' classification error.

There will be costs associated with either type of classification error. In some situations these costs may be quite small, in that classification errors can be easily corrected, while in other situations, where the lives of large numbers of individuals may be affected, if not permanently, at least for a long period of time, the costs of classification errors will be considerable. Furthermore, there may be differential costs associated with different classification errors. That is, in some situations, false positive classifications may be more costly than are false negatives, while in other contexts the reverse might be the case. Consider, for example, a classroom achievement test that will be used as a basis for advancing students to the next higher level in a language course. In this case, false positive errors, that is students who are incorrectly identified as masters, are likely to encounter considerable difficulty in the higher level for which they are not ready, may become frustrated, lose interest and motivation, and consequently do very poorly. False negatives, on the other hand, will simply be given additional instruction that may be redundant, but which nevertheless is less likely to seriously impair their learning. In other situations, where individuals may be denied graduation or employment on the basis of a test, the cost of false negatives may be much higher than that for false positives because of the social stigma that may be attached to the failure to graduate, or the opportunity costs associated with unemployment.

In estimating the dependability of mastery/nonmastery classifications based on a given cut-off score, the test user must consider the types of classification errors that can occur as a result of measurement errors, and make a judgment about their relative seriousness. This judgment is typically reflected in a 'loss ratio', which is the ratio between the seriousness of a false positive error and a false negative error. If, for example, we considered false negative errors to be twice as serious as false positives, the loss ratio would be two, while a loss ratio of one would reflect our judgment that the two error types were of equal seriousness.

Estimating the dependability of mastery/nonmastery classifications

The various approaches to the dependability of mastery/nonmastery classifications all assume that individuals are categorized as masters or nonmasters on the basis of a predetermined cut-off score. These approaches differ in terms of how they treat classification errors. Suppose, for example, that the cut-off score on a CR test were 80 per cent, and two individuals, whose domain scores are actually 75 per cent and 55 per cent, were misclassified as masters on the basis of scores on this test. Are these two misclassifications to be considered equally serious, or is the one with the lower domain score a more serious error? Or suppose another individual, whose domain score is 85, was misclassified as a nonmaster. Is this error equally serious to that of misclassifying the student with a domain score of 75 as a master? Approaches that consider all classification errors as equally serious are referred to as 'threshold loss' agreement indices, while those that consider classification errors to vary depending on how far the misclassified domain score is from the cut-off score are called 'squared-error loss' agreement indices.

Threshold loss agreement indices
Several agreement indices that treat all misclassifications as equally serious have been developed. The most easily understood approach is simply to give the test twice, and then compute the proportion of individuals who are consistently classified as masters and nonmasters on both tests (Hambleton and Novick 1973). This coefficient, symbolized by $\hat{p}_o$, is computed as follows:

$$\hat{p}_o = \frac{n_m}{N} + \frac{n_n}{N} \qquad [27]$$

where n_m is the number of individuals classified as masters on *both* test administrations, n_n is the number of individuals classified as nonmasters on both, and N is the total number of individuals who took the test twice. Another agreement index, $\hat{\kappa}$, that takes into account the probability that a certain proportion of incorrect classifications may be due to chance, has been developed (Swaminathan *et al.* 1974). In addition, several approaches for estimating both $\hat{p}_o$ and $\hat{\kappa}$ on the basis of a single test administration have been developed (Huynh 1976; Subkoviak 1976). Although such approaches are particularly practical for large test administrations in which it is not possible to administer the test twice (Subkoviak 1980; Berk 1984b), they are complex and laborious to compute. Recently Subkoviak (1988) derived a short cut to estimating both $\hat{p}_o$ and $\hat{\kappa}$ from a single test administration. This procedure involves computing a standard score that is a function of the mean, standard deviation and cut-off score, and a classical NR internal consistency estimate, such as KR-20 or coefficient alpha. The standard score and the NR reliability estimate are then used to look up the approximate values for $\hat{p}_o$ or $\hat{\kappa}$ in an appropriate table.

Squared-error loss agreement indices
In contrast to these agreement indices, which treat misclassification errors as all of equal seriousness, a number of agreement indices that

treat misclassification errors near the cut-off score as less serious than those far from the cut-off score have been developed. One index, Φ (c_o) (Brennan and Kane 1977; Brennan 1984), is derived from G-theory and can be computed from the mean and standard deviation of the test scores and the number of items, as follows:

$$\Phi\,(c_o) = 1 - \frac{1}{k-1}\,\frac{\bar{x}_p(1 - \bar{x}_p) - s^2_p}{(\bar{x}_p - c_o)^2 + s^2_p} \qquad [28]$$

where $\bar{x}_p$ is the mean of the proportion scores, s^2_p is the variance of the proportion scores, k is the number of items in the test, and c_o is the cut-off score.

A second agreement index, $\kappa^2(x, T_x)$ (Livingston 1972), is derived from classical true score theory, and can be computed as follows:

$$\kappa^2(x, T_x) = \frac{r_{xx'}\,s^2_x + (\bar{X} - c_o)^2}{s^2_x + (\bar{X} - c_o)^2} \qquad [29]$$

where $r_{xx'}$ is the classical internal consistency reliability coefficient (for example, Guttman split-half, KR–20, or KR–21), and c_o is the cut-off score.

Both types of agreement indices – threshold loss and squared error loss – provide estimates of the probability of making correct mastery/nonmastery classifications. To illustrate the use of $\kappa^2(x, T_x)$, suppose that the cut-off score for an achievement test was 80, the class mean was 80, the standard deviation was 10, and that the NR internal consistency reliability estimate was .60. Computing Livingston's $\kappa^2(x, T_x)$ for a cut-off score of 80 yields a CR agreement index of .60, which is exactly the same as the NR reliability estimate, illustrating the fact that when the cut-off score equals the group mean, the NR and CR reliability estimates will be the same. This value can be interpreted as the probability of a correct decision, given this amount of measurement error and this cut-off score. If this probability is unacceptably low, we could move the cut-off away from the mean. In this particular case, we could either raise or lower the cut-off. If we consider false positive classification errors to be more serious than false negatives, we would raise the cut-off, thereby minimizing the probability of this type of error. If we moved the cut-off score to 90, for example, the value of $\kappa^2(x, T_x)$ would be .80, which would mean that there is an 80 per cent probability that mastery decisions at this cut-off would be correct. If we lowered the cut-off to 70 to minimize false negative classification errors, the agreement index would also be .80.

Standard error of measurement in CR tests

The discussion of the standard error of measurement (SEM) on pp. 197–202 indicated that this statistic can be used to interpret individual observed scores in NR tests. The SEM also has important applications to CR tests. The $SE_{meas}(x_i)$ can be used as a means of computing band scores for interpreting individual observed scores as indicators of domain scores, and several group-specific CR estimates of the SEM have been developed for this interpretation as well (Berk 1984b).

In CR testing situations in which mastery/nonmastery classifications are to be made, the SEM can be used to determine the amount of measurement error at different cut-off scores. The SEMs for different cut-off scores can be estimated by computing the $SE_{meas}(x_i)$ for each cut-off score. These values can then be used to compute band scores, or band interpretations for these scores. Suppose, for example, that we gave a 100-item achievement test based on the content of a course to determine which students will pass the course and go on to the next course in the program, and that we decided to set the cut-off score at 80. Computing the $SE_{meas}(x_i)$ would give us a value of 4.02 which, rounded to the nearest whole number, gives a 68 per cent band score of 76–84. Setting the cut-off higher, at 90, would give a smaller $SE_{meas}(x_i)$, 3.02, and a 68 per cent band score of 87–93 for the cut-off. This illustrates the fact that the value of the $SE_{meas}(x_i)$ decreases as the cut-off is further from 50 per cent, where the $SE_{meas}(x_i)$ is at its maximum value.

In summary, there are two considerations in estimating reliability in CR tests. In virtually all CR interpretations, we need to estimate how dependable the observed score is as an indicator of the individual's domain score, and for this several different dependability coefficients and estimates of the SEM have been developed. In many CR testing situations, we need to estimate the probability of correctly classifying test takers as masters or nonmasters on the basis of a cut-off score. The particular way we estimate this will depend on whether we consider all classification errors as equally serious or whether we consider incorrect decisions to differ in seriousness. In selecting the appropriate CR reliability coefficient, we must first determine which category is of interest for our particular situation and then choose the specific coefficient that has the characteristics and precision that we want, and that can be computed and interpreted easily (Berk 1984c).

Factors that affect reliability estimates

Thus far, different sources of error have been discussed as the primary factors that affect the reliability of tests. In addition to these sources of error, there are general characteristics of tests and test scores that influence the size of our estimates of reliability. An understanding of these factors will help us to better determine which reliability estimates are appropriate to a given set of test scores, and interpret their meaning.

Length of test

For both NR and CR tests, long tests are generally more reliable than short ones, and all of the estimates discussed in this chapter – reliability and generalizability coefficients, test information function, coefficients of dependability, and agreement indices – reflect this. If we can assume that all the items or tasks included are representative indicators of the ability being measured, the more we include, the more adequate our sample of that ability. In the context of measures such as ratings of an oral interview or a written composition, this implies that the reliability of the scores will be affected by the length of the language sample obtained. That is, we would expect that a score based on a 5-minute speech sample would not be as reliable as one from an equivalently obtained 30-minute sample. The adequacy of the sample is of particular importance in the context of CR testing, where we want to interpret a test score as an indication of an individual's level of ability in a given domain. Not only does a longer test tend to provide a more adequate sample of language use, it also tends to minimize the influence of various sources of bias. In a reading comprehension test based on a single passage, for example, there is a high probability that the content of the passage will be biased in favor of some students and against others. This bias due to passage content could be minimized, or at least balanced out, by including several passages with different content.

Difficulty of test and test score variance

If the test is too easy or too difficult for a particular group, this will generally result in a restricted range of scores or very little variance.

As indicated above, this is particularly a problem for NR reliability estimates, which are sensitive primarily to inter-individual score differences. Thus, for NR tests, the greater the score variance, the more reliable they will tend to be.

CR reliability coefficients, on the other hand, are relatively unaffected by restrictions in score variance. Consider the extreme case in which all individuals obtain scores of 100 per cent, where the mean score will be 100 per cent, and the variance will equal zero. In this case, the formula for κ^2 (x, T_x) will reduce to $(\bar{x} - c_o)^2 / (\bar{x} - c_o)^2$. If the cut-off score is not equal to the mean score of 100 per cent, $\kappa^2(x, T_x)$ will equal 1.00. This is reasonable, since we would have considerable confidence in classifying these individuals as masters on the basis of their 100 per cent test scores. We would have equal confidence if the reverse were the case, and everyone obtained a score of zero. However, in either of these two cases, if the cut-off score is equal to the mean score, the equation reduces to 0/0, which is indeterminate.[32] In this case, we may question the appropriateness of either the cut-off score or the level of difficulty of the test.

The value of coefficient $\hat{p}_o$ can also be positive, even though there is no variance in test scores. Again, in the extreme case where all students score 100 per cent on both tests, n_m will equal N and n_n will equal zero, yielding a value of 1.00 for $\hat{p}_o$.

Cut-off score

From the above discussion it is obvious that CR agreement indices are sensitive to differences in cut-off scores. That is, these coefficients will have different values for different cut-off scores. In general, the greater the differences between the cut-off score and the mean score, the greater will be the CR reliability. This is because differences between individuals are likely to be minimal around the mean score, even for a CR test, so that decisions made on the basis of such minimal differences are more likely to be in error. In the limiting case, with the cut-off score equal to the mean, CR reliability will be minimal, and will be entirely a function of the amount of score variance. Livingston (1972) has argued that in NR tests we in effect use the mean as a cut-off score, and that NR reliability is thus a special case of CR reliability, in which we impose the most rigorous standard for judging reliability. Setting the cut-off far from the mean in CR tests, then, has the same effect – increasing reliability – as does maximizing the variance of NR test scores.

Systematic measurement error

As discussed above, one of the weaknesses of classical true score theory is that it considers all error to be random and consequently fails to distinguish between random and systematic error. Within the context of G-theory, systematic error can be defined as the variance component associated with a facet whose conditions are fixed. For example, if every form of a reading comprehension test contained passages from the area of, say, economics, then the facet 'passage content' would be fixed to one condition – economics. To the extent that test scores are influenced by individuals' familiarity with this particular content area, as opposed to their reading comprehension ability, this facet will be a source of error in our measurement of reading comprehension. It is systematic error since it constitutes a part of every score we obtain using this particular test, as opposed to random error, which may affect some scores and not others.

The effects of systematic measurement error

Two different effects are associated with systematic error: a general effect and a specific effect (Kane 1982). The *general effect* of systematic error is constant for all observations; it affects the scores of all individuals who take the test. The *specific effect* varies across individuals; it affects different individuals differentially. In the example above, the passage content, economics, is the same for all tests, and so will have a general effect on all test scores. If individuals differ in their familiarity with economics, this systematic error will have different specific effects for different individuals, increasing some scores and lowering others. In terms of variance components, the *general* effect of systematic error is that associated with a main effect, while the *specific effect* is associated with an interaction between persons and the facet. This specific effect in turn can be distinguished from random error variance, which is associated with residual, or unpredicted variance.

Both the general and the specific effects of systematic error limit the generalizability of test scores as indicators of universe scores. Thus, we would be reluctant to make inferences about reading comprehension in general on the basis of scores from tests containing passages only from the field of economics. We might be willing to accept such scores for students of economics by redefining the ability we are interested in measuring (limiting our universe of generalizability) to reading comprehension of passages in economics. Most of us, however, would object strongly to the obvious bias if such tests were to be used as measures of reading comprehension with individuals from a wide variety of disciplines, including economics.

One way in which systematic error is different from random error, then, is that it introduces bias into our measures. Another way in which systematic error is different from random error is that systematic errors tend to be correlated across measures. What this means is that systematic errors will tend to *increase* estimates of reliability. The problem this creates, however, is that this may also *decrease* validity. If we gave two tests based on economics reading passages to a group of economics students, for example, we might find that the correlation between scores on the two tests was quite high, indicating equivalence reliability. If we had doubts about the validity of our reading tests, we would also give our students a 'general' reading comprehension test and a test of their knowledge of economics that did not involve reading. If we found that scores on our reading tests were correlated more highly with the economics knowledge test scores than with the general reading comprehension test scores, this would suggest that scores on our reading test reflect individuals' knowledge of economics as much as their reading comprehension ability, and were therefore not valid measures of general reading comprehension.

The effects of test method

In obtaining a measure of language ability we observe a sample of an individual's performance *under certain conditions*, which can be characterized by the test method facets described in Chapter 4. If we can assume that test scores are affected by method facets, this means these facets are potential sources of error for every measurement we obtain. This presents two problems: a dilemma in choosing the type of error we want to minimize, and ambiguity in the inferences we can make from test scores.

If test method facets vary from test to test in an uncontrolled manner, these are sources of random error that have been discussed above. One way to minimize this source of random error is to standardize the test method. That is, to measure reading comprehension, we might fix or control the conditions of different method facets so that they are the same for all tests. For example, we might standardize the environment to a particular time of the day and use only familiar space, equipment, and administrative personnel. We could also standardize the input and response by using a single testing technique, say, a cloze test, with passages of equal length, difficulty, and 'neutral' content, allowing the same amount of time and requiring the same type of response from all test takers. This sort of standardization is widely accepted as a means of assuring highly reliable test results (for example, Ebel 1979; Gronlund 1985). The problem standardization creates, however, is that by fixing these facets we are introducing sources of systematic variance into the test scores. In other words, our test might be a better indicator of individuals' ability to take cloze tests than of their reading comprehension ability. This problem is described by Brennan (1983) within the framework of generalizability theory as follows: 'fixing a condition of measurement reduces error and increases the precision of measurements, but it does so at the expense of narrowing interpretations of measurement' (p. 1). The dilemma, then, is that by fixing or standardizing test method facets we reduce *random* errors, thereby increasing reliability, but at the same time we introduce *systematic* errors, thereby decreasing validity.

The influence of test method facets also affects test interpretation, or the inferences we can make about abilities from test scores. If we choose to standardize our test method as suggested above, we introduce a source of systematic variance *in addition to* the systematic variance associated with the ability we wish to measure. That is, when we standardize the testing procedure, we define test method in much the same way that the universe of generalizability defines the ability (Kane 1982: 143).

The presence of two sources of systematic error presents a problem in that we are usually interested in interpreting a language test score as an indicator of an individual's language ability, rather than as an indicator of her ability to take tests of a particular type. If the effect of test method is sizeable, this clearly limits the validity of the test score as an indicator of the individual's language ability. In this case, the test developer may choose to eliminate this test and begin developing a new test in which method facets are less controlled. Or he may choose to accept the presence of systematic method variance and redefine the universe of generalizability by limiting inferences to instances of performance under the conditions specified by the test method.

Consider the example presented earlier, in which reading comprehension test passages were all taken from the discipline of economics. If the test developer were only interested in students' ability to comprehend readings in economics, he would accept scores on such tests as indicators of this more limited ability, and would not attempt to make inferences about general reading ability from these test scores. If, however, he were interested in reading ability in general, he would need to redevelop the test, selecting passages from a wider range of subject matter, recognizing that in so doing he might introduce a source of error. Thus the test developer must sometimes choose whether he wants a minimally reliable measure of an ability, or trait, or a maximally reliable measure of a trait–method combination that may be difficult to interpret in terms of validity. And this choice, as with almost every decision related to test development and test use, will depend upon the specific decisions or interpretations that will be based on the test score.

The interpretation of test scores is particularly problematic when the distinction between trait and method is not clear, as is generally the case with so-called 'performance' tests. Can ratings based on oral interviews, for example, be clearly interpreted as indicators of language competencies, or should they be seen as indicators of an individual's ability to perform well under a particular set of test method conditions? In two studies, Bachman and Palmer attempted to answer this question, and they found that ratings of language abilities based on oral interviews included variance components associated with test method that were substantial, and in some cases actually larger than those associated with the trait measured (Bachman and Palmer 1981a, 1982a).

Beginning with Campbell and Fiske's (1959) classic paper, the effect of test method has been extensively studied in the measurement literature in general and has been well documented as well in the research in language testing (for example, Clifford 1978, 1981; Brütsch 1979; Shohamy 1983b, 1984a). What this research suggests is that there are essentially two options in interpreting scores from tests in which test method facets have a significant effect. First, as has been suggested by most of this research, we can view the effect of test method as a source of error that thereby reduces the reliability and validity of such scores as indicators of language abilities. The other alternative is to recognize this potential limitation of 'performance' tests, and interpret scores from them as reliable and valid indicators of more specific skills. That is, rather than viewing ratings of grammatical competence based on oral interviews as relatively unreliable indicators of this ability, we should probably interpret them more narrowly as indicators of individuals' skill in using grammatical structures accurately *in the context of face-to-face oral interaction.*

The presence of test method effects in language test scores thus has clear implications for the development and use of language tests. First, in developing tests we must clearly define the universe of generalizability, in terms of both traits and method facets, since whether we interpret method variance as a source of error or as part of the skill we are measuring depends upon how we define these factors. Second, we need to design and conduct our reliability studies (G-studies) so as to be able to estimate the effect of test method facets, particularly where these are fixed facets. Finally, in interpreting language test scores, we must be clear about the universe to which we generalize, that is, whether we want to make inferences about a domain of language ability, or whether it is sufficient to be able to generalize to a more limited domain of the performance of language competence under specific conditions.

Summary

Fundamental to the development and use of language tests is being able to identify and estimate the effect of various factors on language test scores. In order to interpret test scores as indicators of a given language ability, we must be sure that they are influenced as much as possible by that ability. Any factors other than the ability being tested that affect test scores are potential sources of error that decrease both the reliability of scores and the validity of their interpretations. Therefore, it is essential that we be able to identify these sources of error and estimate the magnitude of their effect on test scores. Our ability to do this depends upon how we define the various influences on test scores.

Measurement theory provides several models that specify the relationships between measures, or observed scores, and factors that affect these scores. The classical true score model provides several different ways in which we can estimate reliability, but has serious limitations. Generalizability theory is an extension of the classical model that overcomes many of these limitations, in that it enables test developers to examine several sources of variance simultaneously, and to distinguish systematic from random error. Item-response theory presents a more powerful approach in that it can provide sample-free estimates of individual's true scores, or ability levels, as well as sample-free estimates of measurement error at each ability level. But while modern measurement theory has developed beyond the classical true score model, estimates of reliability based on this model are still useful in many situations where neither generalizability theory nor item response theory can be applied because of practical limitations.

Estimates of reliability based on classical measurement theory are inappropriate for use with criterion-referenced (CR) tests because of differences in the types of comparisons and decisions made. In the context of CR testing, reliability is concerned with both the dependability of test scores as indicators of an individual's level of mastery in a given domain of abilities and the dependability of decisions that are based on CR test scores. Several approaches that have been developed for estimating the dependability of CR test scores were discussed.

Systematic error, such as that associated with test method, is different from random error. Systematic error is of particular concern since it introduces bias into test scores and tends to increase estimates of reliability while decreasing validity. Since test method facets affect scores of all tests, it is essential that we clearly distinguish trait from method facets when we define what our tests measure. Likewise, in developing tests, we must employ data collection designs and analytic procedures that enable us to estimate the relative effect of test method on test scores. Finally, in interpreting test results, we must be clear about the extent to which we can make inferences about abilities, as opposed to performance under certain conditions.

We often think of reliability and validity as two distinct but related characteristics of test scores. That is, although validity is the most important characteristic, reliability is a necessary condition to validity. When we consider the systematic effects of test method, however, we can see that this distinction may be somewhat blurred in language tests, since test method facets may affect both reliability and validity. A writing test that is scored largely on the accuracy and completeness of the content, for example, might be an unreliable and hence invalid measure of writing ability, but a valid measure of the test taker's knowledge of a given subject matter. The recognition of this ambiguity, this lack of a clear-cut distinction between reliability and validity for all times and places, leads to a better understanding and appreciation of the fact that the way we interpret language test scores depends upon the uses for which the test is intended. The relationship between reliability and validity will be discussed further in the next chapter.

Notes

All formulae in this chapter are numbered consecutively, and labeled by numbers in brackets, for example, '[1]'.

228 Fundamental Considerations in Language Testing

1 A technical aspect of this assumption is that of *additivity*, that
   the true and error scores add to form the observed score. That
   is, the observed score is assumed to be the *sum* of the true and
   error scores, rather than, say, the product or logarithmic
   function of these scores.

2 Specifically, one assumption states that true and error scores are
   uncorrelated with each other. This assumption can be represented as follows:

$$r_{te} = 0$$

where *r* is the symbol for correlation, and the subscript *te*
indicates that the variables involved in this correlation are the
true score *t* and the error score *e*. This applies to the true and
error scores on the same test, as well as on different tests. That
is, the true score on one test is assumed to be uncorrelated with
the error score on another test.

$$r_{t1e2} = 0$$

where t_1 is the true score on test one and e_2 is the error score on
test two. Another assumption states that the error scores of
different tests are uncorrelated with each other, and can be
represented as follows:

$$r_{e1e2} = 0$$

3 For more precise procedures for determining if two tests are
   parallel, see Gulliksen (1950) pp. 173–92.

4 The classical model also defines 'essentially tau-equivalent' tests
   as tests which have all the characteristics of parallel tests, except
   that their true scores differ by a constant value.

5 The model assumes that the observed score is linear combination of a true score and a random error score. A linear relationship is one that can be represented by an equation of the form:

$$y = ax + c$$

Such a relationship can also be represented graphically by a
straight line. If we were to plot the true scores against observed
scores on a two-dimensional grid, the points of the plot would
fall on a straight line. The point at which the line began on the
vertical axis would be determined by the value of the additive
constant, *c*. One consequence of this assumption is that the
positive square root of the reliability coefficient is equal to the
correlation between the observed and true scores.

6   Most measurement models, including item-response models, assume that individual test items are locally independent. This is a technical assumption which, in item-response theory, implies essentially that a test taker's responses to two different items of the same difficulty are statistically independent, or uncorrelated.

7   For a detailed discussion of different approaches to splitting tests into halves, see Thorndike (1951) pp. 579–86.

8   The general Spearman–Brown prophecy formula is:

$$r_{tt} = \frac{k r_{xx'}}{1 + (k - 1) r_{xx'}}$$

where r_{tt} is the reliability of a test that is k times as long as the test from which the reliability, $r_{xx'}$, was estimated.

9   The number of possible splits can be computed from the number of items by using the following formula:

$$(2k)!/2(k!)^2$$

where k is the number of items on the test.

10 Horst (1953) has developed a correction for unequal item difficulties.

11 In the case where all items are of equal difficulty, KR21 will be equal to KR20. This can be seen in the following equation:

$$KR20 = KR21 + \frac{k^2}{k-1} \left(\frac{(\Sigma p_i - \bar{x}_p)^2}{k s^2_x} \right)$$

where n is the number of items, p_i is the difficulty of a given item, $\bar{x}_p$ is the average difficulty of all the items in the test, and s^2_x is the variance of the test scores. If all the items are of equal difficulty, the expression $p_i - \bar{x}_p$ will be equal to zero, and everything to the right of the + reduces to zero.

12 Reliability estimates that are based on the analysis of components of variance are all variations of Hoyt's (1941) analysis of variance reliability coefficient, and yield what is known as an intraclass correlation coefficient (Stanley 1957).

13 A complete discussion of factorial design and the analysis of variance (ANOVA) and their application to estimating error components in generalizability theory is beyond the scope of this book. Readers interested in factorial designs and ANOVA may find excellent discussions in standard references such as Kirk (1968), Winer (1971), and Shavelson (1988). A discussion of the application of ANOVA to the actual estimation of

variance components in generalizability studies can be found in Cronbach *et al.* (1972) and Brennan (1983).

14 The classical model also regards test scores in this manner (see, for example, Guttman 1953; Stanley 1971). In the classical model, however, the hypothetical universe consists of an indefinitely large set of *undifferentiated* trials or observations over an indefinitely large and equally homogeneous (or at least normally distributed) set of individuals.

15 In some cases, the results of the G-study can be used to estimate what the sizes of the variance components would be under D-study conditions, without actually conducting a D-study.

16 The term 'universe', as used in G-theory, is essentially synonymous with 'total set' or 'whole collection'. Thus, the 'universe of possible measures' is essentially the total set of measures that the test developer or user is willing to accept as indicators of the ability in question. The term 'universe' is used to refer to *conditions*, and 'population' to refer to *persons* (Cronbach *et al.* 1972: 9).

17 This is the simplest case, in which each facet is fixed, and crossed with every other facet. More complex cases, in which facets are random and are nested within each other are discussed in Cronbach *et al.* (1972) and Brennan (1983).

18 A computer program, 'GENOVA', designed specifically to analyze data from G-studies, has been written by Crick and Brennan (1983). This, and other computer programs that can be used to analyze G-study data are discussed in Brennan (1983).

19 While the origins of item response theory can be traced to several different individuals, some of the most influential work, in terms of applications to practical test development and use, has been that of Frederick Lord (for example, Lord and Novick 1968; Lord 1980) and Benjamin Wright (for example, Wright 1968, 1977; Wright and Stone 1979).

20 The more general term for this mathematical formula is the item characteristic function. The item characteristic curve applies to unidimensional IRT models only.

21 A variety of mathematical models have been proposed. Two of the most commonly used are the normal ogive and the logistic models. Detailed discussion of these and other IRT models can be found in Waller (1981), Hulin *et al.* (1983), and Hambledon and Swaminathan (1985).

22 Fortunately for practitioners, computer programs for doing IRT modeling are becoming increasingly available, not only on large

mainframe computers, but also for personal computers. BICAL (Wright and Mead 1976) and Microscale (Wright and Linacre 1984) are two programs that perform one-parameter, or Rasch modeling, while LOGIST (Wingerskey *et al.* 1982) and BILOG (Mislevy and Bock 1982, 1986) perform one-, two-, or three-parameter modeling.

23 A thorough discussion of the limitations of CTS theory and the advantages of IR theory with respect to precision of measurement is provided in Samejima (1977).

24 The fraction in the second term of the Guttman split-half formula reduces to one, since both the numerator and the denominator would be zero. Subtracting one from one equals zero, and zero times $k/(k - 1)$ also equals zero. The same is true for KR20, since if all individuals answer every item correctly, pq will be zero ($p = 1.0, q = 1 - p = 0$).

25 Another, indeed the original, approach to defining the criterion is with reference to specified standards of performance, or degrees of proficiency, as described by Glaser and Klaus (1962) and Glaser (1963).

26 There may exist, of course, domains which are closed and completely specifiable sets, in which case *all* tasks in the domain can be included in the test. Such domains are relatively rare in language testing.

27 See Berk 1980a and 1984c for a review of these methods. Hambleton and Swaminathan (1985) discuss the interpretation of IRT ability estimates within a CR framework, pointing out that if the items in the test are representative of the items in the domain, IRT ability score estimates can provide a basis for *content-referenced interpretation* (Hambleton and Swaminathan 1985: 61–8). The dependability of such ability scores can then be evaluated in terms of their information function. Extensive discussions of the applications of IRT models to criterion-referenced tests can be found in Hambleton (1977) and Cook and Hambleton (1978).

28 Berk (1980c) recommends including a correction in cases where the number of items in the domain is finite. This formula, which should probably be applied when the number of items in the test is large, relative to the domain size, is as follows:

$$SE_{meas}(x_a) = \sqrt{\frac{(N - n)}{n} \quad \frac{x_i (n - x_a)}{n - 1}}$$

where N is the number of items in the domain and n is the number of items in the sample.

29   Brennan (1981) provides a useful table of band scores for different observed scores on tests of different lengths.

30   It is beyond the scope of this discussion to address the range of social, political, legal, and educational issues involved in the debate over standard setting in educational programs. There is an extensive literature on the issues related to minimum competency and minimum competency testing, some of which are referred to in Chapter 7.

31   Discussions of standard setting range from highly critical (Glass 1978), to mildly negative (Shephard 1974), to neutral (Jaeger 1988), to realistically positive (Popham 1978). Perhaps the most objective and factual survey is that of Jaeger (1989), who provides a detailed table comparing the results of over 30 empirical studies using different approaches to standard setting. Brennan (1981) provides a detailed set of non-technical procedures for setting mastery levels and cut-scores, as well as for estimating the dependability of mastery/nonmastery classifications.

32   The formula for $\kappa^2(x, T_x)$ is repeated here:

$$\kappa^2(x, T_x) = \frac{r_{xx'}s^2_x + (\overline{x} - c_o)^2}{s^2_x + (\overline{x} - c_o)^2}$$

If $s^2_x = 0$,

$$\kappa^2(x, T_x) = \frac{r_{xx'}(0) + (\overline{x} - c_o)^2}{0 + (\overline{x} - c_o)^2}$$

or

$$\kappa^2(x, T_x) = \frac{(\overline{x} - c_o)^2}{(\overline{x} - c_o)^2}$$

If $c_o = \overline{x}$

$$\kappa^2(x, T_x) = \frac{0}{0}$$

Further reading

Very readable discussions of classical true-score and item-response theory are given in Allen and Yen (1979), Chapters 3 and 11, respectively. Bolus *et al.* (1982) and van Weeren and Theunissen (1987) provide examples of the application of G-theory to language testing. An extensive treatment of G-theory, including detailed discussion of estimation procedures, is given in Brennan (1983). Henning (1987) provides a useful, non-technical discussion of IRT in general, and of the Rasch model in particular, with reference to language testing. The standard reference for Rasch modeling is Wright and Stone (1979). A general, nontechnical discussion of IRT is provided by Hambleton and Cook (1977), while more extensive treatments can be found in Hulin *et al.* (1983) and Hambleton and Swaminathan (1985). Hambleton (1989) provides a comprehensive review of IRT. Hudson and Lynch (1984) provide an example of applications of CR test development and analysis procedures to language testing. Brown (1989) gives an excellent overview of CR reliability estimates, including practical computational procedures and examples. Brennan (1981) is a non-technical, practical guide to CR test development, including procedures for setting cut-off scores and estimating agreement indices. Articles by Berk, Subkoviak, and Brennan in Berk (1984a) provide comprehensive discussions of CR reliability. Subkoviak (1988) presents practical procedures for estimating CR agreement indices.

Discussion questions

1. If you, as a teacher, know that your students perform poorly on a specific type of test, such as a multiple-choice test, what might you do to minimize the effect of this test method on their test performance?

2. Suppose you are developing a dictation test, and for practical reasons need to be able to estimate its reliability on the basis of a single administration. What potential sources of error must you take into consideration? What classical reliability estimate(s) would you use? What would be the facets of a G-study to estimate generalizability? What would be the design of such a study?

3. Suppose you need to develop a test of speaking ability that must be administered to several thousand individuals in many different locations at the same time. Although an oral interview is not possible, you want to make sure that the testing method you use will yield results that are comparable to those you would obtain from an oral interview. What other testing techniques might you investigate, and what test method facets might you try to examine? How could you use the test method facets described in Chapter 5 to design a G-study to examine

the relative effects of the different facets in which you are interested?

4. Suppose you have developed a 50-item multiple-choice test as an end-of-course achievement test. In order to examine its reliability, you have given it to your students twice at the end of the semester, with three days between administrations. Their scores (x_1, x_2) on the two test administrations, along with the means and standard deviations for the two test administrations, and the correlation between the two sets of scores, are given below:

Student	x_1	x_2
1	47	46
2	47	47
3	46	47
4	46	46
5	46	46
6	46	45
7	46	46
8	45	46
9	45	44
10	45	45
11	45	46
12	44	42
13	44	44
14	44	45
15	42	38
16	41	38
17	40	40
18	38	40
19	38	37
20	37	39

Mean ($\bar{x}$): 43.6 43.4
Standard deviations s: 3.15 3.39
Correlation r_{12}: .89

a. Can these two test administrations be treated as parallel tests? Why or why not?
b. How stable are the scores of this group of students on this test?
c. How internally consistent are the two sets of scores?

(Estimate the internal consistency reliability of each test, using the appropriate approach.) Is this level of reliability acceptable? What factors might affect the size of these reliability estimates?

d. You have decided to set the cut-off for mastery at 40. Estimate the dependability of mastery/nonmastery decisions based on this test. (Use both approaches discussed in this chapter.)

e. What would be the effect of lowering the cut-off score to 38?

7 Validation

Introduction

The primary concern in test development and use is demonstrating not only that test scores are reliable, but that the interpretations and uses we make of test scores are valid. In the previous chapter, we saw that the demonstration of reliability consists of estimating the amount of variation in language test scores that is due to measurement error. This estimation focuses on the effects of test method facets and random factors as sources of unreliability in test scores. If we demonstrate that test scores are reliable, we know that performance on the test is affected primarily by factors other than measurement error. In examining validity, we look beyond the reliability of the test scores themselves, and consider the relationships between test performance and other types of performance in other contexts. The types of performance and contexts we select for investigation will be determined by the uses or interpretations we wish to make of the test results. Furthermore, since the uses we make of test scores inevitably involve value judgments, and have both educational and societal consequences, we must also carefully examine the value systems that justify a given use of test scores.

It has been traditional to classify validity into different types, such as content, criterion, and construct validity. However, measurement specialists have come to view these as aspects of a unitary concept of validity that subsumes all of them. Messick (1989), for example, describes validity as 'an integrated evaluative judgment of the degree to which empirical evidence and theoretical rationales support the *adequacy* and *appropriateness* of *inferences* and *actions* based on test scores' (p. 13). This unitary view of validity has also been clearly endorsed by the measurement profession as a whole in the most recent revision of the *Standards for Educational and Psychological Testing*:

> Validity ... is a unitary concept. Although evidence may be accumulated in many ways, validity always refers to the degree to

which that evidence supports the inferences that are made from the scores. The inferences regarding specific uses of a test are validated, not the test itself.
(American Psychological Association 1985: 9)

We will still find it necessary to gather information about content relevance, predictive utility, and concurrent criterion relatedness, in the process of developing a given test. However, it is important to recognize that none of these by itself is sufficient to demonstrate the validity of a particular interpretation or use of test scores. And while the relative emphasis of the different kinds of evidence may vary from one test use to another, it is only through the collection and interpretation of all relevant types of information that validity can be demonstrated.

The examination of validity has also traditionally focused on the types of evidence that need to be gathered to support a particular meaning or use. Given the significant role that testing now plays in influencing educational and social decisions about individuals, however, we can no longer limit our investigation of validity to collecting factual evidence to support a given interpretation or use. Since testing takes place in an educational or social context, we must also consider the educational and social consequences of the uses we make of tests. Examining the validity of a given use of test scores is therefore a complex process that must involve the examination of both the *evidence* that supports that interpretation or use and the *ethical values* that provide the basis or justification for that interpretation or use (Messick 1975, 1980, 1989).

Although we often speak of a given test's validity, this is misleading, because validity is not simply a function of the content and procedures of the test itself. It might not be valid, for example, to use the *Test of English as a Foreign Language* to measure the English proficiency of beginning level elementary school children studying English as a second language, even though there is considerable evidence supporting the uses of this test with intermediate to advanced level adult learners of English as a foreign language. This is because even though the content and administrative procedures of this test might not vary if it were used with these different groups of individuals, the content of the test – the linguistic features covered, the amount of real-world knowledge assumed – and the administrative procedures followed are inappropriate for elementary school ESL students. Consequently their performance would be likely to vary considerably from that of the group with which the test is intended to be used. Validation must therefore consider, in addition to the test's content and method, how test takers perform.

It is also misleading to speak simply of the validity of test scores, since the interpretation and use we make of test performance may not be equally valid for all abilities and in all contexts. For example, although it may be valid to interpret a rating obtained from an oral interview as an indicator of grammatical accuracy in speaking, it may not be valid to interpret this rating as a measure of sociolinguistic competence. And a rating obtained from a procedure designed to predict success as a member of the diplomatic corps may not provide a valid basis for evaluating the language achievement of college students.

Thus, in test validation we are not examining the validity of the test content or of even the test scores themselves, but rather the validity of the way we interpret or use the information gathered through the testing procedure. To refer to a test or test score as valid, without reference to the specific ability or abilities the test is designed to measure *and* the uses for which the test is intended, is therefore more than a terminological inaccuracy. At the very least, it reflects a fundamental misunderstanding of validity; at worst, it may represent an unsubstantiated claim about the interpretation and use of test scores.

In this chapter I will describe validation as a general process that consists of the marshaling of evidence to support a given interpretation or use, a process that is based on logical, empirical, and ethical considerations (Messick 1981b). I will first discuss the relationship between reliability and validity, viewing the estimation of reliability as an essential requisite of validation. Second, I will outline a framework proposed by Messick (1989) for considering validity as a unitary though multifaceted concept. I will then discuss the evidential basis for validity, including content relevance and criterion related-ness, which have been traditionally called content validity and criterion validity, respectively, and will present arguments that these characteristics are not sufficient evidence to support inferences about ability from test results. Next, I will discuss construct validity as a unified concept that includes both content relevance and criterion relatedness. Then I will discuss the issue of test bias, including culture, test content, personality characteristics of test takers, sex, and age as potential sources of test bias in language tests. Finally, I will discuss the ethical, or consequential basis of test use.

Reliability and validity revisited

In Chapter 6, I pointed out that reliability is a requirement for validity, and that the investigation of reliability and validity can be viewed as complementary aspects of identifying, estimating, and interpreting different sources of variance in test scores (pp. 160–2). The investigation of reliability is concerned with answering the question, 'How much variance in test scores is due to measurement error?' and its complement question, 'How much variance is due to factors other than measurement error?' The variance that is due to factors other than measurement error is what Oller (1979a) has referred to as 'reliable variance'. In order to estimate the relative proportions of error and reliable variance in test scores, we utilize measurement theory as a basis for designing our data collection and for analyzing and interpreting the results. In Chapter 6, generalizability theory was discussed as a means for specifying and empirically examining variance components that are considered sources of measurement error in test scores.

Validity, on the other hand, is concerned with identifying the factors that produce the reliable variance in test scores. That is, validation addresses the question, 'What specific abilities account for the reliable variance in test scores?' Thus, we might say that reliability is concerned with determining how much of the variance in test scores is reliable variance, while validity is concerned with determining what abilities contribute to this reliable variance.

Another way to distinguish reliability from validity is to consider the theoretical frameworks upon which they depend. Generalizability theory provides a framework for identifying and simultaneously examining several sources of error in test scores. When we look at sources of variance that are defined as error within this theory, we are examining reliability. That is, in estimating reliability we are concerned primarily with examining variance in test scores themselves. In validation, on the other hand, we must consider other sources of variance, and must utilize a theory of abilities to identify these sources. That is, in order to examine validity, we need a theory that specifies the language abilities that we hypothesize will affect test performance. The process of validation thus must look beyond reliability and examine the relationship between test performance and factors outside the test itself.

Despite this apparently clear demarcation of the domains of reliability and validity, distinguishing between the two for language tests is not always clear-cut. This is because of problems in clearly distinguishing (1) different test methods from each other, and (2) abilities from test methods. A classic statement of the relationship between reliability and validity is given by Campbell and Fiske (1959):

Reliability is the agreement between two efforts to measure the same trait through maximally similar methods. Validity is represented in the agreement between two attempts to measure the same trait through maximally different methods.
(Campbell and Fiske 1959: 83)

This distinction between reliability and validity is illustrated in Figure 7.1.

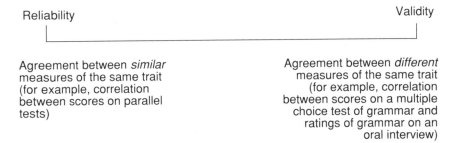

Reliability

Validity

Agreement between *similar* measures of the same trait (for example, correlation between scores on parallel tests)

Agreement between *different* measures of the same trait (for example, correlation between scores on a multiple choice test of grammar and ratings of grammar on an oral interview)

Figure 7.1　Relationship between reliability and validity

If we consider correlations as indicators of agreement, at one end of this continuum we have the correlation between scores on parallel tests, which constitutes the definition of reliability in classical true score theory. At the other end we might have correlations between, say, grammar scores obtained from clearly distinct measures, such as a multiple-choice test and an oral interview.

In many cases, however, the distinctiveness of the test methods is not so clear. For example, is the correlation between concurrent scores on two cloze tests based on different passages to be interpreted as reliability or validity? It depends upon how important we believe (or know, from actually examining this facet) the effect of the difference in passages to be. And what about the correlation between scores on a multiple-choice test of grammar developed by a classroom teacher and scores on the grammar section on a standardized test, such as the *Test of English as a Foreign Language*, assuming the same grammatical structures are included in both? If the item types and formats are similar, and if the tests were administered at about the same time and under the same conditions, it may well be that this correlation is closer to the reliability end of the continuum than to the validity end. Thus, we must carefully consider not only similarities in the test content, but also similarities in the test methods, in order to determine whether correlations between tests should be interpreted as estimators of reliability or as evidence supporting validity.

A second problem, mentioned in Chapter 6 (pp. 160–1), is that of distinguishing the abilities we intend to measure from the facets of the measurement procedure itself. As Stevenson (1981) has noted, this difficulty is particularly serious for language tests:

> Unlike many other areas of testing, language testing has a very special and complex problem when it comes to traits and methods. This problem is simply that what is trait and what is method is very hard to distinguish, and what should be considered as trait and what should be considered as method is very hard to decide. (Stevenson 1981: 53)

In an oral interview test of speaking, for example, the definition of communicative language ability includes the productive modality and oral channel, as does the definition of the response facet of the test method. In this case, these trait and method factors are inextricably bound together, making it impossible to distinguish between them, and hence to make a neat distinction between reliability and validity. (As I will argue in Chapter 8, this matching of trait and method factors is one aspect that contributes to test authenticity.)

In summary, although it is essential to consider both reliability and validity in the development and use of language tests, the distinction between them may not always be clear. Indeed, in many cases, if we insist on distinguishing between these two, the point at which we 'draw the line' may be somewhat arbitrary. However, as I will argue below, our concern in the development and use of language tests is to identify and estimate the relative effects of all the factors that affect test performance. If we can accomplish this, we will have addressed both reliability and validity, and the distinction between them may be incidental.

Validity as a unitary concept

Although validity has traditionally been discussed in terms of different types, as pointed out above, psychometricians have increasingly come to view it as a single, unitary concept. Messick (1980, 1988b) has argued that even viewing different approaches to validation (content, criterion-related, construct) as separate lines of evidence for supporting given score interpretations is inadequate, and that the consideration of values and consequences of score use has an essential role in validity considerations. He proposes a unified framework of validity that

> forestalls undue reliance on selected forms of evidence, that highlights the important though subsidiary role of specific content- and criterion-related evidence in support of construct validity in testing applications, and that formally brings consideration of value implications and social consequences into the validity framework.
> (Messick 1988: 20)

The framework he proposes consists of a four-way classification, described by two facets: (1) the '*source of justification* of the testing', which includes the consideration of either evidence or consequence, or both, and (2) the '*function or outcome* of the testing', which includes either test interpretation or use, or both (Messick 1988b: 20). This framework is illustrated in Table 7.1:

	Function of outcome of testing	
Source of justification	**Test interpretation**	**Test use**
Evidential Basis	Construct validity	Construct validity + Relevance/ Utility
Consequential Basis	Construct validity + Value implications	Construct validity + Relevance/ Utility + Social consequences

Table 7.1   Facets of validity (after Messick 1980, 1988b)

Messick sees this as a *progressive matrix*, with construct validity an essential component in each cell. Thus, for justifying a particular interpretation of a test score, we must gather evidence for construct validity and consider the value implications of this interpretation. If we wish to *use* this test score for a particular purpose, we must justify this by considering not only construct validity and value implications, but also the relevance or utility of the particular use and the social consequences of using the test score in this particular way. If, for example, we wish to interpret a score from an oral interview as an indicator of minimum competency in speaking, and to use this score to make a decision about the employability of a potential language teacher, we must provide the full range of justification. That is, in order to justify the *interpretation* of this test score, we must consider both its construct validity and the value implications of interpreting this score in a particular way. Specifically, we must collect evidence supporting the construct validity of interpreting this score as an indicator of the individual's ability and consider the value implications of various labels we could attach to this interpretation, of the particular theories of language upon which these labels are based, and of the educational or social ideologies in which these theories are embedded. The label 'oral proficiency', for example, has value implications quite different from those of 'communicative language ability', as these are related to very different views of language ability (Lowe 1988), with perhaps different educational and social ideologies as well. In order to justify the *use* of scores from this test as a basis for employment decisions, we must present evidence, or argue coherently that this ability is relevant, indeed essential, to the individual's effectiveness as a language teacher. We must also consider the consequences of the decision that is made on the basis of the test score. What, for example, are the positive benefits to the educational system of adding or retaining highly qualified language teachers and screening out those who are not qualified? What are the possible negative consequences for society at large of preventing individuals from pursuing their chosen careers for which they may have invested considerable time and resources? What are the negative consequences of making wrong decisions?

The evidential basis of validity

In defining validity as 'the appropriateness, meaningfulness, and usefulness of the specific inferences made from test scores' (American Psychological Association 1985: 9), the measurement profession has clearly linked validity to the inferences that are made on the basis of test scores. The process of validation, therefore, 'starts with the inferences that are drawn and the uses that are made of scores. . . . These uses and inferences dictate the kinds of evidence and logical arguments that are required to support judgments regarding validity' (Linn 1980: 548). Judging the extent to which an interpretation or use of a given test score is valid thus requires the collection of evidence supporting the relationship between the test score and an interpretation or use. Messick (1980, 1989) refers to this as the 'evidential' basis for test interpretation and use. The evidence that we collect in support of a particular test use can be grouped into three general types: content relevance, criterion relatedness, and meaningfulness of construct. And while these have typically been discussed as different kinds of validity (content, criterion, and construct), they can be more appropriately viewed as complementary types of evidence that must be gathered in the process of validation.

Content relevance and content coverage (content validity)

One of the first characteristics of a test that we, as prospective test users, examine is its content. If we cannot examine an actual copy of the test, we would generally like to see a table of specifications and example items, or at least a listing of the content areas covered, and the number of items, or relative importance of each area. Likewise, in developing a test, we begin with a definition of the content or ability domain, or at the very least, with a list of content areas, from which we generate items, or test tasks. The consideration of test content is thus an important part of both test development and test use. *Demonstrating* that a test is relevant to and covers a given area of content or ability is therefore a necessary part of validation.

There are two aspects to this part of validation: content relevance and content coverage. The investigation of *content relevance* requires 'the specification of the behavioral domain in question and the attendant specification of the task or test domain' (Messick 1980: 1017). While it is generally recognized that this involves the specification of the *ability* domain, what is often ignored is that examining content relevance also requires the specification of the test method facets. The domain specification that is necessary for examining content relevance is essentially the process of operationally defining constructs, which was discussed in Chapter 2 (pp.42–4). The importance of also specifying the test method facets that define the measurement procedures is clear from Cronbach's description of validation:

> a validation study examines the procedure as a whole. Every aspect of the setting in which the test is given and every detail of the procedure may have an influence on performance and hence on what is measured. Are the examiner's sex, status, and ethnic group the same as those of the examinee? Does he put the examinee at ease? Does he suggest that the test will affect the examinee's future, or does he explain that he is merely checking out the effectiveness of the instructional method? Changes in procedure such as these lead to substantial changes in ability- and personality-test performance, and hence in the appropriate interpretation of test scores. . . . The measurement procedure being validated needs to be described with such clarity that other investigators could reproduce the significant aspects of the procedure themselves.
> (Cronbach 1971: 449)

The necessity of specifying both the ability domain and test method facets is also recognized by proponents of criterion-referenced test development. Popham (1978), for example, includes the following as elements to be specified in test design: (1) 'what it is that the test measures'; (2) the attributes of the stimuli that will be presented to the test taker, and (3) the nature of the responses that the test taker is expected to make. Hambleton (1984) further relates these test design considerations directly to content validity.

The second aspect of examining test content is that of *content coverage*, or the extent to which the tasks required in the test adequately represent the behavioral domain in question. From the perspective of the test developer, if we had a well-defined domain that specified the entire set, or population, of possible test tasks, we could follow a standard procedure for random sampling (or stratified random sampling, in the case of heterogeneous domains) to insure that the tasks required by the test were representative of that domain. And a similar procedure could be followed, drawing multiple samples of tasks from the domain, to determine the extent to which different sets of tasks are equivalent, as a way of demonstrating content coverage.[1]

The problem with language tests, of course, is that we seldom have a domain definition that clearly and unambiguously identifies the set of language use tasks from which possible test tasks can be sampled, so that demonstrating either content relevance or content coverage is difficult. This difficulty applies even to criterion-referenced tests, which are often used to illustrate the sufficiency of content evidence for demonstrating validity. Consider, for example, the case of an oral interview test of speaking ability that is to be used for assigning grades, or for certifying competency, following a course of instruction. In this case, the domain might include not only the teaching points included in the curriculum, but also the 'content' of the instruction itself.[2] This might include a full description of the oral interactions between the teacher and students and among students, including, among other things, grammatical forms used and illocutionary acts performed, communication breakdowns and repairs, and conversational strategies. Also included in this domain might be the physical conditions of the room, the seating arrangement, the time of day, the number of people in the room, and the age, sex, and personality characteristics of the teacher and students. Indeed, even a superficial review of the literature in classroom-centered language research indicates that the list of such factors is virtually endless (for example, Allwright 1980; Long and Sato 1983; Saville-Troike 1984; Saville-Troike *et al.* 1984; Frölich *et al.* 1985; Pica and Long 1986).

There are, of course, domains of language ability that can be specified with greater precision, an example of which might be knowledge of vocabulary, irrespective of how it is acquired. But even here, the domain specification is more than a simple list, since we must specify not only the words that constitute the domain, but the conditions of elicitation and observation that characterize potential test tasks. That is, how will this 'knowledge' of vocabulary be elicited and observed? In a multiple-choice synonym recognition task? A word association task? A free recall task? A count of words used in a composition? A rating of a speech sample? Takala's (1985) study of students' foreign language vocabulary sizes is exemplary of the considerations of domain and task specification, and illustrates how issues such as these can be approached. These two examples, the domains of speaking and vocabulary, illustrate, I believe, the difficulties involved in specifying domains, or 'universes of admissible observations' (Cronbach *et al.* 1972), and hence in demonstrating content relevance and content coverage, in language tests.

Even if we were able to specify content domains of language abilities exhaustively, evidence of content relevance and content coverage will only support interpretations that are limited to the domain specified, such as, 'the subject is able to correctly identify synonyms from among four choices, for 75 per cent of the words in the syllabus, when these words are presented in isolation'. And on the basis of content relevance alone, even such limited interpretations are unidirectional, in that we can only infer what the test taker *can* do; we cannot make any inferences about what he *cannot* do (Messick 1980: 1018). This is because there are a number of possible explanations, other than lack of ability, for why a test taker might fail to perform a given set of tasks successfully:

> Although one may infer from correct performance that the respondents possessed all of the requisite abilities, it is much more tenuous to infer from the absence of correct performance that they lacked some of those abilities. The inference of inability or incompetence from the absence of correct performance requires the elimination of a number of plausible rival hypotheses dealing with motivation, attention, deafness, and so forth. Thus, a report of failure to perform would be valid, but one of inability to perform would not necessarily be valid. The very use of the term *inability* invokes constructs of attribute and process, whereas content-valid interpretation would stick to outcomes.
> (Messick 1975: 960)

This limitation on interpretations that are supported only by content information is particularly problematic in the area of minimum-competency testing, where decisions based on the test often involve the implicit determination of *in*ability, or *in*competency (Madaus 1983b; Linn 1979, 1983).

The major limitation of content relevance as the sole basis for validity, however, is that demonstrating that the contents of a test accurately represent a given domain of ability does not take into consideration, or account for, how individuals actually perform on the test (Cronbach 1971). Even though the content of a given test does not vary across different groups of individuals to which it is given, the performance of these individuals may vary considerably, and the interpretation of test scores will vary accordingly. 'Content validity is a test characteristic. It will not vary across different groups of examinees. . . . However, the validity of test score interpretation *will* vary from one situation to another' (Hambleton, *et al.* 1978: 38–9).

Furthermore, the score of an individual on a given test is not likely to be equally valid for different uses. For example, although a rating from an oral interview may be a valid indicator of speaking ability, it may not be valid as a measure of teaching ability. The primary limitation of content validity, then, is that it focuses on tests, rather than test scores. This limitation has been characterized by Messick in an extended simile:

> content validity is like the barker outside a circus tent touting two bowing aerialists, a waving clown, and a poster of a lady riding a unicorn as a sample of the show you will see inside. It is not just that the sample is not representative of the variety of individuals and animals inside or even an accurate portrayal of them, it is that you do not see any performances.
> (Messick 1975: 961)

In summary, the examination of content relevance and content coverage is a necessary part of the validation process, since the domain specification upon which a test is based provides the means for examining other relationships, such as those between test performance and performance in other contexts. By itself, however, content relevance is not sufficient evidence for validity, since it does not permit inferences about abilities and does not take into consideration how test takers perform.

Criterion relatedness (criterion validity)

Another kind of information we may gather in the validation process is that which demonstrates a relationship between test scores and some criterion which we believe is also an indicator of the ability tested. This 'criterion' may be level of ability as defined by group membership, individuals' performance on another test of the ability in question, or their relative success in performing some task that involves this ability. In some cases this criterion behavior may be concurrent with, or occur nearly simultaneously with the administration of the test, while in other cases, it may be some future behavior that we want to predict.

Concurrent criterion relatedness (concurrent validity)

Information on concurrent criterion relatedness is undoubtedly the most commonly used in language testing. Such information typically takes one of two forms: (1) examining differences in test performance among groups of individuals at different levels of language ability, or (2) examining correlations among various measures of a given ability. If we can identify groups of individuals that are at different levels on the ability in which we are interested, we can investigate the degree to which a test of this ability accurately discriminates between these groups of individuals. Typical groups that have been used for such comparisons are 'native speakers' and 'non-native speakers' of the language (for example, Chihara *et al.* 1977; Alderson 1980; Bachman 1985). Assuming that native speakers are competent in a given component of language ability, for example, sensitivity to cohesive relationships across sentences in written discourse, and non-native speakers are less competent, we would expect that the former would perform significantly better on a test of this component than would the latter.

In designing or interpreting results from such studies, two considerations must be made. First, we must carefully examine the basis on which we assume one group to be more proficient than another. This is particularly important when 'native speakers' are used as a comparison group, since, as indicated in Chapter 2 (pp. 38–40), there are serious problems in determining what kind of language use to consider as the 'native speaker' norm, while the question of what constitutes a native speaker, or whether we can even speak of individuals who are native speakers, is the subject of much debate.[3] Furthermore, there is growing evidence that native speakers perform *neither* uniformly well on tests of all aspects of language ability, *nor* uniformly better than do non-natives (for example, Allen *et al.* 1983; Bachman 1985). Second, we must not assume that since individuals in one group are at a higher level of language ability *in general*, they will therefore be at a higher level on the specific ability in which we are interested. That is, in order to interpret group differences as evidence supporting concurrent validity, we must be sure that the groups differ on the specific ability or abilities that our test measures.

The second type of information on concurrent criterion related-ness, the examination of correlations among different measures of the ability in question, is much more common. Indeed, the literature on language testing research is filled with studies that examine correlations among various measures of language ability. Further-more, one of the first questions test users are likely to ask about a test is whether it is correlated with some standardized test. It is thus not surprising that test developers often feel compelled to administer a standardized test along with their own test in order to find out if scores on the two are correlated. One problem with this, as indicated above in the discussion of validity and reliability, is that these correlations may in fact be best interpreted as indicators of reliability, rather than as evidence of validity, depending on how similar the test methods are.

However, even when the measurement methods are clearly distinct, there are serious problems with accepting a high correlation between two indicators of a given ability as conclusive evidence of validity. One problem is that this assumes that the criterion behavior (test or other performance) can be validly interpreted as an indicator of the ability in question. Frequently evidence for the validity of the criterion itself is that it is correlated with other tests, or other indicators of the ability, which simply extends the assumption of validity to these other criteria, leading to an endless spiral of concurrent relatedness. Thus, without independent evidence support-ing the interpretation of the criterion as an indicator of the ability in question, there is no basis for interpreting a correlation with that criterion as evidence of validity. As Messick, Cronbach, and others have argued, only the process of construct validation can provide this evidential basis of validity. In the absence of evidence from construct validation, the examination of concurrent relevance either becomes circular or eventually appeals to 'real life', or 'natural', or 'normal' language use as a criterion. The problem with this is that although we may be able to make informed comparative judgments about which of two or more tasks is closer to 'real-life' performance, we have no basis for clearly distinguishing where 'real life' language use ends and 'non-real life' language use begins.

The most serious limitation to examining concurrent criterion relevance, however, is that it only considers the extent to which measures of the same ability tend to agree. It ignores the equally important question of the extent to which scores on the test are different from indicators of different abilities. That is, we would not expect scores from measures of language ability to be highly correlated with, say, speed in mathematical computation or knowledge of important dates in history. Thus, if we want to demonstrate that our test scores are valid indicators of a given language ability, we must show not only that they are related to other indicators of that same ability, but also that they are *not* related to measures of other abilities. This suggests that in the validation of language tests we also need to look at the relationships between our language tests and measures of other abilities, such as mathematical computation or knowledge of history. When we look for this sort of divergence, we are in fact embarking on the voyage to construct validation, which will be discussed in greater detail below.[4]

Predictive utility (predictive validity)

Another use of information on criterion relatedness is in determining how well test scores predict some future behavior. Suppose we wanted to use language test scores to predict satisfactory job performance or successful achievement in a course of instruction. Typical examples would be the use of an oral interview for certifying language teachers or of a composition test to place students into a sequence of writing courses. In order to examine the predictive utility of test scores in cases such as these, we would need to collect data demonstrating a relationship between scores on the test and job or course performance. In this case our primary concern is the accuracy with which our test scores predict the criterion behaviors in which we are interested, and our procedures will thus focus on the problems of prediction.

One potential problem with examining predictive utility alone is that it can largely ignore the question of what abilities are being measured. We might find, for example, that scores on a test of signed number problems in mathematics are excellent predictors of performance in language courses. Regardless of such a finding, however, we would not seriously consider using this test as a predictor, because of the obvious mismatch between the ability the test appears to measure and the performance we are trying to predict. That is, in this case we would probably reject predictive utility as evidence supporting the validity of this test use.

The lack of attention to abilities being measured is frequently more subtle than this, however. Consider, for example, the common practice of using multiple-choice grammar tests to place individuals into writing courses, or the use of dictation tests for placement into integrated skills courses. In cases such as these, the mismatch comes not from measuring completely different abilities, but from measuring only limited aspects of the criterion ability. If the use of test scores in these contexts were limited strictly to prediction, such mismatches would be of little concern, since in most cases wrong placement decisions can be fairly easily corrected. Unfortunately, however, the fact that such measures predict placement fairly well is often used as evidence that they measure the abilities that constitute the criterion.

Upshur (1979) has discussed the problems involved in using predictive utility as evidence for interpreting test scores as indicators of ability, and relates these to two ways of viewing language ability, or proficiency: 'Language proficiency is variously conceived in two different ways: as a pragmatic ascription ("Someone is proficient") and as a theoretic construct representing human capacity ("Someone has proficiency")' (p. 76). This distinction is also reflected in the way we use test scores. If we view language ability as a pragmatic ascription, then a test score is seen as an indication that an individual is 'able to do X' in the language. The other view would be to interpret a test score as an indication that an individual 'has ability X'. Upshur's essential argument is that the former view, that of pragmatic ascription, does not require a theoretical description of language ability, and is only sufficient *so long as one is only interested in predicting future performance*. That is, it is possible to find or develop tests that will predict some future behavior, without recourse to any particular theoretical considerations.

In situations where predictive utility is the primary consideration, there is a tendency to simplify, to reduce the number of measures we use to the smallest set, or to the single measure that provides the greatest accuracy of prediction. One reason for this is that in such situations efficiency is also frequently important. For example, if we must select for admission 1,000 individuals from among 50,000 applicants, we need a measure that is not only highly predictive, but also economical. As a result of this need for efficiency, we frequently simplify our tests.

A more important factor that leads to the simplification of

measures, however, is the ultimate indeterminacy of the relationships among several predictors and the behavior to be predicted (Upshur 1979). Cattell (1964) described this problem as follows:

> the correlation of a test now with a criterion next year has a host of determinants among which the properties of the test may well be insignificant. . . . *Future* prediction, after all, requires knowledge of the natural history of the trait, the laws of psychology, and (not least!) the changing life situations, e.g., the stock exchange, which will affect the individual in the interim. If only, say, a tenth, of the variance in estimates of that future behavior is tied to test validity variance, it is absurd to use that behavior to calculate an alleged property of predictive validity in a test.
> (Cattell 1964: 10)

This indeterminacy, which was discussed in Chapter 2 as a limitation in specification (pp. 30–2), is a result of our inability both (1) to identify and measure all the abilities and factors that are relevant to the criterion, and (2) to specify not only whether the predictors are related to each other and to the predicted behavior, but also the strength and type of these relationships. For example, are aptitude, motivation, and current level of ability all equally related to future achievement? Are they related to each other? Are the relationships additive, so that the sum of their effects equals the predicted behavior? Or do they interact with each other, so that the effect of one moderates the effect of the others? And this is not to mention the considerations of situational requirements, such as test method facets and the context of the predicted behavior, which represent an additional dimension of complexity in these relationships. This indeterminacy, or underspecification, is a difficult problem for prediction in general, and is beyond the scope of this book. However, one need only read the literature on attempts to predict academic achievement on the basis of language ability to gain an appreciation of the complexity of examining the predictive utility of language tests (for example, Powers 1980; Alderman 1981; Wilson 1982; Low and Lee 1985; and the studies cited in Hale *et al*. 1984). In the face of such indeterminacy, the theorist tends 'to analyze the test task into as few components as possible – preferably one' (Upshur 1979: 84–5).

The result of such simplification can be the development and use of measures that have no theoretical basis, and which thus provide no explanation of the nature of the ability measured.

In the extreme this [simplification] yields a theory which . . . is simply a trivial exercise in naming: A test score (task value) is a numerical representation of a unidimensional ability (language proficiency) which is a mapping of a single psychological state (language knowledge?), and this ability (proficiency) is applicable to any situation; in the case that some situations require more of it than do others, one simply accepts differential validity coefficients. (Upshur 1979: 85)

The view of language ability as being able to do something, then, is of necessity linked to prediction, and leads to the development of language tests as pragmatic prediction devices that provide an inadequate basis for understanding the nature of the ability we believe we are measuring. The relationships between these two views of language proficiency, their uses or interpretations and the types of evidential support required of each are shown in Figure 7.2 (overleaf).

Prediction is an important and justifiable use of language tests, and evidence that indicates a relationship between test performance and the behavior that is to be predicted provides support for the validity of this use of test results. Prediction, nevertheless, is not 'the only game in town' (Upshur 1979: 99). There is a wide range of situations in which we are not interested in prediction at all, but in determining the levels of abilities of language learners. As indicated in Chapter 3, our primary concerns in most educational settings are with diagnosing and evaluating student abilities. In situations such as these, we must base our tests on a definition of ability, whether this is in the form of a theory of communicative language ability, or of a course syllabus.

The danger that Upshur points out, and which I also see, is the conceptual shift from ability as pragmatic ascription to ability as a theoretical construct, a shift that is inherent in the improper interpretation of measures that have been developed for predictive purposes, as indicators of ability. Language tests that have been developed for purposes of prediction, and whose use for this purpose may be supported by considerable experience and empirical evidence, cannot, on these grounds alone, be interpreted as valid measures of any particular ability. In other words, measures that are valid as predictors of some future performance are not necessarily valid indicators of ability. Demonstrating that a test score is a valid indicator of ability requires an entirely different approach to validation from merely examining predictability. It involves the process of construct validation, which is discussed in greater detail below.

In summary, information about criterion relatedness – concurrent or predictive – is by itself insufficient evidence for validation.

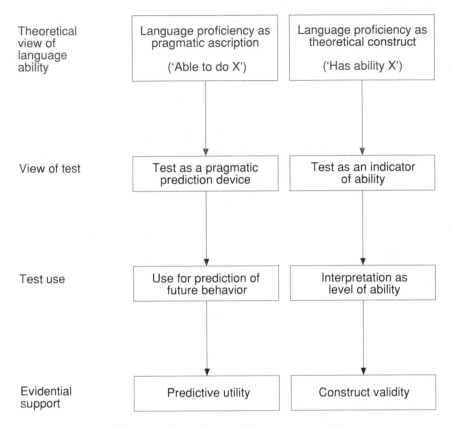

*Figure 7.2   Contrasting views of language proficiency, uses/
interpretations of test results, and validity*

Examining the agreement among concurrent measures of a given
language ability may beg the question of the validity of the criteria,
and ignores the extent to which these measures do not agree with
measures of other abilities. Examining predictive utility is problematic because the criterion behavior that we want to predict is often
a complex one that may depend upon a large number of factors in
addition to language abilities. In addition, predictability does not
constitute evidence for making inferences about abilities.

Construct validation

In discussing the different aspects of validation so far, I have
repeatedly referred to construct validity, and it is high time I
attempted to explain what this is. Construct validity concerns the

extent to which performance on tests is consistent with predictions that we make on the basis of a theory of abilities, or constructs. Historically, the notion of construct validity grew out of efforts in the early 1950s by the American Psychological Association to prepare a code of professional ethics, part of which would address the adequacy of psychological tests (Cronbach 1988).[5] The seminal article that described the need for construct validation and provided the conceptual framework for its investigation is that of Cronbach and Meehl (1955). In the thirty years since, construct validity has come to be recognized by the measurement profession as central to the appropriate interpretation of test scores, and provides the basis for the view of validity as a unitary concept.

Perhaps the easiest place to start in the discussion of construct validity is the following statement by Messick:

> A measure estimates how much of something an individual displays or possesses. The basic question [of construct validation] is, What is the nature of that something?
> (Messick 1975: 957)

In attempting to answer this question, we must identify and define what the 'something' is that we want to measure, and when we define what this is, we are, in effect, defining a construct. For Carroll (1987a), a construct of 'mental ability' is defined in terms of a particular set of mental tasks that an individual is required to perform on a given test. Similarly, Cronbach and Meehl (1955) define a construct as 'a postulated attribute of people, assumed to be reflected in test performance' (p. 283); further, a construct is defined in terms of a theory that specifies how it relates to other constructs and to observable performance. Thus, constructs can be viewed as definitions of abilities that permit us to state specific hypotheses about how these abilities are or are not related to other abilities, and about the relationship between these abilities and observed behavior. Another way of viewing constructs is as a way of classifying behavior.

> Whenever one classifies situations, persons, or responses, he uses *constructs*. The term *concepts* might be used rather than *constructs*, but the latter term emphasizes that categories are deliberate creations to organize experience into general law-like statements. Some constructs are very close to the stuff of ordinary experience – red, for example, or human being. . . . Some constructs (e.g., red-green color blindness) are embedded in well-articulated, well-substantiated theories.
> (Cronbach 1971: 462)

Virtually all test use inevitably involves the interpretation of test scores as indicators of ability, and as soon as we ask the question, 'What does this test really measure?', construct validation is called for. Construct validity is thus seen as a unifying concept, and construct validation as a process that incorporates all the evidential bases for validity discussed thus far:

> Construct validity is indeed the unifying concept that integrates criterion and content considerations into a common framework for testing rational hypotheses about theoretically relevant relationships.
> (Messick 1980: 1015)

Hypotheses

As discussed in Chapter 2, the abilities that we want to measure are not directly observable, but must be inferred on the basis of observed performance. Furthermore, these abilities are theoretical, in the sense that we hypothesize that they affect the way we use language, and how we perform on language tests.[6] The fundamental issue in construct validity is the extent to which we can make inferences about hypothesized abilities on the basis of test performance. In construct validation, therefore, we seek to provide evidence that supports specific inferences about relationships between constructs and test scores. That is, in conducting construct validation, we are empirically testing hypothesized relationships between test scores and abilities.

Construct validation can thus be seen as a special case of verifying, or falsifying, a scientific theory, and just as a theory can never be 'proven', the validity of any given test use or interpretation is always subject to falsification. Construct validation requires both logical analysis and empirical investigation. Logical analysis is involved in defining the constructs theoretically and operationally. This comprises the first two steps in measurement, described in Chapter 2, and provides the means for relating the theoretical definitions of the constructs to observations of behavior – scores on language tests. These definitions can also be considered as hypotheses, in that they comprise conjectural statements about the relationships among constructs (Kerlinger 1986: 17). For example, we might define pragmatic competence as follows: 'the knowledge necessary, in addition to organizational competence, for appropriately producing or comprehending discourse. Specifically, it includes illocutionary competence, or the knowledge of how to perform speech acts, and sociolinguistic competence, or the knowledge of the sociolinguistic conventions which govern language use.' In defining illocutionary and sociolinguistic competence as parts of pragmatic competence, we are, in effect, hypothesizing relationships such as, 'illocutionary and sociolinguistic competence are related to each other' and 'illocutionary and sociolinguistic competence are related to pragmatic competence'.

Our theoretical definitions also provide the basis for stating counterhypotheses regarding relationships among constructs. According to the above definition, for example, reasonable counterhypotheses would be that illocutionary and sociolinguistic competence are not related to organizational competence, or that they are less strongly related to organizational competence than they are to pragmatic competence. The role of counterhypotheses is explicitly recognized in the literature on construct validation (for example, Campbell and Fiske 1959; Campbell 1960; Cronbach 1971, 1980; Messick 1975), and has also been fundamental to much of the construct validation research in language testing. Cronbach (1980) provides the following succinct statement in this regard: 'The job of validation is not to support an interpretation, but to find out what might be wrong with it. A proposition deserves some degree of trust only when it has survived serious attempts to falsify it' (p. 103).

The relationships that we hypothesize among constructs also provide a basis for making hypotheses at an operational level, that is, about *observable* relationships among test scores. When we operationally define constructs as measures of language ability, we are making hypotheses about the relationship between these constructs and test scores, which can thus be viewed as behavioral manifestations of the constructs. The model described in Chapter 4 hypothesizes that communicative language ability comprises a number of specific competencies, such as grammatical, textual, illocutionary, and sociolinguistic competence. These competencies could be operationally defined as language tests in various ways, and we could state hypotheses about the ways in which scores from these language tests would or would not be functionally related (correlated) with each other. For example, ratings of the use of register and of cultural references (two aspects of sociolinguistic competence) from a writing sample should be more highly correlated with each other than with a rating of grammatical competence from a writing sample. Or we would hypothesize that tests that share *two* features of psychophysiological mechanisms, such as two tests involving speaking (auditory channel, productive modality), would be more highly correlated than would two tests that share only *one* feature, such as a test of listening and a test of speaking, which share only the auditory channel.

In examining the effects of test method facets on language test scores, we are also testing hypotheses that are relevant to construct validity. A number of studies (for example, Clifford 1978, 1981; Bachman and Palmer 1981a, 1982a) have addressed this issue as part of construct validation. The framework described in Chapter 5 hypothesizes that test method facets, such as the nature of the input the test taker receives and the type of response required, affect performance on language tests, and hence provide the basis for making further hypotheses about the relationships among test scores. Suppose, for example, that a group of individuals had equal competence in vocabulary and grammar, and that we measured both abilities with a multiple-choice test and a writing sample. If we found that the two multiple-choice tests were more highly correlated with each other than were the multiple-choice and writing tests of grammar, we would attribute this to the effect of test method factors, since the two highly correlated tests of different abilities shared the same multiple-choice test method.

Evidence supporting construct validity

While the examples above involve correlations among test scores, I do not intend to imply that this is the only kind of information that is relevant, or even that observed correlations among language test scores provide sufficient evidence for construct validation. On the contrary, in examining the relationships among different observations of language performance, not all of which will be tests, the test developer involved in the process of construct validation is likely to collect several types of empirical evidence. These may include any or all of the following: (1) the examination of patterns of correlations among item scores and test scores, and between characteristics of items and tests and scores on items and tests; (2) analyses and modeling of the processes underlying test performance; (3) studies of group differences; (4) studies of changes over time, or (5) investigation of the effects of experimental treatment (Messick 1989). Two of these types of evidence, correlational and experimental, are particularly powerful, in my opinion, while I believe a third, the analysis of the process of test taking, holds perhaps the most promise for providing new insights into the factors that affect test performance.

Correlational evidence

Correlational evidence is derived from a family of statistical procedures that examine the relationships among variables, or measures. The approach that has been used most extensively in construct validation studies of language tests is to examine patterns of correlations among test scores, either directly, or, for correlations among large numbers of test scores, through factor analysis. More recently factor analysis, causal modeling, and multiple linear regression analysis have been employed by language testing researchers for investigating relationships at the level of individual tasks or items.

A *correlation* is a functional relationship between two measures. To say that two sets of test scores are correlated with each other is simply to say that they tend to vary in the same way with respect to each other. For example, if students who receive high scores on a test of grammatical competence also earn high grades in writing classes, we could say that the scores on the test and course grades are positively correlated with each other. If the reverse were true, with high grades going to students who do poorly on the test, the two measures would be negatively correlated with each other. A *correlation coefficient* is a single statistic, or number, that tells us 'to what extent variations in one [measure] go with variations in the other' (Guilford and Fruchter 1978: 77).

As indicators of observed functional relationships, correlation coefficients can provide valuable empirical information for supporting or rejecting specific interpretations and uses of test scores.[7] When we interpret a test score as an indicator of a given language ability, we do so on the basis of the hypothesized relationship, specified in the operational definition, between the test score and the ability. Empirical evidence that scores on this test are consistently correlated with other indicators of the same ability provides support for this interpretation. But in addition to demonstrating concurrent relatedness, it is equally important to provide evidence that scores on the test are *not* consistently correlated with indicators of other abilities. We might hypothesize, for example, that scores on a test of reading would not be highly correlated with scores on a test of multiplication, if our theory indicated reading comprehension and competence in multiplication were distinct abilities. It is therefore essential to bear in mind that our uses and interpretations of correlation coefficients must be guided by a theory of constructs. That is, the measures and relationships we choose to examine must be guided by our definitions of these abilities and by the kinds of relationships our theory hypothesizes among them. Specifically, our theory should

provide hypotheses about which measures should be highly correlated with each other, and which should not. In this regard, Kenny
(1979) provides a useful caution:

> The term *correlational inference* should not be taken to mean that
> various statistics are by themselves inferential . . . correlations do
> not, in and of themselves, have an inferential quality. Given a
> plausible model, a statistic can be used for inferential purposes, but
> the statistic itself is merely a passive tool. Inference goes on in the
> head of the researcher, not in the bowels of the computer.
> (Kenny 1979: 2)

Correlational approaches to construct validation may utilize both
exploratory and confirmatory modes. In the exploratory mode, we
attempt to identify the abilities, or traits, that influence performance
on tests by examining the correlations among a set of measures. We
begin with observed functional relationships, or correlations among
test scores, and on the basis of these, we form generalizations, or
hypotheses, about the traits that might account for these correlations.

In the confirmatory mode, we begin with hypotheses about traits
and how they are related to each other, and attempt to either confirm
or reject these hypotheses by examining the observed correlations.
We thus begin with definitions of abilities and hypotheses about how
these are related to each other, develop measures that are operational
definitions of the traits in our theory, hypothesize how scores on
these measures should be correlated, observe the correlations among
the scores, and then determine the extent to which these observed
correlations confirm or provide support for the hypothesized
relationships.[8]

Directly examining patterns of correlations among measures
It is impossible to make clear, unambiguous inferences regarding the
influence of various factors on test scores on the basis of a single
correlation between two tests. For example, if we found that a
multiple-choice test of cohesion were highly correlated with a
multiple-choice test of rhetorical organization, there are three
possible inferences: (1) the test scores are affected by a common trait
(textual competence); (2) they are affected by a common method
(multiple-choice), and (3) they are affected by both trait and
method.[9] These different inferences are illustrated in Figures 7.3a, b,
and c respectively.

Because of the potential ambiguities involved in interpreting a
single correlation between two tests, correlational approaches to

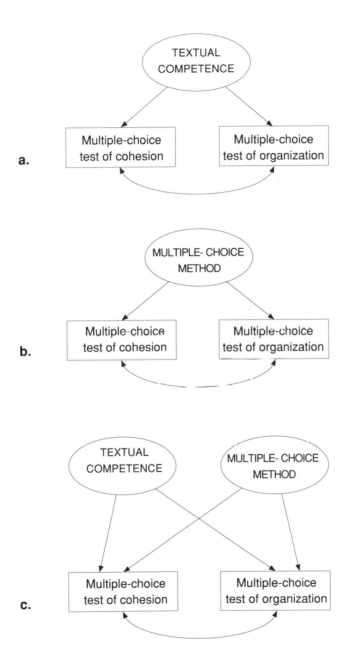

*Figure 7.3   Ambiguity of inferences based on a single correlation
between two tests*

construct validation of language tests have typically involved correlations among large numbers of measures (for example, Carroll 1958, 1967; Carroll *et al.* 1959; Oller 1979b; Scholz *et al.* 1980; Carroll 1983a). One problem with this is that the number of correlations multiplies geometrically with the number of tests, so that it soon becomes extremely difficult to see and interpret patterns. Suppose, for example, that we gave 15 different tests to a single group of subjects in which we expected differences of abilities on a number of different traits. We would have to attempt to find and interpret patterns among 105 correlations.

Factor analysis
A commonly used procedure for interpreting a large number of correlations is factor analysis, which is a group of analytical and statistical techniques 'whose common objective is to represent a set of [observed] variables in terms of a smaller number of hypothetical variables' (Kim and Mueller 1978a: 9). In the context of construct validation, the observed variables are test scores or other measures, while the hypothetical variables are what we attempt to interpret as constructs, test methods, and other influences on performance on language tests. These hypothetical variables, or communalities, that underlie the observed correlations, are called 'factors', and one of the results that are obtained through the factor analytic procedure are factor 'loadings' that indicate the degree of relationship between observed test scores and the various factors that emerge from the analysis.[10]

Starting in the exploratory mode, the language testing researcher may begin with a number of tests that are available and that measure a wide range of language abilities in which she is interested. As patterns of factor loadings emerge, the researcher may formulate hypotheses about similarities and differences among the test scores. Then, on the basis of these hypotheses, the researcher may move to the confirmatory mode, eliminating some tests from further study while designing new tests to examine specific hypotheses. For example, we might extend the study of the single correlation illustrated in Figure 7.4 by adding multiple-choice tests of sensitivity to register and naturalness, in order to disconfirm the hypothesis that test method is a major influence on students' performance on these tests. If we found that these tests were not highly correlated with the other tests, we could probably reject this hypothesis. If we were to further include in our study ratings of cohesion, rhetorical organization, sensitivity to register, and naturalness, based on a writing sample, and found that these were highly correlated with the respective multiple-choice measures of these abilities, but not with each other, this would further support the hypothesis that these test scores are affected primarily by abilities rather than test methods. In this way, we use hypotheses derived from our theoretical definitions of abilities and test method facets, and from exploratory studies, to guide the selection of specific measures to be included in our study. By including these measures and ruling out specific hypotheses, we provide support for a particular interpretation of test scores.

The multitrait–multimethod (MTMM) design
The classic approach to designing correlational studies for construct validation is the multitrait–multimethod (MTMM) matrix, described by Campbell and Fiske (1959). In this approach, each measure is considered to be a combination of trait and method, and tests are included in the design so as to combine multiple traits with multiple methods. One advantage of the MTMM design is that it permits the investigator to examine patterns of both convergence and discrimination among correlations. *Convergence* is essentially what has been referred to above (pp. 248–50) as concurrent criterion relatedness, and is the extent to which different measures of the same trait tend to agree, or converge. *Discrimination* is the extent to which measures of different traits, using either the same or different test methods, tend to produce different results. In the example above, convergence would be indicated by *high positive* correlations between the different measures of the same traits (for textual competence, the tests of cohesion and organization, and for sociolinguistic competence, the tests of register and naturalness). Discrimination, on the other hand, would be indicated by *low* or zero correlations between measures of different traits using different test methods (for example, between a writing test of organization and a multiple-choice test of naturalness). Discrimination would also be demonstrated if tests of different traits using the same test method (for example, a multiple-choice test of cohesion and a multiple-choice test of naturalness) were not correlated with each other. The hypothesized relationships among the tests, abilities, and test methods in this example are illustrated in Figure 7.4.

Data from MTMM correlation matrices can be analyzed in a number of ways, including: (1) the direct inspection of convergent and discriminant correlations, as described by Campbell and Fiske (1959), and as applied to language test data by Clifford (1978, 1980), Brütsch (1979), and Klein-Braley (1981); (2) the analysis of variance, as described by Stanley (1961) and Kavanagh *et al.* (1971), and (3) confirmatory factor analysis, which was first proposed by

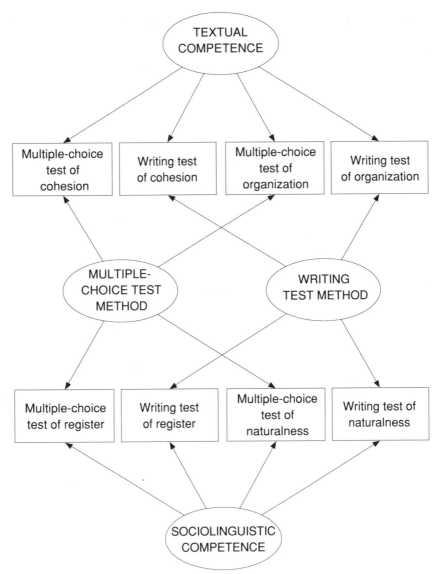

Figure 7.4   Hypothesized relationships among traits, methods, and measures in a MTMM design

Kalleberg and Kluegel (1975) and has been applied to data from language tests by Bachman and Palmer (1981a, 1982a) and Sang *et al* (1986).[11]

Thus far, the discussion has focused on examining patterns of correlations among scores on tests. However, the same types of analyses can be utilized for examining relationships among individual test tasks or items. This is what happens in item response theory (IRT), when we attempt to fit the relationships among items to a particular IRT model. However, because IRT models assume that all the items in a given test measure a single ability, the most that IRT analyses can show is the extent to which items (and persons) do or do not fit on a single dimension. Identifying what that dimension is, in terms of abilities, is beyond its capability. Thus, as Hulin *et al.* (1983) point out, 'IRT can be used to estimate an individual's standing on the latent trait but does not provide guidance for construct validation of the trait' (Hulin *et al.* 1983: 15).

Recently language testing researchers have begun examining patterns of relationships among individual test items or tasks, on the one hand, and between the characteristics of items and performance on items, on the other. Davidson (1988), for example, utilized exploratory factor analysis to examine patterns of relationships among items of so-called 'communicative' language tests. While his analyses revealed that by and large these test items tended to load on a single factor, suggesting unidimensionality, Davidson also points out serious problems with item-level exploratory factor analysis, and recommends using confirmatory factor analysis as well.

Another application of correlational analyses is to examine relationships between characteristics of items, in terms of their content and format, and test takers' performance on these items. Bachman (1982), for example, categorized items on a cloze test on the basis of a linguistic analysis of their relationships to other parts of the cloze passage and used these categories to specify hypotheses for a confirmatory factor analysis of performance on these items. More recently, Perkins and Linnville (1987) used multiple regression analysis to examine relationships between characteristics of vocabulary items on an EFL proficiency test and their difficulty, as indicated by the proportion of test takers who correctly answered an item. The characteristics they investigated included, among others, length of word, word frequency, abstractness, number of syllables, and semantic features. Their results indicate that for the non-native English speakers in their sample, length, frequency and/or distribution of occurrence, abstractness, and the semantic feature 'evaluation', account for the majority of the variance in item performance. As Perkins and Linnville point out, the investigation of relationships between item characteristics and item performance provides another source of evidence in construct validation.

Experimental evidence

While I have discussed the confirmatory mode in correlational analysis as a way of verifying (or falsifying) hypotheses, this is not the only, or even the most appropriate means of testing hypotheses in all situations. The other approach to hypothesis testing, that of classical experimental design, which has a much longer tradition in psychology, can also be applied to construct validation.[12]

In a true experimental design, individuals are assigned at random to two or more groups, each of which is given a different treatment. At the end of the treatment, observations are made to investigate differences among the different groups. In many cases these observations take the form of a post-test. There are two distinguishing characteristics of a true experimental design. The first is that of randomization, which means that (1) a sample of subjects is randomly selected from a population, and (2) the individuals in this random sample are then randomly assigned to two or more groups for comparison. The purpose of randomization is to control for, or equalize, any differences among individuals in the different groups that might affect performance on the post-test. The second characteristic is that of experimental intervention, or treatment. This means that the different groups of subjects are exposed to distinct treatments, or sets of circumstances, as part of the experiment. Assuming that the randomization has been effective, and that the various treatments involved are distinct and do not favor some groups more than others, the researcher can attribute any differences in post-test performance to differences in treatment.[13]

In applied linguistics, experimental (or quasi-experimental) designs have been used most frequently to examine the relative effects of different treatments, with the treatments consisting of different methods or techniques for language teaching, or different contexts of language learning. That is, the focus has generally been on examining the treatments themselves, with the tests that are used being viewed primarily as instruments to detect differences in individuals that can then be attributed to one treatment or another. For example, two groups of language learners, randomly selected and assigned to their groups, could be given different instructional sequences, 'Method X' and the 'Acclaimed and Improved Method' (AIM). (In some cases the researcher may also want to include, for comparison, a third group, which does nothing, as a 'control' group.) After a period of time, at the end of the treatment, all individuals in the experiment are given a test of language abilities, and test score differences among the groups are then attributed to the different treatments. In this example, the experimental hypothesis would be that subjects who had AIM would score higher on the post-test than would subjects who had Method X (who would, in turn, perform better than the 'do nothing' control group).

From this example, it should be clear that such designs must assume that the post-test is a valid measure of the abilities that are affected by the treatment. That is, in order to make inferences about the effect of the treatment on the abilities in question, the measure we use as a post-test must be a valid measure of those abilities. Thus, in the example above, if both AIM and Method X were directed toward improving reading skills, and we wanted to compare their relative effectiveness in achieving this objective, it would make little sense to use a test of listening and speaking as a post-test (except, perhaps, as a means for examining the divergence of scores on these tests with those on tests of reading).

In experimental designs, then, the abilities affected by the treatment must be included in those measured by the post-test. (The post-test may measure other abilities as well, but it must at least measure those abilities that are of concern in the treatment.) This relationship between abilities affected by the treatment and abilities measured by the post-test provides the key to understanding the application of experimental designs to construct validation. In experimental studies aimed at investigating the effects of a given treatment, we typically employ at least one treatment whose effects are *unknown*, and evaluate its effects in terms of performance on a *known* indicator (often a test) of language ability. In construct validation, on the other hand, it is the test, and not the treatment, that is of primary interest. Therefore, since we are examining a test whose validity is as yet *unknown*, we must employ a treatment whose effects are *known*.

Suppose, for example, that we have developed a test of pragmatic implicature, and want to investigate its construct validity. We have already examined its content and test method facets and determined to our satisfaction that the test has content relevance, in terms of theoretical definitions of implicature. We have also investigated the internal consistency of the test, and have determined that this is acceptable. Since we are interested in using this test to place students into a language course that includes, among other things, instruction in implicature, we believe that an experimental design will be the most appropriate way to examine the construct validity of scores on this test. As a basis for comparison, we will use a test of grammar, which has also been determined by competent judges to have content relevance, and which has acceptable internal consistency.

In implementing this experiment, we first identify two sequences of instruction that are known to be distinct (and effective): one focusing on grammar alone, and the other on implicature alone. Next, we select, say, 60 students at random from the program, and then randomly assign these to two groups, 'G' and 'I', with 30 students each. Each group then undergoes a period of instruction, Group G in grammar and Group I in implicature. At the end of the instruction, both groups are given both tests. Our hypothesis would be, of course, that Group G will perform better on the grammar test, and Group I better on the implicature test. There are several possible outcomes to this experiment, only one of which provides convincing support for the construct validity of the implicature test. If there is no difference between the two groups on either test, or if one group does better on both tests, this would tend to disconfirm the validity of the test and, in the absence of other evidence, raise questions about the distinctness of the construct, 'competence in pragmatic implicatures' from grammatical competence. If, on the other hand, our analysis of the results indicates significant differences between the two groups on the two tests, in the direction hypothesized, this would support the construct validity of the test.

In contrast to the number of studies employing correlational approaches, there have been very few experimental construct validation studies of language tests. One study, which was not designed as a construct validation study, but which lends itself to such interpretation, is Palmer (1979). In this research, Palmer employed the experimental design in two different settings and found that differences in performance on different types of language tests – achievement and 'communication' – were related to differences between 'discrete-point accuracy drills' and 'communication activities' as instructional treatments. The results of another experimental study reported by Fischer (1981) suggest that actual practice in taking what he calls communicative tests may lead to better performance on a communicative competence component of a final examination. Another example is a study by Chacevych *et al.* (1982), who found that prior exposure to passage content in the native language was significantly related to differences in performance on ESL cloze tests, thus raising questions about the constructs measured by the cloze. While the number of such studies is quite small, they are illustrative of the application of the experimental approach to construct validation. Perhaps even more intriguing, however, is the potential they suggest for a program of iterative research, in which new teaching methods and new tests are systematically examined so as to evaluate both the effectiveness of the methods and the adequacy of the tests as indicators of language abilities.

Analysis of the processes underlying test performance

While the quantitative analyses of patterns of test performance and of relationships between treatments and test performance constitute powerful methods for investigating specific hypotheses in the process of construct validation, they are relatively limited in their capacity for generating new hypotheses. A more critical limitation to correlational and experimental approaches to construct validation, however, is that these examine only the products of the test taking process – the test scores – and provide no means for investigating the processes of test taking themselves. The importance of investigating these processes has been stated by Messick (1989) as follows:

> in numerous applications of . . . techniques for studying the process, it became clear that different individuals performed the same task in different ways and that even the same individual might perform in a different manner across items or on different occasions. . . . That is, individuals differ consistently in their *strategies and styles of task performance.* [emphasis in original] (Messick 1989: 54)

Messick (1989) discusses a number of approaches to the analysis of the test taking process, including protocol analysis and computer modeling, the analysis of response times and mathematical modeling of these, the analysis of reasons given by test takers for choosing a particular answer, and the analysis of systematic errors.

Recently language testing researchers have begun to utilize qualitative empirical research procedures to better understand the processes involved in taking language tests. Cohen (1984) was one of the first to report on the examination of perceived strategies employed by language test takers and their reactions to different item and test types. Cohen reported on several studies that were based on verbal self-report data and which identified a variety of strategies followed in completing cloze and multiple-choice reading tests. For the cloze these included guessing, using the immediate context, and translating, when the correct answer was not known. For the multiple-choice reading test, subjects reported reading the questions before the passage, reading answer alternatives before the item stem, and choosing answers on the basis of the superficial matching of words and phrases in the stem with those in the passage. Cohen also reported that students at different ability levels reported using different strategies. In addition to these differences in processing strategies, students had different reactions to different tests, in terms of whether they liked them, felt they were difficult, or what they were perceived to measure. More recently, Cohen has utilized verbal report data to examine students' processing of teachers' feedback on compositions (Cohen 1987) and summarization tasks in a foreign language reading comprehension test (Cohen, forthcoming).

In a recent paper, Grotjahn (1986) outlined an integrated program of research that combines quantitative psychometric analyses of test data with qualitative analytic methods. He argues convincingly that the validation of language tests must include, in addition to the quantitative analysis of test takers' responses, the qualitative analysis of test taking processes and of the test tasks themselves. He describes a strategy of 'logical task analysis' that 'can suggest what kind of cognitive processes may be involved when the subject is confronted with the task or that a specific solution may be generated by several alternative processing strategies' (Grotjahn 1986: 165-6). For the investigation of test taking processes, he recommends the types of self-report data (thinking aloud and retrospective interview) utilized by Cohen.

Grotjahn describes an on-going research study into the 'C-test', which is a variant of the cloze test in which the second half of every second word in a reading passage is deleted (Raatz and Klein-Braley 1981; Klein-Braley and Raatz 1984; Klein-Braley 1985). On the basis of self-report data and logical task analysis, Grotjahn has derived a tentative model for the problem-solving process in C-test taking, which includes a classification of different cognitive and metacognitive strategies.

The utilization of self-report data has begun to be applied to language testing research relatively recently. The few studies in which it has been used, however, clearly demonstrate its usefulness for permitting us to better understand what test takers actually do when they take tests, and hence, what it is that our language tests actually measure. It is clear that this research approach has a great deal of potential for providing evidence for construct validation by complementing the quantitative analysis of test and item scores.

In summary, the process of construct validation, of providing evidence for 'the adequacy of a test as a measure of the characteristic it is interpreted to assess' (Messick 1980: 1012), is a complex and continuous undertaking, involving both (1) theoretical, logical analysis leading to empirically testable hypotheses, and (2) a variety of appropriate approaches to empirical observation and analysis. It must consider the content relevance of the test, in terms of both the abilities measured and the method facets of the measurement procedure. Substantial disagreement among competent authorities over the content of the test or the methods used, for example, might be considered sufficient evidence to invalidate its use. The determination of content relevance will be guided by theoretical definitions of abilities, whether in the form of a general framework of language ability, or of a syllabus for language learning, and of the characteristics of the test, including its tasks or items. Finally, hypotheses regarding how the performance of different individuals in different contexts, on other indicators of the abilities in question should or should not be related to performance on tests, must be put to the test of empirical research. The result of this process of construct validation will be a statement regarding the extent to which the test under consideration provides a valid basis for making inferences about the given ability with respect to the types of individuals and contexts that have provided the setting for the validation research.

Test bias

As we have seen, the process of validation is addressed to specific test uses and specific groups of test takers. But within these groups there may be subgroups that differ in ways other than the language ability of interest. These differences may affect their test performance, and hence the validity of inferences we make on the basis of the test scores. Thus, even though the test scores may appear to provide a valid indication of ability for the group of interest, there may be systematic differences in test performance that are the result of differences in individual characteristics, other than the ability being tested, of test takers. When this happens, we speak of *test bias*. If, for example, we found that literature students regularly outperformed other individuals on a test of general reading comprehension, we might conclude that literature students are simply better readers. However, if this difference in test performance were supported by other evidence, such as differences in how well test performance predicted some future criterion for literature students and other individuals, or obvious content bias, we would suspect that the test was biased in their favor. If, on the other hand, the purpose of the test were to measure students' ability to read literature, or literary criticism, we might design the test as a measure of this more specific ability, in which case using it with other, non-literature students would not be so much a case of bias as inappropriate test use.

It is important to note that differences in group performance in themselves do not necessarily indicate the presence of bias, since differences may reflect genuine differences between the groups on the ability in question. Few people would claim, for example, that a language test was biased if native speakers outperformed non-native speakers. However, when systematic differences in test performance occur that appear to be associated with characteristics *not* logically related to the ability in question, we must fully investigate the possibility that the test is biased.

The topic of test bias is a complex one. It may take a wide range of forms, including the misinterpretation of test scores, sexist or racist content, unequal prediction of criterion performance, unfair content with respect to the experience of test takers, inappropriate selection procedures, inadequate criterion measures, and threatening atmosphere and conditions of testing (Nitko 1983: 43–7). The detection of bias is equally complex, since, as noted above, differential performance alone is not sufficient evidence that bias exists. That is, if different groups perform differently on a given test, it may indicate actual inter-group differences in the ability measured. Or it may indicate deficiencies in the instructional program of some groups of test takers (Popham 1981: 181). In language tests, the issue of bias is further complicated by the problem of clearly distinguishing elements of culture and educational background from the language abilities we want to measure. This problem has been articulated by Duran (1989) in discussing problems of assessing individuals of non-English backgrounds in countries where English is the dominant language:

> Assessment of persons with non-English backgrounds is difficult because of the confound existing among culture, language, and thought. . . . Because language-minority persons reflect a different social and cultural heritage from that of mainstream American English speakers, there is always the possibility that unrecognized differences in the backgrounds of examinees might violate assumptions about the nature of the population under assessment. The challenge faced by assessment specialists and educators is to explore and understand how cultural and linguistic factors affect assessment, rather than to deny that such influences might readily exist.
> (Duran 1989: 573–4)

Cultural background

While the issues involved in test bias in general are beyond the scope of this book, I believe an appreciation of potential sources of bias in language tests is essential to both their development and use.[14] Problems related to bias were among the very first to be addressed in the emerging field of language testing. The work of Brière (1968, 1973; Brière and Brown 1971) in developing language tests for use with American Indians in the 1960s is illustrative of an early concern with cultural differences as a potential source of bias in language tests. Other studies that have addressed the problem of cultural content as a potential source of bias in language tests include Plaister (1967) and Condon (1975). More recently, Chen and Henning (1985), employing item response theory, found that some items in a multiple-choice vocabulary test appeared to be biased in favor of members of one linguistic and cultural subgroup. In another recent study, Zeidner (1986) investigated the question of whether English language aptitude tests might be biased toward culturally different groups. On the basis of similarities in psychometric properties (reliability and factor structure) and predictive utility of the test across two groups, he concluded that 'English Language Aptitude scores may be equally applicable for aptitude assessment and prediction functions among varying cultural groups in the Israeli setting' (Zeidner 1986: 94).

Background knowledge

Another source of bias that has been examined is that of prior knowledge of content in tests of reading comprehension. In the study by Chacevych *et al.* (1982) referred to above, prior exposure to passage content was found to explain a significant proportion of variance on cloze test performance. Studies by Erickson and Molloy (1983) and Alderson and Urquhart (1983, 1985a, 1985b), Chavana-chart (1984), and Hale (1988) have provided quite convincing evidence of an interaction between test takers' familiarity with content area and performance on tests of listening and reading comprehension.

The studies by Erickson and Molloy and Alderson and Urquhart were done in the context of English for specific purposes (ESP) testing, and are particularly relevant to the question, raised earlier, of whether content is to be considered a source of bias or a part of the ability measured. These studies all examined the performance of individuals with different content specializations on reading tests that had been developed for different areas of specialization. In general the results indicated that students' performance appeared to be affected as much by their prior background knowledge as by their language proficiency. Alderson and Urquhart (1985a) discuss this as a problem for ESP testing, concluding that a distinction needs to be made between language proficiency and background knowledge, while recognizing that 'it is often extremely difficult, perhaps impossible, to distinguish between generalized and particular knowledge' (Alderson and Urquhart 1985a: 202).

I would concur that the distinctions between language proficiency and background knowledge, and between generalized and particular knowledge are not easy ones. Nevertheless, I would suggest that in designing language tests and interpreting their results, we *must* make such a distinction, and that this will be determined by the way we view language ability and by the intended uses of the test. That is, in an ESP (or any language for specific purposes) setting, we must make a curricular and pedagogical decision fairly early on, it would seem, as to whether we believe the language abilities to be learned are specific to a given purpose or whether students need to learn to apply general language abilities they may already have to a specific language use setting. This distinction may or may not be important with respect to the types of materials and learning activities we include in a language teaching syllabus. However, the distinction has crucial implications for the development and use of language tests and for the interpretation of their results. Thus, if we develop a language for specific purposes reading test under the assumption of specific language abilities, we are, in effect, defining specialized knowledge as part of the language ability to be tested, and this test should properly be used only with individuals whom we believe to have learned those specific abilities to some degree. Furthermore, the scores from this test cannot necessarily be interpreted as indicators of generalized reading ability. Thus, the issue of interpreting scores from such specialized tests as indicators of proficiency in reading is not so much one of test bias as of the improper use and interpretation of language tests. If, on the other hand, we have developed a test that we believe to be a measure of generalized reading ability, we are in effect defining content knowledge as an ability distinct from reading ability. In this case, if it turns out that individuals with different content specializations perform systematically differently, there may be a question of test bias in the interpretation and use of scores from this test.

Cognitive characteristics

A third potential source of bias in language tests that has recently been examined is differences in cognitive characteristics of test takers. There is general agreement among language acquisition researchers and theorists that cognitive factors influence language acquisition (Brown 1987). Furthermore, there is evidence that two of these – field independence and ambiguity tolerance – also influence performance on certain types of language tests. There is no evidence as yet relating performance on language tests to other characteristics such as inhibition, extroversion, aggression, attitude, and motivational orientation, which have been mentioned with regard to second language learning. However, this is not to say that these factors do not affect performance on language tests, and this is an area that is ripe for further research.

Field independence

Witkin *et al.* (1977) define field independence/dependence as 'the extent to which a person perceives part of a field as discrete from the surrounding field as a whole, rather than embedded, or . . . the extent to which a person perceives analytically' (Witkin *et al.* 1977: 7). Chapelle (1988) points out that scores from the most commonly used measure of this cognitive ability, the *Group Embedded Figures Test* (GEFT) (Oltman *et al.* 1971), should properly be interpreted as indicators of high or low field independence, so that the construct is operationally defined as field independence, rather than field independence/dependence. We could hypothesize that persons with a high degree of field independence would perform well on discrete-point tests, in which the items are essentially unrelated to one another and to the overall context in which they occur. Persons with low field independence, on the other hand, might be expected to perform well on integrative tests such as the cloze and the oral interview, in which they are not required to be conscious of discrete items, but can process the test in a global manner.

Hansen and Stansfield (Hansen and Stansfield 1981; Stansfield and Hansen 1983) studied the relationship between field independence and language test performance among American college students studying Spanish as a second language. They analyzed correlations between scores on the GEFT, measures of academic aptitude, and several different indicators of language achievement. After taking into account differences in academic aptitude in mathematics, they found no significant correlations between GEFT scores and final course grades, grades for written and oral Spanish, and teachers' ratings of oral skill. However, they did find a significant correlation between GEFT and cloze test scores. Their results suggest that field independent individuals are better able to complete the blanks in cloze tests than are persons who are field dependent.

Hansen (1984) examined the relationship between field dependence and performance on tests of language proficiency among members of six Pacific island cultures. Her results generally support those of Stansfield and Hansen, in that she found significant positive correlations between GEFT scores and all her measures of language proficiency, the highest of which was that between the GEFT and the cloze.

In a study examining the relationships between cognitive variables and language proficiency among non-native English speaking pre-university students in the United States, Chapelle and Roberts (1986) found significantly high correlations between GEFT scores and scores on a wide range of English proficiency tests, including the *Test of English as a Foreign Language* (TOEFL), a dictation test, a cloze test, and an oral interview. In their study, however, the highest correlations were between the GEFT and multiple-choice tests of structure, although the correlations between the GEFT and the cloze were nearly as high. In addition, they found that for all proficiency measures except the dictation, the correlations between the GEFT and language proficiency tests taken after formal instruction were much higher than those between the GEFT and tests taken before instruction.

In a more recent study, Chapelle (1988) employed multiple linear regression to examine field independence as a predictor of performance in several different tests of English: cloze, dictation, multiple-choice reading, and essay. Her results showed that for the non-native speakers of English in her sample there was no significant relationship between scores on the GEFT and performance on the language tests. In addition, she found that for the native English speaking subjects in her study, once verbal aptitude had been included as a predictor, field independence was significantly related to only one measure, the cloze.

These studies indicate that field independence influences performance on some language tests. What is not quite so clear is the extent to which this influence differs as a function of the testing technique. Thus, while the results discussed above seem to support the hypothesis that highly field independent individuals tend to perform better in general on language tests than do individuals with low field independence, the results are not consistent with regard to the relative effect of field independence on different types of language tests.

Ambiguity tolerance

Ambiguity tolerance can be defined as 'a person's ability to function rationally and calmly in a situation in which interpretation of all stimuli is not clear' (Chapelle and Roberts 1986: 30). Individuals with high ambiguity tolerance might be expected to perform well on cloze tests, in which there are frequently several correct answers and alternative correct interpretations, and in which the correctness of one's answers to early blanks may be called into question as one works through the passage, and on dictation tests, which the test taker is often not able to successfully complete until the passage has been read several times. On the other hand, tolerance for ambiguity might not influence performance on multiple-choice tests in which there is only one correct answer per problem.

In the study previously cited, Chapelle and Roberts also examined the relationship between ambiguity tolerance and language proficiency. Contrary to what we might have expected, they found significant (but low) correlations between scores on a measure of ambiguity tolerance and multiple choice measures of English proficiency, and nonsignificant correlations between ambiguity tolerance test scores and cloze test scores. They also found significant correlations between ambiguity tolerance test scores and dictation test scores. While the results regarding the relationship between ambiguity tolerance and multiple-choice measures of English are by no means as convincing as those with regard to field independence, there does appear to be sufficient evidence to warrant consideration and further research.

Native language, ethnicity, sex, and age

Ethnic, sex, and age biases in the use of tests for selection decisions have been extensively discussed in the measurement literature (for example, Cleary 1968; Cole 1973; Linn 1973; Flaugher 1976). These factors, along with native language background, have also been the focus of research in language testing. In studies examining native language background as a factor in performance on the *Test of English as a Foreign Language* (TOEFL), Swinton and Powers (1980) and Alderman and Holland (1981) both found differential performance across different native language groups. Swinton and Powers found different factor structures for European and non-European language background groups on the structure, written expression, reading, and vocabulary sections of the old five-part

TOEFL. Alderman and Holland compared the performance on individual TOEFL items of individuals whose total TOEFL scores were comparable, and found significant differences across different native language groups. Politzer and McGroarty (1985) investigated relationships between language/cultural background, academic specialization, learning behaviors, and differences in pre- and post-test performance on measures of listening comprehension, speaking, English grammar, and ability to convey information. While they found differences in test performance across language groups, these differences were not uniform, in that one group showed greater gains in listening and speaking, while the other group made greater gains in grammar and the ability to convey information.

Several studies have examined the effects of multiple background characteristics on language test performance. Farhady (1982), for example, found significant relationships between sex, university status, academic major, and nationality, and performance on several measures of language ability. Similarly, Spurling and Ilyin (1985) found that age, language background, and high school graduation have small but significant effects on cloze, reading, and listening tests. Zeidner (1987) examined ethnicity, sex, and age as sources of bias in the use of English language aptitude test scores for selection and placement of students in Israeli colleges and universities. The results of this study indicate significant differences between ethnic groups and sexes in language aptitude test scores, significant differences between ethnic groups in correlations between language aptitude test scores and first-year grade point average, and significant differences among age groups in regressions of grade point average on language aptitude test scores.

To the extent that factors such as these affect performance on language tests, the construct validity of these tests as measures of *language ability* may be diminished. I would repeat here the point made earlier: whether we interpret the effects of these factors to be sources of measurement error, test bias, or part of the language abilities we want to measure will depend on how we define the abilities and what use is to be made of test scores in any given testing situation. Thus, for example, if we consider the language abilities we want to measure to be independent of specific content, then cultural or subject content will be considered a potential source of measurement error to the extent that it affects individuals' performance *unsystematically*. Specific content will be interpreted as a potential source of test bias to the extent that individuals with background knowledge of the culture or subject content *systematically* perform better on the test than do individuals without such prior knowledge. If, on the other hand, we consider either cultural or subject matter content an important component of the ability we want to measure, then we design our tests accordingly and interpret differences in test performance across individuals with different cultural backgrounds or content knowledge not as instances of test bias, but as indicators of different levels on this specific ability to be measured. Thus, the importance of the studies cited above, I believe, is that they raise questions about the extent to which language abilities as constructs are independent of the content and context of the language use elicited in their measurement.

Similarly, if performance on language tests is affected by test takers' characteristics – field independence, tolerance for ambiguity, sex, and age – it may lead us to question their value as measures of language ability. However, as Farhady (1982) has suggested, it may also lead us to reconsider our definition of language ability. That is, the effects of lasting characteristics such as these pose a different problem for the construct validation of language tests. Unlike cultural and subject content, test takers' characteristics are not facets of the test method, and consequently cannot be considered as possible sources of measurement error. The effects of cognitive characteristics on performance in language tests raise questions about the relationships between these constructs and our definitions of language abilities, while the effects of sex and age raise questions about possible differential development of language abilities, and thus lead to the consideration of language abilities from a developmental perspective. Thus, correlations between language test scores and characteristics such as these may tell us something about the characteristics of good language learners and about how language learning varies with age, ethnicity, sex, and other individual characteristics.

The consequential or ethical basis of validity

The considerations of validity discussed thus far have been addressed to demonstrating that a test is an adequate indicator of a given ability. These considerations are essentially scientific and technical, and involve evaluating evidence for the test's psychometric properties (Messick 1980). However, tests are not developed and used in a value-free psychometric test-tube; they are virtually always intended to serve the needs of an educational system or of society at large. Cronbach (1984) has succinctly stated this fact as follows: 'testing of abilities has always been *intended* as an impartial way to perform a political function – that of determining who gets what' (Cronbach 1984: 5).

The uses of language tests reflect in microcosm the role of tests in general as instruments of social policy. We develop and use language tests for the types of educational decisions discussed in Chapter 3 – selection, placement, diagnosis, evaluation. Language tests are also used to make decisions that have broader societal implications, such as the awarding of high school diplomas or the certification of language teachers on the basis of minimum competency tests. However, there is a dearth of published discussion by language testers of these broader issues. Virtually the only language testing researcher to address the ethical considerations of test use is Spolsky (1981), who has questioned whether language testers have enough evidence to be sure of the decisions made on the basis of test scores.

The issues involved in the ethics of test use are numerous and complex, and their impact on test use will vary from culture to culture and from one testing context to another. Nevertheless, issues related to the rights of individual test takers, such as secrecy and access to information, privacy and confidentiality, and consent, as well as the balance between these individual rights and the values of the society at large, go to the very heart of the ethical and political values of any society. Only relatively recently, for example, have such individual rights been recognized and supported by both legislative and judicial actions in the United States. In other cultures, on the other hand, individual rights may be subsumed by, or considered less important than larger societal values such as respect for and responsibility to authority, the preservation of traditions, or the importance of maintaining group, as opposed to individual, values. Furthermore, what is considered to be in the public or societal interest is likely to evolve from one set of values to another over time, just as American society has moved from the *de facto* disregard for the rights of minorities to a concern to redress previous injustices.

As test developers and test users, we must consider the rights and interests of test takers and of the institutions responsible for testing and making decisions based on those tests, and the public interest (Hulin *et al.* 1983). We must recognize that these considerations are essentially political, that they change over time, and that they will differ from one society to another. At the same time, we must also recognize that these considerations will have implications for the practice of our profession, for the kinds of tests we develop and the ways in which we justify their use. In considering the validity of the *uses* of test scores, therefore, we must go beyond the scientific demonstration of empirical and logical evidence to the consideration of the potential consequences of testing. That is, we must move out of the comfortable confines of applied linguistic and psychometric theory and into the arena of public policy. In the words of Hulin *et al.* (1983), 'it is important to realize that testing and social policy cannot be totally separated and that questions about the use of tests cannot be addressed without considering existing social forces, *whatever they are*' (p. 285).

Unlike the demonstration of reliability and construct validity, which can follow a reasonably well understood set of logical and empirical procedures, guidelines for determining whether a given test should be used for a particular purpose in a particular way are much less well defined. Messick (1980, 1988b) has identified four areas to be considered in the ethical use and interpretation of test results. Since test interpretation must inform test use, the first consideration is that of construct validity, or the evidence that supports the particular interpretation we wish to make. In the case of tests of reading, for example, we need to look at the evidence regarding the extent to which prior knowledge of passage content affects performance, or how strongly a test taker's writing performance in a composition test is affected by the topic of the task and any organizational constraints that may be imposed, such as comparing and contrasting. If, for example, we feel it is necessary for language teachers to be competent in oral communication, particularly in conversational discourse, we need to determine what evidence there is that ratings from the oral interview test we intend to use for teacher certification are valid indicators of this ability.

A second area of consideration is that of value systems that inform the particular test use. Test takers, test developers, and test users all have value systems, and in a given testing situation, these systems may coincide completely, overlap to some degree, or be antithetical to each other. How does the test developer, for example, decide to balance the demands of reliability, validity, and practicality against the inevitable limitations on resources for development? If the test user feels that the ability to negotiate meaning by whatever linguistic means is more important than grammatical accuracy, how will this affect the way she interprets and uses scores from tests of these abilities? To what extent does the type of test used reflect the personal bias of the test user, and to what extent does this differ from that of the test taker? If students feel that conversational use of the language is of greatest importance, to what extent is this value reflected in a test that requires the oral reading of literary passages? These individual value systems in turn must be considered within the value systems of the educational program and society at large. Should students be given passing marks and diplomas on the basis of their willingness to persevere in attending what might be an inadequate educational program, or should these be awarded solely on the basis of merit, as determined by a criterion-referenced competency test? And if the latter, whose values inform the determination of the criterion level of acceptable performance?

A third consideration is that of the practical usefulness of the test. If language proficiency tests are to be used for making college admission decisions, for example, what evidence is there to support this test use? Or what evidence is there that scores on a multiple-choice test of vocabulary, which is typically included in tests for selecting secretaries and clerks, are relevant to secretarial activities such as answering the telephone, providing information on course requirements, filing and retrieving information, and maintaining a pleasant disposition in the face of the stresses of registering hundreds of students into courses at the beginning of a semester? Or how do we know that a student's spoken responses to aural stimuli presented via a tape recorder are related to his ability to teach effectively? From the view of validity that has been described in this chapter, the answers to these questions obviously lie in construct validation, and not solely in predictive utility. This view has been clearly articulated by Messick as follows:

> The key inference that is sustainable from a statistically-significant criterion-related validity study is that there is a dependable relationship in the particular setting between the predictor test or tests and the criterion measure. The inference that the practitioner wishes to make, however, is that the test should be used for selection. To reach this conclusion, additional evidence is required bearing on the content relevance and construct meaning of both the predictor and the criterion and on the potential social consequences of the particular selection use.
> (Messick 1988a: 36)

Unfortunately, however, this psychometric viewpoint regarding the relative importance accorded to content relevance and construct validity is not always shared by the legal system. Hulin *et al.* (1983) discuss several legal decisions handed down by courts in the United States in the past decade involving the use of tests for employment decisions. In one such case the court ruled that the evidence for the content relevance of the test was not adequate to justify its use for selection, and in another case ruled that content valid tests could only be used for setting minimum standards but not for ranking applicants for selection. Thus, although measurement specialists, and even government guidelines for employee selection procedures may recognize three methods for establishing validity (criterion relevance, content relevance, and construct validation), Hulin *et al.* (1983) conclude, 'there may be only one safe road, that of criterion-related validity, to the promised land where litigation about selection devices never occurs' (Hulin *et al.* 1983: 267–8). At the same time, they point out the inconsistencies in decisions made by different courts in different cases, and that federal judges are fallible in that they may permit their own value systems to influence their interpretations of the empirical evidence available. Hulin *et al.*'s recommendation is that we, as testing specialists, must provide the best evidence and measurement theory possible, and insist that these be used in deciding issues of appropriate test use (Hulin *et al.* 1983: 285-6).

The fourth area of concern in determining appropriate test use is that of the consequences to the educational system or society of using test results for a particular purpose. Nitko (1983) outlines a set of considerations to be made in this regard. The first was discussed in Chapter 3 as the overriding consideration in test design: listing the intended uses of the test. Next, we might try to list the potential consequences, both positive and negative, of using a particular test. One consequence that has been discussed with respect to language testing, for example, is that of 'washback', or the effect of testing on instruction. Positive washback would result when the testing procedure reflects the skills and abilities that are taught in the course, as, for instance, with the use of an oral interview for a final examination in a course in conversational language use. In many cases, however, there is little or no apparent relationship between the types of tests that are used and instructional practice.

It is not sufficient, however, simply to list the possible conse-quences. We must also rank these in terms of the desirability or undesirability of their occurring. That is, we must assign values to the possible consequences that we have listed. For example, even though we may feel that including a writing sample rather than a multiple-choice test in an entrance test battery will result in a lower predictive utility, we may feel that the potential effect on instruction is important enough to warrant its inclusion. Or, we may feel strongly that it is a more serious error to deny admission to applicants likely to succeed than it is to admit those who will probably fail. Finally, we need to gather information that will help us determine the likelihood of each consequence. This evidence may include prior experience, empirical studies of relationships between similar tests and their consequences, and historical documents, such as school and employment records. With all this information in hand, we are in a position to decide whether to use a test for a given purpose.

Another approach to the examination of consequences is to consider alternatives to testing as a means of achieving the same purposes (Ebel 1964). A fundamental assumption or value that is implicit in the use of tests as instruments of educational and social policy is that the benefits of society should accrue to individuals on the basis of merit (Hulin *et al.* 1983; Cronbach 1984). If we accept this assumption, we may want to consider ways of identifying merit other than ability testing. This is really not a very radical suggestion, since it is the normal state of affairs in most school systems, where factors such as teachers' comments and attendance are regularly considered in making decisions about students. A more radical *sounding* suggestion would be to reject merit as a basis for making decisions about individuals in educational systems and society, thus eliminating the need for tests. But the use of criteria other than merit, such as personal connections or seniority, is also undeniably a fact of life. Which is the less desirable consequence, for example, jeopardizing your family's well-being by failing your boss's son because of a low test score, or temporarily abandoning a personal value that you consider of the greatest importance? Is it better to rescind the certification of a senior colleague because he has not achieved a sufficiently high score on a competency test, or to recognize his many years of teaching and renew his certification?

The questions involved in the appropriate use of tests are not easy ones, but anyone who has used tests has faced them, at one time or another, and they will persist. And while the questions will persist, the appropriate answers will vary across cultures, specific contexts, and time. One suggestion that Hulin *et al.* make for dealing with these questions is to 'explicitly recognize that decision making can be divided into two components: a political component determining [the social value to be implemented by the test] . . . and a psychometric component determining [how that value will be implemented]' (Hulin *et al.* 1983: 269). Spolský (1981) charges language testers with the following responsibilities:

> we're responsible to continue to do everything we can to improve tests in every way we can . . . to avoid mysticism, to keep testing an open process, to be willing to account for our tests, and to

explain to the public and to the people we're testing what we're doing . . . we must make sure that tests are used very carefully. Tests should be labeled just like dangerous drugs: 'Use with care!' (Spolsky 1981: 20)

As test developers and test users, therefore, it is our responsibility to provide as complete evidence as possible that the tests that are used are valid indicators of the abilities of interest and that these abilities are appropriate to the intended use, and then to insist that this evidence be used in the determination of test use.

Post mortem: face validity

Despite the fact that the measurement profession itself has never seriously considered the appearance or appeal of a test to be an aspect of validity, there continues to be considerable misunderstanding of the term 'face validity' among both language testing researchers and practitioners. Over 40 years ago Mosier (1947) made the following observation:

Face validity is a term that is bandied about in the field of test construction until it seems about to become part of accepted terminology. The frequency of its use and the emotional reaction which it arouses – ranging almost from complete contempt to highest approbation – make it desirable to examine its meaning more closely.
(Mosier 1947: 191)

Mosier discusses three meanings of face validity that were then current: 'validity by assumption', 'validity by definition', and 'appearance of validity'. Validity by definition is a special case of what we now call content coverage, in which the tasks required in the test are identical to those that define the domain. Mosier considers the appearance of validity an added attribute that is important with regard to the use of the test, but unrelated to validity. He reserves his harshest criticism for validity by assumption:

The term 'face validity' is thus used to imply that the appearance of a relationship between the test and the external criterion is sufficient evidence of pragmatic validity. This use is a pernicious fallacy. This illegitimate usage has cast sufficient opprobrium on the term as to justify completely the recommendation that it be purged from the test technician's vocabulary. . . . The concept is the more dangerous because it is glib and comforting to those

whose lack of time, resources, or competence prevent them from demonstrating validity (or invalidity) by any other method. . . . This notion is also gratifying to the ego of the unwary test constructor. It implies that his knowledge and skill in the area of test construction are so great that he can unerringly design a test with the desired degree of effectiveness in predicting job success or in evaluating defined personality characteristics, and that he can do this so accurately that any further empirical verification is unnecessary. So strong is this ego complex that if statistical verification is sought and found lacking, the data represent something to be explained away by appeal to sampling errors or other convenient rationalization, rather than by scientific evidence which must be admitted into full consideration.
(Mosier 1947: 194)

Nearly 20 years later, Cattell (1964) also criticized the use of the term:

Face validity would perhaps require nothing but a requiem and a sigh of relief were it not that wishful thinking is too deep in psychologists' reasoning to be easily eradicated. . . . Face validity is part of the callow denial that 'there are more things in heaven and earth than are dreamt of in our philosophy.' In some trivial sense face or faith validity perhaps still has a role, but in diplomacy rather than psychology.
(Cattell 1964: 8)

Finally, Cronbach (1984) has this to say about face validity:

A test that seems relevant to the lay person is said to have 'face validity'. Adopting a test just because it appears reasonable is bad practice; many a 'good-looking' test has had poor validity . . . such evidence as this (reinforced by the whole history of phrenology, graphology, and tests of witchcraft!) warns against adopting a test solely because it is plausible. Validity of interpretations should not be compromised for the sake of face validity.
(Cronbach 1984: 182–3)

This burial of the term can also be seen in the history of the *Standards for Educational and Psychological Testing* (APA 1985). The most recent mention of the term was in the 1974 edition of the 'Standards', which stated that 'so-called "face" validity, the mere appearance of validity, is not an acceptable basis for interpretive inferences from test scores' (American Psychological Association

1974: 26). Final interment of the term is marked by its total absence from the most recent (1985) edition of the 'Standards'.

Nevertheless, the use of the term, and arguments for validity based on the concept continue in the field of language testing. Indeed, the fact that this much space is devoted to a dead concept reflects my concern over its continued use in our field. It is not so much that the field of language testing is ignorant of the concept's demise. Ingram (1977), for example, stated that 'face validity . . . has to do with the surface credibility or public acceptability of a test, and while it is sometimes important, it can be regarded as a public relations problem rather than a technical one' (p. 18). Davies (1977) also recognized that face validity has no theoretical basis, and pointed out one of the most important problems with the concept, a problem often overlooked by those who would claim face validity for their tests:

> The problems of face validity are . . . serious ones; experts often disagree but laymen even more so. Which lay opinion should be taken? This may be a small problem when the audience is small and fairly homogeneous. . . . But a greater problem arises when we try to determine just what lay opinion is in the wider world; often enough in language learning, it represents outmoded, traditionalist attitudes. Thus a test of language to the traditionalist's eye should look like a run through of a set of Latin paradigms. . . . If this is face validity, then it may be more difficult to satisfy than in the more acceptable form of evaluating an essay.
> (Davies 1977: 60)

More recently Stevenson has been both outspoken and eloquent in his frequent criticism of the reliance on faith and face validity in language tests (Stevenson 1981, 1982, 1985a). I, along with colleagues in various places, have also pointed out the problems of accepting so-called 'direct tests' on the basis of their appearance, in lieu of validity (Bachman and Palmer 1979; Bachman 1986; Bachman and Savignon 1986). However, practitioners continue to base interpretations and uses of language tests on 'test appeal'.

Perhaps the reason that this concept and the related notion of 'direct tests' are so persistent in language testing can be found in the dilemma of language testing itself: language is both the object and the instrument of our measurement. That is, we must use language itself as a measurement instrument in order to observe its use to measure language ability. As noted above, this makes it extremely difficult to distinguish the language abilities we want to measure from the method facets used to elicit language. In addition, the more 'authentic' or 'real-life' our testing procedures appear, the more difficult it becomes to distinguish them from the language use that we would like to use as a criterion for validity. The good news in this, as pointed out by John Oller (personal communication) is that in striving to develop tests that are 'direct' or 'face valid', or 'authentic', we may in fact get lucky and develop tests that are also valid, in all the senses discussed in this chapter. The bad news is that we may become complacent, accept the appearance of 'real life', or 'face', for validity, and fail to discharge our duties and responsibilities, as test developers and users, for demonstrating the evidential bases for test interpretation and use.

As can be seen from the quotations above, even those who have argued against 'test appeal' as an aspect of *validity* have at the same time recognized that test appearance has a considerable effect on the acceptability of tests to both test takers and test users. Cattell, for example, grudgingly recognizes that test appearance may be useful for diplomatic reasons, and Ingram cites its importance for public relations, while Cronbach (1984) points out that the tester's task will simply be more difficult if he uses 'mysterious' procedures, rather than methods that are more obvious to test users. With regard to language tests, Davies (1977) clearly articulated the *practical* importance of test appearance to test users:

> whatever may be theoretically trivial is not necessarily trivial from a practical point of view. In education it is often important to seem to be teaching, learning and testing as well as to be actually doing so. Public relations are important both for the pupils and for the public in general.
> (Davies 1977: 60)

In a similar vein Alderson (1981c) states,

> there may be good political or administrative reasons why 'communicative language tests' should look different: if they relate to an innovative curriculum which itself appears to be different, a measure of achievement on that curriculum which looked like traditional measures might engender disbelief in either the validity of the measure or the virtues of the new curriculum.
> (Alderson 1981c: 55)

The 'bottom line' in any language testing situation, in a very practical sense, is whether test takers will take the test seriously enough to try their best, and whether test users will accept the test and find it useful. For these reasons, test appearance is a very important consideration in test use. Recognizing that this is so, unfortunately, does not always answer the questions pointed out by Davies (1977): 'How do we know who will find what type of test task acceptable?' and 'What do we do if test developers, takers and users disagree?'

Summary

The most important quality to consider in the development, interpretation, and use of language tests is validity, which has been described as a unitary concept related to the adequacy and appropriateness of the way we interpret and use test scores. While validity is the most important quality of test use, reliability is a necessary condition for validity, in the sense that test scores that are not reliable cannot provide a basis for valid interpretation and use. In examining reliability we must identify potential sources of measurement error and estimate the magnitude of their effects on test scores. In investigating validity, on the other hand, we examine the extent to which factors other than the language abilities we want to measure affect performance on test scores. Distinguishing between reliability and validity, then, involves differentiating sources of measurement error from other factors that affect test scores. Since the method facets of language tests and the components of communicative language ability overlap, it is not always possible to determine unambiguously whether empirical results should be interpreted as evidence of reliability or of validity. However, we must include, in our development of language tests, provisions for empirically estimating the effects of the factors that we reasonably expect to affect the performance of a given group of individuals on a given test. When we have estimated the effects of these factors, we will have examined both reliability and validity, and the distinction between the two may be incidental.

The process of validation is a continuous one, involving both logical analysis and empirical investigation. Evidence for the validity of test interpretations is of several types, and can be gathered in a number of ways. Content relevance, traditionally called content validity, consists of the specification of domains of content, or ability, and of test facets, and the demonstration that the tasks included on the test are representative of those specified in these domains. A major consideration in demonstrating content relevance is thus the specification of ability and task domains. While the demonstration of content relevance is an important part of the validation process, it by itself is inadequate as a basis for making inferences about abilities, since it looks only at the test, and does not consider the performance of test takers.

Another type of evidence that can be gathered to support the validity of test score interpretations is that of criterion relatedness, traditionally called criterion validity. Demonstration of criterion relatedness consists of identifying an appropriate criterion behavior – another language test, or other observed language use – and then demonstrating that scores on the test are functionally related to this criterion. The criterion may occur nearly simultaneously with the test, in which case we can speak of concurrent criterion relatedness (concurrent validity), or it may consist of some future performance, in which case we speak of predictive utility (predictive validity). The major consideration in collecting evidence of criterion relatedness is that of determining the appropriateness of the criterion. That is, we must ensure that the criterion is itself a valid indicator of the same abilities measured by the test in question. An additional consideration in examining predictive utility is that of determining the importance, relative to a variety of other factors, of the test score as a predictor.

Construct validation is the process of building a case that test scores support a particular interpretation of ability, and it thus subsumes content relevance and criterion relatedness. Construct validation goes beyond these two types of evidence, however, in that it empirically verifies (or falsifies) hypotheses derived from a theory of factors that affect performance on tests – constructs, or abilities, and characteristics of the test method. In general these hypotheses specify how individuals should perform on different tests: that performance on different tests of the same ability should be similar, while performance on tests of different abilities should be dissimilar. For specific tests, hypotheses may be derived from the analysis of test content and task types, and of the processes involved in test taking. These hypotheses can be empirically investigated through a wide range of approaches, such as examining patterns of correlations among different tests, observing the effects of different treatments, such as different courses of language instruction or different language learning contexts, on language test scores, and analyzing the processes of test taking. Construct validity is often mistakenly considered to be of importance only in situations where content relevance cannot be examined because the domain of abilities is not well specified. With reference to language tests, this misconception has generally been applied to the distinction between measures of proficiency, which are theory-based, and measures of achievement, which are syllabus-based. However, because of the limitations on content relevance discussed above, even achievement tests must undergo construct validation if their results are to be interpreted as indicators of ability.

When different groups of individuals who are expected to have the same levels of language ability systematically obtain test scores that are different, we need to consider the possibility that the test is biased. While differential test performance across groups does not necessarily indicate the presence of bias, if these groups differ in characteristics that are not related to the ability in question, we must investigate for possible test bias. Research suggests that in developing and using language tests, we need to consider cultural background, prior knowledge of subject matter, field independence, ambiguity tolerance, native language, ethnicity, sex, and age as characteristics that may cause our tests to be biased for or against various test takers.

Language testing occurs in an educational and social setting, and the uses of language tests are determined largely by political needs that change over time and vary from one society to another. Therefore, we need to move beyond applied linguistic and psychometric theories and consider the social and political functions served by our tests. We must consider the value systems that inform test use — values of test developers, test takers, test users, the educational system, and society at large. We must also consider the practical usefulness of our tests, or the extent to which they are useful for their intended function. We must consider the consequences, both positive and negative, of testing, as well as the relative value attached to these consequences. Finally, we need to consider alternatives to testing, such as other ways of evaluating competence, or entirely different criteria for making decisions about individuals. In all of this, we need to clearly distinguish the political from the psychometric aspects of test use, and recognize that our responsibility as test developers and users is not only to develop tests that meet the standards of adequacy and appropriateness outlined in this chapter, but also to insist that these standards be followed in decisions regarding test use.

Notes

1 Cronbach (1971) describes a parallel test construction experiment as an approach to demonstrating content validity.

2   The notions of 'curricular' and 'instructional' validity are discussed in the papers included in Madaus (1983a).

3   Extensive discussions of the questionable status of the 'native speaker' can be found in Coulmas (1981a) and Paikeday (1985). Variations in native norms are discussed by Kachru (1985), while the problems related to defining native speaker norms are discussed by Lantolf and Frawley (1985). Problems with using native speaker performance as a criterion in language testing are discussed in Bachman and Savignon (1986), Bachman and Clark (1987), and Bachman (1988).

4   Other, perhaps more defensible, uses of information on concurrent criterion relatedness are to determine the utility of a test for specific purposes (Messick 1980: 1017). One such purpose might be in diagnosing areas of strength and weakness, in which case the criterion might be performance in a course of instruction. Another purpose would be as a substitute for a longer, more costly measure, such as a multiple-choice test as a substitute for a written composition. In cases such as these, 'it would be more helpful . . . to characterize the function of the relationship [between the test and the criterion] in terms of utility rather than validity' (Messick 1980: 1017).

5   Messick (1989) provides a detailed discussion of the development of the unitary concept of validity.

6   The question of whether or not we believe these constructs actually exist, in some physical sense, in our brains, is not relevant to construct validation. That is, irrespective of whether these abilities consist of synapses and neurons, or whether they are entities that are part of an abstract theoretical network that provides an explanation for how we use language and perform on language tests, we still need to verify the relationship between these constructs and the behavior we hypothesize they affect. Cronbach (1988) provides a brief discussion of both 'realism' and 'operationalism' in the context of construct validation. A more detailed discussion of differing philosophical positions on the ontology of constructs is given by Messick (1981a).

7   There are, of course, a number of assumptions, regarding the scaling properties and distributions of test scores, that need to be satisfied in the use and interpretation of correlations. These, as well as factors that can affect the size of correlation coefficients, have been discussed by Cziko (1984). More extensive discussions of the nature of data and factors that affect interpretations of correlations can be found in Carroll

(1961b, 1983b), as well as in standard references in multivariate analysis, such as Pedhazur (1982).

8   Although what I have referred to as modes are often discussed as competing approaches to research, they are properly viewed as complementary parts of the 'scientific method'. Very few researchers begin a study with no hypotheses whatsoever about what abilities are being examined, so that most research that is called 'exploratory' begins with some very general hypotheses, and in the process of examining relationships, refines these hypotheses. The primary distinction between exploratory and confirmatory modes is thus not the presence or absence of hypotheses, but rather the status of these hypotheses and the role they play in the design of the study. In exploratory studies, general hypotheses may be refined, and specific hypotheses generated through induction, while in confirmatory studies, specific hypotheses are examined in such a way as to make their falsification (or verification) possible.

9   There is, of course, a fourth possible inference, namely that performance on one test enables subjects to perform well on the second. However, this inference can generally be eliminated through the design of the study, by assuring that the two sets arc experimentally independent of each other, or through the use of counterbalancing to neutralize any practice effect.

10   A full discussion of factor analysis is beyond the scope of this book. However, Carroll (1983a, 1983c, 1985a), has provided excellent introductory-level discussions of factor analysis, one of which (1983a) is within the context of language testing. More extensive, non-technical discussions can be found in Kim and Mueller (1978a, 1978b).

11   Useful reviews of approaches to analyzing MTMM data are provided by Boruch *et al.* (1970); Alwin (1974); Schmitt *et al.* (1977); Avison (1978), and Lomax and Algina (1979).

12   The relative merits of correlational versus experimental approaches to causal inference are beyond the scope of this book. However, extensive discussions can be found in Blalock (1964); Miller (1971); Kenny (1979), and James *et al.* (1982).

13   A detailed discussion of the assumptions and conditions that must be satisfied in order to infer causality from experimental designs can be found in Campbell and Stanley (1972).

14   A comprehensive review of the issues related to bias in test use, including methods for investigating it, is provided by Cole and Moss (1989).

Further reading

One of the most extensive programs of language testing validation research in the world is that conducted on a continual basis by Educational Testing Services as part of the development of *Test of English as a Foreign Language* (TOEFL). The results of this research are available through the *TOEFL Research Reports*, which have been published since 1977. A few exemplary studies listed by topic include: Duran *et al.* (1985); Stansfield (1986b) (content relevance); Clark and Swinton (1980); Powers (1980); Alderman (1981); Wilson (1982); Powers and Stansfield (1983) (concurrent criterion related-ness); Clark and Swinton (1980) (predictive utility).

An example of the use of exploratory factor analysis to examine the traits measured by a test is Swinton and Powers (1980). Carroll (1983a) has provided an excellent introductory level discussion of factor analysis within the context of language testing. Examples of the use of the MTMM in construct validation are Bachman and Palmer (1981b, 1982a). Palmer (1979) provides an example of the interpretation of results from an experimental design as evidence for construct validity. Brown (1987) includes an excellent overview of cognitive factors (Chapter 5) and personality factors (Chapter 6) in language learning. Zeidner (1987) provides an example of both the issues of bias in language tests and the methodology appropriate to investigating bias. Spolsky (1981) discusses ethical considerations in the use of language tests.

Discussion questions

1. How might you specify the communicative language abilities and test method facets involved in a dictation test, as a basis for evaluating its content relevance as a measure of listening comprehension?
2. Suppose you wanted to use a language test for placement into a sequence of courses in academic writing. Discuss the specifications for content and test facets. How would you demonstrate its predictive utility?
3. Discuss the evidence you would need to collect to justify using last semester's listening comprehension test with this semester's students as a basis for grading.
4. You regularly assign grades to students in your high school foreign language class on the basis of quizzes and a final exam based on the course syllabus. A college admissions officer calls

you in regard to one of your 'A' students' applications and requests your evaluation of this student's ability to read college level material in the foreign language. Do you have a basis for making such a recommendation? If so, what? What are the consequences of your declining to make such a recommendation? What are the consequences of your making a wrong prediction?

5. In many countries, nation-wide college entrance examinations include multiple-choice tests of grammar and vocabulary. What are the consequences of this practice for an educational policy aimed at promoting 'communicative' language teaching at the high school level?

6. Views of individual rights vary considerably from culture to culture. How does your culture or educational system view giving students free access to information, including test scores, about themselves? Under what conditions, if any, in your culture would test administrators feel an obligation to obtain students' consent to administer a test? To what extent do the ethical standards discussed in this chapter conflict with values in your society or educational system?

8 Some persistent problems and future directions

Introduction

In the past twenty-five years the field of language testing has been influenced by radical changes in orientation in several interrelated fields. In linguistics, this period has seen Chomsky's theory of syntax come, fade, and more recently re-emerge as a dominant paradigm for describing the formal characteristics of utterances. It has also seen the emergence of a more broadly based inquiry into the nature of language and language use, spearheaded by work in sociolinguistics, pragmatics, and the ethnography of communication. In language teaching, we have moved from an approach that focused on language as formal structure and learning as facilitated by explicit formal instruction, to one that emphasizes language as communication and recognizes the potential for learning and acquisition through communicative language use. Our view of second language acquisition has also broadened from one in which interference from the first language was seen as the major determinant to one that recognizes a variety of influences – cognitive, affective, and contextual.

Advances in the analytic tools available to language testers have been no less marked than the changes mentioned above. In psychometrics, the past two and a half decades have witnessed the development of generalizability theory and item-response theory. They have also seen the birth of criterion-referenced testing and the evolution of a technology for both developing tests and interpreting their results in this approach. In the field of statistics this period has seen the blossoming and refinement of techniques for examining many variables simultaneously – multivariate analysis of variance and covariance structure analysis.

Broader views of language, language use, language teaching, and language acquisition have broadened the scope of language testing, and this presents a challenge that has been articulated by Canale:

> Just as the shift in emphasis from language form to language use has placed new demands on language teaching, so too has it placed

new demands on language testing. Evaluation within a communicative approach must address, for example, new content areas such
as sociolinguistic appropriateness rules, new testing formats to
permit and encourage creative, open-ended language use, new test
administration procedures to emphasize interpersonal interaction
in authentic situations, and new scoring procedures of a manual
and judgemental nature.
(Canale 1984: 79)

This challenge has both practical and theoretical implications for the
field. As language testing researchers, the challenge facing us is to
utilize insights from linguistics, language learning, and language
teaching to develop tests as instruments of research that can lead to a
better understanding of the factors that affect performance on
language tests. As developers and users of language tests, our task is
to incorporate this increased understanding into practical test design,
construction, and use. For both theory and practice, the challenge is
thus to develop tests that reflect current views of language and
language use, in that they are capable of measuring a wide range of
abilities generally associated with 'communicative competence', or
'communicative language ability', and include tasks that themselves
embody the essential features of communicative language use.

Just as advances in applied linguistics have challenged traditional
views of language testing, advances in psychometrics and statistics
are challenging us to ask ourselves difficult questions about test bias
and the effects of test method, and to probe more deeply into the
nature of the abilities we want to measure. The challenge presented
by advances in measurement and statistical analysis is to utilize these
tools appropriately for guiding empirical research in pursuit of the
fundamental goals of language testing. In the development and use of
language tests, this requires demonstrating that test performance is
related to and appropriate for the particular interpretations and uses
for which tests are intended. For language testing research, this
entails validating a theory of language test performance.

These joint challenges from applied linguistics and psychometrics
underscore the interdisciplinary nature of language testing, and the
fact that in pursuing this enterprise language testers must maintain a
balance between these two fields. Thus we cannot, on the one hand,
let psychometric considerations dominate and limit our application
of advanced analytic procedures to the investigation of language tests
that are based on an obsolete theory of language and language use
and that utilize a fairly narrow range of shop-worn testing
techniques, simply because these tests satisfy the assumptions of

current measurement theory. We must also pursue the creative application of these tools both to existing test methods that are compatible with current views of language and language use, and to the development and investigation of innovative methods. Neither, on the other hand, can we place all our faith in applied linguistic theory and throw analytic tools to the wind, so to speak, developing tests based on current views of language and language use, but whose scores and use have no empirical basis. That is, we cannot lull ourselves into believing that the concerns of measurement are exactly the same as those for instruction, and that the essential qualities of reliability and validity therefore need not be demonstrated in language tests. We must have the strength of our convictions and be willing to submit the tests that we develop on the basis of input from language teachers and other applied linguists to the same rigorous standards that are applied to all psychological and educational measurement.

Meeting these challenges will require innovation, and the re-examination of existing assumptions, procedures, and technology. As suggested by the quote from Canale above, one major challenge will be to develop techniques for efficiently administering and scoring authentic language tests. One of the main reasons oral interviews and compositions are not more widely used, for example, is that they are very time-consuming, both to administer and to score. Thus, despite the fact that most of us would agree that these test types can involve authentic language use, considerations of efficiency often take precedence over those of validity and authenticity.

Another major challenge will be either to adapt current measurement models to the analysis of language test scores or to develop new models that are appropriate for such data. This challenge was recently stated as follows:

> if current theoretical frameworks and research describe communicative language ability as involving several distinct but related traits and communicative language performance as occurring in the context of discourse, with interrelated illocutionary acts expressed in a variety of forms, it would seem that language tests would provide both a challenge and an opportunity for psycho-metricians to test the assumptions of current models and to develop more powerful models if needed.
> (Bachman 1986: 85)

These challenges also present an opportunity for us to move the field of language testing forward, to reforge the symbiotic relationship between applied linguistic theory and the tools of psychometrics and statistics that was characteristic of the 'psychometric-structuralist' trend in language testing (Spolsky 1981), and that has, in my opinion, been largely lost sight of in the current 'integrative-sociolinguistic' trend. In a truly productive relationship between a substantive discipline and the tools of research used in that discipline, theoretical advances generate the need for more powerful tools, and the availability of more sophisticated tools can lead to advances in theory. Such a relationship can be seen, for example, in the history of research into human intelligence and factor analysis, as well as in econometrics and causal modeling.

Current theories in applied linguistics view language, language use, and language acquisition as much more complicated phenomena than was the case during the 'psychometric-structuralist' period of language testing, and these views have led to 'communicative' approaches to language testing. The tools of psychometric and statistical analysis are also much more complex and powerful than was the case during the psychometric-structuralist period of language testing. These tools make it possible not only to continue to demonstrate the essential qualities of reliability and validity in language tests, but also to utilize these tests themselves as tools for research into the nature of the abilities we want to measure. What is called for, I believe, is a 'psychometric-communicative' trend in language testing, that appropriately applies the tools of psychometrics and statistics to both the investigation of factors that affect performance on language tests and the development of reliable, valid, and useful tests of communicative language abilities.

Successfully meeting these challenges, or seizing this opportunity, will have both practical and theoretical benefits. The incorporation of more complete views of language use and language abilities into language test development will inevitably lead to better tests and thus provide the basis for better evaluation – for sounder, fairer, and more accountable decisions about individuals and programs. Likewise, applying more sophisticated designs and analytic procedures to language testing research and development can expand our understanding of how individuals perform on language tests. Advances in our understanding of the nature of language use and language abilities, and in the instruments for measuring these abilities, can, in turn, provide empirical support for theories of language use, as well as valuable insights into the process of language learning, and thus be useful for language teaching.

In this chapter I discuss what I consider to be the major issues –

persistent problems, if you will – that must be addressed in pursuing the goals of language testing. These issues have to do with defining what characterizes 'communicative', or 'authentic' tests, whether such tests are attainable, or necessary, and how authenticity is related to validity. I describe some of the dilemmas inherent in the enterprise of language testing, along with some possible avenues for their resolution. I then outline a model of language test performance that I believe provides the conceptual basis for continued research and development in language testing. Finally, I indulge in an introspective analysis of language testing as a profession, including both its strengths and weaknesses, ending with an optimistic view of where we are and where we have the potential to go.

Authentic language tests

One of the main preoccupations in language testing for the past quarter of a century (at least) has been a sincere concern to somehow capture or recreate in language tests the essence of language use, to make our language tests 'authentic'. One of the earliest articulations of this concern is Carroll's often cited distinction between 'integrative' and 'discrete-point' approaches to language testing:

> testing for very specific items of language knowledge and skill . . .
> is the type of approach which is needed and recommended . . .
> where knowledge . . . [is] to be tested. I do not think, however,
> that language testing (or the specification of language proficiency)
> is complete without the use of . . . an approach requiring an
> integrated, facile *performance* on the part of the examinee. It is
> conceivable that knowledge could exist without facility. If we limit
> ourselves to testing only one point at a time, more time is
> ordinarily allowed for reflection than would occur in a *normal
> communication situation*. . . . For this reason I recommend tests in
> which there is less attention paid to specific structure-points or
> lexicon than to the total *communicative effect* of an utterance. . . .
> Indeed, this 'integrative' approach has several advantages over the
> 'discrete structure-point' approach. [emphasis added]
> (Carroll 1961a: 37)

Although the term 'integrative' has, unfortunately, lost much of its original meaning through misapplication and overuse, many language testing researchers and test users continue to believe, as does Carroll (1985b), that in order to obtain a complete measure of an individual's language proficiency, language tests should place the same requirements on test takers as does language performance in non-test situations.

This search for *authenticity* continues to be a major consideration in language testing, and tests described variously as 'direct', 'performance', 'functional', 'communicative', and 'authentic' have been developed and discussed in recent years. The importance of this consideration to language testing was recognized in the convening of an international conference in 1984 whose focus was authenticity, and the dedication of an entire issue of the journal *Language Testing* to the publication of the papers from this meeting (*Language Testing* 2, 1, June 1985). The centrality of this issue to language testing has been summed up by Spolsky (1985) as follows: 'In sum, the criterion of authenticity raises important pragmatic and ethical questions in language testing. Lack of authenticity in the material used in a test raises issues about the generalizability of results' (p. 39).

Defining authenticity

The full ramifications of Carroll's 1961 call for an integrative approach to language testing, in terms of the implicit requirement that 'facile performance', 'normal communication situation', and 'total communicative effect of an utterance' could be characterized or defined, were well beyond both the goals and the capability of linguistic theory of that time. Nevertheless, we can find in Carroll's description the seeds of the two main approaches to defining and operationalizing authenticity that have evolved in recent years. On the one hand, the phrases 'integrated, facile performance' and 'normal communication situation' suggest the reference to 'real-life performance' as a criterion for authenticity. The phrase 'total communicative effect', on the other hand, implies the notion of functionality, or illocutionary purpose as a basis for authenticity. Equipped with broader, more comprehensive theories of language and language use, and a framework for describing language test performance based on these, it may well be that we are now in a position to define more precisely what we mean by authentic language performance, and to examine empirically the implications of these definitions.

What I will call the 'real-life' (RL) approach to defining authenticity essentially considers the extent to which test performance replicates some specified non-test language performance. This approach thus seeks to develop tests that mirror the 'reality' of non-test language use, and its prime concerns are: (1) the appearance or perception of the test and how this may affect test performance and test use (so-called 'face validity'), and (2) the accuracy with which test performance predicts future non-test performance (predictive utility). Test performance is interpreted as an indication of the extent to which the test taker will be able to use language in 'real-life' (RL) situations. This approach does not, in effect, distinguish between language ability and the context in which this ability is observed, since non-test language performance constitutes both the criterion for authenticity and the definition of proficiency. The RL approach has been the dominant one for the past ten years in the area of testing oral proficiency in a foreign language, and its adherents have made substantial contributions to our understanding of the characteristics and uses of tests which attempt to mirror reality. It is this view that underlies what has come to be one of the world's most widely used and emulated approaches to testing speaking ability – the ILR oral interview.

The other approach to defining test authenticity, which I will call the 'interactional/ability' (IA) approach, is in keeping with both the mainstream approach to measuring language as a mental ability and the current view of communicative language use that has been discussed extensively throughout this book. The 'ability' part of the IA approach has a long history in language testing, with roots in early theories of verbal ability, and has appeared in varied manifestations, notably in the skills and components frameworks of Lado (1961) and Carroll (1961a), and in Oller's (1981) 'pragmatic expectancy grammar'. It also continues to inform a great deal of language test development and use, ranging from large-scale institutional testing, such as the *Test of English as a Foreign Language*, to practical classroom language testing all over the world. The 'interactional' aspect of the approach is rooted in the same views of language and language use that have informed communicative language teaching, an aspect that Kramsch (1986) has referred to as 'interactional competence'.

Rather than looking at non-test language performance *per se* as a criterion, the IA approach focuses on what it sees as the *distinguishing characteristic* of communicative language use – the interaction between the language user, the context, and the discourse. It thus attempts to design tests that will involve the test taker in the appropriate expression and interpretation of illocutionary acts. Test performance is interpreted as an indication of the extent to which the test taker possesses various communicative language abilities, and there is a clear distinction in this approach between the abilities to be measured, on the one hand, and the performance we observe and the context in which observations take place, on the other. And while proponents of this approach recognize the importance of the way test takers and test users perceive the test, their primary concern is with demonstrating the extent to which test performance reflects language abilities, or with construct validity.

Both approaches to authenticity are concerned with the context and manner in which we elicit a sample of performance – with the characteristics of the testing methods we use. In order to better understand and investigate the issue of test authenticity, therefore, we need to describe the facets that constitute the test method. That is, just as we must include the features of the language use context in a description of non-test communicative language use, so our description of performance on language tests must include test method facets. In Chapter 5 I discussed a framework of test method facets that I believe may be useful to both approaches to characterizing authenticity. It provides a basis both for comparing language test performance with specific non-test target language performance and for characterizing the nature of the specific interactions involved in test tasks, which should result in more precision in the way we define and examine test authenticity.

Authenticity as 'real-life' language use

While both proficiency and achievement tests have been discussed in the RL approach (for example, Clark 1979), it is with the former that the approach has been most extensively articulated. As indicated above, in this approach proficiency and authenticity are effectively synonymous. There are three interrelated tenets that characterize the RL approach: (1) a view of language ability, or proficiency, as pragmatic ascription (Upshur 1979; see p. 251 above); (2) the reference to 'real-life performance' as a criterion, and (3) the belief that 'face validity', content relevance, and predictive utility are sufficient bases to justify test use. The terms most frequently used by proponents of this approach to characterize authentic tests are 'direct' and 'performance'.

Proficiency as 'real-life' performance

In Clark's (1972) discussion of proficiency tests we find proficiency described as the 'ability to do X' and reference to 'real-life' as the criterion for authenticity:

> Testing procedures . . . may be referred to as proficiency tests in

that they . . . measure his [the student's] ability to use language for
real-life purposes.
(Clark 1972: 5)

The appeal to 'real-life performance' provides the basis for a
distinction between 'direct' and 'indirect' tests of proficiency:

In *direct* proficiency testing, the testing format and procedure
attempts to duplicate as closely as possible the setting and
operation of the real-life situations in which the proficiency is
normally demonstrated.
(Clark 1975: 10)

Indirect measures are not required to reflect authentic language-
use contexts and, indeed, they may in many cases bear little formal
resemblance to linguistic situations that the student would
encounter in real life.
(Clark 1978b: 26)

The terms 'direct' and 'indirect' with reference to language tests have
been used by authors in a wide range of contexts (for example,
Franco 1978; Lowe and Clifford 1980; Lowe and Liskin-Gasparro n.
d.; Perkins 1984; Carroll 1985; Ingram 1985; Low and Lee 1985;
Fok 1985; Rea 1985; Morrow 1986; Henning 1987).

Following essentially the same approach, other researchers (for
example, Jones 1979b, 1985a, 1985b; Bailey 1985; Wesche 1985,
1987) have used the term 'performance test' to characterize
measurement procedures that approximate non-test language performance. Jones' (1985b) definition is representative of this view:

an applied performance test measures performance on tasks
requiring the application of learning in an actual or simulated
setting. Either the test stimulus, the desired response, or both are
intended to lend a high degree of realism to the test situation.
(Jones 1985b: 16)

The difficulty of replicating non-test, or 'real-life' performance in
language tests is recognized by proponents of the RL approach.
Clark (1978b), for example, states that

the most direct procedure for determining an individual's proficiency . . . would simply be to follow that individual surreptitiously over an extended period of time. . . . *It is clearly impossible,
or at least highly impractical, to administer a 'test' of this type in
the usual language learning situation.*
[emphasis added] (Clark 1978b: 23).

Similarly, Jones (1985b) states that

> in a direct assessment the examiner observes, perhaps surreptiti-
> ously, the work of the examinee. . . . Unfortunately, assessing
> second language proficiency in a direct manner such as this is not
> as simple, especially if it is related to a specific task.
> (Jones 1985b: 18)

Recognizing the difficulty of replicating non-test performance in
tests, proponents of performance tests describe authenticity as a
continuum between 'direct' and 'indirect'. Thus Clark (1975) uses
the phrases 'very close facsimile . . . of the real-life language
situations' (p. 11) and 'duplicate as closely as possible . . . real-life
situations' (p. 10) to describe direct tests, and introduces a category
'semi-direct', which is different from both direct and indirect tests in
its characteristics (Clark 1979). Similarly, Jones states that 'the
identifying difference between applied performance and other types
of tests is the degree to which testing procedures approximate the
reality of the situation in which the actual task would be performed'
(Jones 1985b: 16), and discusses a typology of performance tests that
differ in the degree to which their characteristics replicate non-test
language performance. Madsen and Jones (1981) explicitly recognize
a continuum of oral language testing techniques from direct
'communicative discourse', to the 'slightly less direct', 'pseudo-
communicative discourse', to 'the mechanical, discrete items found
on some oral exams' (p. 25). The notion of degrees of directness in
performance tests is vividly summarized by Jones's (1985a) simile:
'Just like equality among George Orwell's animals, some direct oral
tests are more – or less – direct than others' (p. 81).

Proponents of the RL approach thus recognize a continuum of
language tests, from 'direct' to 'indirect', that are characterized by
the extent to which test performance replicates non-test language
use, and have described some of the points on this continuum in
terms of characteristics of test methods. One question that this
approach raises, however, is whether the end-point of the test
performance continuum is 'real-life' non-test language use, or
something short of that. Or, to phrase the question differently, 'Can
language test performance *replicate* "real-life" non-test performance,
or can it only come close?' And if the latter, how close is close?

Validity of 'direct' tests
Since the RL approach defines proficiency as the ability to perform
real-life language tasks, it is not surprising to find that discussions of
validity within this approach focus on the extent to which test

performance mirrors or predicts real-life performance. The primary validity concerns of this approach are with predictive utility, so-called 'face validity', and content relevance and coverage.

From discussions of both the purpose of 'direct' proficiency tests and their validity, it is clear that a primary concern is with predictive utility. Numerous writers have mentioned the prediction of future performance as the primary purpose of proficiency tests (for example, Davies 1968b; Spolsky 1968; Clark 1975; Jones 1979b, 1985b; Weir 1981). Wesche (1985) states that predictive utility is the major concern of performance tests: 'performance tests . . . are expected to predict how successfully the examinee will be able to communicate using the second language in certain target situations, rather than to establish his or her general proficiency level or to provide diagnostic feedback for the classroom' (p. 1).

The fact that 'direct' tests appear to mirror 'real-life', their 'face validity', has also been claimed by some proponents of the RL approach as their most important quality. Clark (1980), for example, states, 'the great strength of direct speaking tests of the FSI interview type as measures of global proficiency lies precisely in the highly realistic testing format involved' (p. 38), and 'the direct proficiency interview enjoys a very high degree of face validity' (ibid.).

Finally, we also find content validity stressed as the most important concern with direct tests. Clark (1978b), for example, arguing for the centrality of content validity for direct tests, states, 'since a direct proficiency test is, in effect, its own criterion, it must necessarily be evaluated by informed inspection rather than through statistical means' (p. 23). He then proceeds to describe what he considers to be the most important measurement property of direct tests: 'The formal correspondence between the setting and operation of the testing procedure and the setting and operation of the real-life situation constitutes the face/content validity of the test – the basic psychometric touchstone for direct proficiency tests' (p. 23). This combining of the notions of test appearance ('face validity') and content representativeness (content validity) reflects the overlap between test method and ability that is inherent in defining proficiency in terms of actual performance. This overlap is also reflected in other terms, such as 'representational validity' (Clark 1980) and 'genuine validity' (Caulfield and Smith 1981), that have been used by proponents of the RL approach.

Content validity, in the conventional measurement sense, is the extent to which the content of the test constitutes a representative sample of the domain to be tested, and the main problems in demonstrating content representativeness are related to the adequacy of the sample. Proponents of the RL approach explicitly recognize the problem of sampling. Jones (1985b), for example, states, 'language behavior is very complex, and [in a direct assessment situation] it would be necessary to make observations over a relatively long period of time before one could be satisfied that an adequate sample had been obtained' (p. 18). Similarly, with regard to achievement tests, Clark states:

> the specification of test content, in virtually every instance, must involve sampling, from among an extremely large number of potentially testable elements, those which can be considered to stand in for a wide number of similar elements not formally tested. Unfortunately, the identification of meaningful domains of 'similar' elements is an extremely complex matter.
> (Clark 1978b: 19)

While discussions of content representativeness within the RL approach come up against the thorny question of sampling, this nevertheless constitutes one type of evidence for validity. Some writers, however, have made more general, stronger, claims implying that direct tests are inherently valid. Thus Jones (1985b) states, 'the test is valid if the elicited performance is representative of what actually takes place on the job' (p. 20), and Griffin (1985) simply asserts that 'validity is enhanced by directness of measure' (p. 149), without indicating how or why this should be so. Probably the most sweeping claim is that of Rea (1985), who extends the notion of directness to include both content and construct validity: 'construct and content validity are assured to the extent that a test mirrors dimensions of performance' (p. 26).

In summary, the 'real-life' approach defines language proficiency as the ability to perform language tasks in non-test situations, and authenticity as the extent to which test tasks replicate 'real-life' language use tasks. Since non-test language use is the criterion for both, proficiency and authenticity are thus virtually identical. Test tasks, or methods, are seen as constituting a continuum between 'direct' tests, which are absolute replications of non-test language use, and 'indirect' tests, which are not characteristic of non-test language use. Validity in this approach is also essentially synonymous with authenticity: 'face validity' is the appearance of real life; content relevance is the representation of real life, and predictive utility is essentially precluded without authenticity (Jones 1979b: 51).

Criticisms of the RL approach

Language testing researchers have pointed out several problems with the use of non-test language performance as a criterion for defining proficiency and authenticity. One problem is that the failure to distinguish between the trait or ability measured and the observation of behavior limits the interpretation and use of test results. A second problem is that the RL approach provides an inadequate basis for examining validity. As pointed out in Chapter 7, arguments supporting test appearance, content relevance, and predictive utility do not by themselves provide sufficient evidence to justify test use. With respect to content relevance, several researchers (for example, Weir 1981; Alderson 1981c; Shohamy and Reves 1985; Stevenson 1985a) have argued that the RL approach provides no basis for defining the domain of non-test performance so as to distinguish it from test performance, and that the replication of non-test performance in language tests is unattainable.

Failure to distinguish ability from behavior

The distinction between language ability and the actual performance of that ability has been at the same time a central axiom and a dilemma for language testing. Carroll (1968), for example, states that 'the single most important problem confronted by the language tester is that he cannot test competence in any direct sense; he can measure it only through manifestations of it in performance' (p. 51). The distinction is also implicit in Spolsky's (1968) statement that a 'serious problem in choosing a test technique is deciding whether it is a valid representation of the skill we want to test' (p. 148), as well as in the title of his paper, 'What does it mean to know a language: or, how do you get someone to perform his competence?' (Spolsky 1973).

As mentioned in Chapter 7, Upshur (1979) pointed out the problem of failing to distinguish between language ability and performance, arguing that defining proficiency as pragmatic ascription limits test interpretation and use to the prediction of future behavior. While prediction is an important use of tests in many situations, Upshur's main concern was that proponents of the RL approach might ignore this limitation, and on the basis of arguments about test appearance and predictive utility inappropriately seek to interpret scores from language tests developed through this approach as indicators of ability. That this concern is warranted is clearly demonstrated by claims for the inherent validity of direct tests, such as those that have been cited above.

The crux of the problem lies in identifying performance, or behavior, with trait, or ability, and this is most apparent in the term 'direct test'. The argument in support of direct tests is intuitively appealing. An observation of performance, someone speaking, for example, quite clearly constitutes a sample of language use, and *if we accept a sample of behavior as the ability itself*, that observation of performance becomes a direct observation of the ability. This is what Messick (1981a) has called the 'operationist approach to measurement', which he criticizes because it 'identifies not just the meaning of the test score but the meaning of the construct with the scoring operations, thereby confusing the test with the construct and the measurement model with substantive theory' (p. 578). This 'operationalist orthodoxy' has never been espoused by very many measurement specialists, and has been virtually rejected by the measurement profession as a whole (Cronbach 1988). Because of its relevance to the RL approach to language testing, Cronbach's summation is worth quoting in its entirety:

> Operationalism lingers in the hearts of some specialists in achievement testing. . . . For them, interpretation begins and ends with a highly specific definition of the kinds of tasks the examinee should be faced with; a test sampling from the defined domain is valid by fiat. This program is coherent but shortsighted. For understanding poor performance, for remedial purposes, for improving teaching methods, and for carving out more functional domains, process constructs are needed.
> (Cronbach 1988: 22)

One problem with the RL approach, then, is that it treats the behavioral manifestation of an ability as the trait itself. Language tests, however, like all mental measures, are *indirect* indicators of the abilities in which we are interested. That is, we are not generally interested so much in how an individual performs on a particular test task in a specified setting on a given day, as in what that performance indicates about that individual's ability. The identification of trait with performance, however, does not permit us to make inferences beyond the testing context, and thus severely limits both the interpretation and use of test results and the type of evidence that can be brought forth in support of that interpretation or use.

Inadequate basis for validation
A concern with the inadequacy of claims for the 'face validity', content relevance, and predictive utility of language tests has been

clearly voiced by a number of language testing researchers (for example, Carroll 1973; Lado 1975; Bachman and Palmer 1979; Upshur 1979; Stevenson 1981, 1982, 1985a, 1985b; Alderson 1981c, 1983; Skehan 1984; Bachman and Savignon 1986; Bachman 1988a). Many of these researchers cite the standards established by specialists in educational and psychological measurement (American Psychological Association 1974, 1985) in rejecting 'face validity' as a basis for justifying test interpretation. Stevenson (1985b) summarizes statements by several measurement specialists as follows: 'Each [statement] emphasizes that face validity is the mere appearance of validity and that face validity judgments are naive because appearances in testing are treacherous, and well-established deceivers' (p. 114).

Critics of the RL approach have also questioned the possibility of demonstrating the content representativeness of 'direct tests'. As indicated in Chapter 7, the fundamental requirement for content relevance and coverage is demonstrating that the tasks included in the test constitute a representative sample of tasks from a well-defined target domain. The first consideration is that of defining real-life language use, which is complex, variable, and context dependent. The problems posed for the design of language tests by the complexity of language use were first discussed by Cooper (1968), who pointed out that components of language use will co-vary as a function of social contexts. Peterson and Cartier (1975) pointed out the problem this complexity poses for predictive validity: 'For a complex concept such as "language proficiency", a large number of behaviors are implied, and no single criterion measure can be regarded as adequate to establish the predictive validity of the test' (p. 108). The constraints on language tests imposed by variability in language use have recently been discussed by Olshtain and Blum-Kulka (1985) and Shohamy and Reves (1985), and Spolsky (1986), who points out the complexity of the conditions that determine how a given speech act is realized in an utterance:

> we can study the pragmatic value and sociolinguistic probability of choosing each of these structures in different environments – the goal of an ethnography of communication, which starts its analysis with functions – but the complexity is such that we cannot expect ever to come up with anything like a complete list from which sampling is possible.
> (Spolsky 1986:150)

What any attempt to define authenticity by sampling 'real-life' language use fails to recognize, ultimately, is that instances of language use are by definition context dependent and hence unique. This has been recognized by Stevenson (1985a), for example, who points out that 'any single sociolinguistic form or item is not, by definition, appropriate across situations or within any situation, without consideration of the whom, who, when, why, where, and so on' (p. 43). The implication of this is that the domain of language use is a finite open set, consisting of a potentially infinite number of instances (Spolsky 1986), and hence definable only in terms of distinguishing characteristics or features.

Related to the problem of domain specification is that of content coverage, or the adequate sampling of tasks from the domain. Hughes (1981) has pointed out that a representative sampling of language skills is very difficult to achieve because of the inadequate analyses of students' language needs and the absence of a descriptive framework of language use (p. 206). In the context of testing English for specific purposes, where we would expect to find well-defined domain specifications, Skehan (1984) makes the following observation about the sampling problem:

> This viewpoint [that communicative tests should mimic or simulate 'real' communicative events] . . . confuses naturalness of setting with sufficiency. A large part of the problem in testing is in sampling a sufficiently wide range of language to be able to generalize to new situations. Merely making an interaction 'authentic' does not guarantee that the sampling of language involved will be sufficient, or the basis for wide-ranging and powerful predictions of language behaviour in other situations.
> (Skehan 1984: 208)

These criticisms contrast sharply with Jones' (1979b) optimism about the comparative ease and applicability of job analysis for the domain specification of target language use and subsequent test development:

> The job analysis is basically a determination of the relationship between the skills being tested and the job as a whole. If, for example, we were designing a language performance test for airline stewardesses, we would first need to examine carefully how language is used in their work. . . . It can be quickly determined that within the scope of their official duties the language universe is rather restricted. . . . The test must be representative of typical job-related situations, and short enough to be practical.
> (Jones 1979b: 52–3)

Wesche (1987), however, is more moderate in recognizing the limitations on applicability that the complexities of domain specification place on performance tests in stating that 'a performance approach can only be used where second language needs are relatively homogeneous and identifiable' (p.35).

Consideration of specifying domains of job-related language use reminds me of a testing workshop I conducted in Thailand a few years ago, where one group of Thai language teachers decided to undertake, as their project, the design of a hypothetical test to certify the English ability of taxi drivers seeking licenses to operate in the international airport in Bangkok. We all naively thought that this relatively restricted language use context would be quite easy to specify, since the conversational discourse should be straightforward. The essentials would consist of a request by the customer to be taken to a particular place, agreement by the driver to take the customer, or perhaps a request for directions followed by an agreement, and finally a statement of the fare by the driver, and a polite 'thank you' upon receipt of the fare. We began making lists of the actual utterances the taxi drivers needed to control, such as interpreting, 'Excuse me, could you take me to the Oriental Hotel?', 'I need to go to the Oriental Hotel', and 'Do you know the way to the Oriental Hotel?' all as requests to be driven to the hotel in question, and were immediately struck by the inadequacy of our discourse plan. One typically negotiates more than meaning with Bangkok taxi drivers; the fare itself is a point of bargaining. This made us realize that there was probably an infinite variety of conversational exchanges that might take place, depending on the familiarity of the hypothetical English-speaking customer with the custom of bargaining over the fare, her expertise at this, her calculation of the advantages and disadvantages of waiting until the end of the ride to bargain with this particular driver, the weather, time of day or night, the condition of the streets, traffic, and a host of other contextual factors that routinely determine language use in this 'real life' situation.

While this example may be esoteric, its point, that routine, everyday, 'real-life' language use is extremely complex, can be supported, I believe, by a careful analysis of the pragmatics of virtually any language use context that goes beyond formulaic greetings. This is also Skehan's (1984) point: 'any language performance that is worthy of interest will be complex and multidimensional'. He supports this statement by showing that 'waiter behaviour [which] might seem to be a straightforward affair' is in fact complex and multidimensional (p. 216).

Accommodations to the RL approach

While critics have pointed out the deficiencies of the RL approach in defining authenticity in language tests, they have not, in my opinion, provided a viable alternative. Rather, what one finds in the literature are attempts to deal with authenticity that essentially sidestep the central problems without really solving them. One such attempt has been to list the characteristics of authentic, or 'communicative' tests. Examples of this include Morrow (1979), Alderson (1981b), Harrison (1983), Porter (1983), and Swain (1985). While these lists of characteristics are valuable, and constitute a partial description of authenticity, they do not, I believe, provide a comprehensive framework for telling us how to identify an authentic test when we see one, and raise more questions than they answer. Which list, for example, should we choose, or should we attempt to collate all the lists and come up with a comprehensive list of features? Or should we compile a list of features common to all? Must a test possess all the characteristics of a given list in order to be authentic? What if it possesses 75 per cent of the desired characteristics? Are language tests that possess more characteristics than others thus more authentic?

The other attempt, which entails the *de facto* identification of authenticity with 'real-life', has been to argue that language tests are by definition inauthentic. Thus Klein-Braley (1985) states that 'if authenticity means real-life behaviour, then any language testing procedure is non-authentic' (p. 76), while Alderson (1981b) argues as follows:

> Does not the very fact that the setting is one of assessment disauthenticate most 'language tests'? Are there not some language tasks which are authentic in a language test, which would be inauthentic outside that domain?
> (Alderson 1981b: 48)

Similarly, Spolsky (1985), citing Searle's distinction between real questions and exam questions, states:

> from this analysis we are forced to the conclusion that testing is not authentic language behaviour, that examination questions are not real, however much like real-life questions they seem, and that an examinee needs to learn the special rules of examinations before he or she can take part in them successfully.
> (Spolsky 1985: 36)

Caught on the horns of a dilemma, those who claim that tests are inherently inauthentic have offered two solutions: (1) accept 'real-life' as the criterion for authenticity and modify our testing methods so that they do not impinge on the language use observed, or (2) recognize that test language is different from real-life language, and attempt to define what constitutes 'authentic test language'. As possible ways of observing 'real-life' language unobtrusively, Spolsky (1985) discusses the 'planted encounter' and ethnographic techniques of observation from the field of sociolinguistics, concluding that, 'long, patient and sympathetic observation by observers who care to help seems the only full solution' (p. 39). Shohamy and Reves (1985) also suggest the unobtrusive observation of language use in 'natural situations' as one solution to obtaining authenticity in language tests.

Such suggestions are tantamount to a total acceptance of the RL approach, since they are exactly what proponents of the RL approach have characterized as the ultimate 'direct' tests. As indicated in the quote above (p. 304), Clark (1978b) considers the surreptitious observation of an individual over a period of time 'the most direct procedure for determining an individual's proficiency' (p. 23). In a similar vein, Jones (1985a) states that 'a real [sic] direct test of a person's oral performance would require surreptitious observation over a period of several days or even weeks' (p. 81). These characterizations of direct tests differ from Spolsky's suggestion only in that they make no mention of helpful caring on the part of the examiner.

The main problem with extensive naturalistic observation of non-test language use is that of practicality. Spolsky and Shohamy and Reves recognize, as do Clark and Jones, that such techniques are time-consuming, cumbersome and expensive, and hence not feasible in most language testing situations. A different but perhaps more important problem pointed out by Spolsky (1985) concerns the serious ethical questions raised by using information obtained surreptitiously, without individuals' knowledge, for making decisions about them.

The other attempt to solve the dilemma is to argue that language tests have an authenticity of their own, as illustrated by Alderson's (1981b) statement:

the authenticity argument . . . seems to assume that the domains of language teaching and language testing do not have their own set of specifications for language use which are distinct from the specifications of other domains. Thus 'What is this? – It's a pencil'

is authentic language teaching language, and so on. If one does not accept this, then authentic tasks are in principle impossible in a language testing situation, and communicative language testing is in principle impossible.
(Alderson 1981b: 48)

While the argument that language tests possess an authenticity of their own, based on the specific domain of test language use, is an appealing one, it really does not buy us much in terms of solving the problems of validity associated with the RL approach to defining authenticity. If we can define 'face validity' in terms of authentic *test* language can we then raise this concept from its psychometric grave? In defining the content domain as that of test language use, we may have made progress toward solving the problems of domain specification and domain sampling. However, we have also isolated test language use from 'communicative' language use, and have thus placed severe limitations on any inferences we can make on the basis of language test scores. This problem is recognized by Alderson (1981c), who states, 'anything that happens in a testing situation, must be authentic in its own terms: the problem comes when one tries to relate that testing situation to some other communicative situation' (p. 57). This argument applies equally to the predictive utility of such tests. How can we justify using a measure of test language use to predict communicative language use in other situations? And what about construct validity? Is our primary interest really individuals' ability to take language tests?

Authenticity as interactive language use

Virtually every attempt to come to grips with the problems of defining authenticity discussed above, by both proponents and critics of the RL approach, has involved, either implicitly or explicitly, the identification of distinguishing characteristics of language use. Jones (1979b), for example, recommends the use of a checklist which 'outlines the critical performance factors that are to be observed', (p. 53), while Wesche (1987) speaks of 'crucial aspects of the language use situations' (p. 37). As indicated above, one approach that critics of the RL approach have taken is to list characteristics of authentic tests. What is lacking in all of these, however, is a theoretical framework that provides a coherent rationale for the identification and definition of critical features of language use, whether this be in test or non-test contexts. The need for such a framework has been voiced by several language testing researchers. Bachman and Clark (1987), for example, state that 'there is a pressing need for the development of a theoretical framework, or domain specification, of factors that affect performance on language tests' (p. 21). Alderson (1983) is more specific about what such a framework should include:

> The criteria for helping one answer those questions [about validity] come from theory, from what one knows and believes about language and communicative abilities, and from what one knows and believes about communication with and through language. Like it or not, we need theory to help us decide when a communicative language test is or is *not* a communicative language test.
> (Alderson 1983: 91)

These statements imply that the characterization of authenticity in language tests must take cognizance of the critical features, or essential characteristics of communicative language use, rather than attempting to capture holistic language use situations. Furthermore, they imply that this theoretical description must include not only features of the context, but also the language abilities of language users. This is clear from Canale's statement of minimal requirements of measures of communication:

> an adequate test of communication must satisfy two main conditions. First, it must be based on a sound description of communication and proficiency in communicating, or what is often referred to as 'communicative competence.' . . . Second, these descriptions must be reflected not only in test content – that is, what is to be measured – but also in test method – that is, how content is to be measured.
> (Canale 1984: 81)

In Chapter 4 the distinguishing feature of communicative language use was described as the dynamic interaction between the language user(s), the discourse, and the context. In the context of reading, Widdowson (1978) has described this interaction as authenticity: 'Authenticity is a characteristic of the relationship between the passage and the reader and it has to do with appropriate response' (p. 80). I would propose to adopt this as a basis for describing authenticity in language testing as well. This notion of authenticity is very similar to Oller's (1979b) description of a 'pragmatic' test as:

any procedure or task that causes the learner to process sequences of elements in a language that conform to the normal contextual constraints of that language, and which requires the learner to relate sequences of linguistic elements via pragmatic mapping to extralinguistic context.
(Oller 1979b: 38)

Authenticity is thus a function of the *interaction* between the test taker and the test task. If we could develop a means of classifying test tasks on the basis of dimensions, or factors that we abstract from authentic language use, we should be able to characterize the relative authenticity of a given test task in terms of its potential for generating an authentic interaction with the abilities of a given group of test takers. Test authenticity thus becomes essentially synonymous with what we consider communicative language use, or the negotiation of meaning.

This definition of authenticity may appear to be a mere terminological sleight of hand, in that 'real-life' language use necessarily involves such communicative interactions. One difference between this and the RL approach, however, lies in the way in which we operationalize the concept. Thus, rather than attempting to replicate actual instances of non-test language use, the IA approach uses a theoretical framework of factors affecting test performance to construct tests that include features of language use that are relevant to both the interpretations and uses to be made of test scores. Our major consideration thus shifts from that of attempting to sample actual instances of non-test language use to that of determining what combination of test method facets is most likely to promote an appropriate interaction of a particular group of test takers with the testing context. The second difference is that unlike the RL approach, the IA approach must necessarily consider the abilities of the test taker. That is, in the RL approach language ability need not be a consideration, since it is performance on real-life tasks that provides the *de facto* definition of ability.

By now it should be clear that I am proposing the theoretical frameworks of communicative language ability and test method facets described in Chapters 4 and 5 as the basis for this approach to authenticity. The identification of these two aspects of authentic language tests is, it turns out, consistent with much that has been written 'around' the topic of authenticity. It reflects Canale's minimum requirements, quoted above, as well as Swain's (1985) principle of 'starting from somewhere', by which she means a theoretical framework of 'constructs [that] guide the development of the stimulus material, the tasks to which the test-taker must respond, the scoring procedures and the subsequent analyses and interpretation of the data' (pp. 37-8). Spolsky (1985) also distinguishes authenticity of content from authenticity of task, emphasizing the importance of the latter, while Porter (1983) states that 'communicative testing is characterized by the centrality which it accords to the nature of the test task' (p. 191).

At this point I believe that a discussion is in order of how the characteristics of authenticity that have been mentioned in the literature can be addressed by these frameworks. Let us begin with the basic premise of the IA view of authenticity: two factors, the test taker and the characteristics of the test method, will jointly co-determine the extent to which a given test or test task is authentic. The need to consider the characteristics of the test taker in developing language tests is, I believe, one point upon which all agree, and should go without saying. We obviously must begin with the consideration of the language abilities of the test takers that we want to measure. In addition, we must consider, to the extent allowed by our knowledge of the test takers, all the other characteristics that may affect their performance, such as cognitive and personality characteristics, domains of real world knowledge, interests and aspirations, motivation to succeed, prior experience with tests in general, and expectations regarding language tests, in particular, to mention a few.

In the characterization of authenticity, we also need to consider the features, or facets, of the test method. One set of test facets are those related to the testing environment. For example, the familiarity of the place, equipment, and personnel administering the test may affect the authenticity of the test to the extent that the test taker feels threatened or ill at ease. It is simply good testing practice to attempt to lower the test taker's anxiety. This, unfortunately, is all too often *not* followed by examiners who place a higher priority on maintaining an authoritarian attitude in the belief that this will prevent or at least minimize problems of collaboration and breaches of test security. After many years of practical experience in administering hundreds of tests, including multiple-choice tests, dictations, and writing samples to groups of test takers, as well as individual oral interviews to thousands of test takers, I refuse to accept the criticism that taking tests is necessarily an unpleasant experience. Humanizing the facets of the testing environment is perhaps the single most effective means for reducing test anxiety.

Shohamy and Reves (1985) have pointed out that the relationship between the participants (test takers and testers), and the setting of the test often leads to interactions that are 'artificial, awkward and difficult' (p. 55). While I agree that this is certainly a potential threat to authenticity, I do not consider it a necessary condition of testing. I believe that a sensitivity to this problem on the part of the tester, and careful consideration of how to control the facets of the testing environment so as to minimize this problem can create a testing environment that will promote authentic interaction.

The facet that is probably most directly related to the issues of authenticity that have been discussed above is the nature of the language of input and response. Widdowson (1978) has argued that comprehensibility is a requisite for authentic interaction with discourse. Since the comprehensibility of the language of test input will be largely a function of its propositional content and organizational characteristics, we can maximize comprehensibility in our tests by carefully selecting or simplifying the input language, considering our knowledge (or best guess) of the test takers' general level of ability. The degree of contextualization, distribution, and type of information will all influence comprehensibility. A single test item that has insufficient relevant contextual information may be partially incomprehensible to test takers. An item such as the following, for example, may be inauthentic simply because of the test taker's lack of appropriate background knowledge, even though it focuses on a discrete aspect of grammar, correct prepositional usage:

Pterodactyls first appeared on the earth _____ the Jurassic Period, some 150 million years ago.
    a. at
    b. during
    c. when
    d. and

For the test taker who attempts to process this item as an instance of language use but does not know the meanings of 'pterodactyls' and 'Jurassic Period', this item is likely to be context-reduced, and hence difficult. 'Test-wise' test takers, on the other hand, may find such items relatively easy, if they employ a strategy of focusing on the local context around the blank and then deciding which of the four choices is correct, thus avoiding problems in processing the entire stem.

Widdowson (1978) and Mountford (1976) have described a number of ways in which the organizational and illocutionary characteristics of discourse can be simplified or recreated to facilitate comprehensibility *without* resulting in inauthentic language. And although these approaches to simplification are discussed in the context of language teaching, their applicability to language testing is well worth exploring.

Swain (1985) indicates that the content of communicative language tests should also be motivating, substantive, integrated, and interactive. These desirable characteristics can be maximized by the selection of appropriate topics, including Swain's recommendation for opinions or controversial ideas, and by including content that has a substantial ratio of new to known information, which will contribute to the 'information gap' that several others have also mentioned as a characteristic of communicative language tests (for example, Morrow 1979; Harrison 1983; Canale 1984). In addition, integration is attainable through the planned control of these test method facets in different items or in various parts of the test. In *The Ontario Test of English as a Second Language*, for example, this type of integration is achieved by basing several different test tasks (reading passages, audio-taped lecture, dictation, and structured composition) on a common theme related to either science and technology or social sciences (Wesche 1987; Wesche *et. al.* 1987). Similarly, in the *A Vous la Parole* testing unit described by Swain (1985), the central theme of summer employment provides the integrating motif for test tasks that include reading about typical summer living conditions and discussing potential problems that might arise when several people who do not know each other share a bathroom, kitchen, and living room. This thematic integration of test tasks is also an integral part of the *English Language Testing Service* (ELTS) (British Council and the University of Cambridge Local Examinations Syndicate n.d.; Alderson 1988) and the *Test in English for Educational Purposes* (Associated Examining Board 1987), both of which provide test takers with a 'sourcebook' that provides the basis for a variety of tasks, including multiple-choice and short answer items, compositions, listening comprehension questions and, in the case of ELTS, an oral interview.

Another 'threat' to authenticity that Shohamy and Reves (1985) mention pertains to the 'goal of the interaction'. They make the strong claim that 'in a test . . . both the tester and the test taker know that the *only* purpose of the interaction is to obtain an assessment of the test taker's language performance' (p. 55). This criticism is also made by Spolsky (1985), who maintains that 'however hard the tester might try to disguise his purpose, it is not to engage in genuine conversation with the candidate, . . . but rather to find out something about the candidate in order to classify, reward, or punish him/her' (p. 36). Morrow (1979) and Canale (1984) also imply that lack of appropriate purpose is a characteristic of inauthentic tests.

The discussion of test method facets in Chapter 5 includes the input and response facets of 'illocutionary characteristics', and recognizes that the primary function performed by tests is that of a request for information about the test taker's language ability. However, I believe that *in addition to* this function, it is quite possible to engage test takers in authentic illocutionary acts. An example of this occurred during the interviewing for the 'Utah Study' (Bachman and Palmer 1982b), in which one candidate became so involved in the informal telephone role play that she completely forgot herself and began confiding quite personal information to the interviewer who was playing the role of her best friend. It is also possible for an interviewee to recognize when communication is *not* the object of the conversation. During the 'Illinois Study' (Bachman and Palmer 1981a), for example, one of the interviewees captivated us with a detailed description of how to prepare a stir-fry vegetable dish. This was done with a combination of gestures, facial expressions, and words from her native language, but *with virtually no English*. Although this person was obviously a very effective communicator, it was clear that her proficiency in English was limited, and that this topic was not going to provide a sample of English that we could evaluate. We therefore decided to try to determine the extent of her English vocabulary, and at the cost of bringing a very interesting and informative description of stir-fry cooking to a close, I politely interrupted and began questioning her:

'What is this?' (indicating my suit jacket).

'Shirt?' she replied, a bit surprised.

'And what is this?' I resolutely continued, pointing to my tie.

'Tie?' she offered hesitantly, still not quite sure of what was happening.

'Yes, and what do you wear on your feet?'

'Floor?'

'No, *on* your *feet*,' I repeated.

'Shoes? You crazy!' came her reply, and we all broke into laughter, realizing what a silly, *inauthentic* conversation this had become.

While these examples from oral interview tests may seem exceptional, they are by no means rare, and they do illustrate the point that language tests do not necessarily have to be without communicative purpose. Again, the key is the selection or creation of

322   *Fundamental Considerations in Language Testing*

language whose content is interesting and relevant enough to the test taker to be engaging.

Perhaps the adjective that is used most frequently to describe language tests is 'artificial'. The perception of artificiality is probably the sum total of the features discussed thus far that contribute to inauthenticity. However, as discussed in Chapter 5 (pp. 144–8), language tests may also impose restrictions on the test taker's response that are uncharacteristic of the restrictions imposed by contexts in non-test language use. While the examples given there illustrate the kinds of inappropriate restrictions that can result in tests of reduced authenticity, they also suggest ways in which the conditions of this test facet can be manipulated to result in more appropriate response tasks.

In summary, the IA approach views authenticity as residing in the interaction between the test taker, the test task, and the testing context. The primary consideration, according to this view, in developing and using authentic, or communicative, language tests is to construct or select tests or test tasks that reflect our knowledge of the nature of language abilities and language use. Both the development and selection of authentic language tests is thus based on a theoretical framework that includes the language abilities of the test taker and the characteristics of the testing context.

I have proposed the frameworks described in Chapters 4 and 5 as a guide for both the development and selection of authentic language tests, and have suggested ways in which these frameworks can be applied to these activities. And while I have discussed their application primarily in the context of the IA view of authenticity, I believe they can be used to describe the characteristics of 'direct' or 'performance' tests as well. In some tests the mode and channel of the *input* match that of the language ability being tested. An example of this would be a test of listening comprehension (receptive mode, aural channel) in which test takers must respond to input that is presented aurally. In this case the mode (receptive) and channel (aural) facets of the test input match the aspects of the psychophysiological mechanisms associated with ability in listening. It is also possible for the mode and channel of the *response* to match that of the language ability being tested, as in a composition test, where the mode (productive) and channel (visual) of the response match those of the ability being measured, writing.

This matching between *test method* mode and channel and *language ability* mode and channel would appear to be characteristic of so-called 'direct' or 'performance' tests, such as an oral interview as a measure of speaking ability or a composition test as a measure of writing ability. I would suggest that this type of test can be adequately described in terms of a match between the test method facet, 'expected response channel', and the language ability channel, without resorting to the term 'direct'. Furthermore, tests that Clark (1979) has termed 'semi-direct', because they involve ' "nonhuman" ' elicitation procedures' (p. 36), can be characterized in terms of the test method facet, 'vehicle of input presentation'. In a test in which test takers listen to tape-recorded aural input and respond into a tape recorder, for example, the vehicle of presentation is 'canned'. Finally, the term 'indirect' simply refers to tests in which neither the input nor the response channel matches the ability channel. Thus, the terms 'direct', 'semi-direct', and 'indirect', refer not really to different types of tests, so much as different patterns of relationships between the abilities we want to measure and the methods we use to measure them.

Authenticity and validity

In the discussion above it was quite explicit that the 'real-life' approach to authenticity is concerned primarily with 'face validity' and predictive utility. The status of content relevance in this approach is ambiguous, with the term 'face/content validity' some-times being used. However, this conflation of terms reflects one of Mosier's (1947) four meanings of face validity, that is, 'validity by definition', which can be seen as a special case of content validity:

> Validity by definition . . . is applicable . . . to the situation, very frequent in educational measurement, in which the only available measure of the criterion (that which the test is intended to measure) is, because of the nature of the criterion, directly and intimately related to the test questions themselves. If the objective of measurement is the pupils' skill in forming the elementary number combinations in addition, a test consisting of the one hundred possible combinations is presumably valid by definition. (Mosier 1947: 195)

While predictive utility itself will be of interest in the IA view of authenticity if prediction is one of the uses that are to be made of test scores, this, along with content relevance, will also provide valuable evidence supporting construct validity, which is the primary concern of this approach. The consideration of construct validity forces us to ask difficult questions, such as whether inauthentic and authentic tests measure different abilities. Given what we know about the effects of test methods on test performances in general, and the differential interactions between test methods and abilities, it is clear that the construct validity of a test will be partly a function of the authenticity of the test. This is implicit in Alderson's (1983) description of test tasks:

> a test and the testing situation is an Activity Type in its own right – it has its own defining characteristics, its own rules and purposes. The purposes of the participants in this Activity Type have their own 'validity', their own authenticity.
> (Alderson 1983: 89)

Another difficult question is whether a given test or test task measures the same ability in different individuals, or even in the same individual, at different times. As Messick has pointed out, research on the test taking process indicates that test task processing strategies and styles vary not only across individuals, but within the same individual (Messick 1988b: 54). This finding is consistent with the way the IA approach defines authentic interactions, in that these are essentially *individually* determined, so that the relative authenticity of a given test task will undoubtedly vary from one test taker to another. In this regard Douglas and Selinker's (1985) discussion of discourse domains is useful. They present data from both interlanguage (IL) research and a test of speaking to support their general hypothesis that test takers create individual 'discourse domains', which are a function of the discourse domains they have already created in their IL use. They also present a specific hypothesis about validity: 'The validity of a particular test as a test will be limited by the extent to which it engages discourse domains which learners have already created in their IL use' (p. 218). The implication of this evidence and line of reasoning is that the construct validity of a given test score will vary from individual to individual, which complicates the process of construct validation considerably.

The IA approach also raises the question of whether a test must be authentic in order to measure communicative language ability. We are not always interested in measuring the entire range of competencies included in communicative language ability. The answer to this question, therefore, is that it depends on what aspects of communicative language ability we want to measure and for what purpose, as has been pointed out by numerous writers. It is quite conceivable, for example, that in some situations we are only interested in measuring individuals' grammatical competence, while in others we may only be interested in assessing their ability to read technical articles in a particular discipline. Stevenson (1982) has pointed out that the variety of language tests that have been developed reflect not only different views of what language ability is, but equally important, the wide variety of purposes for which language tests are needed, and concludes that it is unreasonable to condemn tests that were not designed for a particular purpose: 'To state that there is only one proper goal of testing, or that a test with any other goal cannot be valid is to pursue rhetoric that has very little to do with scientific validity and validation' (p. 10). The unanswered question, of course, is whether such narrowly focused tests do, in fact, measure the abilities we think they do. That is, can tests that are not authentic, and that focus on only a narrow aspect of communicative language ability, actually provide valid indicators of that specific component? Given what we know about the nature of communicative language use, it is unlikely that tasks that do not elicit authentic interactions will involve all aspects of the test taker's communicative language ability. From this it is clear that *if* we do, indeed, want to measure communicative language ability in its entirety, our testing methods must be authentic, or communicative. Whether such tests accomplish this purpose, and whether we can measure parts of communicative language ability without involving the whole are empirical questions that can only be answered by a program of construct validation research.

Real-life and interactional/ability approaches to oral proficiency testing: an illustrative comparison

The RL and IA approaches to defining language ability and authenticity do not necessarily lead to different types of language tests, but they do have clearly distinct implications for both the design and interpretation of a given type of language test. These differences can be illustrated by comparing two different approaches to oral interview testing. For purposes of comparison, the RL approach is exemplified by the ILR *Language Skill Level Descriptions* (Lowe 1982) and the *ACTFL Proficiency Guidelines* (American Council on the Teaching of Foreign Languages 1986) and the oral interview test, the 'Oral Proficiency Interview' (OPI), based upon them (Lowe 1982), while the IA approach is exemplified by the *Oral Interview Test of Communicative Proficiency in English* (Bachman and Palmer 1983a). The ILR oral interview is used by various agencies of the United States government to measure proficiency in foreign languages, while the ACTFL oral interview is widely used in secondary and tertiary level foreign language programs in the United States. The Bachman–Palmer oral interview was developed primarily for research purposes, and has been used as a criterion measure of oral English proficiency in a number of studies in second language acquisition (for example, Day 1984, 1985; Chapelle and Jamieson 1986; Chapelle and Roberts 1986).

The salient differences between these two tests appear in the rating scales that are used to measure samples of spoken language elicited during the interview procedure. For purposes of exposition, the scale definitions for ILR level two and the ACTFL 'advanced' level, which are considered to be comparable (Clark and Clifford 1988), are presented below:

> ILR Level Two:
> Can handle with confidence but not with facility most social situations including introductions and casual conversations about current events, as well as work, family, and autobiographical information; can handle limited work requirements, needing help in handling complications or difficulties. Can give directions from one place to another.
> (Lowe 1982: 5)

> ACTFL Advanced Level:
> Able to satisfy the requirements of everyday situations and routine school and work requirements. Can handle with confidence but not with facility complicated tasks and social situations, such as elaborating, complaining, and apologizing. Can narrate and describe with some details, linking sentences together smoothly. Can communicate facts and talk casually about topics of current public and personal interest, using general vocabulary.
> (American Council on the Teaching of Foreign Languages 1986: 2)

The Bachman–Palmer scales are given in Tables 8.1a, b, and c.

Grammatical competence

Rating	Range	Accuracy
0	No systematic evidence of morphologic and syntactic structures	Control of few or no structures; errors of all or most possible types
1	Limited range of both morphologic and syntactic structures, but with some systematic evidence	Control of few or no structures; errors of all or most possible types

(Rating)	(Range)	(Accuracy)
2	Limited range of both morphologic and syntactic structures, but with some systematic evidence	Control of some structures used, but with many error types
3	Large, but not complete, range of both morphologic and syntactic structures	Control of some structures used, but with many error types
4	Large, but not complete, range of both morphologic and syntactic structures	Control of most structures used, with few error types
5	Complete range of morphologic and syntactic structures	Control of most structures used, with few error types
6	Complete range of morphologic and syntactic structures	No systematic errors

Table 8.1a   Scale of grammatical competence (Bachman and Palmer 1983a)

Pragmatic competence

Rating	Vocabulary	Rating	Cohesion
0	*Extremely limited vocabulary* (A few words and formulaic phrases. Not possible to discuss any topic, due to limited vocabulary.)	0	*No cohesion* (Utterances completely disjointed, or discourse too short too judge.)
1	*Small vocabulary* (Difficulty in talking with examinee because of vocabulary limitations.)	1	*Very little cohesion* (Relationships between utterances not adequately marked; frequent confusing relationships among ideas.)
2	*Vocabulary of moderate size* (Frequently misses or searches for words.)	2	*Moderate cohesion* (Relationships between utterances generally marked; sometimes confusing relationships among ideas.)
3	*Large vocabulary* (Seldom misses or searches for words.)	3	*Good cohesion* (Relationships between utterances well-marked.)
4	*Extensive vocabulary* (Rarely, if ever, misses or searches for words. Almost always uses appropriate word.)	4	*Excellent cohesion* (Uses a variety of appropriate devices; hardly ever confusing relationships among ideas.)

Table 8.1b   Scales of ability in vocabulary and cohesion (Bachman and Palmer 1983a)

Sociolinguistic competence

R	Distinguishing of registers	R	Nativeness	R	Use of cultural references
0	Evidence of only one register	1	*Frequent* non-native but grammatical structures or Impossible to judge because of interference from other factors	0.5	No evidence of ability to use cultural references
1	Evidence of two registers			2.5	Some evidence of ability to use cultural references appropriately
2	Evidence of two registers *and* control of either formal or informal register			4	Full control of appropriate cultural references
3.5	Control of *both* formal and informal registers	3	*Rare* non-native but grammatical structures		
		4	*No* non-native but grammatical structures		

Table 8.1c   Scales of sociolinguistic competence (Bachman and Palmer 1983a)

One difference between the RL and AI approaches that these scales reflect is their different views of language proficiency. In the ILR and ACTFL rating scales, language proficiency is viewed as a unitary ability, with scores 'expressed in a single global rating of general language ability' (Lowe 1988: 12), while the Bachman–Palmer test includes three main scales, 'grammatical competence', 'pragmatic competence', and 'sociolinguistic competence', each with subscales, corresponding to the different components of language ability that they hypothesized in their model of communicative language proficiency (Bachman and Palmer 1982a).

The second difference is in the relationship between the contextual features of the elicitation procedure and the ability to be measured. As has been pointed out by Bachman and Savignon (1986) and Bachman (1988), in the ILR and ACTFL scales, there is no distinction between the ability to be measured and the features of the context in which language performance takes place. This can be seen, for example, in the definition for ACTFL 'advanced' level, which includes references to specific language use contexts ('everyday situations', 'school and work requirements', 'social situations'); specific topics ('current public and personal interest, information'), and specific functions ('elaborating', 'complaining', 'apologizing', 'narrate', 'describe', 'communicate facts'). The Bachman–Palmer scales, on the other hand, are defined in terms of levels on the various component abilities, with no reference to specific contextual features.

These differences derive quite logically from the differences between the RL and IA definitions of language proficiency and test authenticity. If language proficiency is defined in terms of language performance, as is the case in the RL approach, there is no basis for distinguishing separate abilities. That is, abilities cannot be directly observed in performance, and if we define proficiency as perform-ance, then it follows that separate abilities cannot be measured as part of proficiency. It should be noted that proponents of the ILR/ ACTFL oral interview implicitly recognize the multicomponential nature of language proficiency when they speak of the 'functional trisection' of functions, content, and accuracy that characterizes the scale definitions (Higgs and Clifford 1982), and when they provide raters with profile checklists as aids to ratings (for example, Lowe 1982). Nevertheless, to the best of my understanding, none of these components is actually reported in the scores. If, on the other hand, one chooses to define language proficiency in terms of component abilities, as is the case with the IA approach, then the implication is that we should attempt to measure these component abilities and report scores for these measures separately.[1]

Similarly, if test authenticity is defined in terms of 'real-life' language performance, then it is appropriate to include features of the language use context, that is, facets of the test elicitation procedure, in scale definitions. If, on the other hand, one chooses to define authenticity in terms of the interaction between the abilities of the language user and the features of the language use context, scale definitions of abilities must necessarily exclude facets of the test method.

While the ILR/ACTFL and Bachman–Palmer rating scales have been discussed as examples of the RL and IA approaches to the design of oral interview tests of language proficiency, these are not the only language tests that manifest these two approaches. The ILR model has formed the basis for other rating scales of oral proficiency, such as the *Australian Second Language Proficiency Ratings* (Ingram and Wylie 1982; Ingram 1984), as well as for scales for testing reading (for example, Carton and Kaya-Carton 1986; Dandonoli 1987); writing (for example, Herzog 1988), and for batteries for testing all four skill modalities (Freed 1987; Lange 1987). Another exemplar of the RL approach are the rating scales for oral interaction and academic writing developed by B. J. Carroll (1980).

Examples of the IA approach are equally numerous. The various tests of speaking and writing that were developed as part of the Language Monitoring Project in the United Kingdom consist of several sets of tasks, or elicitation procedures, and separate rating scales for these tasks (Portal 1986b; Gorman 1986). These tests were used in surveys of foreign language (French, German, and Spanish) performance in schools in England, Wales, and Northern Ireland (for example, Gorman *et al.* 1985; Dickson *et al.* 1985, 1986). Raffaldini (1988) reports on an innovative oral situation test, in which speaking tasks that are presented to students as situations are rated on separate scales of discourse, sociolinguistic, and linguistic abilities. Another example is the widely used approach to ESL writing assessment described by Jacobs *et al.* (1981), which clearly distinguishes elicitation procedures from the scales that are used for rating aspects of writing ability.

Toward a synthesis of approaches

The characterization of authenticity is undoubtedly one of the most difficult problems for language testing, as it necessarily involves the consideration of not only the context in which testing takes place, but also of the qualities of the test taker and of the very nature of language ability itself. To use Conrad's phrase, authenticity is at 'the heart of the matter' of language testing. The consideration of authenticity has taken language testers in two distinct directions in the development and use of language tests. And, given the complexity of the issues, both approaches are fraught with problems. At the same time, however, each has its advantages. Furthermore, these approaches are not mutually exclusive in their applications, nor will they necessarily result in different types of language tests.

The RL approach has proven to be a useful means for guiding practical test development. For classroom teachers, and for many other testing situations in which the decisions to be made about individuals are not irreversible or of monumental importance, this approach is perhaps sufficient. It provides a relatively easy way to develop tests that 'look good' and may have some predictive utility. As Wesche (1987) has indicated, its application is limited to situations in which the criterion domain of language use is relatively homogeneous and identifiable. Its primary limitation, however, is that it cannot provide much information about language abilities, and hence, cannot demonstrate validity, in the broad sense that this quality is currently conceived by most measurement specialists (Bachman 1988). And this is the ever present danger in its use:

many language testers who follow this approach will inevitably make inferences about abilities on the basis of test scores, even when there is no evidential basis for such inferences.

The IA approach, on the other hand, is much more demanding. It must incorporate a model of abilities and test method facets for both test development and the interpretation of test results. It requires a complex process of theory falsification – construct validation – to provide an evidential basis for validity. But the pay-off is well worth the effort, since this approach provides the only means, in my opinion, of making inferences about the abilities we think we are measuring.

These two approaches do not necessarily lead to different types of language test tasks. The elicitation procedures used in the Bachman–Palmer oral interview, for example, are similar, in many respects, to those employed in the ILR oral interview, even though it was developed from a theoretical framework of language abilities that is quite different from the domain of 'real-life' tasks that the ILR is intended to reflect. Similarly, reading comprehension tests developed by selecting texts and tasks that are believed to represent 'real-life' reading activities may not appear to be very much different from tests developed on the basis of a theory of reading comprehension abilities. Thus, while tests developed by these two approaches differ in design, they may include similar features in their elicitation procedures, so that differences in their appearance, or even in their relative authenticity, may be slight. Tests developed by the RL approach can and do involve authentic interactions between test takers and the testing context. Similarly, tests developed from a theory of language abilities and test method facets will not necessarily be complex, cumbersome, and inauthentic.

Language testers thus need not be presented with a true–false question in deciding what type of test to develop or use. As has been repeatedly stressed throughout this discussion, the fundamental consideration is that we use the right test for the right purpose. What we are faced with, essentially, is what Spolsky (1986) has called a multiple-choice question of matching appropriate testing methods to the various and changing needs of educational systems and society. He has proposed a 'multiple branching' approach to test use and development based on Jackendoff's (1983) preference model, as a solution to the problem of language test development and use. According to this approach, we would accept the outcomes of language learning as a complete set of preferences, which would be ordered and weighted according to the demands of the particular testing situation. The features to be included in the test would then be determined on the basis of this prioritization of preferences:

> For any given learning goal, weightings determine which features should be included. Thus, in the training of a telephone operator for a multilingual business, the probability of languages, topics, requests and responses will all contribute to a final description. Language learning theory will provide some notion of suitable ordering of items; . . . Beyond this minimum, a 'needs assessment survey' will have to be used to set up the scale.
> (Spolsky 1986: 155)

While Spolsky does not elaborate on the details of implementing this approach, it is clear that such an approach will need to include a description of language abilities and characteristics of language use tasks. To the extent that this description enables us to identify the critical features of authentic language use tasks, this approach may point the direction to a synthesis between the RL and IA approaches to authenticity.

As with many debates in applied linguistics, the debate over the nature of authentic or communicative tests has too often focused on the worst, or extreme cases, rather than examining the best examples from each side. It is true that many artificial and inauthentic language tests have been developed on the basis of various theories of language ability. It is also true that many tests based on some notion of what constitutes 'real-life' tasks have been used to make inferences about individuals' abilities. However, there have been success stories on both sides, and as Stevenson (1982) has pointed out, it is counterproductive to criticize tests because they do not satisfy a set of conditions and purposes for which they were not intended.

The difference between the two approaches lies primarily in the way we can interpret and use the results of language tests. If the RL approach has produced tests that are acceptable to test takers and test users, and which are perceived as being useful for their intended purposes (which it has), it would seem reasonable to embark on a program of research to examine the validity of scores based on these tests through the process of construct validation. By the same token, if the IA approach has produced tests with demonstrated validity but which are none the less inauthentic (which it has), it would seem reasonable to explore the possibility of achieving the same results with test tasks that have greater potential for authenticity. The recent re-examination of the *Test of English as a Foreign Language* reported in Duran *et al.* (1985) and Stansfield (1986b) is an example of this type of activity.

The answers to the questions raised by the consideration of authenticity are not to be found, in my opinion, in further speculation and debate. The logical dilemmas have been recognized and the lines of the debate drawn for years, as Alderson noted in 1981:

> There would appear to be a variety of dimensions of language in use that existing language tests do not tap . . . existing tests may be unsatisfactory to the extent that they do not cover psycholinguistic abilities . . . or features of language. . . . Such features or dimensions derive from two possible sources: either from our theories of language use – that is, our developing theories of the use of language for and in communication generate the dimensions which are to be operationalized in language tests; or they derive from 'real-life': from observations of the world around us. (Alderson 1981c: 55)

The anwers are to be found, I believe, in continued construct validation research, employing the full range of approaches available. We need to employ both logical analysis and empirical investigation, including a variety of observation techniques, from ethnographic observation to controlled elicitation, along with all the appropriate qualitative and quantitative analytic procedures that are at our disposal. I believe that only through such a broad-based program of research will we continue to expand our understanding of the factors that affect performance on language tests, and more important, of the language abilities that are involved in communicative language use. Herein lies the future of language testing research, and it is to this that we now turn.

Some future directions

It goes without saying, I believe, that language testing research and development must be addressed to both the needs for language tests that may arise in education and society at large, and to the needs of applied linguistics, especially language acquisition and attrition research, and language teaching methodology. But while the field of language testing has historically been closely associated with language teaching, and has contributed a multitude of practical instruments for use in instructional programs, I do not believe that its potential as an approach to applied linguistic research has been fully realized. Indeed, the field of language testing research may be unique in that it constitutes both an approach to applied linguistic research and a means for developing practical measurement instruments for other types of research and for use in making decisions about individuals and educational programs.

While it is tempting to become expansive and speculate about where future research and development will lead us, I believe it will be more constructive to focus on two areas in which I see the needs as being particularly pressing. First, I believe that our highest priority must be given to the continued development and validation of authentic tests of communicative language ability. This is essential because of the need for practical tests for use in 'communicative' language teaching in making decisions about the employability of language teachers, and in language acquisition and attrition research. Validation research is also important in its own right because of its potential for providing insights into the nature of communicative language ability and communicative language use.

Related to validation research, or perhaps within it, is a second area of need: the development of criterion-referenced measures of communicative language ability. In many foreign language programs there has been a movement toward the use of some form of competency-based evaluation, and this has led to the need for measures of language ability based on a 'common yardstick'. At the same time, the proliferation of approaches to foreign and second language teaching has increased the need for measures for use in evaluating the relative effectiveness of these approaches. As has been pointed out by Bachman and Clark (1987) and Bachman (1989b), norm-referenced tests are inadequate for either of these needs, and criterion-referenced tests are required.

Validation of authentic tests of communicative language ability

In Chapter 7 construct validation was described as an on-going process, involving a wide range of approaches to gathering evidence that scores from a given test can be inferred as indicators of a particular ability. Much of the progress that we have seen in the field of language testing in the past two and a half decades has grown out of this type of research, whether it was explicitly called that or not, and as I have indicated above, I believe future progress will be possible only if we continue and expand this type of research. This expansion will come from two sources: (1) an expanded framework of communicative language ability (CLA) and test method facets, such as those presented in Chapters 4 and 5, and (2) a greater variety of approaches to construct validation.

Expanded frameworks of CLA and test method facets will depend heavily on continued input from both theoretical and applied linguistics. An understanding both of language as a system, and of language in use, in all its complexity, must be the basis for any theory of language ability. As our understanding of these expands, so our framework of CLA will expand, and hence, the hypotheses that form the basis for construct validation research. Applied linguistics research provides what Shohamy (1984b) has called the 'input component' and what Stevenson (1985a) has called the 'sociolinguistic principle' of language testing research. Our framework of test method facets will also depend to a large extent upon these fields, particularly those aimed at investigating language in use, since the factors that affect the use of language in language tests must surely be a subset of the factors that determine language use in general. That is, I would not expect a set of test method facets that is incongruous with a theory of language use to be particularly productive, either for generating hypotheses for construct validation research, or as a basis for practical test development.

While construct validation studies of language tests have employed a variety of approaches, by far the majority have examined only the *product* of language tests – test scores. Furthermore, such studies have been largely quantitative in their approach and analyses, and have examined primarily group performance. However, if we are to begin to understand what makes language tests authentic, and how this is related to test performance, we must also examine the *processes* or strategies utilized in test-taking as well, and this must be at the level of the *individual*, rather than of the group.

The need to examine process as well as product has been recognized and discussed in the context of language program evaluation (for example, Bachman 1981; Long 1984; Beretta 1986b). In Chapter 7 studies by Cohen (1984, 1987, forthcoming) and Grotjahn (1986) were cited as exemplars of the usefulness of this approach to the construct validation of language tests (pp. 269–71).

As Cohen (1986) points out, there is a wide range of techniques that can be utilized to elicit introspective data about the processes or strategies which individuals employ in taking language tests. The work of Douglas and Selinker (1985) also illustrates the potential for this kind of research, and the hypotheses they have articulated with respect to the construction of discourse domains by test takers should provide a fruitful direction for future research of this type. Douglas and Selinker analyzed responses to a task from the *Speaking Proficiency English Assessment Kit* (SPEAK) (Educational Testing

Service 1985) in which test takers were asked to describe the components of a perfect meal, and discovered five different specific strategies for responding to this task, such as naming the specific foods that would make up a perfect meal, describing the nutritional characteristics of a perfect meal, and describing the process of cooking the perfect meal.

I believe that the computer administration of language tests also has a great deal of potential for providing information on the process of taking language tests. Computers have been used to collect data of relevance to second language acquisition (for example, Garrett 1980; Chapelle and Jamieson 1986), and are being used increasingly to administer language tests (for example, studies reported in Stansfield 1986a). The major application of computer technology to language testing has been that of improving the psychometric qualities of test scores and maximizing the efficiency of test administration, rather than as a means of collecting data on the process of test-taking. However, some information regarding test-taking processes can be gleaned, it seems, from the examination of individual response patterns, utilizing item-response theory (for example, Henning 1987; Madsen 1987; Pollitt and Hutchinson 1987), although this, too, has tended to focus on products – the identification of responses that fail to fit item-response curves.

An approach to investigating test-taking processes through the analysis of test takers' responses has been developed by Tatsuoka and her associates (for example, Birenbaum and Tatsuoka 1980, 1983; Tatsuoka 1983, 1984, 1986; Tatsuoka and Tatsuoka 1987). Using a combination of information obtained through content-based error analysis, introspection by test takers, and expert teachers' knowledge of student error patterns, Tatsuoka has developed a statistical 'rule-space model' for diagnosing the application of erroneous rules from test response patterns (Tatsuoka 1983). Tatsuoka and Tatsuoka (1987) describe rules and how they can be developed as follows:

> A rule is a description of a set of procedures or operations that one can use in solving a problem in some well-defined procedural domain. . . . A right rule . . . produces the right answer to every item on a test, but an erroneous rule may fortuitously yield the right answer for some subset of items. Logical analysis of cognitive tasks – identifying subtasks for solving the problems correctly, investigating possible solution paths and constructing a subtask tree or process network for a well-defined procedural domain – is

often an important prerequisite to developing a cognitive error-diagnostic test.
(Tatsuoka and Tatsuoka 1987: 194).

Tatsuoka's model has been developed from and applied primarily to tests involving mathematical problem solving. However, to the extent that we can describe the 'rules' individuals apply in taking language tests, this model may have important applications to the analysis of the process of taking language tests. It may be that Selinker and Douglas's notion of individual learner discourse domains, for example, can be characterized in terms of different sets of idiosyncratic rules, the application of which may be reflected in differential patterns of responses.

It is well known that computers can perform iterative tasks both unerringly and endlessly, characteristics that are sometimes used to anthropomorphize them as 'trustworthy' and 'patient'. The advantage of these characteristics for the investigation of process in language testing is that computers can compile and categorize larger amounts of data from 'integrative' language tests than would be feasible through introspection or self-report. Consider, for example, a cloze test administered by computer. Test takers are given the standard instructions: that they should read the passage through completely before beginning the test, that they can use only one word per blank, and that they may go back and change their answers as they go along. We have the technology to record information on both response latencies and patterns of response. That is, we can find out how long an individual spent on a given item, what his first response was, at what point he went back and changed that response, and so forth. The analysis of this type of data would be useful for generating hypotheses about how individuals take cloze tests, and perhaps for testing some of Douglas and Selinker's hypotheses about the construction of discourse domains. It could also provide a valuable guide for collecting introspective and self-report data, since the test taker could be led through his actual response pattern, and could thus focus on recalling his reasons for that particular pattern. Another computer-administered test that could provide similar data is the 'copytest', which is essentially a dictation presented in visual mode on a computer screen (Cziko 1982; Cziko and Lin 1984).

In summary, the examination of the processes that individuals utilize in taking language tests adds an essential and exciting dimension to construct validation research, and may provide a missing piece in helping complete the puzzle of test authenticity.

Combining the analysis of test-taking strategies with existing methods for examining relationships among test scores may also let us begin to glimpse that most elusive aspect of communicative language ability, what I have called strategic competence.

Criterion-referenced tests of communicative language ability

The need for criterion-referenced (CR) measures of language abilities for certain specific uses has been recognized for some time. Cartier (1968), in a seminal article, argued for the usefulness of CR measures as a basis for designing language courses, and more recently the needs for CR tests for minimum competency testing and language program evaluation have been described (Bachman and Clark 1987). Despite these recognized needs, however, applications of CR measurement to language testing have been relatively sparse, and have generally been limited to the measurement of achievement (for example, Hudson and Lynch 1984; Hughes 1986). One of the main reasons CR measurement has not been more widely applied to the measurement of language proficiency, I believe, is because of the problems related to domain specification, which have been discussed above with respect to the real-life approach to authenticity, and the difficulty encountered in defining criterion levels of ability, problems that some language testers view as virtually intractable (for example, Skehan 1984).

One source of recent interest in the development of CR tests of foreign language proficiency is the need for a measurement instrument that could be used as a basis for establishing standards for competency-based foreign language instruction and minimum competency requirements for foreign language teachers. The issue of minimum competency testing is a complex one, and far beyond the scope of this book. Suffice it to say that minimum competency testing is a controversial topic in education in general. The evidence seems to indicate that minimum competency testing is neither the universal panacea for educational ills that some of its proponents have claimed, nor the end to excellence in education, as many of its critics see it. (See, for example, Jaeger and Tittle 1980 and Lazarus 1981 for extensive discussions of the issues.)

If we accept the proposition that *for a given language program* minimum competency testing will result in better educational practice and learner outcomes, both cognitive and affective, then we can follow established procedures for developing CR achievement tests based on a domain specified by the learning outcomes of the program. However, when the educational plan is to establish standards for minimum competency that will apply to a wide range of language programs, different languages and different types of language learners, such procedures become more problematic, in that both the domain and criterion levels of achievement become more difficult to specify. Consider, for example, the problems involved in attempting to develop CR tests for several languages, such as Spanish, French, and German, not only for high school and college students, but for teachers of these languages as well, and you can begin to appreciate the complexities, both educational and political, involved in this issue. Some of these issues are discussed by Bachman and Savignon (1986) with respect to the explicit claims by proponents of the ACTFL oral interview that it provides a basis for the criterion-referenced measurement of language proficiency.

A similar need can be found in the evaluation of language programs. As with minimum competency decisions, so long as we are only interested in evaluating the effectiveness of a given program in successfully achieving its stated objectives for a specific group of language learners, standard procedures for CR test development can be followed. However, if we want to examine the extent to which these objectives themselves are worthwhile, or if we want to compare the relative effectiveness of different programs, with different sets of objectives, we encounter problems of domain specification, and issues of fairness (Beretta 1986a; Bachman 1989b).

A third area of need is in second language acquisition (SLA) research, where criterion measures of language abilities that can be used to assess learners' progression through developmental sequences are still largely absent (Brindley 1986). Several researchers (for example, Brindley and Singh 1982; Clahsen 1985; Ingram 1985; Pienemann *et al.* 1988) have begun investigating the relationship between regularities in SLA and performance on language tests, with the intention of incorporating information about developmental sequences into procedures for assessing language proficiency. Since most of this work has been limited to the assessment of grammatical competence, it is not yet clear whether this approach will extend to other aspects of language ability (Bachman 1989a).

One solution that has been proposed to meet the various needs of competency-based foreign language instruction, language program evaluation, and SLA research is the development of a 'common metric' of language proficiency (Woodford 1978, 1981; B. J. Carroll 1980; Clark 1980). Clark (1980) describes a common measure of speaking proficiency as follows: 'a uniform testing procedure that could be used with diverse groups of examinees in a variety of language-learning and language-use situations, with testing results reported on a uniform scale' (p. 15). The distinguishing features of a common metric would be: (1) its independence of course-specific objectives, and (2) its comparability across different languages, contexts, times, and groups (Bachman and Clark 1987). Clark's 1980 discussion of the considerations involved in developing common measures of speaking ability includes a carefully laid-out plan of research and development, the main elements of which are the basis of a broad agenda for language testing research and development subsequently proposed by Bachman and Clark (1987). They argue that the NR approach to test development and interpretation is not adequate for the purpose of developing common measures, in that 'it fails to reflect the degree of mastery of specific objectives and since both the score norms and the content may be inappropriate to [the different] . . . groups that are being compared' (p. 27). They further argue that a common metric scale of language proficiency must be criterion-referenced:

> Unlike norm-referenced test scores, the interpretation of CR test scores is independent of the performance of other individuals on the test. A CR test is one that can be interpreted as an indication of an individual's attainment with respect to a given domain of proficiency.
> (Bachman and Clark 1987: 28)

If we accept Bachman and Clark's argument about the inadequacies of NR tests for these purposes and the need to develop CR tests of language abilities, our primary concerns must be: (1) to identify the essential characteristics of such tests, and (2) to define these characteristics in a way that is consistent with considerations that must be made with respect to validity and authenticity.

Essential characteristics of common metric scales of communicative language ability

Many different definitions of CR tests have been proposed, and in his review of the literature Nitko (1984) synthesizes these into two general categories, within which he lists nine different approaches. These are listed in Figure 8.1. The major differences in these approaches have to do with how the domain is specified and whether the objectives or behaviors in the domains are ordered with respect to each other. The category of CR tests based on ordered domains is

WELL-DEFINED AND ORDERED DOMAINS	WELL-DEFINED AND UNORDERED DOMAINS
Basis for scaling or ordering the domain	**Basis for delineating the behavior domain**
1 Judged social or esthetic quality of the performance	6 Stimulus properties of the domain and the sampling plan of the test
2 Complexity or difficulty of the subject matter	7 Verbal statments of stimuli and responses in domain
3 Degree of proficiency with which complex skills are performed	8 Diagnostic categories of performance
4 Prerequisite sequence for acquiring intellectual and psychomotor skills	9 Abstractions, traits, constructs
5 Location on an empirically defined latent trait	

Figure 8.1   Categories of criterion-referenced tests (adapted from Nitko 1984: 15, 18–19)

most directly relevant to the development of language tests, since most language teaching is based on the assumption that language acquisition and learning is a cumulative process, with learners gradually increasing in their levels of proficiency, an assumption that is supported, by and large, by research into second and foreign language learning. Furthermore, one particular type of ordered domain, that based on the 'degree of proficiency with which complex skills are performed' (3 in Figure 8.1 above), incorporates the notion of an *absolute* scale of proficiency, and provides, I believe, the key to the development of 'common-metric' measures of language proficiency.

Glaser and Klaus (1962) first used the term 'criterion-referenced' to refer to the type of information derived from proficiency tests. Their discussion makes explicit the notion of an underlying absolute scale of proficiency:

Underlying the concept of proficiency measurement is a continuum

of skill ranging from no proficiency at all to perfect performance. In these terms, an individual's proficiency at a given task falls at some point on the continuum, as measured by the behaviors he displays during testing. The degree to which his proficiency resembles desired performance at any specified level is assessed by *criterion-referenced measures* of proficiency.
(Glaser and Klaus 1962: 421)

This concept of zero and perfect levels as the defining end-points of a criterion-referenced scale was also explicit in Glaser's often quoted definition, which he adapted to fit the context of school learning, in contrast to the military training environments that he and Klaus had addressed:

Underlying the concept of achievement measurement is the notion of a continuum of knowledge acquisition ranging from no proficiency at all to perfect proficiency. An individual's achievement level falls at some point on the continuum as indicated by the behaviors he displays during testing. The degree to which his achievement resembles desired performance at any specified level is assessed by criterion-referenced measures of achievement or proficiency.
(Glaser 1963: 519)

In subsequent CR definitions that have continued to include the notion of an *ordered* domain, the absolute nature of that domain has been lost, or omitted. Thus, Glaser and Nitko (1971) give the following general definition:

A criterion-referenced test is one that is deliberately constructed to yield measurements that are directly interpretable in terms of specified performance standards. . . . [CR tests] are specifically constructed to support generalizations about an individual's performance relative to a specified domain of tasks.
(Glaser and Nitko 1971: 653)

The other approach to CR test development that has evolved, that of an *unordered* domain, has perhaps become the dominant because of its relevance and importance to the development of achievement tests based on instructional objectives. The approach is defined by Popham (1978) as follows:

A criterion-referenced test is used to ascertain an individual's status with respect to a well-defined behavioral domain.
(Popham 1978: 93)

This domain-referenced approach to CR test development is particularly relevant to instructional settings in which domains can be reasonably specified. Indeed, much of the development effort in this approach is aimed at the specification of domains of instructional objectives (for example, Hively *et al.* 1973; Popham 1984). As noted above, this approach may be quite usable in the context of developing measures of language abilities based on a given set of learning objectives, that is, for achievement tests. Recall, from Chapter 3 (pp. 71–2), that the primary difference between tests of language achievement and language proficiency lies in the origin of their 'content' domain. Thus, while a language achievement test is based on a specific course syllabus, or set of learning objectives, a proficiency test is based on a general theory of language proficiency, such as the framework of communicative language ability presented in Chapter 4. Because of the problems involved in specifying the domain of language proficiency, or communicative language ability, as a set of behaviors, however, I believe this approach is not applicable to the development of tests of this ability, and that we must utilize the notion of criterion-referencing defined in terms of ordered levels of language proficiency.

One scale for measuring language proficiency, that originally defined in the *Absolute Language Proficiency Ratings* (Foreign Service Institute (FSI) 1968), was developed in the spirit of the original Glaser CR definition of proficiency as constituting a continuum of skill ranging from absolute zero to perfect mastery: 'The S-rating for speaking proficiency and the R-rating for reading proficiency are based on the absolute criterion of the command of an educated native speaker of the language' (Wilds 1975: 36). However, there is a flaw in these definitions, with respect to the claim that they constitute an 'absolute' scale of language proficiency: the reference to the 'educated native speaker' as the criterion for perfect proficiency. In the two decades since these ratings were first articulated, the applied linguists' view toward the 'native speaker' has changed considerably. As has been pointed out above (pp. 38–40, 248–9), the very concept of 'native speaker' as actual individuals has been rejected by many scholars, and the problems of identifying the characteristics that might be used to define even the prototypical native speaker are virtually impossible to resolve. Furthermore, given the empirical evidence that 'native speakers' vary considerably in their control of different aspects of language proficiency, it is unreasonable to consider them as any more than a norm group, in which case a scale based on actual native speaker performance becomes, by definition, a norm-referenced scale. All this is not to say that rating scales based on the original FSI definitions, such as the ILR scale (Lowe 1982) and the *ACTFL Proficiency Guidelines* (ACTFL 1986) are not of value, but simply that they are, in fact, norm-referenced scales. Thus, while they may be of use for purposes of comparing an individual's level of proficiency with reference to other 'norm' levels, they are not adequate as bases for a 'common metric' scale, or for the uses in program evaluation and minimum competency testing that have been described above.

Another problem with the FSI-type scale definition as a basis for a 'common metric' is the characteristic, discussed above (pp. 328–9), that it does not distinguish abilities from test method facets. So long as we are only interested in predicting whether an individual can perform language use tasks within a fairly narrowly defined domain, this may not present a problem. However, it means that such definitions may not be adequate for making inferences about performance in other domains. A crucial question, then, is how broad a domain of performance we are interested in predicting.

In summary, in order to satisfy the needs of a 'common metric' measure of language proficiency, we must develop criterion-referenced scales, with criteria consisting of *absolute* levels, defined in terms of components of language proficiency, rather than with respect to actual language performance or actual language users, 'native' or otherwise. Furthermore, if we want this measure to be comparable across different languages, contexts, and groups of language users, we must distinguish the components of proficiency from the facets of the measurement procedure.

Absolute scales of measurement

The problem of determining the number of levels for any given measurement scale is essentially an empirical one, and this is a problem that has been of concern to measurement specialists for the better part of this century. Reviews of this literature can be found in Flanagan (1951), Angoff (1971), and Peterson *et al.* (1988). Of particular interest to the proposal to develop CR tests of language proficiency are the attempts that have been made to develop absolute scales of measurement, in which the problem is one of defining the zero, or end point of the scale.

While the distinction between relative and absolute scales of measurement is generally attributed to Thorndike (for example, Berk 1984b; Carroll 1987b), it was Thurstone's early work in the measurement of intelligence that resulted in a procedure for actually developing absolute scales of measurement (Thurstone 1925, 1927b, 1928). Thurstone demonstrated, essentially, that an absolute scale could be developed by plotting the frequency distributions of different groups of individuals who are at different levels on a given ability, on a single base line. Although Thurstone's method of absolute scaling was developed with data from tests of primary mental abilities on different age groups, and was based on assumptions that may be overly restrictive (for example, that the ability is normally distributed in each of the different age groups), the principle of using different ability groups as a basis for absolute scale development lends itself, I believe, to the development of CR scales of language proficiency. It may be possible to accomplish this by combining the notion of theoretically defined criterion levels of ability with IRT techniques of scale calibration.

The Bayesian approach to estimates of ability within the framework of IRT may provide the basis for the development of criterion-referenced scales with meaningful zero and perfect end points. In the Bayesian approach to estimating ability, the test developer or user makes use of prior information about the characteristics of the test items or about the ability levels of the test takers, or both, to improve estimates of ability. That is, the test developer may specify certain values for item parameters based on prior information about the characteristics of the test, or for ability levels, based on prior definitions of the ability to be measured (Hambleton and Swaminathan 1985: 141–4). Lord (1980) discusses the use of prior levels of low and high ability upon which judges (presumably subject matter specialists) can agree as a basis for the development and use of mastery tests (Lord 1980, Chapter 11). It is well known that the scale on which ability ('θ') is measured is largely arbitrary, and that ability estimates can be transformed in a number of ways to make such scores more meaningful to test users (Hambleton and Swaminathan 1985). While it is common practice to define the ability scale so that the mean is equal to zero and the standard deviation equal to one, it would appear to be equally feasible to specify a prior level of ability as zero and use this point as the basis for scale calibration. This procedure may be enhanced by the utilization of Carroll's 'person characteristic functions' (Carroll 1980, 1983b, 1987a). It is essentially this line of research and development that Nitko (1984) has identified as a priority area for CR testing:

> Research related to such test development [referencing test scores to a domain that can be ordered as levels of proficiency . . . along a

novice–expert continuum] will need to focus initially on describing the nature of competence in a specific kind of performance or knowledge area and the relation of competent performance to cognitive process. Such research will undoubtedly reveal that there is not an underlying unidimensional continuum, and thus existing mathematical models will be difficult, if not impossible, to apply to this psychometric problem. Defining and measuring competence seems to be an important societal concern, however, even though a scientific understanding of the psychological processes differentiating levels of competence is still largely lacking. . . . Once an operational version of a test has been developed it will be possible to explore the potential uses of competence measures in classroom practice, thereby moving cognitive-psychology process research out of the laboratory and into the school.
(Nitko 1984: 23)

In this call for future research, Nitko is clearly concerned about the potential lag between theory and practice, and urges a program of empirical research to begin the narrowing of that gap.

An approach to the definition of criterion-referenced scales of language proficiency

The approach to the development of CR scales of language proficiency that I propose is based on the definition of levels in terms of the relative presence or absence of abilities that constitute the domain. At the defining ends of each ability scale we have the absolute levels, 'perfect' at the top and 'zero' at the bottom, *which may or may not be found in actual language users*. It is possible, for example, that a 'native speaker' of a particular variety of a given language will be perfect in his control of the syntax of the language, but below this level in his lexical ability. At the other end of the scale, we may find second or foreign language learners who are at some intermediate level in their ability to use the formal characteristics of the language, but who may be near the zero level in terms of sociolinguistic conventions of language use. In the majority of foreign or second language testing situations, we are likely to find that virtually none of our test takers are at the top level of any given ability, and very few (hopefully) are at the zero level. The concern about whether individuals at these levels actually exist, however, is a norm-referenced one, and the point to keep in mind is that the 'zero' and 'perfect' levels represent the criterion reference points, or ability levels, against which individual performance is to be compared. That is, the end points are essentially hypothetical levels that function as a basis for scale definition and calibration, but which may or may not have observable manifestations in the performance of individuals.

An initial attempt to incorporate these principles into operational measures of language proficiency can be found in the tests developed by Bachman and Palmer (1982a) for use in research into the nature of language proficiency. The scales upon which Bachman and Palmer based these tests, given in Table 8.1 (pp. 326–8), are examples of how this approach to criterion-referenced scale definition might be implemented. The scales themselves are defined solely in terms of language abilities, while facets of the test method were included in the description of different elicitation procedures: a multiple-choice test, a set of writing tasks, an oral interview, and a self-rating questionnaire.

As these examples demonstrate, although scales of different abilities will all have zero and perfect end points, the number of intermediate levels may vary from one scale to another, depending on the results of empirical calibration procedures. The determination of the number of levels between the end points of any given ability scale is essentially an empirical question to be answered through a program of research and development. It might be useful at this point to discuss briefly what the research implications of this approach are.

The development of language tests according to the approach just outlined requires the initial definition of absolute levels (zero, perfect) of proficiency for each of the components of communicative language ability that are to be measured. These definitions would be stated in terms of the abilities to be measured, without reference to either the actual performance of actual individuals or the facets of the measurement procedure. In addition to defining the end points, the scale definitions would include a provisional division of the ability continuum into several intermediate levels.

Next, several sets of elicitation procedures, specifying the conditions for all the relevant test method facets so as to maximize the potential for authentic interaction, would be designed to be applicable to several different groups of individuals, ranging from 'novices', or those with little or no ability, to 'experts', or those with a high level of ability. Then, through a program of systematically eliciting authentic language use by the different methods across several different ability levels, and rating these samples of language use on the ability scales, it would be possible to begin calibration of both the abilities and the scale points.

It should be obvious that such a program of research and development fits squarely into the process of construct validation that has been discussed above. Thus, in addition to yielding practical 'common metric' instruments for measuring communicative language ability, this research should advance our understanding of this ability as well. This research and development is also consistent with recent calls from language testers for a 'unified' agenda for language testing (for example, Bachman and Clark 1987; Clark and Clifford 1988; Clark and Lett 1988). Furthermore, the battery of tests that would result from such a program of research would be a step toward satisfying Nevo's (1986) recommendation that we develop a 'multipurpose–multimethod' approach to language testing, in which 'everyone's language skills can be appropriately tested for various purposes provided that an appropriate testing method is being used' (p. 241).

A general model for explaining performance on language tests

As a means of synthesizing much of the discussion in this book, and as a possible beginning model for the implementation of the research and development activities I have proposed in this chapter, I will describe a general model for explaining performance on language tests. This model is essentially an elaboration of the factors presented in Figure 6.1 (p. 165), with the inclusion of an attempt to provide a means for operationalizing the relationships represented there.

The inferences we can make from measures of language abilities depend directly upon the way in which we define the universes to which we wish to generalize. That is, in order to make inferences about individuals' language abilities on the basis of test scores, it is essential that we clearly define those abilities. Given what we know about the effect of test methods, we must also clearly define test method facets so as to be able to distinguish them from components of language ability. The frameworks presented in Chapters 4 and 5 provide a basis for formulating hypotheses about factors that affect performance on language tests and for defining these factors so as to make them more clearly distinguishable.

The four categories of influences on language test scores included in this model are communicative language ability, test method facets, personal characteristics, and random measurement error. Although personal characteristics have often been considered either sources of error or test bias, and thus not directly treated in measurement models, I believe there is sufficient evidence about their influence on language test scores to treat them as a separate group of factors.[2] Furthermore, explicitly including these factors in the model will hopefully have two salutary effects on language testing. First, this may lead both developers and users of language tests to consider these factors when designing language tests and interpreting test scores. Second it may stimulate further search into their effects on language test performance, thus furthering our understanding of these, and perhaps enabling us to more effectively control the influence of these factors through the careful design of appropriate test method facets. In addition to acting as individual influences on test performance, components of communicative language ability, test method facets, and personal attributes may interact with each other, constituting additional sources of variation, as described in Chapter 6, in the discussion of estimating variance components in G-theory. These interactions may thus constitute essentially random influences, to the extent that we are not able to control them in our test design. These different sources of variance are illustrated in Figure 8.2. Using this framework, we can formulate a model, or hypothesis for describing the variance in a set of language test scores:

$$s^2_x = s^2_a + s^2_m + s^2_p + s^2_{am} + s^2_{ap} + s^2_{mp} + s^2_{amp} + s^2_e$$

where:

s^2_a = variance due to components of CLA

s^2_m = variance due to TMFs

s^2_p = variance due to personal attributes

s^2_{am} = variance due to interactions between components of CLA and TMFs

s^2_{ap} = variance due to interactions between components of CLA and personal attributes

s^2_{amp} = variance due to interactions among components of CLA, TMFs, and personal attributes

s^2_e = residual error variance

This framework is presented not as a definitive model, but rather as a means for generating empirical hypotheses about sources of variance in language test scores. The examination of these hypotheses through generalizability theory and multivariate analytic procedures will hopefully result in a better understanding of what language tests measure, and provide a more solid basis for examining both the reliability and validity of language test scores. In addition, the detailed specification that this model requires for its application

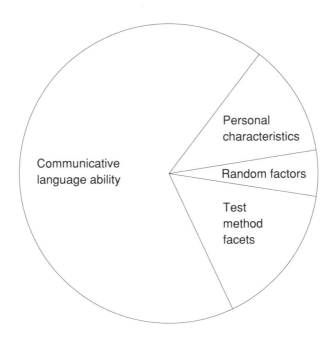

I. COMMUNICATIVE LANGUAGE ABILITY (CLA)
A Language competencies
  1   Grammatical competence
  2   Textual competence
  3   Illocutionary competence
  4   Sociolinguistic competence
B Strategic competence
C Psychophysiological mechanisms

II. TEST METHOD FACETS (TMF)
A   Environment
B   Rubric
C   Input
D   Expected response
E   Relationships between
   input and response

III. PERSONAL CHARACTERISTICS
A   Cultural background
B   Background knowledge
C   Cognitive abilities
D   Sex
E   Age

IV. RANDOM FACTORS
A   Interactions among components
   of CLA, test method facets, and
   personal characteristics
B   Measurement error

Figure 8.2   Sources of variation in language test scores

should lead to language tests that are designed with more careful attention to the language abilities that are to be measured and the test method facets that characterize the procedures used to elicit measurable language performance.

Apologia et prolegomenon

There seems to be perennial discontent, both among language teachers and among developers of language tests themselves, with the enterprise of language testing. This discontent was the motivation for one of the first conferences devoted to the topic of foreign language testing:

> The idea for the meeting grew out of private and public expressions of dissatisfaction by a number of people who are involved in test production and who depend on test results – dissatisfaction with the quality and range of foreign language tests available, with the uses to which tests often are put, and with the ends they are made to serve.
> (Upshur 1968: vii)

This dissatisfaction has been voiced since, and is clearly evident in much of the discussion of communicative or authentic tests that has taken place since Morrow's (1979) seminal and controversial paper entitled, 'Communicative language testing: revolution or evolution?' In a recent review article, Canale (1988) discusses a number of problems that continue to perplex the field, not the least of which are related to how we define language ability and how to gather information that is relevant to its assessment. But as Canale also points out, there have been solid achievements in these areas as well. To the credit of language testers, the debate about the fundamental considerations of language testing over the years has been motivated and informed, by and large, by both a sincere interest in better understanding the nature of language abilities and their measure-ment, and a genuine desire to develop language tests that better reflect our knowledge of what language and language use are, that exhibit the essential psychometric qualities of reliability and validity, and which are also usable. That we are not well understood by our clients and fellow applied linguists is to be expected, since it is merely a reflection of our own uncertainties. That we are sometimes viewed as either callous and indifferent to the larger issues of language teaching, applied linguistics, and educational policy, or as pie-in-the-sky ivory-tower number crunchers is simply misinformed and unfair.

Nevertheless, the burden is upon us, as a profession, to alter this image, and this will come neither through faith nor the recitation of correlation coefficients. Language teachers and applied linguists will no longer be intimidated or convinced by misguided statistical analyses, no matter how sophisticated. And we can no longer find safe haven by simply asserting that our tests are based on 'experience', 'real life', or the 'intuitions of language teachers', or that they measure 'communicative language ability' and are 'authentic'. To echo Stevenson's (1981) call, the burden of proof is upon us to demonstrate our good intentions in the form of 'good works'. And these works will have to be in the form of useful tests whose authenticity and validity we can *demonstrate* to our clients.

A number of writers have noted the two disciplines that come together in language testing: applied linguistics and psychometrics (for example, Stevenson 1981, 1985a; Spolsky 1986). Stevenson (1985a) has referred to these as 'sociolinguistic' and 'psychometric' principles, while Shohamy (1984b) has called them the 'input' and 'output' components of language testing, respectively.

> The two domains – language learning and measurement – have different, yet complementary roles and purposes in producing language tests. Language learning theories can bring the INPUT component into language testing, i.e., defining *what* should be tested and what the appropriate language behaviours are. Measurement theories on the other hand can bring the OUTPUT component of the test, i.e. how can language performance and proficiency turn into tests of these constructs. . . .

> The language tester's role is to integrate the input and the output components. The language tester needs to construct testing tasks based on the input, that lend themselves to testing and that will also possess the needed measurement properties.
> (Shohamy 1984b: 162, 164)

Her point, in the context of this chapter, would appear to be self evident. That it needs to be made, however, reflects the fact that both views do not always inform testing practice. Indeed, I would go a step further and suggest that much of the dissatisfaction with language testing over the years can be attributed to the emphasis, in test development and use, on one or the other of these two principles, to the virtual exclusion of the other.

We language testers thus cannot allow ourselves the delusion that current views of language use and language learning can be ignored because this simplifies the problems of measurement. Nor can we afford the luxury of placing all our confidence in the correctness of our applied linguistic theories, in the hope that the measurement issues will thus evaporate. Progress does not lie in the direction of more sophisticated psychometric analyses of theoretically unjustified tests. Nor will we advance if we ignore fundamental measurement considerations in our striving to capture authenticity in our testing procedures. The challenge will be to address the perennial dilemmas of language testing with both an open mind and a healthy respect for the complexity of the abilities we want to measure, and a continued commitment to utilize the best and most appropriate psychometric theories and statistical tools at our disposal so as to assure that we can be held accountable for the uses we and others make of our tests.

The 'up' side of this challenge to language testing research is the opportunity it presents for providing insights of its own into the nature of language and language use. The excitement in the field is that we are now dealing with a more complex and comprehensive view of language abilities and language use, and have at our disposal much more sophisticated tools – both qualitative and quantitative – for empirically examining these views. One can sense this *élan* in Spolsky's (1986) statement: 'Communicative tests are exciting in the practical and theoretical problems they present: they still refuse to fit neatly into the psychometrist's neat formulas, offering thus promise of the humanism we have come to expect in postmodern language testing' (p. 157).

While the future of language testing will most likely be marked by the greater synthesis of applied linguistic and psychometric theories in the development of language tests, I believe it will also come into its own as an area of research, contributing to each. The potential for language testing research for providing insights into the nature of language abilities has already been mentioned. However, I believe this potential will be fully realized only when combined with other approaches to research into the nature of language ability and language learning.

Allen *et al.* (1983) in their conclusion to *Development of Bilingual Proficiency: Second Year report* ('DBP Study') have described three stages of development in the history of empirical research into the nature of language abilities (pp. 55–8). The first stage was characterized by the use of exploratory factor analysis as the primary statistical tool, beginning with John Carroll's work on verbal abilities in the 1940s, and culminating in the 'g-factor' studies of John Oller and his students in the 1970s. The major development during this stage was the change in applied linguistic theory regarding the nature of language proficiency. Thus, while early researchers focused primarily on the formal characteristics of language, Oller's research has been based on the axiom that the functional, or pragmatic dimension of language is fundamental.

The second stage, toward the end of which the DBP study falls, has been characterized not only by increasingly complex and comprehensive frameworks of language ability, but also by sophisticated (and exhausting) research designs and statistical analyses. As the investigators correctly observe, this was the 'state of the art' when they designed their study at the turn of the 1980s. In the years that followed, a number of other studies also demonstrated what, it seems to me, is one of the major outcomes of the DBP Study: that both background characteristics of language learners and test method effects can influence test performance as strongly as the abilities we wish to examine, and that there are thus limitations on the *ex post facto* analysis of test performance as a paradigm for research into the nature of language proficiency. While there may still be a researcher or two out there who secretly hope for the opportunity to conduct a 'really big' MTMM study, the DBP Study may have marked the passing of a paradigm for large-scale language research, much as did the Pennsylvania (Smith 1970) and GUME (Lindblad and Levin 1970; Levin 1970) studies for quasi-experimental method comparison research.

The third stage, whose onset has been spurred on in no small degree by the DBP Study itself, will be marked, according to Allen *et al.*, by the interpretation of language performance 'explicitly in terms of how different aspects of communicative competence have developed as a function of specific language acquisition/learning experiences' (p. 58). This stage will draw on both abstract models of language use and theories of language acquisition/learning. It will also be marked by the use of a much wider range of research approaches and analytic procedures. I would further speculate that this stage will see the marriage of language testing research and second language acquisition research in designs that will permit the full application of the tools of multivariate analysis. The usefulness of such designs and analyses has already been demonstrated in studies such as Bachman and Palmer (1983b), Gardner (1983), Gardner *et al.* (1983), Fouly (1985), Bachman and Mack (1986), Sang *et al.* (1986), and Wang (1988), which have examined the complex relationships among learner characteristics and different aspects of language proficiency.

It is in this perspective that the future of language testing research can be properly considered. Studies such as these have provided us with a sobering reaffirmation of the complexity of language proficiency at a time when overly simplistic views have gained ground in both second language acquisition research and foreign language testing. More important, however, these studies point the way to a broader agenda for research into the nature of language proficiency, an agenda that promises to further enrich our under-standing of both this ability and its acquisition.

Finally, I am optimistic that the future will also see greater collaboration between language testers and the consumers of language tests – not only other researchers, but the whole range of individuals involved in the enterprise of language teaching: learners, teachers, program developers, materials writers, publishers, admini-strators, legislators. This view has also been expressed by Cooper (1986) in reflecting on the future of language testing:

> we can best encourage the development of [language testing] by facilitating interaction among researchers who need language tests to solve their problems and also between them and other consumers of language tests. The most useful conference on [language testing] in the next 25 years will address not testing issues but rather issues which require language tests.
> (Cooper 1986: 240)

It is human nature to consider one's own time and place of great significance, and I suppose language testers are no different. The optimists among us can look back in hindsight and justifiably relish our accomplishments. Those of a slightly more realistic bent will also be aware of the commitments yet to be fulfilled, to the users of language tests. In view of past accomplishments and current capabilities, however, most language testers share a feeling of confidence that with our increased knowledge and technical expertise the major breakthroughs are yet to come. This confidence is essential, since when we look into the future we can quite easily become overwhelmed by the complexity of the issues, and the enormity of the task ahead can lead us to hearken back wistfully to what now seem simpler times. However, the problems have always been complex, the dilemmas real, and the solutions elusive, and they will persist. But, as with Milton's shepherd, perhaps we have benefited from the confrontation with these issues, and will be able to address more wisely those that lie ahead.

He touch't the tender stops of various Quills.
With eager thought warbling his *Doric* lay:
And now the Sun had stretch't out all the hills,
And now was dropt into the Western bay;

At last he rose, and twitch't his Mantle blue:
Tomorrow to fresh Woods and Pastures new.
(Milton, 'Lycidas')

Summary

The most complex and persistent problems in language testing are those presented by the consideration of the relationship between the language use required by tasks on language tests and that which is part of our everyday communicative use of language. That there must be a relationship between the language used on tests and that used in 'real life' cannot be denied, since if there is no such relationship, our language tests become mere shadows, sterile procedures that may tell us nothing about the very ability we wish to measure.

Two distinct approaches for attempting to describe this vital relationship, or test 'authenticity', have been followed by language testers. In one approach we identify the 'real-life' language use that we expect will be required of test takers, and with this as a criterion, attempt to design test tasks that mirror this. Our primary concerns in this approach are the degree to which language test tasks look and operate like the 'real life' language use tasks we have identified as criteria, and the extent to which language test scores predict future language performance. This approach provides a description of the relationship between test language and 'real-life' language use that is helpful in designing practical language tests for groups of individuals whose language use needs are fairly homogeneous and identifiable. However, because of the complexities of 'real-life' language use, this approach is likely to be extremely difficult to implement in situations in which test takers' language use needs are diverse. Furthermore, because of the limited types of information that can be gathered, the construct validity of test scores obtained through this approach cannot be examined. For this reason, tests developed through this approach cannot be used to make inferences about levels of language *ability*.

The other approach also examines actual non-test communicative language use, in an attempt to identify the critical, or essential features of such language use. The features identified are of two types: the abilities required for successful communicative language use and the characteristics of the situation that determine the nature of the interaction between the language user, the context, and the discourse. These essential features become the basis for a framework describing communicative language abilities and language test method facets, which in turn guide the design and development of language test tasks. The primary concerns in this approach are with designing test tasks that engage the test taker in communicative language use, and with the construct validity of test scores. This approach is more demanding, in that it requires both a theoretical framework with which to begin, and a program of construct validation research. However this approach can provide empirical evidence for interpreting test scores as indicators of language abilities.

While these approaches are distinct in terms of how we design and develop language tests, and how we can interpret and use test scores, they do not necessarily lead to different types of language tests or test tasks. An integration of the two approaches would involve the analysis of test tasks developed through the 'real-life' approach, using a framework of language abilities and test method facets, along with the designing of a wide range of test tasks according to specifications of language abilities and test method facets, followed by a program of construct validation research.

There are pressing needs for language tests suitable for uses in making minimum competency decisions about foreign language learners and language teachers, and in the evaluation of foreign language teaching methods. These needs can best be met by the development of a set of 'common metric' tests that would yield scores that would be both independent of the objectives of specific language courses and comparable across a wide range of languages and language use contexts. Such tests would need to be based on criterion-referenced scales of language abilities, defined in terms of ordered levels, from zero to perfect. The development of such scales would involve a program of empirical research to determine both the number of intermediate levels on each scale and the applicability of such scales across different groups of language learners.

Given the complexities of both the language abilities we wish to measure and the facets of the procedures we must use to measure these abilities, along with the need for language tests that are usable, the challenges facing language testers are immense. However, we have a wide range of research approaches and analytic tools at our disposal, and the prospect of combining language testing research with other approaches to the investigation of language ability and language use is an exciting one, promising ever better understanding of these, and better, more useful authentic tests of communicative language ability.

Notes

1   As has been emphasized throughout this book, the question of how many component abilities there are, and how, if at all, they are related to each other, is essentially an empirical one. The specific component abilities included in the Bachman–Palmer scale are given here primarily for illustrative purposes, and not as a definitive model of language proficiency. Indeed, Bachman and Palmer's own research indicates that this particular configuration of components is only partially supported by empirical results.

2   I must acknowledge a comment by Roger Hawkey that first led me to begin thinking about personal characteristics as other than random error variance. At a language testing conference in Bangkok in 1986, if I remember correctly, at the beginning of his presentation, Roger said something like, 'Everything I studied in my Ph.D. dissertation, [1982] and that I'm going to talk about today is what Lyle Bachman calls "random error".'

Further reading

Examples of tests developed through the 'real-life' approach, along with discussions of issues related to this approach, can be found in Clark (1978a) and Hauptman *et al.* (1985). Discussions of the problems in defining 'communicative' or 'authentic' language tests can be found in Alderson and Hughes (1981), Hughes and Porter (1983), and *Language Testing* 2, No. 1 (June 1985). Popham (1978) provides a comprehensive treatment of the issues and procedures of criterion-referenced testing. A more technical discussion of these issues can be found in Berk (1984a).

Discussion questions

1.   Consider a situation in which language must be used to reach an understanding of a concept that is not quite the same in two different cultures. For example, how would a speaker of English and a speaker of German explain to each other the similarities and differences between 'world view' and 'Weltanschauung'? Discuss the language abilities involved in this interaction, and the features of the context that will determine what is said.

2.   Analyze the language abilities and contextual features involved in ordering a meal in a foreign culture and language.

3. What kind of test tasks might you employ to measure an individual's ability to successfully complete the tasks involved in questions 1 and 2 above?

4. Consider the scales of grammatical competence, vocabulary and cohesion, and sociolinguistic competence developed by Bachman and Palmer (pp. 326–8 above). Discuss appropriate testing methods for measuring these abilities in: (a) bilingual elementary school children; (b) college foreign language students, and (c) adult immigrants.

Bibliography

Adams, M. L. 1980. 'Five co-occurring factors in speaking proficiency' in Frith 1980: 1–6.

Adams, R. J., P. E. Griffin, and L. Martin. 1987. 'A latent trait method for measuring dimension in second language proficiency.' *Language Testing* 4,1:9–27.

Alderman, D. L. 1981. *Language Proficiency as a Moderator Variable in Testing Academic Aptitude.* TOEFL Research Report 10. Princeton, NJ: Educational Testing Service.

Alderman, D. L. and P. W. Holland. 1981. *Item Performance across Native Language Groups on the Test of English as a Foreign Language.* TOEFL Research Report, No. 9. Princeton, NJ: Educational Testing Service.

Alderson, J. C. 1979a. 'The cloze procedure and proficiency in English as a foreign language.' *TESOL Quarterly* 13,2:219–28.

Alderson, J. C. 1979b. 'The effect on the cloze test of changes in deletion frequency.' *Journal of Research in Reading* 2,2:108–19.

Alderson, J. 1980. 'Native and non-native performance on cloze tests.' *Language Learning* 30,2:219–23.

Alderson, J. C. 1981a. 'Introduction' in Alderson and Hughes 1981: 5–8.

Alderson, J. C. 1981b. 'Reaction to Morrow paper (3)' in Alderson and Hughes 1981: 45–54.

Alderson, J. C. 1981c. 'Report of the discussion on communicative language testing' in Alderson and Hughes 1981: 55–65.

Alderson, J. C. 1983. 'Response to Harrison: who needs jam?' in Hughes and Porter 1983: 87–92.

Alderson, J. C. 1988. 'New procedures for validating proficiency tests of ESP? Theory and practice.' *Language Testing* 5,2:220–32.

Alderson, J. C. and A. Hughes. (eds.) 1981. *Issues in Language Testing.* ELT Documents 111. London: The British Council.

Alderson, J. C. and A. H. Urquhart. 1983. 'The effect of student background discipline on comprehension: a pilot study' in Hughes and Porter 1983: 121–7.

Alderson, J. C. and A. H. Urquhart. 1985a. 'The effect of students' academic discipline on their performance on ESP reading tests.' *Language Testing* 2,2:192–204.

Alderson, J. C. and A. H. Urquhart. 1985b. 'This test is unfair: I'm not an economist' in Hauptman *et al.* 1985: 15–24.

Allen, J. P. B. and **A. Davies** (eds.) 1977. *Testing and Experimental Methods. The Edinburgh Course in Applied Linguistics*, Vol. 4. London: Oxford University Press.

Allen, M. J. and **W. M. Yen.** 1979. *Introduction to Measurement Theory.* Monterey, Calif.: Brooks/Cole.

Allen, P., E. Bialystok, J. Cummins, R. Mougeon, and **M. Swain.** 1982. *Development of Bilingual Proficiency: Interim Report on the First Year of Research.* Toronto, Ont.: The Ontario Institute for Studies in Education.

Allen, P., J. Cummins, R. Mougeon, and **M. Swain.** 1983. *Development of Bilingual Proficiency: Second Year Report.* Toronto, Ont.: The Ontario Institute for Studies in Education.

Allwright, R. L. 1980. 'Turns, topics and tasks: patterns of participation in language teaching and learning' in Larsen–Freeman 1980: 188–98.

Alwin, D. F. 1974. 'Approaches to the interpretation of relationships in the multitrait-multimethod matrix' in H. L. Costner (ed.): *Sociological Methodology 1973–1974.* San Francisco, Calif.: Jossey-Bass: 79–105.

American Council on the Teaching of Foreign Languages. 1986. *ACTFL Proficiency Guidelines.* New York: American Council on the Teaching of Foreign Languages.

American Psychological Association. 1974. *Standards for Educational and Psychological Testing.* Washington, DC: American Psychological Association.

American Psychological Association. 1985. *Standards for Educational and Psychological Testing.* Washington, DC: American Psychological Association.

Angoff, W. H. 1971. 'Scales, norms and equivalent scores' in Thorndike 1971: 508–600.

Associated Examining Board. 1987. *Test in English for Educational Purposes (TEEP).* Aldershot, Hampshire: Associated Examining Board.

Austin, J. L. 1962. *How to Do Things with Words.* Oxford: Clarendon Press.

Avison, W. R. 1978. 'Auxiliary theory and multitrait-multimethod validation: a review of two approaches.' *Applied Psychological Measurement* 2,3:433–9.

Bachman, L. F. 1981. 'Formative evaluation in ESP program development' in R. Mackay and J. D. Palmer (eds.): *Languages for Specific Purposes: Program Design and Evaluation.* Rowley, Mass.: Newbury House: 106–16.

Bachman, L. F. 1982. 'The trait structure of cloze test scores.' *TESOL Quarterly* 16,1:61–70.

Bachman, L. F. 1985. 'Performance on cloze tests with fixed-ratio and rational deletions.' *TESOL Quarterly* 19,3:535–56.

Bachman, L. F. 1986. 'The test of English as a foreign language as a measure of communicative competence' in Stansfield 1986b: 69–88.

Bachman, L. F. 1988. 'Problems in examining the validity of the ACTFL oral proficiency interview.' *Studies in Second Language Acquisition* 10,2:149–64.

Bachman, L. F. 1989a. 'Language testing–SLA interfaces' in R. B. Kaplan (ed.): *Annual Review of Applied Linguistics*, Vol. 9. New York: Cambridge University Press: 193–209.

Bachman, L. F. 1989b. 'The development and use of criterion-referenced tests of language proficiency in language program evaluation' in R. K. Johnson (ed.): *The Second Language Curriculum*. Cambridge University Press: 242–58.

Bachman, L. F. and J. L. D. Clark. 1987. 'The measurement of foreign/second language proficiency.' *Annals of the American Academy of Political and Social Science* 490:20–33.

Bachman, L. F., F. Davidson, and B. Lynch. 1988. 'Test method: the context for performance on language tests.' Paper presented at the Annual Meeting of the American Association for Applied Linguistics, New Orleans, December 1988.

Bachman, L. F., F. Davidson, B. Lynch, and K. Ryan. 1989. 'Content analysis and statistical modeling of EFL proficiency tests.' Paper presented at the 11th Annual Language Testing Research Colloquium, San Antonio, Texas, March 1989.

Bachman, L. F., F. Davidson, K. Ryan, and I. Choi 1989. *The Cambridge-TOEFL Comparability Study: Final Report*. Cambridge: University of Cambridge Local Examinations Syndicate.

Bachman, L. F., A. Kunnan, S. Vanniarajan, and B. Lynch. 1988. 'Task and ability analysis as a basis for examining content and construct comparability in two EFL proficiency test batteries.' *Language Testing* 5,2:128–59.

Bachman, L. F. and M. Mack. 1986. 'A causal analysis of learner characteristics and second-language proficiency.' Paper presented at the 1986 TESOL Convention, Anaheim, California.

Bachman, L. F., and A. S. Palmer 1979. 'Convergent and discriminant validation of oral language proficiency tests' in Silverstein 1979: 53–62.

Bachman, L. F. and A. S. Palmer. 1981a. 'The construct validation of the FSI oral interview.' *Language Learning* 31,1:67–86.

Bachman, L. F. and A. S. Palmer. 1981b. *Self-assessment of Communicative Competence in English*. Salt Lake City, Utah: Mimeograph.

Bachman, L. F. and A. S. Palmer. 1982a. 'The construct validation of some components of communicative proficiency.' *TESOL Quarterly* 16,4:449–65.

Bachman, L. F. and A. S. Palmer. 1982b. 'A scoring format for rating components of communicative proficiency in speaking.' Paper presented at the Pre-conference on Oral Proficiency Assessment, Georgetown University, Washington, DC.

Bachman, L. F. and A. S. Palmer. 1982c. *Test of Communicative Competence in English: Multiple-Choice Method*. Salt Lake City, Utah: Mimeograph.

Bachman, L. F. and A. S. Palmer. 1982d. *Test of Communicative Competence in English: Writing Sample Method.* Salt Lake City, Utah: Mimeograph.

Bachman, L. F. and A. S. Palmer. 1983a. *Oral Interview Test of Communicative Proficiency in English.* Urbana, Ill.: Photo-offset.

Bachman, L. F. and A. S. Palmer. 1983b. 'The relationship between background and learner variables and aspects of communicative proficiency.' Paper presented at the 1983 TESOL Convention, Toronto.

Bachman, L. F. and A. S. Palmer. 1988. 'The construct validation of self-ratings of communicative language ability.' Paper presented at the 10th Annual Language Testing Research Colloquium, Urbana, Illinois, March 1988.

Bachman, L. F. and S. J. Savignon. 1986. 'The evaluation of communicative language proficiency: a critique of the ACTFL oral interview.' *The Modern Language Journal* 70,4:380–90.

Bailey, K. M. 1985. 'If I had known what I know now: performance testing of foreign teaching assistants' in Hauptman *et al.* 1985: 153–80.

Bailey, K. M., T. L. Dale, and R. T. Clifford. (eds.) 1987. *Language Testing Research: Selected Papers from the 1986 Colloquium.* Monterey, Calif.: Defense Language Institute.

Baker, E. L. 1974a. 'Beyond objectives: domain-referenced tests for evaluation and instructional improvement.' *Educational Technology* 10–16.

Baker, E. L. 1974b. 'Formative evaluation of instruction' in Popham 1974a: 533–85.

Beretta, A. 1986a. 'Program-fair language teaching evaluation.' *TESOL Quarterly* 20,3:431–44.

Beretta, A. 1986b. 'Toward a methodology of ESL program evaluation.' *TESOL Quarterly* 20,1:144–55.

Berk, R. A. 1980a. 'A consumer's guide to criterion-referenced reliability.' *Journal of Educational Measurement* 17, 323–49.

Berk, R. A. (ed.) 1980b. *Criterion-Referenced Measurement: The State of the Art.* Baltimore, Md.: Johns Hopkins University Press.

Berk, R. A. 1980c. 'Estimation of test length for domain-referenced reading comprehension tests.' *Journal of Experimental Education* 48:188–93.

Berk, R. A. (ed.) 1984a. *A Guide to Criterion-Referenced Test Construction.* Baltimore, Md.: The Johns Hopkins University Press.

Berk, R. A. 1984b. 'Introduction' in Berk 1984a:1–7.

Berk, R. A. 1984c. 'Selecting the index of reliability' in Berk 1984a: 231–66.

Berkowitz, S. and B. Taylor. 1981. 'The effects of text types and familiarity on the nature of information recalled by readers' in M. L. Kamil (ed.): *Directions in Reading: Research and Instruction.* Washington, DC: National Reading Conference: 157–61.

Besnier, N. 1986. 'Register as a sociolinguistic unit: defining formality' in J. Connor–Linton, J. Hall, and M. McGinnis (eds.): *Social and Cognitive*

Perspectives on Language. Southern California Occasional Papers in Linguistics 11. Los Angeles, Calif.: University of Southern California: 25–63.

Birenbaum, M. and K. K. Tatsuoka. 1980. 'The use of information from wrong responses in measuring students' achievement.' Office of Naval Research, *Research Report* 80–1. Urbana, Ill.: University of Illinois, Computer-based Education Research Laboratory.

Birenbaum, M. and K. K. Tatsuoka. 1983. 'The effect of a scoring system based on the algorithm underlying students' response patterns on the dimensionality of achievement test data of the problem solving type.' *Journal of Educational Measurement* 20,1:17–26.

Blalock, H. M. 1964. *Causal Inferences in Nonexperimental Research.* Chapel Hill, NC: University of North Carolina Press.

Bolus, R. E., F. B. Hinofotis, and K. M. Bailey. 1982. 'An introduction to generalizability theory in second language research.' *Language Learning* 32,2:245–58.

Bormuth, J. R. 1964. 'Experimental applications of cloze tests.' *International Reading Association Conference Proceedings* 9: 303–6.

Boruch, R. F., J. D. Larkin, L. Wolins, and A. C. MacKinney. 1970. 'Alternative methods of analysis: multitrait-multimethod data.' *Educational and Psychological Measurement* 30: 833–53.

Bowen, J. D. 1978. 'The effect of environment on proficiency testing.' *Workpapers in Teaching English as a Second Language* XII. University of California at Los Angeles: 57–61.

Brennan, R. L. 1981. *Some Statistical Procedures for Domain-Referenced Testing: A Handbook for Practitioners. ACT Technical Bulletin* 38. Iowa City, Iowa: The American College Testing Program.

Brennan, R. L. 1983. *Elements of Generalizability Theory.* Iowa City, Iowa: The American College Testing Program.

Brennan, R. L. 1984. 'Estimating the dependability of scores' in Berk 1984a: 292–334.

Brennan, R. L. and M. Kane. 1977. 'An index of dependability for mastery tests.' *Journal of Educational Measurement* 14:277–89.

Brière, E. 1968. 'Testing ESL among Navajo children' in Upshur and Fata 1968: 11–21.

Brière, E. 1973. 'Cross cultural biases in language testing' in Oller and Richards 1973: 214–27.

Brière, E. and R. H. Brown. 1971. 'Norming tests of ESL among Amerindian children.' *TESOL Quarterly* 5,4:327–34.

Brière, E. J. and F. B. Hinofotis. (eds.) 1979a. *Concepts in Language Testing: Some Recent Studies.* Washington, DC: TESOL.

Brière, E. J. and F. B. Hinofotis. 1979b. 'Cloze test cutoff points for placing students in ESL classes' in Brière and Hinofotis 1979a: 12–20.

Brindley, G. P. 1986. *The Assessment of Second Language Proficiency: Issues and Approaches.* NSCR Research Series. Adelaide: National Curriculum Resource Centre.

Brindley, G. P. and **K. N. Singh.** 1982. 'The use of second language learning research in ESL proficiency assessment.' *Australian Review of Applied Linguistics* 5,1:84–111.

British Council and the **University of Cambridge Local Examinations Syndicate.** n.d. *English Language Testing Service: Specimen Materials Booklet.* London: The British Council.

Brown, G. 1989. 'Making sense: the interaction of linguistic expression and contextual information.' *Applied Linguistics* 10, 1:97–108.

Brown, G. and **G. Yule.** 1983. *Discourse Analysis.* Cambridge: Cambridge University Press.

Brown, H. D. 1987. *Principles of Learning and Teaching.* Second edition. Englewood Cliffs, NJ: Prentice-Hall.

Brown, J. 1985. 'An introduction to the uses of facet theory' in Canter 1985a: 17–57.

Brown, J. D. 1989. 'Short-cut estimates of criterion-referenced test reliability.' Paper presented at the 11th Annual Language Testing Research Colloquium, San Antonio, March 1989.

Brown, W. 1910. 'Some experimental results in the correlation of mental abilities.' *British Journal of Psychology* 3: 296–322.

Brütsch, S. M. 1979. 'Convergent-discriminant Validation of Prospective Teacher Proficiency in Oral and Written French by Means of the MLA Cooperative Language Proficiency Test, French Direct Proficiency Tests for Teachers (TOP and TWP), and Self-ratings.' Unpublished Ph.D. dissertation, University of Minnesota.

Burt, M. K., H. C. Dulay, and **E. Hernández-Chávez.** 1975. *Bilingual Syntax Measure.* New York: Harcourt Brace Jovanovich.

Campbell, D. T. 1960. 'Recommendations for APA test standards regarding construct, trait, or discriminant validity.' *American Psychologist* 15:546–53.

Campbell, D. T. and **D. W. Fiske.** 1959. 'Convergent and discriminant validation by the multitrait-multimethod matrix.' *Psychological Bulletin* 56:81–105.

Campbell, D. T. and **J. C. Stanley.** 1972. *Experimental and Quasi-Experimental Designs in Research.* New York: Harcourt Brace Jovanovich.

Canale, M. 1983. 'On some dimensions of language proficiency' in Oller 1983b: 333–42.

Canale, M. 1984. 'Testing in a communicative approach' in Gilbert A. Jarvis (ed.): *The Challenge for Excellence in Foreign Language Education.* Middlebury, Vt.: The Northeast Conference Organization: 79–92.

Canale, M. 1988. 'The measurement of communicative competence' in R. B. Kaplan (ed.): *Annual Review of Applied Linguistics.* Vol. 8, 1987: 67–84.

Canale, M. and **M. Swain.** 1980. 'Theoretical bases of communicative approaches to second language teaching and testing.' *Applied Linguistics* 1,1:1–47.

Candlin, C. N. 1986. 'Explaining communicative competence limits of testability?' in Stansfield 1986b: 38–57.

Canter, D. 1983. 'The potential of facet theory for applied social psychology.' *Quality and Quantity* 17:35–67.

Canter, D. (ed.) 1985a. *Facet Theory: Approaches to Social Research*. New York: Springer–Verlag.

Canter, D. 1985b. 'Editor's introduction: the road to Jerusalem' in Canter 1985a: 1–13.

Canter, D. 1985c. 'How to be a facet researcher' in Canter 1985a: 265–75.

Carrell, P. L. 1982. 'Cohesion is not coherence.' *TESOL Quarterly* 16:479–88.

Carrell, P. L. 1986. 'A view of the written text as communicative interaction: implications for reading in a second language' in J. Devine, P. Carrell, and D. Eskey (eds.): *Research in Reading ESL*. Washington, DC: TESOL.

Carrell, P. 1987. 'Content and formal schemata in ESL reading.' *TESOL Quarterly* 21,3:461–81.

Carroll, B. J. 1980. *Testing Communicative Performance*. London: Pergamon Institute of English.

Carroll, B. J. 1985. 'Second language performance testing for university and profession contexts' in Hauptman *et al.* 1985: 73–88.

Carroll, J. B. 1941. 'A factor analysis of verbal abilities.' *Psychometrika* 6:279–307.

Carroll, J. B. 1958. 'A factor analysis of two foreign language aptitude batteries.' *Journal of General Psychology* 59:3–19.

Carroll, J. B. 1961a. 'Fundamental considerations in testing for English language proficiency of foreign students' in *Testing the English Proficiency of Foreign Students*. Washington, DC: Center for Applied Linguistics: 30–40.

Carroll, J. B. 1961b. 'The nature of data, or how to choose a correlation coefficient.' *Psychometrika* 26,4:347–72.

Carroll, J. B. 1964. *Language and Thought*. Englewood Cliffs, NJ: Prentice–Hall.

Carroll, J. B. 1967. 'The foreign language attainments of language majors in the senior year: a survey conducted in US colleges and universities.' Cambridge, Mass.: Harvard Graduate School of Education. ERIC ED 013 343.

Carroll, J. B. 1968. 'The psychology of language testing' in Davies 1968a: 46–69.

Carroll, J. B. 1973. 'Foreign language testing: will the persistent problems persist?' in M. C. O'Brien (ed.): *Testing in Second Language Teaching: New Dimensions*. Dublin: ATESOL-Ireland: 6–17.

Carroll, J. B. 1979. 'Psychometric approaches to the study of language abilities' in C. J. Fillmore, D. Kempler, and S-Y. Wang (eds.): *Individual*

Differences in Language Ability and Language Behavior. New York: Academic Press: 13–51.

Carroll, J. B. 1980. 'Measurement of abilities constructs' in US Office of Personnel Management and Educational Testing Service, *Construct Validity in Psychological Measurement: Proceedings of a Colloquium on Theory and Application in Education and Employment.* Princeton, NJ: Educational Testing Service: 23–41.

Carroll, J. B. 1981. 'Twenty-five years of research on foreign language aptitude' in K. C. Diller (ed.): *Individual Differences and Universals in Language Learning Aptitude.* Rowley, Mass.: Newbury House: 83–118.

Carroll, J. B. 1983a. 'Psychometric theory and language testing' in Oller 1983b: 80–107.

Carroll, J. B. 1983b. 'The difficulty of a test and its factor composition revisited' in H. Wainer and S. Messick (eds.): *Principles of Modern Psychological Measurement: A Festschrift for Frederic M. Lord.* Hillsdale, NJ: Lawrence Erlbaum Associates: 257–82.

Carroll, J. B. 1983c. 'Studying individual differences in cognitive abilities: through and beyond factor analysis' in R. F. Dillon and R. R. Schmeck (eds.): *Individual Differences in Cognition.* Vol. 1. New York: Academic Press: 1–33.

Carroll, J. B. 1985a. 'Exploratory factor analysis: a tutorial' in D. K. Detterman (ed.): *Current Topics in Human Intelligence: Vol. 1, Research Methodology.* Norwood, NJ: Ablex: 25–58.

Carroll, J. B. 1985b. 'LT + 25, and beyond? Comments.' *Language Testing* 3,2:123–9.

Carroll, J. B. 1987a. 'New perspectives in the analysis of abilities' in R. R. Ronning, J. A. Glover, J. C. Conoley, and J. C. Witt (eds.): *The Influence of Cognitive Psychology on Testing.* Hillsdale, NJ: Lawrence Erlbaum Associates: 267–84.

Carroll, J. B. 1987b. 'Measurement and educational psychology: beginnings and repercussions' in J. A. Glover and R. R. Ronning (eds.): *Historical Foundations of Educational Psychology.* New York: Plenum: 89–106.

Carroll, J. B., A. S. Carton, and C. P. Wilds. 1959. 'An investigation of cloze items in the measurement of achievement in foreign languages.' Cambridge, Mass.: Harvard Graduate School of Education. ERIC ED 021 513.

Carroll, J. B. and S. M. Sapon. 1959. *Modern Language Aptitude Test.* New York: Psychological Corporation.

Cartier, F. 1968. 'Criterion-referenced testing of language skills.' *TESOL Quarterly* 2,1:27–32.

Carton, A. S. and E. Kaya-Carton. 1986. 'Multidimensionality of foreign language reading proficiency: preliminary considerations in assessment.' *Foreign Language Annals* 19:95–102.

Cattell, R. B. 1964. 'Validity and reliability: a proposed more basic set of concepts.' *Journal of Educational Psychology* 55:1–22.

Caulfield, J. and W. C. Smith. 1981. 'The reduced redundancy test and the cloze procedure as measures of global language proficiency.' *Modern Language Journal* 65:54–8.

Chacevych, A., C. Delva, F. Houle, R. Moon, and J. A. Upshur. 1982. 'Language testing and content predictability.' Paper presented at the Third Annual Language Testing Research Colloquium, Honolulu, Hawaii, May 1982.

Chapelle, C. 1988. 'Field independence: a source of language test variance?' *Language Testing* 5,1:62–82.

Chapelle, C. and J. Jamieson. 1986. 'Computer-assisted language learning as a predictor of success in acquiring English as a second language.' *TESOL Quarterly* 20,1:27–46.

Chapelle, C. and C. Roberts. 1986. 'Ambiguity tolerance and field dependence as predictors of proficiency in English as a second language.' *Language Learning* 36:27–45.

Chaudron, C. 1988. *Second Language Classrooms: Research on Teaching and Learning.* Cambridge: Cambridge University Press.

Chavanachart, P. 1984. 'The Effect of Explicitly and Implicitly Presented Rhetorical Functions on the Comprehension of Scientific Discourse: A Multitrait-multimethod Construct Validation Study of EST Reading Comprehension.' Unpublished Ph.D. dissertation, University of Illinois.

Chavez-Oller, M. A., T. Chihara, K. A. Weaver, and J. W. Oller. 1985. 'When are cloze items sensitive to constraints across sentences?' *Language Learning* 35:181–206.

Chen, Z. and G. Henning. 1985. 'Linguistic and cultural bias in language proficiency tests.' *Language Testing* 2,2:155–63.

Cherry, C. 1957. *On Human Communication.* Cambridge, Mass.: MIT Press.

Chihara, T., J. W. Oller, K. A. Weaver, and M. A. Chavez-Oller. 1977. 'Are cloze items sensitive to constraints across sentences?' *Language Learning* 27,1:63–73.

Chomsky, N. 1965. *Aspects of the Theory of Syntax.* Cambridge, Mass.: MIT Press.

Clahsen, H. 1985. 'Profiling second language development: a procedure for assessing L2 proficiency' in Hyltenstam and Pienemann 1985: 283–331.

Clark, H. H. and E. V. Clark. 1977. *Psychology and Language.* New York: Harcourt Brace Jovanovich.

Clark, J. L. D. 1972. *Foreign Language Testing: Theory and Practice.* Philadelphia, Pa.: Center for Curriculum Development, Inc.

Clark, J. L. D. 1975. 'Theoretical and technical considerations in oral proficiency testing' in Jones and Spolsky 1975: 10–24.

Clark, J. L. D. (ed.) 1978a. *Direct Testing of Speaking Proficiency: Theory and Application.* Princeton, NJ: Educational Testing Service.

Clark, J. L. D. 1978b. 'Interview testing research at Educational Testing Service' in Clark 1978a: 211–28.

Clark, J. L. D. 1979. 'Direct vs. semi-direct tests of speaking ability' in Brière and Hinofotis 1979a: 35–49.

Clark, J. L. D. 1980. 'Toward a common measure of speaking proficiency' in Frith 1980: 15–26.

Clark, J. L. D. 1982. 'Measurement considerations in language attrition research' in Lambert and Freed 1982: 138–52.

Clark, J. L. D. and R. T. Clifford. 1988. 'The FSI/ILR/ACTFL Proficiency scales and testing techniques: development, current status, and needed research' in Valdman 1988: 129–47.

Clark, J. L. D. and J. Lett. 1988. 'A research agenda' in Lowe and Stansfield 1988: 53–82.

Clark, J. L. D. and S. Swinton. 1980. *The Test of Spoken English as a Measure of Communicative Ability in English-Medium Instructional Settings*. Princeton, NJ: Educational Testing Service.

Cleary, T. A. 1968. 'Test bias: prediction of grades of Negro and white students in integrated colleges.' *Journal of Educational Measurement* 5:115–24.

Clifford, R. T. 1978. 'Reliability and validity of language aspects contributing to oral proficiency of prospective teachers of German' in Clark 1978a: 191–209.

Clifford, R. T. 1980. 'Foreign Service Institute factor scores and global ratings' in Frith 1980: 27–30.

Clifford, R. T. 1981. 'Convergent and discriminant validation of integrated and unitary language skills: the need for a research model' in Palmer *et al.* 1981: 62–70.

Cohen, A. D. 1980. *Testing Language Ability in the Classroom*. Rowley, Mass.: Newbury House.

Cohen, A. D. 1984. 'On taking tests: what the students report.' *Language Testing* 1,1:70–81.

Cohen, A. D. 1986. 'Comments on Grotjahn: test validation and cognitive psychology: some methodological considerations.' *Language Testing* 3,2:186–7.

Cohen, A. D. 1987. 'Student processing of feedback on their compositions' in A. Wenden and J. Rubin (eds.): *Learner Strategies in Language Learning*. Englewood Cliffs, NJ: Prentice-Hall.

Cohen, A. D. Forthcoming. 'English testing in Brazil: problems in using summary tasks' in C. Hill and K. Parry (eds.): *From Testing to Assessment: English as an International Language*. London: Longman.

Cohen, A. D. and E. Aphek. 1981. 'Easifying second language learning.' *Studies in Second Language Acquisition* 3,2:221–35.

Cohen, A. D. and E. Olshtain. 1980. 'Developing a measure of socio-cultural competence: the case of apology.' *Language Learning* 31:113–34.

Cole, N. S. 1973. 'Bias in selection.' *Journal of Educational Measurement* 10:237–55.

Cole, N. S. and P. A. Moss. 1989. 'Bias in test use' in Linn 1989: 201–19.

Condon, E. C. 1975. 'The cultural context of language testing' in Palmer and Spolsky 1975: 205–17.

Cook, L. and R. K. Hambleton. 1978. 'Application of latent trait models to the development of norm-referenced and criterion-referenced tests.' *Laboratory of Psychometric and Evaluative Research Report No. 72.* Amherst, Mass.: University of Massachusetts, School of Education.

Cooper, R. L. 1968. 'An elaborated language testing model' in Upshur and Fata 1968: 57–72.

Cooper, R. L. 1986. 'Panel discussion: the next 25 years?' *Language Testing* 3,2:239–40.

Corder, S. P. 1983. 'Strategies of communication' in Færch and Kasper 1983a: 15–19.

Coulmas, F. (ed.) 1981a. *A Festschrift for Native Speaker.* The Hague: Mouton.

Coulmas, F. (ed.) 1981b. *Conversational Routine. Explorations in Standardized Communication Situations and Pre-patterned Speech.* The Hague: Mouton.

Coulthard, M. 1977. *An Introduction to Discourse Analysis.* London: Longman.

Courchene, R. J. and J. I. de Bagheera. 1985 'A theoretical framework for the development of performance tests' in Hauptman *et al.* 1985: 45–58.

Crick, J. E. and R. L. Brennan. 1983. *Manual for GENOVA: a GENeralized analysis Of VAriance system* (ACT Technical Bulletin No. 43). Iowa City, Ia.: American College Testing Program.

Criper, C. and A. Davies. 1988. *ELTS Validation Project Report.* London: The British Council and the University of Cambridge Local Examinations Syndicate.

Cronbach, L. J. 1951. 'Coefficient alpha and the internal structure of tests.' *Psychometrika* 16,292–334.

Cronbach, L. J. 1971. 'Validity' in Thorndike 1971: 443–597.

Cronbach, L. J. 1980. 'Validity on parole: how can we go straight?' *New Directions for Testing and Measurement* 5:99–108.

Cronbach, L. J. 1984. *Essentials of Psychological Testing.* Fourth edition. New York: Harper and Row.

Cronbach, L. J. 1988. 'Construct validation after thirty years' in Robert L. Linn (ed.): *Intelligence: Measurement, Theory, and Public Policy.* Urbana, Ill.: University of Illinois Press: 147–71.

Cronbach, L. J., G. C. Gleser, H. Nanda, and N. Rajaratnam. 1972. *The Dependability of Behavioral Measurements: Theory of Generalizability for Scores and Profiles.* New York: John Wiley.

Cronbach, L. J. and P. E. Meehl. 1955. 'Construct validity in psychological tests.' *Psychological Bulletin* 52,4:281–302.

Cronbach, L. J., N. Rajaratnam, and G. C. Gleser. 1963. 'Theory of generalizability: a liberalization of reliability theory.' *British Journal of Statistical Psychology* 16, 137–63.

Culhane, T., C. Klein-Braley, and D. K. Stevenson. (eds.) 1981. *Practice and Problems in Language Testing 4. Occasional Papers,* No. 26. Colchester, Essex: Department of Language and Linguistics, University of Essex.

Culhane, T., C. Klein-Braley, and D. K. Stevenson. (eds.) 1984. *Practice and*

Problems in Language Testing 7. Occasional Papers, No. 29. Essex: Department of Language and Linguistics, University of Essex.

Cummins, J. P. 1980a. 'The cross-lingual dimensions of language proficiency: implications for bilingual education and the optimal age question.' *TESOL Quarterly* 14:175–87.

Cummins, J. P. 1980b. 'Psychological assessment of immigrant children: logic or intuition.' *Journal of Multilingual and Multicultural Development* 1:97–111.

Cummins, J. P. 1983. 'Language proficiency and academic achievement' in Oller 1983b: 108–26.

Cziko, G. A. 1978. 'Differences in first and second language reading: the use of syntactic, semantic, and discourse constraints.' *Canadian Modern Language Review* 39:473–89.

Cziko, G. A. 1981. 'Psychometric and edumetric approaches to language testing.' *Applied Linguistics* 2, 1:27–43.

Cziko, G. A. 1982. 'Improving the psychometric, criterion-referenced, and practical qualities of integrative language tests.' *TESOL Quarterly* 16,3:367–79.

Cziko, G. A. 1984. 'Some problems with empirically-based models of communicative competence.' *Applied Linguistics* 5,1:23–38.

Cziko, G. A. and N-H. J. Lin. 1984. 'The construction and analysis of short scales of language proficiency: classical psychometric, latent trait, and nonparametric approaches.' *TESOL Quarterly* 18,4:627–47.

Dandonoli, P. 1987. 'ACTFL's current research in proficiency testing' in H. Byrnes and M. Canale (eds.): *Defining and Developing Proficiency: Guidelines, Implementations, and Concepts*. Lincolnwood, Ill.: National Textbook Company: 75–96.

Darnell, D. K. 1970. 'Clozentropy: a procedure for testing English language proficiency of foreign students.' *Speech Monographs* 37:36–46.

Davidson, F. 1988. 'An Exploratory Modeling Survey of the Trait Structures of Some Existing Language Test Datasets.' Unpublished Ph.D. dissertation. Department of Applied Linguistics, University of California at Los Angeles.

Davidson, F. and G. Henning. 1985. 'A self-rating scale of English proficiency: Rasch scalar analysis of items and rating categories.' *Language Testing* 2,2:164–79.

Davidson, F., T. Hudson, and B. Lynch. 1985. 'Language testing: operationalization in classroom measurement and L2 research' in M. Celce-Murcia (ed.): *Beyond Basics: Issues and Research in TESOL*. Rowley, Mass.: Newbury House: 137–52.

Davies, A. (ed.) 1968a. *Language Testing Symposium. A Psycholinguistic Perspective*. London: Oxford University Press.

Davies, A. 1968b. 'Introduction' in Davies 1968a: 1–18.

Davies, A. 1977. 'The construction of language tests' in Allen and Davies 1977: 38–194.

Davies, A. 1984. 'Validating three tests of English language proficiency.' *Language Testing* 1,1:50–69.

Day, R. R. 1984. 'Student participation in the ESL classroom, or some imperfections in practice.' *Language Learning* 7:78–93.

Day, R. R. 1985. 'The use of the target language in context and second language proficiency' in S. M. Gass and C. G. Madden (eds.): *Input in Second Language Acquisition*. Rowley, Mass.: Newbury House: 257–71.

Dickson, P., C. Boyce, B. Lee, M. Portal, and M. Smith. 1985. *Foreign Language Performance in Schools: Report on 1983 Survey of French, German and Spanish*. London: Department of Education and Science.

Dickson, P., C. Boyce, B. Lee, M. Portal, and M. Smith. 1986. *Foreign Language Performance in Schools: Report on 1984 Survey of French*. London: Department of Education and Science.

Douglas, D. 1986. 'Communicative competence and tests of oral skills' in Stansfield 1986b: 156–74.

Douglas, D. and L. Selinker. 1985. 'Principles for language tests within the "discourse domains" theory of interlanguage: research, test construction and interpretation.' *Language Testing* 2,2:205–26.

Duran, R. P. 1989. 'Testing linguistic minorities' in Linn 1989: 573–87.

Duran, R. P., M. Canale, J. Penfield, C. W. Stansfield, and J. Liskin-Gasparro. 1985. *TOEFL from a Communicative Viewpoint on Language Proficiency: A Working Paper*. TOEFL Research Report 17. Princeton, NJ: Educational Testing Service.

Ebel, R. L. 1964. 'The social consequences of educational testing' in *Proceedings of the 1963 Invitational Conference on Testing Problems*. Princeton, NJ: Educational Testing Service: 130–43.

Ebel, R. L. 1979. *Essentials of Educational Measurement*. Third edition. Englewood Cliffs, NJ: Prentice-Hall.

Educational Testing Service. 1985. *Guide to SPEAK*. Princeton, NJ: Educational Testing Service.

Eisner, E. W. 1985. *The Educational Imagination*. Second edition. New York: Macmillan.

Erickson, M. and J. Molloy. 1983. 'ESP test development for engineering students' in Oller 1983b: 280–8.

Færch, C. and G. Kasper. 1983a. *Strategies in Interlanguage Communication*. London: Longman.

Færch, C. and G. Kasper. 1983b. 'Plans and strategies in foreign language communication' in Færch and Kasper 1983a: 20–60.

Færch, C. and G. Kasper. 1984. 'Two ways of defining communication strategies.' *Language Learning* 34,1:45–63.

Farhady, H. 1980. 'Justification, Development, and Validation of Functional Language Tests.' Unpublished Ph.D. dissertation, University of California at Los Angeles.

Farhady, H. 1982. 'Measures of language proficiency from the learner's perspective.' *TESOL Quarterly* 16,1:43–59.

Farhady, H. 1983. 'New directions for ESL proficiency testing' in Oller 1983b: 253–68.

Feldt, L. S. and **R. L. Brennan.** 1989. 'Reliability' in Linn 1989: 105–46.

Finegan, E. and **N. Besnier.** 1988. *Language: An Introduction to Its Structure and Use.* San Diego, Calif.: Harcourt Brace Jovanovich.

Firth, J. R. 1957. 'Personality and language in society' in J. R. Firth: *Papers in Linguistics: 1934–1951.* London: Oxford University Press: 177–89.

Fischer, R. A. 1981. 'Towards a practical model of a communicative competence testing program' in T. Culhane *et al.* 1981: 35–47.

Flanagan, J. C. 1951. 'Units, scores and norms' in E. F. Lindquist (ed.): *Educational Measurement.* Washington, DC: American Council on Education: 695–763.

Flaugher, R. L. 1976. 'The new definitions of test fairness in selection: developments and implications' in W. A. Mehrens (ed.): *Readings in Measurement and Evaluation in Education and Psychology.* New York: Holt, Rinehart and Winston: 359–67.

Fok, A. C. Y. 1985. 'Language proficiency and related factors' in Lee *et al.* 1985: 127–36.

Foreign Service Institute. 1968. *Absolute Language Proficiency Ratings.* Washington, DC: Foreign Service Institute.

Fouly, K. A. 1985. 'A Confirmatory Multivariate Study of the Nature of Second Language Proficiency and its Relationship to Learner Variables.' Unpublished Ph.D. dissertation, University of Illinois.

Franco, R. B. 1978. 'Direct testing of speaking skills in a criterion-referenced mode' in Clark 1978a: 41–64.

Fraser, B. and **W. Nolan.** 1981. 'The association of deference with linguistic form.' *International Journal of the Sociology of Language* 27:93–109.

Freed, B. F. 1987. 'Issues in establishing and maintaining a language proficiency requirement' in Valdman 1987: 263–73.

Frith, J. R. (ed.) 1980. *Measuring Spoken Language Proficiency.* Washington, DC: Georgetown University Press.

Fröhlich, M., N. Spada, and **P. Allen.** 1985. 'Differences in the communicative orientation of L2 classrooms.' *TESOL Quarterly* 19:27–57.

Gardner, R. C. 1982. 'Social factors in language retention' in Lambert and Freed 1982: 24–43.

Gardner, R. C. 1983. 'Learning another language: a true social psychological experiment.' *Journal of Language and Social Psychology* 2, 3, and 4:219–39.

Gardner, R. C., R. N. Lalonde, and **J. MacPherson.** 1985. 'Social factors in second language attrition.' *Language Learning* 35,4:519–40.

Gardner, R. C., R. N. Lalonde, and **R. Moorcroft.** 1985. 'The role of attitudes and motivation in second language learning: correlational and experimental considerations.' *Language Learning* 35,2:207–27.

Gardner, R. C., R. N. Lalonde, and R. Pierson. 1983. 'The socio-educational model of second language acquisition: an investigation using LISREL causal modeling.' *Journal of Language and Social Psychology* 2,1:1–15.

Gardner, R. C. and W. E. Lambert. 1972. *Attitudes and Motivation in Second Language Learning.* Rowley, Mass.: Newbury House.

Garrett, N. 1980. 'In search of interlanguage: a study of second-language acquisition of German syntax.' Unpublished Ph.D. dissertation, University of Illinois at Urbana-Champaign.

Genesee, F., G. R. Tucker, and W. E. Lambert. 1975. 'Communication skills of bilingual children.' *Child Development* 46:1010–14.

Glaser, R. 1963. 'Instructional technology and the measurement of learning outcomes: some questions.' *American Psychologist* 18:519–21.

Glaser, R. and D. J. Klaus. 1962. 'Proficiency measurement: assessing human performance' in R. M. Gagne (ed.): *Psychological Principles in System Development.* New York: Holt, Rinehart, and Winston: 419–74.

Glaser, R. and A. J. Nitko. 1971. 'Measurement in learning and instruction' in Thorndike 1971: 625–70.

Glass, G. V. 1978. 'Standards and criteria.' *Journal of Educational Measurement* 15:237–61.

Gleser, G. C., L. J. Cronbach, and N. Rajaratnam. 1965. 'Generalizability of scores influenced by multiple sources of variance.' *Psychometrika* 30,395–418.

Gorman, T. P. 1986. *The Framework for the Assessment of Language.* Windsor: NFER-Nelson.

Gorman, T. P., J. White, and G. Brooks. 1986. *Language Performance in Schools: Review of Language Monitoring, 1979–83.* London: Department of Education and Science.

Gradman, H. L. and B. Spolsky. 1975. 'Reduced redundancy testing: a progress report' in Jones and Spolsky 1975: 59–66.

Greenbaum, S. 1985. *The English Language Today.* Oxford: Pergamon.

Grice, H. P. 1975. 'Logic and conversation' in P. Cole and J. Morgan (eds.): *Syntax and Semantics: Speech Acts,* Vol. 3. New York: Academic Press: 41–58.

Griffin, P. E. 1985. 'The use of latent trait models in the calibration of tests of spoken language in large-scale selection-placement programs' in Lee *et al.* 1985: 149–61.

Griffin, P. E., R. J. Adams, L. Martin, and B. Tomlinson. 1988. 'An algorithmic approach to prescriptive assessment in English as a second language.' *Language Testing* 5,1:1–18.

Gronlund, N. E. 1985. *Measurement and Evaluation in Teaching.* Fifth edition. New York: Macmillan.

Grotjahn, R. 1986. 'Test validation and cognitive psychology: some methodological considerations.' *Language Testing* 3,2:159–85.

Guilford, J. P. 1954. *Psychometric Methods.* Second edition. New York: McGraw-Hill.

Guilford, J. P. and **B. Fruchter.** 1978. *Fundamental Statistics in Psychology and Education.* Sixth edition. New York: McGraw-Hill.
Gulliksen, H. 1950. *Theory of Mental Tests.* New York: John Wiley.
Guttman, L. 1945. 'A basis for analyzing test-retest reliability.' *Psychometrika* 10,4:255–81.
Guttman, L. 1953. 'Reliability formulas that do not assume experimental independence.' *Psychometrika* 18,3:225–39.
Guttman, L. 1970. 'Integration of test design and analysis' in *Proceedings of the 1969 Invitational Conference on Testing Problems.* Princeton, NJ: Educational Testing Service: 53–65.
Guttman, L. 1980. 'Integration of test design and analysis: status in 1979.' *Directions for Testing and Measurement* 5:93–98.

Hale, G. 1988. 'Student major field and text content: interactive effects on reading comprehension in the Test of English as a Foreign Language.' *Language Testing* 5,1:49–61.
Hale, G. A., C. W. Stansfield, and **R. P. Duran.** 1984. *Summaries of Studies Involving the Test of English as a Foreign Language, 1963–1982.* TOEFL Research Report 16. Princeton, NJ: Educational Testing Service.
Haley, J. 1963. *Strategies of Psychotherapy.* New York: Grune and Stratton.
Halliday, M. A. K. 1973. 'Relevant models of language' in M. A. K. Halliday: *Explorations in the Functions of Language.* New York: Elsevier North-Holland.
Halliday, M. A. K. 1976. 'The form of a functional grammar' in G. Kress (ed.): *Halliday: System and Function in Language.* Oxford: Oxford University Press.
Halliday, M. A. K. and **R. Hasan.** 1976. *Cohesion in English.* London: Longman.
Halliday, M. A. K., A. McIntosh, and **P. Strevens.** 1964. *The Linguistic Sciences and Language Teaching.* Bloomington, Ind.: Indiana University Press.
Hambleton, R. K. 1977. 'Contributions to criterion-referenced test theory: on the uses of item characteristic curves and related concepts.' *Laboratory of Psychometric and Evaluative Research Report No. 51.* Amherst, Mass.: University of Massachusetts, School of Education.
Hambleton, R. K. 1984. 'Validating the test scores' in Berk 1984a: 199–230.
Hambleton, R. K. 1989. 'Principles and selected applications of item response theory' in Linn 1989: 147–200.
Hambleton, R. K. and **L. L. Cook.** 1977. 'Latent trait models and their use in the analysis of educational test data.' *Journal of Educational Measurement* 14,2:75–96.
Hambleton, R. K. and **M. R. Novick.** 1973. 'Toward an integration of theory and method in criterion-referenced tests.' *Journal of Educational Measurement* 10,159–70.

Hambleton, R. K. and H. Swaminathan. 1985. *Item Response Theory: Principles and Applications*. Boston: Kluwer-Nijhoff.
Hambleton, R. K., H. Swaminathan, J. Algina, and D. B. Coulson. 1978. 'Criterion-referenced testing and measurement: A review of technical issues and developments.' *Review of Educational Research* 48:1–47.
Hansen, J. and C. Stansfield. 1981. 'The relationship between field dependent-independent cognitive styles and foreign language achievement.' *Language Learning* 31:349–67.
Hansen, L. 1984. 'Field dependence-independence and language testing: evidence from six Pacific island cultures.' *TESOL Quarterly* 18:311–24.
Harley, B., J. P. Allen, J. Cummins, and M. Swain. 1987. *The Development of Bilingual Proficiency: Final Report*. Toronto, Ont.: Modern Language Centre, Ontario Institute for Studies in Education.
Harris, C. W., M. C. Alkin, and W. J. Popham. (eds.) 1974. *Problems in Criterion-Referenced Evaluation. CSE Monograph Series in Evaluation, No. 3*. Los Angeles, Calif.: Center for the Study of Evaluation, University of California at Los Angeles.
Harrison, A. 1983. 'Communicative testing: jam tomorrow?' in Hughes and Porter 1983: 77–85.
Hatch, E. 1978. 'Discourse analysis and second language acquisition' in E. Hatch (ed.): *Second Language Acquisition: A Book of Readings*. Rowley, Mass.: Newbury House: 401–35.
Hatch, E. and M. H. Long. 1980. 'Discourse analysis, what's that?' in D. Larsen-Freeman 1980: 1–40.
Haughton, G. and L. Dickinson. 1988. 'Collaborative assessment by masters candidates in a tutor-based system.' Paper presented at the 10th Annual Language Testing Research Colloquium, Urbana, Illinois, March 1988.
Hauptman, P. C., R. LeBlanc, and M. B. Wesche. (eds.) 1985. *Second Language Performance Testing*. Ottawa: University of Ottawa Press.
Hawkey, R. 1982. 'An Investigation of Interrelationships between Cognitive/affective and Social Factors and Language Learning. A Longitudinal Study of Twenty-seven Overseas Students Using English in Connection with their Training in the United Kingdom.' Unpublished Ph.D. dissertation. University of London.
Heaton, G. B. 1975. *Writing English Language Tests*. London: Longman.
Heaton, G. B. (ed.) 1982. *Language Testing*. Hayes, Middx.: Modern English Publications.
Henning, G. 1984. Review of Arthur Hughes and Don Porter (eds.): *Current Developments in Language Testing. Language Testing* 1,2:237–41.
Henning, G. 1987. *A Guide to Language Testing*. Cambridge, Mass.: Newbury House.
Henning, G., T. Hudson, and J. Turner. 1985. 'Item response theory and the assumption of unidimensionality.' *Language Testing* 2,2:141–54.
Herzog, M. 1988. 'Issues in writing proficiency assessment: the government scale' in Lowe and Stansfield 1988: 149–77.

Higgs, T. V. (ed.) 1982a. *Curriculum, Competence, and the Foreign Language Teacher. The ACTFL Foreign Language Education Series, Vol. 13.* Skokie, Ill.: National Textbook Company.

Higgs, T. V. 1982b. 'What can I do to help?' in Higgs 1982a: 1–11.

Higgs, T. V. and **R. T. Clifford.** 1982. 'The push toward communication' in Higgs 1982a: 57–79.

Hively, W., G. Maxwell, G. Rabehl, D. Sension, and **S. Lundlin.** 1973. *Domain-Referenced Curriculum Evaluation: A Technical Handbook and Case Study from the Minnemast Project. CSE Monograph Series in Evaluation, Vol. 1.* Los Angeles, Calif.: Center for the Study of Evaluation, University of California at Los Angeles.

Horst, P. 1953. 'Correcting the Kuder-Richardson reliability for dispersion of item difficulties.' *Psychological Bulletin* 50:371–4.

Hoyt, C. 1941. 'Test reliability estimated by analysis of variance.' *Psychometrika* 6:153–60.

Hudson, T. and **B. Lynch.** 1984. 'A criterion-referenced measurement approach to ESL.' *Language Testing* 1,2:171–201.

Hughes, A. 1981. 'Epilogue' in Alderson and Hughes 1981: 206–9.

Hughes, A. 1986. 'A pragmatic approach to criterion-referenced foreign language testing' in Portal 1986a: 31–40.

Hughes, A. and **D. Porter.** 1983. *Current Developments in Language Testing.* London: Academic Press.

Hughes, A., D. Porter, and **C. Weir.** (eds.) 1988. *ELTS Validation Project: Proceedings of a Conference Held to Consider the ELTS Validation Project Report.* London: The British Council and the University of Cambridge Local Examinations Syndicate.

Hulin, C. L., F. Drasgow, and **C. K. Parsons.** 1983. *Item Response Theory: Application to Psychological Measurement.* Homewood, Ill.: Dow Jones-Irwin.

Huynh, H. 1976. 'On the reliability of decisions in domain-referenced testing.' *Journal of Educational Measurement* 13:253–64.

Hyltenstam, K. and **M. Pienemann.** (eds.) 1985. *Modelling and Assessing Second Language Acquisition.* Clevedon, Avon: Multilingual Matters.

Hymes, D. H. 1964. 'Introduction: toward ethnographies of communication' in J. Gumperz and D. Hymes (eds.): *The Ethnography of Communication. American Anthropologist* 66,6:1–34.

Hymes, D. H. 1972a. 'Models of interaction of language and social life' in J. J. Gumperz and D. H. Hymes (eds.): *Directions in Sociolinguistics: The Ethnography of Communication.* New York: Holt, Rinehart and Winston: 35–71.

Hymes, D. H. 1972b. 'On communicative competence' in J. B. Pride and J. Holmes (eds.): *Sociolinguistics.* Harmondsworth: Penguin: 269–93.

Hymes, D. H. 1973. *Toward Linguistic Competence. Texas Working Papers in Sociolinguistics, Working Paper No. 16.* Austin, Tex.: Center for Intercultural Studies in Communication, and Department of Anthropology, University of Texas.

Hymes, D. H. 1982. *Toward Linguistic Competence*. Philadelphia, Pa.: Graduate School of Education, University of Pennsylvania. (Mimeo).

Ilyin, D. 1972. *Ilyin Oral Interview*. Rowley, Mass.: Newbury House.
Ingram, D. E. 1984. *Australian Second Language Proficiency Ratings*. Canberra, NSW: Department of Immigration and Ethnic Affairs.
Ingram, D. E. 1985. 'Assessing proficiency: an overview of some aspects of testing' in Hyltenstam and Pienemann 1985: 215–76.
Ingram, D. E. and E. Wylie. 1982. *Australian Second Language Proficiency Ratings (ASLPR)*. Brisbane, Qld.: Australian Department of Immigration and Ethnic Affairs.
Ingram, D. E. 1977. 'Basic concepts in testing' in Allen and Davies 1977: 11–37.

Jackendoff, R. 1983. *Semantics and Cognition*. Cambridge, Mass.: MIT Press.
Jacobs, H. J., S. A. Zingraf, D. R. Wormuth, V. F. Hartfiel, and J. B. Hughey. 1981. *Testing ESL Composition: A Practical Approach*. Rowley, Mass.: Newbury House.
Jaeger, R. M. 1989. 'Certification of student competence' in Linn 1989: 485–514.
Jaeger, R. M. and C. K. Tittle. 1980. *Minimum Competency Achievement Testing: Motives, Models, Measures and Consequences*. Berkeley, Calif.: McCutchan.
James, L. R., S. A. Mulaik, and J. M. Brett. 1982. *Causal Analysis: Assumptions, Models and Data*. Beverly Hills, Calif.: Sage.
Johnson, K. 1982. 'Some communicative processes' in K. Johnson (ed.): *Communicative Syllabus Design and Methodology*. Oxford: Pergamon.
Johnson, K. and D. Porter. (eds.) 1983. *Perspectives in Communicative Language Teaching*. London: Academic Press.
Johnson, P. 1981. 'Effects on reading comprehension of language complexity and cultural background of a text.' *TESOL Quarterly* 15:169–81.
Jones, R. L. 1979a. 'The oral interview of the Foreign Service Institute' in Spolsky 1979: 104–15.
Jones, R. L. 1979b. 'Performance testing of second language proficiency' in Brière and Hinofotis 1979a: 50–7.
Jones, R. L. 1985a. 'Second language performance testing: An overview' in Hauptman *et al.* 1985: 15–24.
Jones, R. L. 1985b. 'Some basic considerations in testing oral proficiency' in Lee *et al.* 1985: 77–84.
Jones, R. L. and B. Spolsky. (eds.) 1975. *Testing Language Proficiency*. Arlington, Va.: Center for Applied Linguistics.
Jonz, J. 1976. 'Improving the basic egg: the multiple-choice cloze.' *Language Learning* 26:255–65.
Joos, M. 1967. *The Five Clocks*. New York: Harcourt Brace Jovanovich.

Kachru, B. J. 1985. 'Standards, codification and sociolinguistic realism: the English language in the outer circle' in R. Quirk and H. G. Widdowson (eds.): *English in the World: Teaching and Learning the Language and Literatures.* Cambridge: Cambridge University Press: 11–30.

Kachru, B. J. 1986. *The Alchemy of English: The Spread, Functions and Models of Non-native Englishes.* Oxford: Pergamon.

Kalleberg, A. L. and J. R. Kluegel. 1975. 'Analysis of the multitrait-multimethod matrix: some limitations and an alternative.' *Journal of Applied Psychology* 60,1:1–9.

Kane, M. T. 1982. 'A sampling model for validity.' *Applied Psychological Measurement* 6:125–160.

Kane, M. T. and R. L. Brennan. 1980. 'Agreement coefficients as indices of dependability for domain-referenced tests.' *Applied Psychological Measurement* 4:219–40.

Kavanagh, M. J., A. C. MacKinney, and L. Wolins. 1971. 'Issues in managerial performance: multitrait-multimethod analyses of ratings.' *Psychological Bulletin* 75, 1:34–49.

Kenny, D. 1979. *Correlation and Causality.* New York: Wiley.

Kerlinger, F. N. 1986. *Foundations of Behavioral Research.* Third edition. New York: Holt, Rinehart and Winston.

Kim, J.-O. and C. W. Mueller. 1978a. *Introduction to Factor Analysis: What It Is and How To Do It.* Beverly Hills, Calif.: Sage.

Kim, J-O. and C. W. Mueller. 1978b. *Factor Analysis: Statistical Methods and Practical Issues.* Beverly Hills, Calif.: Sage.

Kirk, R. E. 1968. *Experimental Design: Procedures for the Behavioral Sciences.* Monterey, Calif.: Brooks/Cole.

Klein-Braley, C. 1981. 'Empirical Investigations of Cloze Tests: an Examination of the Validity of Cloze Tests as Tests of General Language Proficiency in English for German University Students.' Unpublished Ph.D. dissertation. University of Duisburg.

Klein-Braley, C. 1985. 'A cloze-up on the c-test: a study in the construct validation of authentic tests.' *Language Testing* 2,1:76–104.

Klein-Braley, C. and U. Raatz. 1984. 'A survey of research on the c-test.' *Language Testing* 1:134–46.

Klein-Braley, C. and D. K. Stevenson. (eds.) 1981. *Practice and Problems in Language Testing 1.* Frankfurt: Verlag Peter D. Lang.

Kohonen, V., H. von Essen, and C. Klein-Braley. (eds.) 1985. *Practice and Problems in Language Testing 8.* Tampere, Finland: Finnish Association for Applied Linguistics.

Kohonen, V. and A. J. Pitkanen. (eds.) 1985. *Language Testing in School.* Tampere, Finland: Finnish Association for Applied Linguistics.

Kramsch, C. 1986. 'From language proficiency to interactional competence.' *The Modern Language Journal* 70,4:366–72.

Krashen, S. D. 1982. *Principles and Practice in Second Language Acquisition.* Oxford: Pergamon.

Krashen, S. D. 1985. *Issues and Insights.* Haywood, Calif.: Alemany Press.

Kuder, G. F. and **M. W. Richardson.** 1937. 'The theory of the estimation of test reliability.' *Psychometrika* 2:151–60.

Labov, W. 1972. *Sociolinguistic Patterns.* Philadelphia, Pa.: University of Pennsylvania Press.

Lado, R. 1957. *Linguistics Across Cultures.* Ann Arbor, Mich.: University of Michigan Press.

Lado, R. 1961. *Language Testing.* New York: McGraw-Hill.

Lado, R. 1975. 'Comment on Clark's paper' in Jones and Spolsky 1975: 25.

Lambert, R. D. and **B. F. Freed.** (eds.) 1982. *The Loss of Language Skills.* Rowley, Mass.: Newbury House.

Lange, D. L. 1987. 'Developing and implementing proficiency oriented tests for a new language requirement at the University of Minnesota: issues and problems in implementing the ACTFL/ETS/ILR proficiency guidelines' in Valdman 1987: 274–90.

Lantolf, J. P. and **W. Frawley.** 1985. 'Oral proficiency testing: a critical analysis.' *The Modern Language Journal* 69:337–45.

Larsen-Freeman, D. (ed.) 1980. *Discourse Analysis in Second Language Research.* Rowley, Mass.: Newbury House.

Larson, J. W. 1987. 'Computerized adaptive language testing: a Spanish placement exam' in Bailey *et al.* 1987: 1–19.

Lazarus, M. 1981. *Goodbye to Excellence: A Critical Look at Minimum Competency Testing.* Boulder, Colo.: Westview Press.

LeBlanc, R. and **G. Painchaud.** 1985. 'Self-assessment as a second language placement instrument.' *TESOL Quarterly* 19,4:673–87.

Lee, Y. P., A. C. Y. Fok, R. Lord, and **G. Low.** (eds.) 1985. *New Directions in Language Testing.* Oxford: Pergamon Press.

Levin, L. 1970. *Implicit and Explicit: A Synopsis of Three Parallel Experiments in Applied Psycholinguistics, Assessing Different Methods of Teaching Grammatical Structures in English as a Foreign Language.* Gothenburg, Sweden: Gothenburg School of Education.

Likert, R. 1932. 'A technique for the measurement of attitudes.' *Archives of Psychology, No. 140*:1–55.

Lindblad, T. and **L. Levin.** 1970. *Teaching Grammar: An Experiment in Applied Psycholinguistics, Assessing Three Different Methods of Teaching Grammatical Structures in English as a Foreign Language.* Gothenburg, Sweden: Gothenburg School of Education.

Linn, R. L. 1973. 'Fair test uses in selection.' *Review of Educational Research* 43:139–61.

Linn, R. L. 1979. 'Issues of validity in measurement for competency-based programs' in M. A. Bunda and J. R. Sanders (eds.): *Practices and Problems in Competency-based Measurement.* Washington, DC: National Council on Measurement in Education: 108–23.

Linn, R. L. 1980. 'Issues of validity for criterion-referenced measures.' *Applied Psychological Measurement* 4,4:547–61.

Linn, R. L. 1983. 'Curricular validity: convincing the court that it was taught without precluding the possibility of measuring it' in Madaus 1983a: 115–32.

Linn, R. L. (ed.) 1989. *Educational Measurement*. Third edition. New York: American Council on Education/Macmillan.

Liskin-Gasparro, J. 1984. 'The ACTFL proficiency guidelines: A historical perspective' in T. V. Higgs (ed.): *Teaching for Proficiency, the Organizing Principle*. Lincolnwood, Ill.: National Textbook Company.

Livingston, S. A. 1972. 'Criterion-referenced applications of classical test theory.' *Journal of Educational Measurement* 9:13–26.

Lomax, R. G. and J. Algina. 1979. 'Comparison of two procedures for analyzing multitrait-multimethod matrices.' *Journal of Educational Measurement* 16,3:177–86.

Long, M. H. 1984. 'Process and product in ESL program evaluation.' *TESOL Quarterly* 18,3:409–25.

Long, M. H. and C. J. Sato. 1983. 'Classroom foreigner talk discourse: forms and functions of teachers' questions' in W. Seliger and M. Long (eds.): *Classroom-oriented Research in Second Language Acquisition*. Rowley, Mass.: Newbury House: 268–85.

Lord, F. M. 1980. *Applications of Item Response Theory to Practical Testing Problems*. Hillsdale, NJ: Lawrence Erlbaum.

Lord, F. M. 1983. 'Estimating the imputed social cost of errors in measurement.' *Research Report* 83–33–ONR. Princeton, NJ: Educational Testing Service.

Lord, F. M. and M. R. Novick. 1968. *Statistical Theories of Mental Test Scores*. Reading, Mass.: Addison-Wesley.

Low, G. D. and Y. P. Lee. 1985. 'How shall a test be referenced?' in Lee *et al.* 1985: 119–26.

Lowe, P. Jr. 1982. *ILR Handbook on Oral Interview Testing*. Washington, DC: DLI/LS Oral Interview Project.

Lowe, P. Jr. 1983. 'The ILR oral interview: origins, applications, pitfalls, and implications.' *Die Unterrichtspraxis* 60: 230–44.

Lowe, P. Jr. 1985. 'The ILR proficiency scale as a synthesizing research principle: the view from the mountain' in C. J. James (ed.): *Foreign Language Proficiency in the Classroom and Beyond*. Lincolnwood, Ill.: National Textbook Company.

Lowe, P. Jr. 1986. 'Proficiency: panacea, framework, process? a reply to Kramsch, Schulz, and, particularly, to Bachman and Savignon.' *The Modern Language Journal* 70,4:391–7.

Lowe, P. Jr. 1988. 'The unassimilated history' in Lowe and Stansfield 1988: 11–51.

Lowe, P. Jr. and R. T. Clifford. 1980. 'Developing an indirect measure of overall oral proficiency' in Frith 1980: 31–9.

Lowe, P. Jr. and J. Liskin-Gasparro. n.d. 'Testing speaking proficiency: The oral interview.' ERIC Clearinghouse on Languages and Linguistics, *Q & A*. Washington, DC: Center for Applied Linguistics.

Lowe, P. Jr. and **C. W. Stansfield.** (eds.) 1988. *Second Language Proficiency Assessment: Current Issues.* Englewood Cliffs, NJ: Prentice-Hall.
Lutjeharms, M. and **T. Culhane.** (eds.) 1982. *Practice and Problems in Language Testing* 3. Brussels: Free University of Brussels.

MacKay, R. 1974. 'Standardized tests: objective/objectified measures of "competence"' in A. V. Cicourel *et al.*: *Language Use and School Performance.* New York: Academic Press: 218–47.
Mackey, W. F. 1968. 'The typology, classification and analysis of language tests' in Upshur and Fata 1968: 163–6.
Madaus, G. F. 1983a. *The Courts, Validity, and Minimum Competency Testing.* Boston, Mass.: Kluwer-Nijhoff.
Madaus, G. F. 1983b. 'Minimum competency testing for certification: the evolution and evaluation of test validity' in Madaus 1983a: 21–61.
Madsen, H. S. 1982. 'Determining the debilitative impact of test anxiety.' *Language Learning* 32:133–43.
Madsen, H. S. 1987. 'Utilizing Rasch analysis to detect cheating on language examinations' in Bailey *et al.* 1987: 11–23.
Madsen, H. S. and **R. L. Jones.** 1981. 'Classification of oral proficiency tests' in Palmer *et al.* 1981: 15–30.
Madsen, H. S. and **J. W. Larson.** 1986. 'Computerized Rasch analysis of item bias in ESL tests' in Stansfield 1986a: 47–67.
McCrimman, J. M. 1984. *Writing with a Purpose.* Eighth edition. Boston, Mass.: Houghton Mifflin.
Messick, S. A. 1975. 'The standard problem: meaning and values in measurement and evaluation.' *American Psychologist* 30:955–66.
Messick, S. A. 1980. 'Test validity and the ethics of assessment.' *American Psychologist* 35:1012–27.
Messick, S. A. 1981a. 'Constructs and their vicissitudes in educational and psychological measurement.' *Psychological Bulletin* 89:575–88.
Messick, S. A. 1981b. 'Evidence and ethics in the evaluation of tests.' *Research Report* 81–9. Princeton, NJ: Educational Testing Service.
Messick, S. A. 1988. 'The once and future issues of validity: assessing the meaning and consequences of measurement' in H. Wainer and H. I. Braun (eds.): *Test Validity.* Hillsdale, NJ: Lawrence Erlbaum.
Messick, S. A. 1989. 'Validity' in Linn 1989: 13–103.
Miller, A. D. 1971. 'Logic of causal analysis: from experimental to nonexperimental designs' in H. Blalock (ed.): *Causal Models in the Social Sciences.* Chicago, Ill.: Aldine-Atherton: 273–94.
Miller, G., E. Galanter, and **K. H. Pribram.** 1960. *Plans and the Structure of Behavior.* New York: Holt, Rinehart, and Winston.
Millman, J. 1974. 'Criterion-referenced measurement' in Popham 1974: 309–97.
Mislevy, R. J. and **R. D. Bock.** 1982. *BILOG: Maximum Likelihood Item Analysis and Test Scoring with Logistic Models for Binary Items.* Mooresville, Ind.: Scientific Software.

Mislevy, R. J. and **R. D. Bock.** 1986. *PC-BILOG: Item Analysis and Test Scoring with Binary Logistic Models.* Mooresville, Ind.: Scientific Software.

Morrow, K. 1977. *Techniques of Evaluation for a Notional Syllabus.* London: Royal Society of Arts.

Morrow, K. 1979. 'Communicative language testing: revolution or evolution?' in C. J. Brumfit and K. Johnson (eds.): *The Communicative Approach to Language Teaching.* Oxford: Oxford University Press: 143–57.

Morrow, K. 1986. 'The evaluation of tests of communicative performance' in Portal 1986a: 1–13.

Mosier, C. I. 1947. 'A critical examination of the concepts of face validity.' *Educational and Psychological Measurement* 7:191–205.

Mountford, A. 1976. 'The notion of simplification: its relevance to materials preparation for English for science and technology' in J. C. Richards (ed.): *Teaching English for Science and Technology.* Singapore: Regional English Language Centre: 143–62.

Munby, J. 1978. *Communicative Syllabus Design.* Cambridge: Cambridge University Press.

Nevo, D. 1986. 'Panel discussion: the next 25 years?' *Language Testing* 3,2:240–2.

Nitko, A. J. 1983. *Educational Tests and Measurement: An Introduction.* New York: Harcourt Brace Jovanovich.

Nitko, A. J. 1984. 'Defining the criterion-referenced test' in Berk 1984a: 8–28.

Nitko, A. J. 1989. 'Designing tests that are integrated with instruction' in Linn 1989: 447–74.

Ohnmacht, F. W. and **J. T. Fleming.** 1974. 'Further effects of selected deletion strategies and varying contextual constraints on cloze performance' in the *23rd Yearbook of the National Reading Conference.* Clemson, SC: The National Reading Conference: 163–71.

Oller, J. W. Jr. 1972. 'Scoring methods and difficulty levels for cloze tests of proficiency in ESL.' *Modern Language Journal* 56:151–8.

Oller, J. W. Jr. 1975. 'Cloze, discourse and approximations to English' in M. K. Burt and H. Dulay (eds.): *New Directions in TESOL.* Washington, DC: Teachers of English to Speakers of Other Languages: 345–56.

Oller, J. W. Jr. 1976. 'Evidence of a general language proficiency factor: an expectancy grammar.' *Die Neuren Sprachen* 76: 165–74.

Oller, J. W. Jr. 1979a. 'Explaining the reliable variance in tests: the validation problem' in Brière and Hinofotis 1979a: 61–74.

Oller, J. W. Jr. 1979b. *Language Tests at School: A Pragmatic Approach.* London: Longman.

Oller, J. W. Jr. 1983a. 'A consensus for the eighties?' in Oller 1983b: 351–6.

Oller, J. W. Jr. (ed.) 1983b. *Issues in Language Testing Research*. Rowley, Mass.: Newbury House.

Oller, J. W. Jr. 1986. 'Communication theory and testing: what and how' in Stansfield 1986b: 104–55.

Oller, J. W. Jr. and F. B. Hinofotis. 1980. 'Two mutually exclusive hypotheses about second language ability: indivisible and partly divisible competence' in Oller and Perkins 1980: 13–23.

Oller, J. W. Jr. and K. Perkins. (eds.) 1978. *Language in Education: Testing the Tests*. Rowley, Mass.: Newbury House.

Oller, J. W. Jr. and K. Perkins. (eds.) 1980. *Research in Language Testing*. Rowley, Mass.: Newbury House.

Oller, J. W. Jr. and C. Richards. (eds.) 1973. *Focus on the Learner: Pragmatic Perspectives for the Language Teacher*. Rowley, Mass.: Newbury House.

Olshtain, E. and S. Blum-Kulka. 1985. 'Crosscultural pragmatics and the testing of communicative competence.' *Language Testing* 2,1:16–30.

Oltman, P., E. Raskin, and H. Witkin. 1971. *Group Embedded Figures Test*. Palo Alto, Calif.: Consulting Psychologists Press.

Ontario Ministry of Education. 1980. *The Ontario Assessment Instrument Pool: French as a Second Language, Junior and Intermediate Divisions*. Toronto, Ont.: Ontario Ministry of Education.

Oskarsson, M. 1978. *Approaches to Self-Assessment in Foreign Language Learning*. Strasbourg: Council of Europe.

Oskarsson, M. 1988. 'Self-assessment of language proficiency: rationale and applications.' Paper presented at the Tenth Annual Language Testing Research Colloquium. Urbana, Illinois, March 1988.

Oxford, R. L. 1982. 'Technical issues in designing and conducting research on language skill attrition' in Lambert and Freed 1982: 119–37.

Paikeday, T. M. 1985. *The Native Speaker is Dead!* Toronto, Ont.: Paikeday.

Palmer, A. S. 1972. 'Testing communication.' *International Review of Applied Linguistics and Language Teaching* 10:35–45.

Palmer, A. S. 1979. 'Compartmentalized and integrative control: an assessment of some evidence for two kinds of competence and implications for the classroom.' *Language Learning* 29:169–80.

Palmer, A. S. 1981. 'Measurements of reliability and validity of two picture-description tests of oral communication' in Palmer *et al.* 1981: 127-39.

Palmer, A. S., P. J. M. Groot, and G. A. Trosper. (eds.) 1981. *The Construct Validation of Tests of Communicative Competence*. Washington, DC: TESOL.

Palmer, L. and B. Spolsky. (eds.) 1975. *Papers in Language Testing: 1967–74*. Washington, DC: TESOL.

Pawley, A. and F. H. Syder. 1983. 'Two puzzles for linguistic theory: nativelike selection and nativelike fluency' in Richards and Schmidt 1983a: 191–225.

Pedhazur, E. J. 1982. *Multiple Regression in Behavioral Research.* Second edition. New York: Holt, Rinehart, and Winston.

Perkins, K. 1984. 'A regression analysis of direct and indirect measures of English as a second language writing compositions' in Culhane *et al.* 1984: 113–23.

Perkins, K. and **S. E. Linnville.** 1987. 'A construct definition study of a standardized ESL vocabulary test.' *Language Testing* 4,2:125–41.

Peterson, C. R. and **F. A. Cartier.** 1975. 'Some theoretical problems and practical solutions in proficiency test validity' in Jones and Spolsky 1985: 105–13.

Peterson, N. S., M. J. Kolen, and **H. D. Hoover.** 1989. 'Scaling, norming and equating' in Linn 1989: 221–62.

Pica, T. and **M. H. Long.** 1986. 'The linguistic and conversational performance of experienced and inexperienced teachers' in R. R. Day (ed.): *Talking to Learn: Conversation in Second Language Acquisition.* Rowley, Mass.: Newbury House: 85–98.

Pienemann, M., M. Johnston, and **G. Brindley.** 1988. 'Constructing an acquisition-based procedure for second language assessment' in Valdman 1988: 121–243.

Pike, L. W. 1979. *An Evaluation of Alternative Item Formats for Testing English as a Foreign Language.* TOEFL Research Report 2. Princeton, NJ: Educational Testing Service.

Pilliner, A. E. G. 1968. 'Subjective and objective testing' in Davies 1968b: 19–35.

Pimsleur, P. 1966. *Language Aptitude Battery.* New York: Harcourt, Brace Jovanovich.

Plaister, T. H. 1967. 'Testing aural comprehension: a culture fair approach.' *TESOL Quarterly* 1,3:17–19.

Politzer, R. L. and **M. McGroarty.** 1985. 'An exploratory study of learning behaviors and their relationship to gains in linguistic and communicative competence.' *TESOL Quarterly* 19,1:103–23.

Pollitt, A. and **C. Hutchinson.** 1987. 'Calibrating graded assessments: Rasch partial credit analysis of performance in writing.' *Language Testing* 4,1:72–92.

Popham, W. J. 1969. 'Objectives and instruction' in W. J. Popham, E. W. Eisner, H. J. Sullivan, and L. L. Tyler (eds.): *Instructional Objectives. AERA Monograph Series on Curriculum Evaluation, No. 3.* Chicago, Ill.: Rand McNally: 32–52.

Popham, W. J. 1974a. *Evaluation in Education: Current Applications.* Berkeley, Calif.: American Educational Research Association.

Popham, W. J. 1974b. 'Selecting objectives and generating test items for objectives-based tests' in Harris *et al.* 1974:13–25.

Popham, W. J. 1978. *Criterion-Referenced Measurement.* Englewood Cliffs, NJ: Prentice-Hall.

Popham, W. J. 1981. *Modern Educational Measurement.* Englewood Cliffs, NJ: Prentice-Hall.

Popham, W. J. 1984. 'Specifying the domain of content or behaviors' in Berk 1984a: 29–48.

Portal, M. (ed.) 1986a. *Innovations in Language Testing.* Windsor, Berks.: NFER-Nelson.

Portal, M. 1986b. 'Methods of testing speaking in the Assessment of Performance Unit (APU) French surveys' in Portal 1986a: 41–54.

Porter, D. 1983. 'Assessing communicative proficiency: the search for validity' in Johnson and Porter 1983: 189–204.

Powers, D. E. 1980. *The Relationship between Scores on the Graduate Management Admission Test and the Test of English as a Foreign Language.* TOEFL Research Report 5. Princeton, NJ: Educational Testing Service.

Powers, D. E. and **C. W. Stansfield.** 1983. *The Test of Spoken English as a Measure of Communicative Ability in the Health Professions.* Princeton, NJ: Educational Testing Service.

Purcell, E. T. 1983. 'Models of pronunciation accuracy' in Oller 1983b: 133–51.

Raatz, U. 1981. 'Are oral tests tests?' in Klein-Braley and Stevenson 1981: 197–212.

Raatz, U., and **C. Klein-Braley.** 1981. 'The c-test – a modification of the cloze procedure' in Culhane *et al.* 1981: 113–38.

Raffaldini, T. 1988. 'The use of situation tests as measures of communicative ability' in Valdman 1988: 197–216.

Ramanauskas, S. 1972. 'The responsiveness of cloze readability measures to linguistic variables operating over segments of text longer than a sentence.' *Reading Research Quarterly* 8,1:72–91.

Rea, P. M. 1985. 'Language testing and the communicative teaching curriculum' in Lee *et al.* 1985: 15–32.

Read, A. S. (ed.) 1981. *Directions in Language Testing. Anthology Series,* No. 9. Singapore: SEAMEO Regional Language Centre.

Richards, J. C. and **R. W. Schmidt.** (eds.) 1983a. *Language and Communication.* London: Longman.

Richards, J. C. and **R. W. Schmidt.** 1983b. 'Conversational analysis' in Richards and Schmidt 1983a: 117–53.

Richards, J. C. and **M. Sukwiwat.** 1983. 'Language transfer and conversational competence.' *Applied Linguistics* 4,2:113–25.

Rivera, C. (ed.) 1984. *Communicative Competence Approaches to Language Proficiency Assessment: Research and Application.* Clevedon, Avon: Multilingual Matters.

Roid, G. H. 1984. 'Generating the test items' in Berk 1984a: 49–77.

Samejima, F. 1977. 'A use of the information function in tailored testing.' *Applied Psychological Measurement* 1:233–47.

Samson, D. M. M. 1983. 'Rasch and reading' in J. van Weeren (ed.): *Practice and Problems in Language Testing.* Arnhem: CITO.

Sang, F., B. Schmitz, H. J. Vollmer, J. Baumert, and **P. M. Roeder.** 1986. 'Models of second language competence: a structural equation approach.' *Language Testing* 3,1:54–79.

Savard, J-G. 1968. 'A proposed system for classifying language tests' in Upshur and Fata 1968: 167–74.

Savignon, S. J. 1972. *Communicative Competence: An Experiment in Foreign Language Teaching*. Philadelphia, Pa.: Center for Curriculum Development.

Savignon, S. J. 1983. *Communicative Competence: Theory and Classroom Practice*. Reading, Mass.: Addison-Wesley.

Saville-Troike, M. 1984. 'What *really* matters in second language learning for academic achievement?' *TESOL Quarterly* 18:199–219.

Saville-Troike, M., E. McClure, and **M. Fritz.** 1984. 'Communicative tactics in children's second language acquisition' in F. R. Eckman, L. H. Bell, and D. D. Nelson (eds.): *Universals of Second Language Acquisition*. Rowley, Mass.: Newbury House: 60–71.

Schmitt, N., B. W. Coyle, and **B. B. Saari.** 1977. 'A review and critique of analyses of multitrait-multimethod matrices.' *Multivariate Behavioral Research* 12:447–78.

Scholz, G., D. Hendricks, R. Spurling, M. Johnson, and **L. Vandenburg.** 1980. 'Is language ability divisible or unitary? A factor analysis of 22 English language proficiency tests' in Oller and Perkins 1980: 24–33.

Scott, M. L. 1986. 'Student affective reactions to oral language tests.' *Language Testing* 3,1:99–118.

Scott, M. L. and **H. S. Madsen.** 1983. 'The influence of retesting on test affect' in Oller 1983b: 270–9.

Scriven, M. 1967. 'The methodology of evaluation' in R. W. Tyler, R. M. Gagné, and M. Scriven (eds.): *Perspectives of Curriculum Evaluation*. Chicago, Ill.: Rand McNally and Co: 39–83.

Searle, J. R. 1969. *Speech Acts: An Essay in the Philosophy of Language*. Cambridge: Cambridge University Press.

Seaton, I. 1981. 'A review of issues raised in the production of the English Language Testing Service' in Culhane *et al.* 1981: 139–45.

Seaton, I. 1983. 'The English Language Testing Service (ELTS): two issues in the design of the new "non-academic module" in Hughes and Porter 1983: 129–39.

Shavelson, R. J. 1988. *Statistical Reasoning for the Behavioral Sciences*. Second edition. Boston, Mass.: Allyn and Bacon.

Shephard, L. A. 1974. 'Setting performance standards' in Berk 1984a: 169–98.

Shohamy, E. 1982. 'Affective considerations in language testing.' *The Modern Language Journal* 66:13–17.

Shohamy, E. 1983a. 'Interrater and intrarater reliability of the oral interview and concurrent validity with cloze procedure in Hebrew' in Oller 1983b: 229–36.

Shohamy, E. 1983b. 'The stability of oral proficiency assessment on the oral interview testing procedure.' *Language Learning* 33:527–40.

Shohamy, E. 1984a. 'Does the testing method make a difference? The case of reading comprehension.' *Language Testing* 1,2:147–70.

Shohamy, E. 1984b. 'Input and output in language testing' in Culhane *et al.* 1984: 159–66.

Shohamy, E. and T. Reves. 1985. 'Authentic language tests: where from and where to?' *Language Testing* 2,1:48–59.

Silverstein, R. (ed.) 1979. *Proceedings of the Third International Conference on Frontiers in Language Proficiency and Dominance Testing.* Carbondale, Ill.: Department of Linguistics, Southern Illinois University.

Sinclair, J. M. and M. Coulthard. 1975. *Towards an Analysis of Discourse.* Oxford: Oxford University Press.

Skehan, P. 1984. 'Issues in the testing of English for specific purposes.' *Language Testing* 1,2:202–20.

Smith, P. D. 1970. *A Comparison of the Cognitive and Audiolingual Approaches to Foreign Language Instruction: The Pennsylvania Foreign Language Project.* Philadelphia, Pa.: Center for Curriculum Development.

Spearman, C. 1910. 'Correlation calculated from faulty data.' *British Journal of Psychology* 3:271–95.

Spolsky, B. 1968. 'Language testing: the problem of validation.' *TESOL Quarterly* 2,2:88–94.

Spolsky, B. 1973. 'What does it mean to know a language? Or, how do you get someone to perform his competence?' in Oller and Richards 1973: 164–76.

Spolsky, B. (ed.) 1978a. *Approaches to Language Testing. Advances in Language Testing Series: 2.* Arlington, Va.: Center for Applied Linguistics.

Spolsky, B. 1978b. 'Introduction: linguistics and language testers' in Spolsky 1978a: v–x.

Spolsky, B. 1979. *Some Major Tests. Advances in Language Testing Series: 1.* Arlington, Va.: Center for Applied Linguistics.

Spolsky, B. 1981. 'Some ethical questions about language testing' in Klein-Braley and Stevenson 1981: 5–21.

Spolsky, B. 1985. 'The limits of authenticity in language testing.' *Language Testing* 2, 1:31–40.

Spolsky, B. 1986. 'A multiple choice for language testers.' *Language Testing* 3,2:147–58.

Spolsky, B., P. Murphy, W. Holm, and A. Ferrel. 1972. 'Three functional tests of oral proficiency.' *TESOL Quarterly* 63:221–35.

Spolsky, B., B. Sigurd, M. Sato, E. Walker, and C. Aterburn. 1968. 'Preliminary studies in the development of techniques for testing overall second language proficiency' in Upshur and Fata 1968: 79–98.

Spurling, S. and D. Ilyin. 1985. 'The impact of learner variables on language test performance.' *TESOL Quarterly* 19,2:283–301.

Stake, R. E. 1970. 'Objectives, priorities, and other judgment data.' *Review of Educational Research* 40:181–212.

Stake, R. E. 1978. 'The case study method in social inquiry.' *Educational Researcher* 7:5–8.

Stanley, J. C. 1957. 'K–R 20 as the stepped-up mean item intercorrelation' in the *14th Yearbook of the National Council on Measurement in Education*. New York: National Council on Measurement in Education: 78–92.

Stanley, J. C. 1961. 'Analysis of unreplicated three-way classifications, with applications to rater bias and trait independence.' *Psychometrika* 26, 2:205–19.

Stanley, J. C. 1971. 'Reliability' in Thorndike 1981: 356–442.

Stansfield, C. W. (ed.) 1986a. *Technology and Language Testing* (Collected papers from the 1985 Colloquium.) Washington, DC: TESOL.

Stansfield, C. W. (ed.) 1986b. *Toward Communicative Competence Testing: Proceedings of the Second TOEFL Invitational Conference.* Princeton, NJ: Educational Testing Service.

Stansfield, C. and J. Hansen. 1983. 'Field dependence-independence as a variable in second language cloze test performance.' *TESOL Quarterly* 17:29–38.

Steffensen, M. S., C. Joad-dev, and R. C. Anderson. 1979. 'A cross-cultural perspective on reading comprehension.' *Reading Research Quarterly* 15:10–29.

Stevenson, D. K. 1981. 'Beyond faith and face validity: the multitrait-multimethod matrix and the convergent and discriminant validity of oral proficiency tests' in Palmer *et al.* 1981: 37–61.

Stevenson, D. K. 1982. 'The sociolinguistics of language testing: a tester's perspective' in Lutjeharms and Culhane 1982: 4–22.

Stevenson, D. K. 1985a. 'Authenticity, validity and a tea party.' *Language Testing* 2, 1:41–7.

Stevenson, D. K. 1985b. 'Pop validity and performance testing' in Lee *et al.* 1985: 111–18.

Stufflebeam, D. L. 1973. 'An introduction to the PDK book' in Worthen and Sanders 1973: 128–42.

Subkoviak, M. J. 1976. 'Estimating reliability from a single administration of a mastery test.' *Journal of Educational Measurement* 13:265–76.

Subkoviak, M. J. 1980. 'Decision-consistency approaches' in Berk 1980b: 129–85.

Subkoviak, M. J. 1984. 'Estimating the reliability of mastery-nonmastery decisions' in Berk 1984a: 267–91.

Subkoviak, M. J. 1988. 'A practitioner's guide to computation and interpretation of reliability indices for mastery tests.' *Journal of Educational Measurement* 25:47–55.

Swain, M. 1985. 'Large-scale communicative language testing: a case study' in Lee *et al.* 1985: 35–46.

Swales, J. 1988. 'Discourse communities, genres and the teaching of English as an international language.' *World Englishes* 7, 2:211–20.

Swaminathan, H., R. K. Hambleton, and J. Algina. 1974. 'Reliability of criterion-referenced tests: a decision-theoretic formulation.' *Journal of Educational Measurement* 11:263–7.

Swinton, S. S. and D. E. Powers. 1980. *Factor Analysis of the Test of English as a Foreign Language for Several Language Groups.* TOEFL Research Report 6. Princeton, NJ: Educational Testing Service.

Takala, S. 1985. 'Estimating students' vocabulary sizes in foreign language teaching' in Kohonen *et al.* 1985: 157–65.

Tarone, E. E. 1981. 'Some thoughts on the notion of communication strategy.' *TESOL Quarterly* 15:285–95.

Tatsuoka, K. K. 1983. 'Rule space: an approach for dealing with misconceptions based on item response theory.' *Journal of Educational Measurement* 20,4:345–54.

Tatsuoka, K. K. 1984. 'Caution indices based on item response theory.' *Psychometrika* 49,1:95–110.

Tatsuoka, K. K. 1989. 'Toward an integration of item-response theory and cognitive error diagnoses' in Fredericksen, Glaser, Lesgold, and Shafto (eds.): *Diagnostic Monitoring of Skill and Knowledge Acquisition.* Hillsdale, NJ: Lawrence Erlbaum Associates .

Tatsuoka, K. K. and M. M. Tatsuoka. 1987. 'Bug distribution and statistical pattern classification.' *Psychometrika* 52,2:193–206.

Test of English as a Foreign Language. 1987. *TOEFL Test and Score Manual.* Princeton, NJ: Educational Testing Service.

Thorndike, R. L. 1951. 'Reliability' in E. F. Lindquist (ed.): *Educational Measurement.* Washington, DC: American Council on Education: 560–620.

Thorndike, R. L. (ed.) 1971. *Educational Measurement.* Second edition. Washington, DC: American Council on Education.

Thorndike, R. L. and E. P. Hagen. 1977. *Measurement and Evaluation in Psychology and Education.* Fourth edition. New York: John Wiley and Sons.

Thurstone, L. L. 1925. 'A method of scaling psychological and educational tests.' *Journal of Educational Psychology* 16:433–51.

Thurstone, L. L. 1927a. 'A law of comparative judgment.' *Psychological Review* 35:273–86.

Thurstone, L. L. 1927b. 'The unit of measurement in educational scales.' *Journal of Educational Psychology* 18:505–24.

Thurstone, L. L. 1928. 'The absolute zero in intelligence measurement.' *Psychological Review* 35:175–97.

Torgerson, W. S. 1958. *Theory and Methods of Scaling.* New York: John Wiley.

University of Cambridge Local Examinations Syndicate. 1987. *English as a Foreign Language: General Handbook*. Cambridge: University of Cambridge Local Examinations Syndicate.

Upshur, J. A. 1968. 'Introduction' in Upshur and Fata 1968: vii–xii.

Upshur, J. A. 1971. 'Productive communication testing: a progress report' in G. Perren and J. L. M. Trim (eds.): *Applications in Linguistics.* Cambridge: Cambridge University Press:435–42.

Upshur, J. A. 1973. 'Context for language testing' in Oller and Richards 1973: 200–13.

Upshur, J. A. 1979. 'Functional proficiency theory and a research role for language tests' in Brière and Hinofotis 1979a: 75–100.

Upshur, J. A. and **J. Fata.** (eds.) 1968. *Problems in Foreign Language Testing. Language Learning Special Issue.* No. 3. Ann Arbor, Mich.: Research Club in Language Learning.

Valdman, A. (ed.) 1987. *Proceedings of the Symposium on the Evaluation of Foreign Language Proficiency.* Bloomington, Ind.: Center for Research and Development in Language Instruction, Indiana University.

Valdman, A. (ed.) 1988. *The Assessment of Foreign Language Oral Proficiency. Studies in Second Language Acquisition* 10,2.

van Dijk, T. A. 1977. *Text and Context: Explorations in the Semantics and Pragmatics of Discourse.* London: Longman.

van Weeren, J. and **T. J. J. Theunissen.** 1987. 'Testing pronunciation: an application of generalizability theory.' *Language Learning* 37:109–22.

Venneman, T. 1975. 'Topic, sentence accent and ellipsis: a proposal for their formal treatment' in E. L. Keenan (ed.): *Formal Semantics of Natural Language.* Cambridge: Cambridge University Press.

Vincent, R. J. 1978. 'Psychophysical scaling of the language proficiency interview: a preliminary report' in Clark 1978a: 229–53.

Von Elek, T. 1985. 'A test of Swedish as a second language: an experiment in self-assessment' in Lee *et al.* 1985: 47–58.

Waller, M. I. 1981. 'A procedure for comparing logistic latent trait models.' *Journal of Educational Measurement* 18:119–25.

Wang, L-S. 1988. 'A Comparative Analysis of Cognitive Achievement and Psychological Orientation among Language Minority Groups: A Linear Structural Relations (LISREL) Approach.' Unpublished Ph.D. dissertation. University of Illinois.

Weir, C. J. 1981. 'Reaction to Morrow paper (1)' in Alderson and Hughes 1981: 26–37.

Weir, C. J. 1983. 'The Associated Examining Board's test of English for academic purposes: an exercise in content validation events' in Hughes and Porter 1983: 147–53.

Weiss, C. H. 1972. *Evaluation Research: Methods for Assessing Program Effectiveness.* Englewood Cliffs, NJ: Prentice-Hall.

Wesche, M. 1981. 'Communicative testing in a second language.' *Canadian Modern Language Review* 37,3:551–71.

Wesche, M. 1985. 'Introduction' in Hauptman *et al.* 1985: 1–12.

Wesche, M. 1987. 'Second language performance testing: the Ontario Test of ESL as an example.' *Language Testing* 4,1:28–47.

Wesche, M., M. Canale, E. Cray, S. Jones, D. Mendelsohn, M. Tumpane, and M. Tyacke. 1987. *The Ontario Test of English as a Second Language (OESL): A Report on the Research.* Ottawa: Ontario Ministry of Colleges and Universities.

Widdowson, H. G. 1978. *Teaching Language as Communication.* Oxford: Oxford University Press.

Widdowson, H. G. 1983. *Learning Purpose and Language Use.* London: Oxford University Press.

Wilds, C. P. 1975. 'The oral interview test' in R. L. Jones and B. Spolsky (eds.): *Testing Language Proficiency.* Washington, DC: Center for Applied Linguistics: 29–38.

Wilson, K. M. 1982. *GMAT and GRE Aptitude Test Performance in Relation to Primary Language and Scores on TOEFL* TOEFL Research Report 12. Princeton, NJ: Educational Testing Service.

Winer, B. J. 1971. *Statistical Problems in Experimental Design.* Second edition. New York: McGraw-Hill.

Wingerskey, M. S., M. A. Barton, and F. M. Lord. 1982. *LOGIST User's Guide.* Princeton, NJ: Educational Testing Service.

Witkin, H. A., C. A. Moore, D. R. Goodenough, and P. W. Cox. 1977. 'Field-dependent and field-independent styles and their educational implication.' *Review of Educational Research* 47:1–67.

Witkin, H. A., P. K. Oltman, E. Raskin, and S. A. Karp. 1971. *A Manual for the Embedded Figures Test.* Palo Alto, Calif.: Consulting Psychologists Press.

Woodford, P. 1978. 'Let's speak the same language.' Paper presented at the National Conference on New Directions in Foreign Language Studies and Language Policy, Wayne, NJ, November 17, 1978.

Woodford, P. 1981. 'A common metric for language proficiency: final report.' Princeton, NJ: Educational Testing Service.

Worthen, B. R. and J. R. Sanders. 1973. *Educational Evaluation: Theory and Practice.* Worthington, OH: Charles A. Jones.

Wright, B. D. 1968. 'Sample-free test calibration and person measurement' in *Proceedings of the 1967 Invitational Conference on Testing Problems.* Princeton, NJ: Educational Testing Service: 85–101.

Wright, B. D. 1977. 'Solving measurement problems with the Rasch model.' *Journal of Educational Measurement* 14:97–166.

Wright, B. D. and J. M. Linacre. 1983. *Microscale Manual for Microscale Version 1.2.* Westport, Conn.: Mediax Interactive Technologies.

Wright, B. D. and R. Mead. 1976. *BICAL. Calibrating Rating Scales with the Rasch Model. Research Memorandum No. 23.* Chicago, Ill.: University of Chicago, Statistical Laboratory, Department of Education.

Wright, B. D. and **M. H. Stone.** 1979. *Best Test Design.* Chicago, Ill.: MESA Press.

Zeidner, M. 1986. 'Are English language aptitude tests biased towards culturally different minority groups? Some Israeli findings.' *Language Testing* 3,1:80–95.

Zeidner, M. 1987. 'A comparison of ethnic, sex and age biases in the predictive validity of English language aptitude tests: some Israeli data.' *Language Testing* 4,1:55–71.

Author index

Subject index

as quality of test scores 24
relation to quantification of observations 49
relationship with validity 240 (7.1)
as reliable variance 239
as requirement for validity 160, 238–9
remedial instruction 65–7
representational validity 306
requesting
    strategies for 91
residual variance 193
resource grammar 85
response 116–17
    actual response 125–6
    definition 125–6
    constructed response 129
    degree of contextualization 131–4
    dialect 142–3
    distribution of new information 134–5
    expected response, *see* expected response
    illocutionary force 140–2
    length of language sample 130
    organizational character 139–40
    register 143–4
    selected response 129
    sociolinguistic characteristics 142
    vocabulary 131
response, reciprocal, *see* reciprocal response
rhetorical organization 88
RL, *see* real life
rules and procedures (measurement) 20
rule-space model 336–7

sampling
    of tasks from domain 311
scale calibration 345–6
    end points 346–7
    research 347–8
scales of measurement 26–30
scales of measurement, absolute, *see* absolute
    scales of measurement
scoring
    as influence of strategic competence on test
        performance 105–6
second language acquisition 2–3, 69, 339
    developmental sequence 3, 339
selected response 129
selection tests 70
self-ratings 148
    as indicators of language abilities 148
self-weighting 122
SEM, *see* standard error measurement
semi-direct test 127
sexism in language 16–17 (n 3)
similes
    interpretation 98
SLA, *see* second language acquisition
sociocultural orientation 84
sociolinguistic competence 42, 85, 87 (4.2),
    94–8
    scale 328 (8.1c)
sociolinguistic principle
    of language testing research 335
sociosemantic basis of linguistic knowledge
    84

sources of error
    and approaches to estimating reliability
        171–2
    examination under classical test theory
        197
    examination under generalizability theory
        197
    see also measurement error
SPEAK, *see* Speaking Proficiency in English
    Assessment Kit
Speaking Proficiency in English Assessment
    Kit 335–6
Spearman-Brown prophecy formula 174,
    229 (n 8)
Spearman-Brown split-half estimate 174–5,
    177–8
speech acts
    theory of 90
speech events
    language used in different 112
speech production
    psycholinguistic model 100
speededness 128–9
speeded tests 121, 123
split-half reliability coefficient 174–5
    see also Spearman-Brown split-half;
        Guttman split-half
split-half reliability estimates 172–5
    difficulties in splitting tests 173–4
squared-error loss agreement indices 217–19
stability 181–2, 184
standard deviation
    defined 106, 166
standard error of measurement 198–202
    and band interpretations in criterion-
        referenced measurement 219–20
    confidence intervals 200 (6.5)
    criterion-referenced 213–14
    estimation from theorems of classical
        measurement model 199–200
    group specific estimate 214
    for individual test takers 213–4
standardization of test method 224
standardized test 74
standard setting 232 (n 30)
Standards for Educational and Psychological
    Testing definition of validity 236
    on face validity 286–7
statistical analysis 299
stimulus 116–17
strategic competence 84, 98–107
    assessment component 100–1
    definition 99–100
    execution component 103–4
    function of 102
    influence on language test performance
        104–6
    measurement of 106–7
    planning component 101–2
style of discourse 96
subjective measure 51 (n 4)
subjective test 76
subjectivity
    of language tests 37–8